Causes of War

A volume in the series

CORNELL STUDIES IN SECURITY AFFAIRS

edited by Robert Jervis, Robert J. Art, *and* Stephen M. Walt

A full list of titles in the series appears at the end of the book.

Causes of War

Power and the Roots of Conflict

Stephen Van Evera

Cornell University Press

ITHACA AND LONDON

Copyright © 1999 by Cornell University

First published 1999 by Cornell University Press.

Printed in the United States of America.

Library of Congress Cataloging-in-Publication Data

Causes of war : power and the roots of conflict /
Stephen Van Evera.
p.   cm.
Includes index.
ISBN 0-8014-3201-4 (cloth : alk. paper).
1. War. 2. Balance of power. 3. International relations—Case studies. I. Title
U21.2.V34   1999   355.02'7—dc21   98-43650

Cornell University Press strives to use environmentally responsible suppliers and materials to the fullest extent possible in the publishing of its books. Such materials include vegetable-based, low-VOC inks and acid-free papers that are recycled, totally chlorine-free, or partly composed of nonwood fibers. Books that bear the logo of the FSC (Forest Stewardship Council) use paper taken from forests that have been inspected and certified as meeting the highest standards for environmental and social responsibility. For further information, visit our website at www.cornellpress.cornell.edu.

Cloth printing   10 9 8 7 6 5 4 3 2 1

Contents

[v]

Tables

Diagrams

Acknowledgments

Many people gave me important help with this book. Shai Feldman and Barry Posen shared key ideas that shaped my thinking. My many arguments with Marc Trachtenberg and John Mearsheimer seldom had winners, but much was learned—at least on my side. They also gave indispensable substantive and editorial advice on the manuscript, as did Robert Art. For insightful comments and suggestions I also thank Miriam Avins, Nazli Choucri, Charles Glaser, Robert Jervis, Chaim Kaufmann, Carl Kaysen, Teresa Johnson Lawson, Jack Levy, Peter Liberman, Michael Mandelbaum, Steven Miller, Sofia Mortada, William Rose, Michael Salman, Richard Samuels, Margaret Sevčenko, Glenn Snyder, Jack Snyder, Mark Torrey, Stephen Walt, and Kenneth Waltz. Leon Navickas and Rich Brennan provided crucial logistical help. And I received important education on subjects covered here from my students at the University of California at Davis, Tufts, Princeton, and MIT.

Generous support for my research came from the MIT Security Studies Program, the Harvard Belfer Center for Science and International Affairs, and the Woodrow Wilson Center of the Smithsonian Institution.

S. V. E.

Causes of War

[1]

Introduction

QUESTIONS ADDRESSED, WHY THEY ARISE

What caused the great wars of modern times? Of those causes, which were preventable? What are the likely causes of future wars, and how can those wars best be prevented?

These are the questions I address. They are not new. Devising schemes to prevent war has been a philosophers' industry for centuries. Dante Alighieri, William Penn, the abbé de Saint Pierre, Immanuel Kant, Jeremy Bentham, and James Mill all gave it a try.[1] Later, the goal of war prevention helped inspire the founder of the first modern school of political science, a U.S. Civil War veteran who sought to prevent war and hoped the study of politics would offer answers.[2] Still later, the international politics subfield embraced war prevention as a prime focus during its rapid growth after World War I.[3]

Sadly, though, scholars have made scant progress on the problem. A vast literature on the causes of war has appeared,[4] but this literature says little

[1] A survey of writings on war prevention from the fourteenth century through World War I is F. H. Hinsley, *Power and the Pursuit of Peace* (Cambridge: Cambridge University Press, 1967), pp. 13–149.

[2] The Columbia University graduate school of political science was founded in 1880 by John Burgess, who had vowed during an 1863 battle that if he survived he would devote his life to the search for peace. See John W. Burgess, *Reminiscences of an American Scholar* (New York: Columbia University Press, 1934), pp. 28–29, 69, 86, 141, 197.

[3] Edward Hallett Carr, *The Twenty Years' Crisis, 1919–1939: An Introduction to the Study of International Relations* (1939; New York: Harper & Row, 1964), p. 8.

[4] The best recent review of hypotheses on the causes of war is Jack S. Levy, "The Causes of War: A Review of Theories and Evidence," in Philip E. Tetlock, Jo L. Husbands, Robert Jervis, Paul C. Stern, and Charles Tilly, eds., *Behavior, Society, and Nuclear War*, 2 vols. (New York: Oxford University Press, 1989, 1991), 1:209–333; updated by Levy, "The Causes of War and the Conditions of Peace," *Annual Review of Political Science* 1998, 1:139–65. As Levy notes (1989,

about how war can be prevented.[5] Most of the many causes that it identifies cannot be manipulated (for example, human instinct, the nature of the domestic economic or political systems of states, or the distribution of power among states). Many hypotheses that identify manipulable causes have not been tested, leaving skeptics free to reject them. Accordingly, these writings are largely ignored by opinion leaders, policymakers, and peace groups.[6] Meanwhile, failed peace ideas—for example, disarmament, pacifism, and large reliance on international institutions to resolve conflict—remain popular for lack of better alternatives.

In short, our stock of hypotheses on the causes of war is large but unuseful. Those culling it for tools to prevent war will find slim pickings. Accordingly, my main purpose here is to propose prescriptively useful hypotheses on war's causes—that is, hypotheses that point to war causes that can feasibly be reduced or addressed by countermeasures. Toward this goal I elab-

---

1991, p. 212), other surveys of hypotheses on the causes of war are few, and none are really comprehensive. Other useful surveys include Greg Cashman, *What Causes War? An Introduction to Theories of International Conflict* (New York: Lexington Books, 1993); Seyom Brown, *The Causes and Prevention of War* (New York: St. Martin's Press, 1987); and Keith Nelson and Spencer C. Olin, Jr., *Why War? Ideology, Theory, and History* (Berkeley: University of California Press, 1979). Valuable older surveys include the classic Kenneth N. Waltz, *Man, the State, and War* (New York: Columbia University Press, 1959); and Geoffrey Blainey, *The Causes of War* (New York: Free Press, 1973). Shorter surveys include T. C. W. Blanning, *The Origins of the French Revolutionary Wars* (London: Longman, 1986), pp. 1–35; and Bernard Brodie, *War and Politics* (New York: Macmillan, 1973), pp. 276–340. A partial survey and application is John Lewis Gaddis, "The Long Peace: Elements of Stability in the Postwar International System," *International Security* 10 (Spring 1986): 99–142. Collections of theoretical writings include Robert I. Rotberg and Theodore K. Rabb, eds., *The Origins and Prevention of Major Wars* (New York: Cambridge University Press, 1989); Richard A. Falk and Samuel S. Kim, eds., *The War System: An Interdisciplinary Approach* (Boulder: Westview, 1980); Manus I. Midlarsky, ed., *Handbook of War Studies* (Boston: Unwin Hyman, 1989); Leon Bramson and George W. Goethals, *War: Studies from Psychology, Sociology, Anthropology*, rev. ed. (New York: Basic Books, 1968); John A. Vasquez and Marie T. Henehan, eds., *The Scientific Study of Peace and War: A Text Reader* (New York: Lexington Books, 1992); and Charles W. Kegley, Jr., ed., *The Long Postwar Peace: Contending Explanations and Predictions* (New York: HarperCollins, 1991).

[5] Concurring, A. F. K. Organski and Jacek Kugler lamented in 1980 that "despite the vast literature devoted to war, little is known on the subject that is of practical value." *The War Ledger* (Chicago: University of Chicago Press, 1980), p. 13. J. David Singer offered a broader criticism of causes-of-war studies in 1986, arguing that "nothing worthy of the name has yet emerged in the way of a compelling theory of war . . . we have no adequate theory as yet." "Research, Policy, and the Correlates of War," in Øyvind Østerud, ed., *Studies of War and Peace* (Oslo: Norwegian University Press, 1986), pp. 44–58 at 50–51. Jack S. Levy likewise concluded in 1983 that "our understanding of war remains at an elementary level. No widely accepted theory of the causes of war exists and little agreement has emerged on the methodology through which these causes might be discovered." *War in the Modern Great Power System, 1495–1975* (Lexington: University Press of Kentucky, 1983), p. 1.

[6] Paul Nitze states a common view among policymakers: "Most of what has been written and taught under the heading of 'political science' by Americans since World War II has been . . . of limited value, if not counterproductive, as a guide to the actual conduct of policy." *Tension Between Opposites: Reflections on the Practice and Theory of Politics* (New York: Scribner's, 1993), p. 3.

orate existing hypotheses that have been underappreciated or underdeveloped, and I propose a few new ones. I also test these hypotheses and apply them to explain history, infer policy prescriptions, and predict the future.

I use three criteria to select the hypotheses I explore:

1. *Explanatory power*. How much war can the hypothesis explain? How well? The explanatory power of a hypothesis is a function of three attributes: its importance, its explanatory range, and its real-world applicability. *Importance*: How strongly does the causal phenomenon of the hypothesis affect the caused phenomenon?[7] An important hypothesis points to a strong cause—that is, one that has large effects. The greater the effect produced, the greater the explanatory power. *Explanatory range*: How many classes of phenomena does the cause affect? The wider the range of affected phenomena, the greater the explanatory range of the hypothesis. Most social science theories have narrow range, but a few gems explain many diverse domains.[8] *Applicability*: Is the causal phenomenon that the hypothesis identifies common in the real world? How common are the conditions that it needs to operate? The more prevalent the cause and its conditions, the greater the explanatory power. Even important (that is, strong) causes have little explanatory power if they are rare in the real world or if they require rare hothouse conditions to operate. A weaker cause can have more explanatory power if the cause and its required conditions are common. The past prevalence of the causes and conditions of a hypothesis governs its ability to explain history; their current and future prevalence governs its ability to explain present and future events.

2. *Prescriptive richness*. Can the war cause that the hypothesis identifies be manipulated? If not, can its effects be mitigated by feasible countermeasures? Prescriptively rich hypotheses point to causes that can be manipulated or whose effects can be mitigated.

3. *Degree of satisfaction*. How well does the hypothesis satisfy our curiosity? The further the cause stands from its proposed effect, the greater the

[7] A theory's importance can be measured in "theoretical" or "dispersion" terms. A theoretical measure of importance asks: how many units of change in the value on the dependent variable (DV) are caused by a unit of change in the value on the independent variable (IV)? For example, how many additional votes can a candidate gain by spending an additional campaign dollar on television ads? A dispersion measure asks: what share of the DV's total variance in a specific data set is caused by variance of this IV? For example, what percentage of the variance in the votes received by various congressional candidates is explained by variance in their television spending? I use importance in the former sense, to refer to theoretical importance. A discussion is Christopher H. Achen, *Interpreting and Using Regression* (Beverly Hills: Sage, 1982), pp. 68–77.

[8] Examples of wide-range social science theories include Mancur Olson's theory of public goods, and Stanislav Andreski's military-participation ratio (MPR) explanation for social stratification. See Mancur Olson, *The Logic of Collective Action* (Cambridge: Harvard University Press, 1971); and Stanislav Andreski, *Military Organization and Society* (Berkeley: University of California Press, 1971), pp. 20–74.

[3]

satisfaction it offers. A politician once explained her election loss: "I didn't get enough votes!" This is true but unsatisfying. A good explanation would reveal why she did not get enough votes.

I ask five questions of the hypotheses I examine: (1) How can they be tested? What predictions can be inferred from each, and what tests of these predictions might be devised? (2) Do they pass preliminary tests? I test three hypotheses using single case studies (in Chapters 3, 4, 6, and 7). (3) How great is their explanatory power? That is, how large is their importance, how wide is their explanatory range, and how well can they explain recent and current international politics? (4) Are they satisfying? (5) What policy prescriptions follow from them?

ARGUMENTS ADVANCED, ANSWERS OFFERED

This book concentrates on war causes related to the character and distribution of national power. Power factors deserve attention because they strongly influence the probability and intensity of war, they are relatively malleable, and they remain understudied and underappreciated, despite a growing literature that addresses them.[9] Thomas Schelling notes that there is "something we might call the 'inherent propensity toward peace or war' embodied in weaponry, the geography, and the military organization of the time."[10] This volume develops Schelling's idea by exploring five specific hypotheses:

H1. War is more likely when states fall prey to false optimism about its outcome.
H2. War is more likely when the advantage lies with the first side to mobilize or attack.
H3. War is more likely when the relative power of states fluctuates sharply—that is, when windows of opportunity and vulnerability are large.
H4. War is more likely when resources are cumulative—that is, when the control of resources enables a state to protect or acquire other resources.
H5. War is more likely when conquest is easy.

These hypotheses have been discussed before, but they have not been fully developed and their strength has been underestimated. None have

---

[9] Marc Trachtenberg notes the general dismissal of military factors as war causes by diplomatic historians, who "as a rule never paid much attention to the military side of the story.... We all took it for granted that war was essentially the outcome of political conflict.... Purely military factors, such as the desire to strike before being struck ... were seen as playing at best a very marginal role." *History and Strategy* (Princeton: Princeton University Press, 1991), p. viii.

[10] Thomas C. Schelling, *Arms and Influence* (New Haven: Yale University Press, 1966), p. 234.

been well tested. (For a detailed summary of these hypotheses, see the Appendix.)

Chapter 2, "False Optimism," argues that war is more likely when governments exaggerate their own chances of winning crises and wars, or when they underestimate the cost of war. If the losing side could foresee the outcome, it would often decline to fight. Crystal balls that revealed the future to national leaders would prevent many wars.

Chapter 3, "Jumping the Gun," argues that war is markedly more likely when the first side to mobilize or attack has the advantage. A first-move advantage rarely causes a reciprocal fear of surprise attack—the main danger ascribed to it—but it does raise other serious dangers. It leads states to launch preemptive attacks to prevent an opponent from getting in the first blow. It also leads states to conceal their capabilities and grievances, from fear that open displays of strength or grievance could trigger another's preemptive attack. These deceptions impede diplomacy and make false optimism and inadvertent war more likely. Since 1740, some seven major wars have plausibly stemmed from dangers raised by real or perceived first-move advantages: the 1740 War of Austrian Succession, World War I, Hitler's 1940 attack on Norway, the U.S.-China clash during the Korean War, and the Arab-Israeli wars of 1956, 1967, and 1973.

Chapter 4, "Power Shifts," argues that fluctuations in the relative power of states ("windows") cause war by tempting states to launch preventive attack, by accelerating diplomacy to unsafe speeds, and by making agreements less valuable. If declining states think war is likely later, they strike because they prefer war now to war later. Or they hurry diplomacy, hastening to resolve disputes before their power wanes, often making war-causing mistakes of haste in the process. Or they give up on diplomacy altogether because they doubt the value of agreements, fearing that the rising state will break agreements made today after it grows stronger. As a result, diplomacy breaks down and disputes fester, waiting to erupt in war. Nine major wars since 1756 have arguably stemmed from dangers raised by windows or by false perceptions of windows.

Chapter 5, "Cumulative Resources," argues that war is more likely when resources are cumulative (that is, are highly additive). Some resources are highly cumulative: they can be readily used to seize more resources. Others are less so. States must compete more fiercely for control of more cumulative resources, because their gain or loss spells further gains or losses. Hence the greater the cumulativity of conquerable resources, the greater the risk of war.

Chapter 6, "Offense, Defense, and the Security Dilemma," argues that war is far more likely when conquest is easy. Easy conquest is a master cause of other potent causes of war, raising all the risks they pose. States adopt more expansionist foreign policies, for both defensive and opportunistic reasons, when conquest is easy. They resist other states' expansion more fiercely. First-move advantages and windows of opportunity and vulnerability are larger, hence preemptive and preventive wars are more common. Secrecy is tighter, hence false optimism is more common. States adopt more dangerous styles of diplomacy (specifically, fait accompli tactics), and arms racing is more intense. Diplomatic blunders have larger and less reversible consequences. In short, easy conquest is a mainspring that drives many mechanisms of war. Previous scholarship has warned against it, but has understated the dangers it raises and the range of phenomena it explains. Most wars of modern times were fueled by dangers stemming from the perception that conquest was feasible.

Chapter 7 tests the hypotheses advanced in Chapter 6, using the outbreak of World War I as a single case study. This case supplies a strong test of offense-defense theory and corroborates its main elements.

Chapter 8 applies the hypotheses developed in Chapters 2–6 to assess the impact of the nuclear revolution. It argues that nuclear weapons are Janus-faced: their effects depend heavily on the nature of the nuclear states. Nuclear weapons pacify a world of normal states—mainly by abating the causes of war outlined in this book—but they make a world of neurotic rogue states even more violent than it would otherwise be. Chapter 8 also argues that there is no safe escape from the current nuclear order (often called MAD—mutual assured destruction), in which the major nuclear powers can annihilate each other even after absorbing an all-out surprise attack. Proposed alternatives—such as nuclear disarmament or deployment of defenses that would protect populations from nuclear attack—would raise far greater dangers than they removed. We are stuck with MAD and must learn to live with it.

How much war can these five hypotheses explain? I argue that the causes of war they identify are potent when present, but four of the five (first-move advantage, windows, resource cumulativity, and easy conquest—all except false optimism) are rather rare in the real world, especially in the modern world. Thus they explain only a moderate amount of history as such. They explain a great deal of history, however, if they are recast as hypotheses on the effects of false *perceptions* of the dangers they frame. In fact, these misperceptions are common: states often exaggerate the size of first-move advantages, the size of windows of opportunity and vulnerability, the degree of resource cumulativity, and the ease of conquest. They then adopt war-causing policies in response to these illusions.

Thus the structure of power per se is benign and causes rather few wars, but the structure of power as perceived is often malignant and explains a good deal of war.

Realism argues that international politics is largely shaped by states' pursuit of power and by the distribution (or perceived distribution) of power among states.[11] Scholars have long quarreled over the value of the Realist approach. This book supports five arguments that bear on the value of Realism.

1. The structure of international power, and perceptions of that power structure, strongly affect the probability of war. When these factors incline states toward war, the risk of war is far greater. Hence Realism's focus on power and its distribution is well placed.

2. The *fine-grained* structure of power has far greater impact on the risk of war than does the *gross* structure of power. Realists have focused on the gross structure of power—that is, the distribution of aggregate capabilities. Is it bipolar or multipolar? Is power equally or unequally distributed across

---

[11] Robert Keohane's summary of the elements of the Realist paradigm aptly distills other definitions: (1) "States are the most important actors in world politics"; (2) States are "unitary rational actors, carefully calculating costs of alternative courses of action and seeking to maximize their expected utility, although doing so under conditions of uncertainty and without necessarily having sufficient information about alternatives or resources (time or otherwise) to conduct a full review of all possible courses of action"; and (3) "States seek power . . . and they calculate their interests in terms of power." "Theory of World Politics: Structural Realism and Beyond," in Robert O. Keohane, ed., *Neorealism and Its Critics* (New York: Columbia University Press, 1986), pp. 158–203 at 163–65. Stephen Walt includes a fourth element: "Realists believe that the external environment heavily shapes the foreign policies of states." "Alliances, Threats, and U.S. Grand Strategy: A Reply to Kaufman and Labs," *Security Studies* 1 (Spring 1992): 448–82 at 474n. Together these summaries suggest that the Realist theory family includes causes lying in the structure of international power and in misperceptions of that structure, although rather limited room is allowed for misperceptions.

Other summaries of the Realist paradigm include Michael Joseph Smith, *Realist Thought from Weber to Kissinger* (Baton Rouge: Louisiana State University Press, 1986), pp. 1–2; Sean M. Lynn-Jones and Steven E. Miller, "Preface," in Michael E. Brown, Sean M. Lynn-Jones and Steven E. Miller, eds., *The Perils of Anarchy: Contemporary Realism and International Security* (Cambridge: MIT Press, 1995), pp. ix–xxi at ix–x; and Benjamin Frankel, "Restating the Realist Case: An Introduction," *Security Studies* 5(Spring 1996): ix–xx.

Two schools of Realism are often distinguished: Classical and Neorealist (or Structural Realist). Classical Realism is associated with the writings of Hans J. Morgenthau and E. H. Carr, especially Morgenthau's *Politics among Nations*, 5th ed. (1948; New York: Knopf, 1973), and Carr's *Twenty Years' Crisis*. Others in the Classical Realist tradition include Norman Graebner, John Herz, George Kennan, Henry Kissinger, Reinhold Niebuhr, Nicholas Spykman, Martin Wight, and Arnold Wolfers. A useful discussion of some of these is Smith, *Realist Thought*; see also James E. Dougherty and Robert L. Pfaltzgraff, Jr., *Contending Theories of International Relations: A Comprehensive Survey*, 3d ed. (New York: HarperCollins, 1990), chap. 3. Neorealism refers mainly to the work of Kenneth N. Waltz, especially his *Theory of International Politics* (Reading, Mass.: Addison-Wesley, 1979). Others in the Neorealist tradition include John Mearsheimer and John Lewis Gaddis. A collection of assessments of Neorealism is Keohane, *Neorealism and Its Critics*. The two schools differ on two main issues: (1) What causes conflict: human nature (Classical Realists) or the anarchic nature of the international system (Neorealists)? (2) What is the prime goal of states: power (Classical Realists) or security (Neorealists)?

states and coalitions? Is the distribution of international privileges apportioned to the gross distribution of international power? Realists compare gross quantities of power but rarely distinguish types of power. In contrast, this book addresses the fine-grained structure of power—that is, the distribution of particular types of power. We can distinguish offensive power from defensive power, and the power to strike first from the power to retaliate after taking a first strike. We can further distinguish rising power, waning power, and the power to parlay gains into further gains. The distribution of these capacities defines the fine-grained structure of power. I argue that the gross structure of power explains little; the fine-grained structure explains far more.

Realism has been criticized for offering few hypotheses on the causes of war,[12] or for proposing hypotheses of uncertain validity and strength.[13] This weakness stems from Realists' focus on the gross structure of power. When Realism is expanded to include the fine-grained structure of power, its net explanatory power is vastly increased.

3. The fine-grained structure of power is more malleable than the gross structure; hence hypotheses that point to the fine-grained power structure yield more policy prescriptions. The bipolar or multipolar structure of the international system is fairly immutable. In contrast, the relative power of attackers and defenders can be shaped by national foreign and military policies.

Realism has been rightly criticized for failing to provide prescriptively useful explanations for the war problem. Even if Realist theories are valid, the argument goes, they are barren of solutions. Thus Robert Keohane complains that "Realism . . . is better at telling us why we are in such trouble than how to get out of it." It "helps us determine the strength of the trap" set by international anarchy, "but does not give us much assistance in seeking an

---

[12] Morgenthau identified two roots of conflict: the human desire for power and the desire for scarce goods. Beyond this he said little. His *Politics among Nations* has no extended discussion of the causes of war—there is no entry for "war, causes of" in the index—although it implies many hypotheses. A summary of Morgenthau is Kenneth N. Waltz, "The Origins of War in Neorealist Theory," in Rotberg and Rabb, *Origins and Prevention of Major Wars*, pp. 39–52 at 40–41. Carr's *Twenty Years' Crisis* advances one main hypothesis on war's causes: that the risk of war is greater when strong states enjoy less privilege than their power would allow them to seize or defend. This risk, he argues, can be reduced by granting greater rights to underprivileged states. See *Twenty Years' Crisis*, chap. 13. Carr's argument, essentially a brief for appeasement, was toned down after the book's first edition (1939). For the passages omitted from later editions see Smith, *Realist Thought*, pp. 83–84. Waltz's *Theory of International Politics* advances one prime hypothesis: the risk of war is greater in a multipolar world than in a bipolar one.

[13] Arguing that Realist theories have failed empirical tests is Stephen A. Kocs, "Explaining the Strategic Behavior of States: International Law as System Structure," *International Studies Quarterly* 38 (1994): 535–56 at 548–49.

escape."[14] This book offers Realist explanations that yield practical policy prescriptions.

4. The fine-grained structure of power is quite benign. The war-causing power structures identified below are rare in the real world. Two implications follow. First, the fine-grained power structure explains only a moderate amount of modern war. It explains more war than the gross structure of power, but its absolute explanatory power is only middling. Second, Realists who claim that the structure of international power rewards belligerent policies are wrong.[15] In fact the structure of international power provides more disincentives than incentives for aggression. Aggressors are more often punished than rewarded. Even successful aggression offers few benefits. Moreover, aggression seldom succeeds. Aggressor states usually are contained or destroyed.

5. The fine-grained structure of power is widely misperceived. Governments often think it more malignant than in fact it is. These misperceptions are a common cause of war and provide a strong explanation for past wars.

Realism thus is most powerful—that is, it explains the most international politics—if we repair it by shifting its focus (a) from the gross to the fine-grained structure of power and (b) from power itself to national perceptions of power.

This discussion suggests the need to define two new variants of Realism in addition to the "Classical Realism" and "Neorealism" (or "Structural Realism") that now dominate the landscape. A number-letter system might be used to distinguish these four Realisms:

[14] Keohane, "Theory of World Politics," pp. 198–99. For these reasons Keohane finds Realism morally objectionable: "Realism sometimes seems to imply, pessimistically, that order can *only* be created by hegemony," a conclusion that is "morally unacceptable" since it leaves the danger of nuclear war unaddressed. "No serious thinker could, therefore, be satisfied with Realism as the correct theory of world politics, even if the scientific status of the theory were stronger than it is." Instead "we need to focus . . . on variables that to some extent can be manipulated by human action" (ibid.).

Realist writings are not wholly devoid of prescriptions for war prevention. Morgenthau offers sensible advice for the conduct of diplomacy, and Carr recommends appeasement. See Morgenthau, *Politics among Nations*, pp. 540–48; and Carr, *Twenty Years' Crisis*, pp. 208–23. However, Keohane is correct that Realism is generally pessimistic about the preventability of war, and offers few prescriptions.

[15] For example, John Mearsheimer, an archetypal Neorealist, argues that "conflict is common among states because the international system creates powerful incentives for aggression." "Back to the Future: Instability in Europe after the Cold War," *International Security* 15 (Summer 1990): 5–56 at 12. As Robert Gilpin notes, Mearsheimer's view is common among Realists. Many hold that international anarchy compels the state "to expand its power and attempt to extend its control over the international system"; states that do otherwise suffer "severe penalties." *War and Change in World Politics* (New York: Cambridge University Press, 1981), p. 86. An attack on this view is Charles L. Glaser, "Realists as Optimists: Cooperation as Self-Help," *International Security* 19 (Winter 1994/95): 50–90.

Type I Realism (formerly "Classical Realism"): the Realism of Hans Morgenthau and E. H. Carr. It posits that states seek power as a prime goal for reasons rooted in human nature. It locates the causes of war largely in this power drive and in situations where states enjoy greater or lesser privilege than their power could justify.[16]

Type II Realism (formerly "Neorealism" or "Structural Realism"): the Realism of Kenneth Waltz and John Mearsheimer.[17] It posits that states seek security as a prime goal, for reasons rooted in the anarchic nature of the international system. It locates the causes of war largely in the gross structure of international power. *Type IIA Realism*, following Waltz's argument in *Theory of International Politics*, holds that the polarity of the international system governs the risk of war: multipolar systems are more war prone than bipolar systems.[18] *Type IIB Realism* suggests other ways that the gross structure of power can shape the risk of war. Some Type IIB Realists reverse the Type IIA argument to assert that multipolarity is safer than bipolarity.[19] Some argue that an equal distribution of power between opposing states or coalitions is safer than inequality, and some argue oppositely that equality is more dangerous.[20]

Type III Realism ("fine-grained structural Realism"?) posits, like Type II Realism, that states seek security as a prime goal, for reasons rooted in the anarchic nature of the international system. It locates the causes of war in the fine-grained structure of international power—in the offense-defense balance, the size of first-move advantages, the size and frequency of power fluctuations, and the cumulativity of resources.[21]

---

[16] See notes 11 and 12, above.

[17] My Realist categories are not mutually exclusive, and many scholars fall in several Realist camps at the same time. Thus Kenneth Waltz, the prime exemplar of Type II Realism, has also endorsed Type III Realist ideas (on these see below) in his post-1979 writings, and John Mearsheimer endorses both Types II and III ideas. See, for example, Kenneth N. Waltz, *The Spread of Nuclear Weapons: More May Be Better*, Adelphi Papers no. 171 (London: International Institute for Strategic Studies, 1981), pp. 5–6; Waltz, "Origins of War," p. 50; Mearsheimer, "Back to the Future," pp. 13–20. However, there is some degree of clustering around one worldview or the other. Most Type I and Type II Realists who endorsed Type III ideas did so rather slowly and not very strongly.

[18] Waltz, *Theory of International Politics*, pp. 161–76. Concurring are Gaddis, "Long Peace," pp. 105–10; and Mearsheimer, "Back to the Future," pp. 13–19, 21–29.

[19] Discussing literature on both sides of this question is Levy, "Causes of War," pp. 232–35.

[20] Discussing literature on both sides of this question is Levy, "Causes of War," pp. 231–32, 240–43. See also, arguing for the peacefulness of equality, Mearsheimer, "Back to the Future," pp. 18–19; and arguing the opposite, Blainey, *Causes of War*, pp. 109–14.
Some Type II realists pay some attention to misperceptions of the gross structure of power as a war cause. See, for example, Waltz, *Theory of International Politics*, p. 168; Waltz argues that miscalculations of the gross balance of power are more likely in a multipolar world, and such miscalculations raise the risk of war. This suggests a third class of Type II realism (Type IIC), which addresses the causes and effects of misperceptions of the gross structure of power. However, misperceptions are a minor theme in Type II realist writings, hence Type IIC is a minor current relative to Types IIA and IIB.

[21] Type III Realist ideas began developing in the 1960s and 1970s, but these ideas have not been located in the Realist paradigm by their authors, by other Realists, or by critics of Real-

Type IV Realism ("misperceptive fine-grained structural Realism"?) posits, like Type II and III Realism, that states seek security as a prime goal, for reasons rooted in the anarchic nature of the international system. It locates the causes of war in national misperceptions of the fine-grained structure of international power—in exaggeration of the power of the offense, the size of first-move advantages, the size and frequency of power fluctuations, and the cumulativity of resources.

Type I Realism is largely barren of useful hypotheses on the causes of war. Type II Realism is only marginally more useful.

Type III Realism has some value. Its hypotheses have large importance and very wide explanatory range. They have only moderate real-world applicability, however, because the causes they identify are rare. Conquest rarely is easy, moving first seldom provides much reward, windows are few, seldom are large, and resources seldom are highly cumulative. Hence these hypotheses explain only a middling amount of modern history. They have some prescriptive utility, because the causes they identify are somewhat manipulable, but not a great deal, because these causes are rare to begin with.

If these hypotheses are restated as theories of misperception, to become Type IV Realist hypotheses—for example, "war is more likely when states *believe* that conquest is easy"—they acquire great explanatory and prescriptive power. As noted above, the misperceptions they identify are common, hence they explain a sizable amount of history. These misperceptions are also more manipulable than power realities. Thus Type IV Realism is the most useful of the four Realisms.

In sum, this book both faults and repairs Realism. It faults Realism for failing to explain war and to prescribe solutions, and repairs it by offering Realist hypotheses that fill these gaps.

METHODS

The prime purpose of this book is to develop hypotheses, but I also test three hypotheses (those on the effects of first-move advantages, windows, and easy conquest—H2, H3, and H5) in ten single-case studies. These studies proceed by comparing the case to normal conditions and by drawing

---

ism. The 1986 exchange on Neorealism in Keohane, *Neorealism and Its Critics*, illustrates this point: neither proponents nor opponents of Realism mentioned Type III ideas except in a very brief aside (p. 175). Realists nevertheless can be distinguished by their views of Type III Realist ideas. Most important, we can distinguish offensive Realists, who think conquest is easy and security is scarce, from defensive Realists, who think conquest is difficult and security is abundant. A discussion of these schools is Frankel, "Restating the Realist Case," pp. xv–xviii.

[11]

within-case comparisons across time and space. Cases are selected for three attributes: data richness, extreme high or low values on the causal variable (that is, the cause either is present in unusual abundance or is strikingly absent in the case), and large within-case variance in values on the causal variable. Cases with these characteristics allow stronger tests because theories make more certain and more unique predictions about them.

How strong are the tests that my case studies supply? Believers in orthodox social science methodology would fault them for weakness. The orthodox methodology creed presumes that case studies are weaker than large-*n* tests. It doubts the value of single case studies, arguing that only explicit comparison of pairs or groups of cases can tell us much. It requires that cases not be selected on the dependent variable. For example, theories of war cannot be tested by studying only cases of war; cases of peace must also be studied.[22] It warns against testing theories with cases from which a theory was inferred.[23] It warns against selecting atypical cases that are overloaded with the causal phenomenon. An abundant cause is bound to create visible effects (the argument goes), so theories are bound to pass tests in cases where their causes are abundant, so these tests are weak. I have never found these rules useful, and my case studies break them all. Readers can judge if my recalcitrance did any harm.[24]

In these case studies, I frame predictions inferred from the test theory and ask if these predictions are congruent or incongruent with the evidence from the case. I also remark on the strength or weakness of the test that this comparison sets up. Most practitioners of case studies are less explicit. Test predictions are often left unstated, the congruence of predictions with observed evidence is seldom assessed, and the strength or weakness of tests is left undiscussed. However, I see no way to add up the results of case studies—that is, to decide what we have learned from them—except to actively address these issues. Has a theory passed a test? We cannot tell without assessing the congruence of its predictions with observed evidence. How much weight should a specific case study be given? We cannot tell without assessing the strength of the test that it presents. This book would be shorter without these assessments, but key judgments would be missing.

In testing hypotheses H2, H3, and H5, I consider two classes of evidence: data on the correlates of *actual* first-move advantages, windows, and offense dominance; and data on the correlates of *perceptions* of these phenomena. I consider the latter evidence for two reasons. First, the correlates of these

[22] See, for example, Gary King, Robert O. Keohane, and Sidney Verba, *Designing Social Inquiry: Scientific Inference in Qualitative Research* (Princeton: Princeton University Press, 1994), pp. 108–9, 129–32, 137–38, 140–49.

[23] Ibid., pp. 21–23, 46, 141.

[24] I summarize my doubts about these rules in Stephen Van Evera, *Guide to Methods for Students of Political Science* (Ithaca: Cornell University Press, 1997), pp. 45–47, 50–55, 66–67, 79–81.

perceptions are a sound guide to the impact of actual power realities. Power realities create outcomes through their impact on perceptions of power realities, which in turn shape outcomes. Therefore, perceptions of reality will correlate with outcomes that objective realities cause. Hence we can gauge the impact of first-move advantages, windows, and offense-dominance by asking what follows when they are believed present, whether or not they actually are. Second, evidence on the effects of perceptions sheds light on the scope and effects of misperceptions of these phenomena. Do hypotheses H2, H3, and H5 gain strength if recast to frame dangers that arise when first-move advantages, windows, and offense dominance are falsely perceived? We can address this question by tracking the scope and effects of these perceptions.

As background for the book I also examined a number of other wars and surveyed European international history since the French Revolution. Thirty wars were surveyed in all, including those examined in case studies.[25] I focused on modern wars rather than ancient wars; modern war is more relevant to the prevention of future war, since its causes are more prone to recur.

PLAN OF THE BOOK

This book starts with immediate causes of war and then moves to more remote causes of these causes. Chapter 2 frames a danger (false optimism) that stems in part from dangers outlined in Chapters 3 and 6 (first-move advantage and easy conquest). The dangers framed in Chapters 3, 4, and 5 (first-move advantage, windows, and resource cumulativity) also stem partly from easy conquest.

This ordering principle is not followed precisely. Some phenomena mentioned early cause phenomena mentioned later. But in general the book moves from immediate to more remote causes, and the problem of easy conquest is framed as a prime cause of other dangers.

[25] The wars surveyed, with their year of outbreak in parentheses, were the Peloponnesian War (460 B.C.E., 431 B.C.E., 415 B.C.E.); Second Punic War (218 B.C.E.); War of Austrian Succession (1740); Seven Years' War, Prussian-Russian-Austrian-French conflict (1756); Seven Years' War, Anglo-French conflict (1756); French Revolutionary War of 1792; War of 1812; U.S.-Mexican War (1846); U.S. Civil War (1861); Crimean War (1853); Austro-Prussian War (1866); Franco-Prussian War (1870); Spanish-American War (1898); Russo-Japanese War (1904); World War I (1914); Russo-Polish War (1920); Finnish-Soviet War (1939); World War II in Europe, outbreak and escalation (1939–41); World War II in the Pacific (1941); Arab-Israeli War (1947–48); Korean War, outbreak (1950); Korean War, U.S. vs. China (1950); Arab-Israeli War (1956); Indochina War (1965); Arab-Israeli War (1967); Arab-Israeli War (1970); Arab-Israeli War (1973); Arab-Israeli war in Lebanon (1982); Falklands/Malvinas War (1982); and Persian Gulf War (1991).

[2]

False Optimism:
Illusions of the Coming War

Hypothesis 1. War is more likely when states fall prey to false optimism about its outcome.

FALSE HOPE AND WAR

Wars would be fewer if the losers could foretell their defeat and if both sides could foresee the cost of fighting. If governments had crystal balls that revealed the future, they would fight only wars that improved their situation. Since few wars improve things for both sides, war would be scarce. Future losers would settle on the future winner's terms, and all would settle to avoid costly wars. Thus a root cause of war lies in the opacity of the future and in the optimistic illusions that this opacity allows. These illusions lead states to fight in false hope of victory, or for Pyrrhic victories.

Other chapters in this book argue that much war is driven by fears—fear of surprise attack, fear of relative decline, fear of conquest by others. This chapter dwells on the opposite danger, the risk of war raised by false hopes. States can have false hopes about the winner of war or the cost of war. I argue that both errors are common and dangerous, leading states to fight many wars they would avoid if they saw the future clearly.

False hopes of wartime victory raise the risk of war in two ways. First, such hopes lead losers to join wars they would avoid if they foresaw their defeat. War is a trial of strength. If its results were foretold, the weaker could yield to the stronger and achieve the same result without suffering the pain of war.[1] But often relative strength cannot be measured without a battlefield

---

[1] As Ralph Hawtry noted, "War means the imposition of the will of the stronger on the weaker by force. But if their relative strength is already known, a trial of strength is unnecessary. The weaker will yield to the stronger without going through the torments of conflict

test. If states agree on their relative power, this test is unnecessary; but if they disagree, a contest of arms can offer the only way to persuade the weaker side that it is the weaker and must concede.

Second, false hopes of wartime victory lead states to join more crises and to drive these crises over the brink more often. Optimistic states join crises more boldly and conduct them more recklessly because they are more willing to risk the war that a crisis could spawn. They also join crises from false hopes that the other side will concede ("They know they are too weak to confront us, so they will fold"), giving them a peaceful victory. Then they dismiss the adversary's real threats as bluff ("They know they will lose a fight, so their threat to fight must be empty"), push the crisis too far, and trigger inadvertent war.

Underestimating the cost of war causes war in similar ways. States are less anxious to avoid cheap wars than expensive wars. Hence the cheaper states expect war will be, the more likely they are to opt for war, to join war-risking crises, and to adopt war-risking stands during crises.

False optimism is not necessary for war, and its opposite, false pessimism, can also cause war. War can occur without false optimism if governments that expect defeat see value in fighting just to preserve their honor and credibility,[2] or if they believe that even a lost war will bolster their regime domestically by diverting public hatred toward outsiders. Governments that expect defeat can also find themselves at war without making a conscious choice to fight, if they unwittingly trigger another's surprise attack. Examples of such wars are rare, however. In most wars, losers have false hopes of avoiding defeat. Moreover, even the winners would avoid many wars if they foresaw the price of victory.

False fear of defeat can cause war if it leads states to exaggerate the hostility of others' intentions—"They gained military superiority; does this mean they intend aggression?"—feeding a spiral of reciprocal hostility. It can lead states to launch a preemptive attack if they think they can avert defeat only by striking first, or to launch preventive war if they think they can avert later defeat only by striking at the peak of their power. It can also lead status quo powers to appease when deterrence would prevent war better.[3] However,

---

to arrive at a conclusion foreknown from the beginning." Quoted in Robert Gilpin, *War and Change in World Politics* (Cambridge: Cambridge University Press, 1981), pp. 31–32. On false optimism also see Geoffrey Blainey, *The Causes of War*, 3d ed. (New York: Free Press, 1988), pp. 35–56, 114, 293; and Jack S. Levy, "Misperception and the Causes of War," *World Politics* 36 (October 1983): 76–99 at 82–86, 91–96.

[2] Making this argument is Robert Jervis, "War and Misperception," in Robert I. Rotberg and Theodore K. Rabb, eds., *The Origins and Prevention of Major Wars* (New York: Cambridge University Press, 1989), pp. 101–26 at 103–4.

[3] For example, Britain appeased Germany in 1938 partly because British civilians exaggerated the strength of German airpower. This appeasement set the stage for deterrence failure in 1939. A summary is P. M. H. Bell, *The Origins of the Second World War in Europe* (London: Longman, 1986), pp. 180–81, 234, 242. See also pp. 209–10 on the 1936 Rhineland crisis.

these effects are usually overridden by the caution that false pessimism creates. States absorbed in false pessimism may be more fearful and more hostile, but they are also more cautious by an even larger measure.

Thus false optimism is not necessary for war, but is nearly necessary; and its opposite is also dangerous, but less so.

The following sections distinguish types of false optimism, speculate on their causes, and survey the role of false optimism in history. This survey indicates that false optimism correlates closely with war and that it accompanies the outbreak of the vast majority of wars. I have not systematically measured false optimism or pessimism in peacetime, but it nevertheless seems fair to conclude, on the basis of a general reading of history, that false optimism is markedly less common in peacetime than before the outbreak of war.

Thus false optimism seems a potent and pervasive cause of war. States are far more warlike when they are in the thrall of false optimism. Moreover, false optimism is a fairly common phenomenon, hence a pervasive cause of war, hence a cause of many wars. Hence its control or abatement would prevent many wars.

ILLUSIONS OF VICTORY

False hopes of victory can arise when opposing states misread their relative military strength, their relative will, or the relative number, power, and will of each side's allies. These misreadings are considered in turn.

The balance of military power

Unduly rosy estimates of relative military power infect the belligerents before the vast majority of wars. At least some false optimism about relative power preceded every major war since 1740, as well as many lesser and ancient wars.

Pericles told Athenians they should "feel confident of final victory" as they started down the road to ruin by launching war against Sparta in 431 B.C.E.[4] Athenians later were oblivious of the size and power of Syracuse, believing their ill-fated expedition against it was "an absolutely safe thing."[5] Hannibal of Carthage likewise dared to invade Rome in 218 B.C.E., bringing calamity to Carthage, because he wrongly thought Rome was ripe for rebellion and defeat.[6]

[4] Thucydides' summary, in Thucydides, *History of the Peloponnesian War*, trans. Rex Warner (Harmondsworth: Penguin, 1954), p. 133.
[5] Ibid., p. 425.
[6] R. M. Errington, *The Dawn of Empire: Rome's Rise to World Power* (Ithaca: Cornell University Press, 1972), p. 64.

[16]

Austria expected easy victory over Frederick the Great's invading Prussian armies in 1740. Austria's queen later wrote that her government had assumed that a "few soldiers could contain the inexperienced Prussians"—but the Prussians handily won the First Silesian War.[7] In 1756 Frederick attacked again with rosy visions of another smooth victory,[8] but Prussia barely survived a harrowing war that left it ravaged, depopulated, and nearly destroyed.

Britain held its American colonists' fighting abilities in contempt and expected easy victory in 1775–76. Britain's General Thomas Gage declared that "there is not a man amongst [the colonists] capable of taking command or directing the motions of any Army." A Colonel Grant told the House of Commons that the Americans "did not possess any of the qualifications necessary to make a good soldier" and "would never dare face an *English* army."[9]

Both revolutionary France and its conservative enemies were supremely confident of a quick victory in 1792. French revolutionaries argued that Prussia and Austria were tottering near collapse and would crumble at a tap, while these conservative regimes thought the revolution had destroyed French power.[10] T. C. W. Blanning notes that the French revolutionaries had "a sense of invincibility" that stemmed from their belief in the superiority of their principles. The conservative powers suffered a symmetric overconfidence: their aristocratic assumptions "made it impossible for them even to conceive that a 'citizen army' could resist, let alone defeat, an army of professionals."[11] One cocky Prussian leader told Prussian officers, "Do not buy too many horses, the comedy will not last long. The army of lawyers will be annihilated in Belgium and we shall be home by autumn."[12]

The United States falsely expected easy victory in the War of 1812. Thomas Jefferson smugly wrote that the conquest of Canada was just "a mere matter of marching," and John C. Calhoun predicted American seizure of all Upper Canada and part of Lower Canada in just four weeks.[13] Before their Mexican War debacle (1846–48), Mexicans talked of invading Louisiana, arming the American slaves, and organizing an American Indian rebellion.

---

[7] Queen Maria Teresa, quoted in Karl A. Roider, Jr., ed., *Maria Teresa* (Englewood Cliffs, N.J.: Prentice-Hall, 1973), p. 20.

[8] Christopher Duffy, *Frederick the Great: A Military Life* (London: Routledge & Kegan Paul, 1985), p. 87.

[9] Neil R. Stout, *The Perfect Crisis: The Beginning of the Revolutionary War* (New York: New York University Press, 1976), p. 175, Grant's emphasis in original.

[10] T. C. W. Blanning, *The Origins of the French Revolutionary Wars* (London: Longman, 1986), pp. 73, 79–80; see also 100, 108, 110, 115–16, 123, 153–54.

[11] Ibid., pp. 208–9.

[12] Johann von Bischoffwerder, quoted in ibid., p. 116.

[13] Thomas A. Bailey, *A Diplomatic History of the American People*, 9th ed. (Englewood Cliffs, N.J.: Prentice-Hall, 1974), p. 138; T. Harry Williams, *The History of American Wars from 1745 to 1918* (New York: Alfred A. Knopf, 1981), p. 98.

One Mexican officer boasted that his cavalry could break American infantry squares with the lasso.[14]

Before its crushing 1866 loss to Prussia, Austria exaggerated its own strength and underestimated every category of Prussian military strength—quantity of trained troops and quality of leadership, tactics, military technology, and logistics.[15] Four years later, France was so certain of victory against Prussia that the French Army issued maps of Prussia but not France to its officers.[16] French Minister of Foreign Affairs Duc de Gramont boasted that "in a few days we will be on the Rhine" shortly before the Prussian Army routed French forces and besieged Paris.[17] French military advisors assured Empress Eugénie that "our offensive across the Rhine will be so shattering that it will cut Germany in two and we will swallow Prussia in one gulp."[18]

Russian leaders approached their 1904 drubbing by Japan with high confidence. Minister of War A. N. Kuropatkin assured the Czar that his armies would quickly expel Japan from Manchuria and Korea and end the war with a "landing in Japan, annihilation of the Japanese territorial army . . . and capture of the Mikado."[19] Hence he dismissed Japan's prewar threats as bluff: "The Japanese will not dare to fight, they are unprepared, they are only putting on airs, thinking that we shall be frightened and believe them."[20] One member of the Russian general staff forecast that "we will only have to throw our caps at them and they will run away."[21] Russian Navy Chief of Staff E. I. Alekseiev declared that "I personally cannot admit the possibility of the destruction of the Russian fleet by the Japanese" shortly before Russian flotillas were beaten at Port Arthur and crushed at Tsushima.[22]

---

[14] Bailey, *Diplomatic History of the American People*, p. 259.

[15] Richard Smoke, *War: Controlling Escalation* (Cambridge: Harvard University Press, 1977), p. 98.

[16] Blainey, *Causes of War*, p. 45.

[17] Michael Howard, *The Franco-Prussian War: The German Invasion of France, 1870–1871* (London: Granada, 1961), p. 54.

[18] John Bierman, *Napoleon III and His Carnival Empire* (New York: St. Martin's, 1988), p. 335.

[19] Quoted in Richard Ned Lebow, *Between Peace and War: The Nature of International Crisis* (Baltimore: Johns Hopkins University Press, 1981), p. 245. The Russian military attaché in Tokyo reported that "it would take perhaps hundreds of years for the Japanese army to acquire the moral foundations necessary to put it on a par with even the weakest European force." Ibid., p. 246. Other prewar Russian reports described the Japanese as an "army of sucklings" that "could not be compared to any major European army, least of all the Russians." Ibid. A racist assumption of oriental ineptitude informed these illusions: for example, the Czar privately referred to Japanese as "short-tailed monkeys." Bruce W. Menning, *Bayonets before Bullets: The Imperial Russian Army, 1861–1914* (Bloomington: Indiana University Press, 1992), p. 152.

[20] Lebow, *Between Peace and War*, p. 246.

[21] Ibid.

[22] Alfred Vagts, *Defense and Diplomacy: The Soldier and the Conduct of Foreign Relations* (New York: Kings Crown Press, 1956), p. 357.

Both the Triple Entente (Britain, France, and Russia) and the Central Powers (Germany and Austria-Hungary) expected a quick victory in 1914. Alfred Vagts notes "the belief of the soldiers and sailors of *all* the Powers and of the statesmen acting on their advice . . . that the war could be won by their own side."[23] In early August the German kaiser told departing troops: "You will be home before the leaves have fallen from the trees."[24] The German general staff expected to crush France in four weeks and finish off the rest of the Triple Entente in four months.[25] Other Germans talked of victory in eight or ten weeks.[26] A German officer expressed the typical view: "The chances of achieving a speedy victory in a major European war are . . . very favorable for Germany."[27] As he left for the front, another German officer declared that he expected to breakfast at the Café de la Paix in Paris on Sedan Day (September 2). A third told a colleague in early August: "You and I will be meeting again in England."[28] This false confidence led Germans to underrate both the dangers that war posed and the risk that German-Austrian belligerence would cause it. On the eve of war, one German official declared that "Russia is not now ready to strike," hence "the more boldness Austria displays, the more strongly we support her, the more likely is Russia to remain quiet."[29]

The Russians had parallel dreams of quick triumph, talking of victory in two or three months. Some Russian officers even boasted that they would reach Berlin in six weeks.[30] French leaders expected a swift victory,[31] and a

---

[23] Ibid., p. 307; see also pp. 365–76; and Blainey, *Causes of War*, pp. 35–40.

[24] Barbara W. Tuchman, *The Guns of August* (New York: Dell, 1962), p. 142.

[25] Tuchman, *Guns of August*, p. 142; Bernadotte E. Schmitt, *The Coming of the War, 1914*, 2 vols. (New York: Scribner's, 1930), 2:264. As war erupted on July 31, the Bavarian ambassador in Berlin recorded that "the Prussian general staff looks forward to war with France with great confidence, counts on being able to conquer France in four weeks; no effective spirit in the French army," and that "military circles here are in the best of spirits." Ibid. On August 2 he recorded that "the feeling in military circles here is one of absolute confidence." Ibid., 2:324.

[26] Tuchman, *Guns of August*, p. 142. See also Fritz Fischer, *Germany's Aims in the First World War* (New York: Norton, 1967), pp. 54–55, 59–60.

[27] Major-General Georg von Waldersee, in May 1914, quoted in John C. G. Röhl, "Germany," in Keith Wilson, ed., *Decisions for War 1914* (New York: St. Martin's, 1995), pp. 27–54 at 45.

[28] Count Häseler and Count Hochberg, quoted in Tuchman, *Guns of August*, p. 142. Kurt Riezler, Bethmann-Hollweg's top aide, later explained that "the General Staff declared that the war against France would be over in 40 days. All this played its part" in forming Germany's bellicose policy in 1914. Quoted in Röhl, "Germany," pp. 33–34.

[29] German Secretary of State for the Foreign Office Gottlieb von Jagow, on July 18, 1914, quoted in Luigi Albertini, *The Origins of the War of 1914*, 3 vols., trans. and ed. Isabella M. Massey (1952–57; reprint, Westport: Greenwood Press, 1980), 2:158; see also 2:159–61, 301–2; and Schmitt, *Coming of the War*, 1:317–20.

[30] Tuchman, *Guns of August*, p. 142.

[31] Christopher M. Andrew, "France and the German Menace," in Ernest R. May, ed., *Knowing One's Enemies: Intelligence Assessment before the Two World Wars* (Princeton: Princeton Uni-

British officer declared Germany would be "easy prey" for Britain and France.[32] Austria and Russia each expected to defeat the other.[33] Even the Turks caught the mood: in late 1914 the Turkish war minister confided that after victory in the Caucasus, Turkey might march through Afghanistan to India.[34]

Similar illusions prevailed before World War II. Japanese planners disdained Chinese military capabilities before launching their 1937 invasion of China. Japan's army boasted that it could defeat China in three months with no more than five divisions.[35] The Japanese Army minister forecast that "we'll send large forces, smash them in a hurry and get the whole thing over with quickly," and even claimed that the Army could conquer China in less than a month.[36] But China was still unsubdued when Japan surrendered in 1945.

Poland vastly exaggerated its own military power in the late 1930s. Some Poles boastfully predicted a "cavalry ride to Berlin" if Poland fought Germany,[37] and Polish officials thought they could hold off Germany alone for six months, until Britain and France could move in the west.[38] The Polish vice-minister for war boasted that Poland "certainly" was militarily superior to Germany and that Germany's armed forces were "one big bluff."[39] But Polish forces proved little more than a speed bump for Hitler's invading armies.

In 1939, Soviet leaders thought Soviet forces could race through Finland in a few hours. Soviet diplomats boasted that "in three days it will all be over." Advance units of the Red Army were warned not to cross the Swedish border by mistake.[40] This warning proved unnecessary, as strong Finnish forces checked the Soviet invasion near its jumping-off point and locked Soviet invaders in grueling combat through the winter of 1939–40.

In May 1940 France and the Low Countries foresaw success against

---

versity Press, 1986), pp. 127–49 at 146. The French general staff foresaw "the prospect of a victory permitting [the Triple Entente] to redraw the map of Europe." Ibid.

[32] General Sir James M. Grierson, quoted in Vagts, *Defense and Diplomacy*, p. 366.

[33] Samuel R. Williamson, Jr., *Austria-Hungary and the Origins of the First World War* (New York: St. Martin's, 1991), p. 119.

[34] M. S. Anderson, *The Eastern Question, 1774–1923* (London: Macmillan, 1966), p. 315.

[35] Robert J. C. Butow, *Tojo and the Coming of the War* (Stanford: Stanford University Press, 1969), p. 109; Saburo Ienaga, *The Pacific War, 1931–1945* (New York: Pantheon, 1978), p. 85.

[36] Ienaga, *Pacific War*, p. 85; and Edwin P. Hoyt, *Japan's War: The Great Pacific Conflict, 1853 to 1952* (New York: McGraw-Hill, 1986), pp. 144, 277.

[37] B. H. Liddell Hart, *History of the Second World War*, 2 vols. (New York: G. P. Putnam's Sons, 1972), 2:12.

[38] Gordon Wright, *The Ordeal of Total War, 1939–1945* (New York: Harper & Row, 1968), p. 8.

[39] In March 1938, quoted in Yohanan Cohen, *Small Nations in Times of Crisis and Confrontation* (Albany: State University of New York Press, 1989), p. 85.

[40] Max Jakobson, *The Diplomacy of the Winter War* (Cambridge: Harvard University Press, 1961), p. 168.

Hitler's western onslaught. The Dutch expected to hold the Grebbe line, their main fortification barrier, for three months—enough time for decisive Franco-British help to arrive.[41] It fell in three days, the Netherlands in four. The Belgians hoped their frontier defenses would delay the Germans for a lengthy period, and some Belgians even dreamed of victory: General Van Overstraeten forecast that a German attack on Belgium would face decisive defeat.[42] Germany crushed Belgium in eighteen days. The French approached their sudden rout by Germany with confidence. Most French officers expected victory; the French commander, General Gamelin, actually hoped for a German attack.[43] But French forces were shattered in less than a week, and France surrendered in six weeks.

Hitler held the Soviet Union in contempt and expected easy victory over Soviet forces in 1941. After crushing France, he told German officers that "a campaign against Russia would be like a child's game in a sandbox by comparison" and that "we have only to kick in the door and the whole rotten structure will come crashing down."[44] Hitler also dismissed American military power: the United States, he believed, was a "decayed country" incapable of waging war.[45] American society was "half Judaized, the other half Negrified," hence "I don't see much future for the Americans."[46] Hence he dismissed both the danger that U.S. intervention would pose and the likelihood that it would occur, arguing in 1938 that the United States was too weak to dare going beyond empty gestures in international affairs.[47]

Both Japan and the United States underestimated the other during their 1940–41 approach to war. Japanese leaders were not confident of victory but saw some chance of it. Navy Minister Koshiro Oikawa argued in September 1940 that "if we aim at a quick war and a quick victory, we have a

[41] J. S. Van Wieringen, "The Grebbe Line: A Long Defence Line with a Long History," *Fort* 19 (1991): 73–92 at 87.

[42] Brian Bond, *Britain, France and Belgium 1939–1940* (London: Brassey's, 1990), pp. 31–32.

[43] Bell, *Origins of the Second World War*, p. 173; and Bond, *Britain, France and Belgium*, p. 54.

[44] Albert Speer, *Inside the Third Reich* (New York: Avon, 1970), p. 238; and William L. Shirer, *The Rise and Fall of the Third Reich: A History of Nazi Germany* (New York: Simon & Schuster, 1960), p. 856. Conversely, Soviet military leaders falsely expected to halt a German attack at the Soviet border and promptly carry the war into the German empire. J. M. Mackintosh, "The Development of Soviet Military Doctrine since 1918," in Michael Howard, ed., *The Theory and Practice of War* (Bloomington: Indiana University Press, 1965), pp. 247–70 at 257.

[45] Shirer, *Rise and Fall*, p. 895n; and Gerhard L. Weinberg, "Hitler's Image of the United States," *American Historical Review* 69 (July 1964): 1006–21 at 1012.

[46] His view in early 1942; see Shirer, *Rise and Fall*, p. 895n. Gerhard Weinberg notes that Hitler thought the United States was "deprived by its racial composition of the ability to produce an effective military force." Weinberg, "Hitler's Image of the United States," p. 1011. In 1940 he assured his generals that U.S. rearmament would not be effective before 1945, long after Germany had conquered Europe. Ibid., p. 1015. Mussolini approached war with the United States with a similar contempt. His experts claimed that the United States had almost no defense industrial capacity, and he argued that U.S. military capability was negligible. Denis Mack Smith, *Mussolini's Roman Empire* (Harmondsworth: Penguin, 1977), p. 245.

[47] Weinberg, "Hitler's Image of the United States," p. 1012.

good chance to win"; another senior Navy official later was "confident that we can defeat the United States."[48] Meanwhile, U.S. officials underestimated Japanese forces and expected a quick, easy U.S. victory.[49]

Before attacking South Korea in June 1950, North Korean dictator Kim Il Sung assured Stalin that he was "absolutely certain of success" and that North Korea's army could have the war won in three days, before the United States could intervene against him.[50] Conversely, U.S. Secretary of State Dean Acheson blithely assumed that "South Korea could now take care of any trouble that was started solely by North Korea."[51] Then, during the fall of 1950, the United States dismissed China's threat to intervene in Korea as bluff, partly because U.S. officials thought China too weak to carry it out. General Douglas MacArthur predicted in October that "if the Chinese tried to get down to Pyongyang there would be the greatest slaughter," shortly before Chinese armies routed his forces to Pyongyang and far beyond.[52] He dismissed Chinese Foreign Minister Zhou Enlai's October 3 warning of Chi-

[48] Jun Tsunoda, "The Navy's Role in the Southern Strategy," in James William Morley, ed., *The Fateful Choice: Japan's Advance into Southeast Asia, 1939–1941* (New York: Columbia University Press, 1980), pp. 241–95 at 275, 277; see also 251.

[49] Roberta Wohlstetter, *Pearl Harbor: Warning and Decision* (Stanford: Stanford University Press, 1962), pp. 264, 336–38; and William L. Neumann, "The Open Door Closed Tight," in Robert A. Goldwyn and Harry M. Clor, eds., *Readings in American Foreign Policy*, 2d ed. (New York: Oxford University Press, 1971), pp. 274–89 at 283–84. U.S. racial arrogance fed this overconfidence. David Kahn notes that before 1941 Americans held a "belief in the superiority of the white race" and "looked upon the Japanese as bucktoothed, bespectacled little men." David Kahn, "United States Views Germany and Japan in 1941," in May, *Knowing One's Enemies*, pp. 476–502 at 476. Thus U.S. naval intelligence in 1937 claimed that the Japanese had "a natural ineptitude" at building aircraft carriers. Stephen E. Pelz, *Race to Pearl Harbor: The Failure of the London Naval Conference and the Onset of World War II* (Cambridge: Harvard University Press, 1974), p. 200. The British naval attaché in Tokyo argued in 1935 that the Japanese navy was inefficient because "the Japanese have peculiarly slow brains." Ibid., p. 182.

[50] Nikita Khrushchev's paraphrase of Kim, quoted in Nikita Khrushchev, *Khrushchev Remembers*, trans. and ed. Strobe Talbott (Boston: Little, Brown, 1970), p. 368; and Sergei N. Goncharov, John W. Lewis and Xue Litai, *Uncertain Partners: Stalin, Mao, and the Korean War* (Stanford: Stanford University Press, 1993), p. 144. Kim meant that he would be in a winning position in three days. He thought the actual conquest of South Korea would take three to four weeks. His military plan of operation foresaw victory in 22–27 days, and he promised Mao victory within a month. Ibid., pp. 137n, 146; and see also p. 155.

[51] In January 1950; quoted in John Lewis Gaddis, "The Strategic Perspective: The Rise and Fall of the 'Defense Perimeter' Concept, 1947–1951," in Dorothy Borg and Waldo Heinrichs, eds., *Uncertain Years: Chinese-American Relations, 1947–1950* (New York: Columbia University Press, 1980), pp. 61–118 at 106.

[52] *Foreign Relations of the United States, 1950*, vol. 7, *Korea* (Washington, D.C.: U.S. Government Printing Office, 1976), p. 953. General Almond, commander of U.S. X corps, told his troops that they faced "a bunch of Chinese laundrymen" as China began its devastating attack in late November. Quoted in Michael Doyle, "Endemic Surprise? Strategic Surprises in First World–Third World Relations," in Klaus Knorr and Patrick Morgan, eds., *Strategic Military Surprise: Incentives and Opportunities* (New Brunswick, N.J.: Transaction Books, 1983), pp. 77–110 at 99.

nese intervention as "just blackmail" because Zhou "must realize [my] vastly greater potential in the air, on the ground, and on the sea."[53]

U.S. officials recurrently underestimated their opponents in Vietnam. In 1961 Secretary of Defense Robert McNamara and the Joint Chiefs of Staff thought 205,000 U.S. troops could achieve U.S. goals; 543,000 later proved insufficient.[54] Argentina seized the Falkland Islands in 1982 wrongly believing that Britain lacked the military power to recover them; hence it thought a British military campaign of recovery was "inconceivable," as Argentine junta leader General Leopoldo Galtieri later confided.[55] Before Iraq's crushing 1991 defeat, Saddam Hussein believed Iraqi forces could hold their own against the U.S.-led coalition. In July 1990 Saddam told the U.S. ambassador, "Yours is a society that cannot accept 10,000 dead in one battle," as if Iraq could inflict such casualties. He later predicted that Americans would "swim in their own blood."[56]

The Arab-Israeli wars were rife with false optimism. Before their disastrous defeat in the 1948 war, most Arabs were certain of Arab military superiority.[57] In 1956 Britain and France wrongly thought their attack would quickly topple Nasser's government.[58] In 1967 Nasser expected not the crushing defeat he suffered, but a stalemate; the Israelis might capture parts of the Western Sinai, but Egypt would capture Eilat.[59] Egyptian pilots, who were routed in the war, thought they could destroy the Israeli air force in a matter of hours.[60] In 1973 Israel believed the Arabs so weak they would never attack, hence Israel need not negotiate. Deputy Prime Minister Yigael

[53] MacArthur paraphrased by Alvary Gascoigne, quoted in Peter Lowe, *The Origins of the Korean War* (London: Longman, 1986), p. 192.

[54] Larry Berman, *Planning a Tragedy: The Americanization of the War in Vietnam* (New York: Norton, 1982), p. 21. When George Ball warned in July 1965 that the war might require half a million troops, McNamara called the figure "outrageous." George C. Herring, *America's Longest War: The United States in Vietnam, 1950–1975*, 2d ed. (New York: McGraw-Hill, 1986), p. 143.

[55] Richard Ned Lebow, "Miscalculation in the South Atlantic: The Origins of the Falkland War," *Journal of Strategic Studies* 6 (March 1983): 3–35 at 22.

[56] Norman Cigar, "Iraq's Strategic Mindset and the Gulf War: Blueprint for Defeat," *Journal of Strategic Studies* 25 (March 1992): 1–29 at 5; see also pp. 1, 14–16.

[57] Jon Kimche and David Kimche, *A Clash of Destinies: The Arab-Jewish War and the Founding of the State of Israel* (New York: Frederick A. Praeger, 1960), pp. 151–52, 164, 232–33; Nadav Safran, *From War to War: The Arab-Israeli Confrontation, 1948–1967* (New York: Pegasus, 1969), p. 29.

[58] Nadav Safran, *Israel: The Embattled Ally* (Cambridge: Harvard University Press, 1979), p. 355.

[59] Janice Gross Stein, "The Arab-Israeli War of 1967: Inadvertent War Through Miscalculated Escalation," in Alexander L. George, ed., *Avoiding War: Problems of Crisis Management* (Boulder: Westview, 1991), pp. 126–59 at 135; see also pp. 134, 136, 156n; and Richard B. Parker, *The Politics of Miscalculation in the Middle East* (Bloomington: Indiana University Press, 1993), p. 82.

[60] David Kimche and Dan Bawley, *The Six-Day War* (New York: Stein and Day, 1971), p. 97; see also pp. 110, 167.

Allon declared that "Egypt has no military option at all," as Egypt and Syria quietly prepared a nasty war that would badly bloody Israeli forces.[61] In 1982, Israeli General Ariel Sharon, architect of the Lebanon War, forecast that Israeli troops would be back from Lebanon in six weeks. They remained three bloody years.[62]

The false optimism observed in the run-ups to these wars exceeds what we see in typical peacetime. Even odd examples of such false optimism are uncommon when war is not imminent. The more common peacetime error is to overestimate the opponent's power and underestimate one's own. Examples include the three nineteenth-century British naval panics (1847–48, 1851–53, 1859–61), the U.S. Cold War "bomber gap" and "missile gap" episodes (1955–57, 1957–61), the U.S. "window of vulnerability" (1978–82), and the chronically too pessimistic U.S. assessments of the Cold War conventional military balance.[63] If these examples typify the peacetime norm, this demonstrates a clear correlation between false optimism and war.

What causes this false optimism? Two causes—first-move advantage and offense dominance—are discussed below. Anything that fosters the feigning of military weakness, the maintenance of tight military secrecy, or rapid military change causes false optimism by confusing assessments of military capabilities. First-move advantages cause states to feign weakness in order to lull their opponents and thus ripen them for surprise attack. The lulled opponent is bound to adopt an unduly rosy view of the military balance. Offense dominance causes states to maintain tighter military secrecy. This raises the risk that opponents will underestimate concealed capabilities. Offense dominance also fosters arms racing, which muddies the military balance by quickening the pace of military change.[64]

[61] Donald Neff, *Warriors Against Israel* (Brattleboro, Vt.: Amana Books, 1988), p. 123.

[62] Ze'ev Schiff and Ehud Ya'ari, *Israel's Lebanon War*, trans. Ina Friedman (New York: Simon and Schuster, 1984), p. 46.

[63] Good accounts of the naval panics are Richard Cobden, "The Three Panics," in Richard Cobden, *The Political Writings of Richard Cobden* (London: Cassell & Co., 1886), pp. 537–704; and F. W. Hirst, *The Six Panics and Other Essays* (London: Methuen, 1913). On the bomber and missile gaps see Chapter 6, note 89. On the window of vulnerability see Michael Salman, Kevin J. Sullivan, and Stephen Van Evera, "Analysis or Propaganda? Measuring American Strategic Nuclear Capability, 1969–1988," in Lynn Eden and Steven E. Miller, eds., *Nuclear Arguments: Understanding the Strategic Nuclear Arms and Arms Control Debates* (Ithaca: Cornell University Press, 1989), pp. 172–263 at 172–221; and Fred M. Kaplan, *Dubious Specter: A Skeptical Look and the Soviet Nuclear Threat*, rev. ed. (Washington, D.C.: Institute for Policy Studies, 1980), pp. 24–54.

Gloomy views of the European conventional military balance prevailed in the Western popular media throughout the Cold War, while in-depth studies were more optimistic but gained little attention. Among the latter are Matthew Evangelista, "Stalin's Postwar Army Reappraised," *International Security* 7 (Winter 1982–83): 110–38 (on the late 1940s); Alain C. Enthoven and K. Wayne Smith, *How Much Is Enough? Shaping the Defense Program 1961–1969* (New York: Harper & Row, 1971), pp. 132–56 (on the late 1950s and early 1960s); and John J. Mearsheimer, "Why the Soviets Can't Win Quickly in Central Europe," *International Security* 7 (Summer 1982): 3–39 (on the late 1970s and early 1980s).

[64] On these points see Chapter 3 at notes 47–53, and Chapter 6 at notes 69–98, 104–13.

The chauvinist myths embedded in many nationalisms are another source of false optimism. These chauvinist myths often foster arrogance and contempt: "We are strong and brave, our enemies are cowardly and incompetent, perhaps even subhuman, hence easily beaten." Thus Wilhelmine-era German nationalists proclaimed that Germans were "the greatest civilized people known to history" and that "the German should feel himself raised high above all the peoples who surround him and whom he sees at an immeasurable depth below him."[65] Germans were assured that "the French Army lacks the . . . united spirit which characterizes the German army, the tenacious strength of the German race, and the esprit de corps of the officers."[66] The French likewise claimed that "we, the French, possess a fighter, a soldier, undeniably superior to the one beyond the Vosges in his racial qualities, activity, intelligence, spirit, power of exaltation, devotion, patriotism."[67] A French schoolbook later informed students that in war "one Frenchman is worth ten Germans."[68] The wide currency of such nationalist chest-pounding in prewar Europe goes far to explain the rosy optimism that infected both sides as they rode to war in 1914.

The balance of will

Which adversary will pay a higher price for victory? The answer can decide a war's winner; hence a misreading of relative will can foster false optimism. States rarely exaggerate their own will, but they often underestimate the enemy's. As a result, they misjudge the endurance or the matériel that each will commit to the war, seeing an illusory balance in their own favor. This fosters false expectations of victory.

Alcibiades wrongly claimed in 415 B.C.E. that the Sicilians would offer little resistance to the Athenians, being a polyglot collection of tribes that lack "the feeling that they are fighting for their own fatherland," and would "make separate agreements with us."[69] Britain's Major John Pitcairn wrote from the rebellious American colonies in 1775 that "one active campaign, a smart action, and burning two or three of their towns, will set everything to rights."[70] In 1899, British leaders thought the Boers would quit without a fight: in the words of Alfred Milner, British High Commissioner in South

---

[65] General Friedrich von Bernhardi, *Germany and the Next War*, trans. Allen H. Powles (London: Edward Arnold, 1914; first published in Germany in 1912), p. 14; and Professor Werner Sombart, in 1915, quoted in William Roscoe Thayer, ed., *Out of Their Own Mouths* (New York: D. Appleton, 1917), p. 60.

[66] Bernhardi, *Germany and the Next War*, p. 146.

[67] Ferdinand Foch, *The Principles of War* (London: Chapman & Hall, 1918), p. 285.

[68] A. Mironneau, *Choix de Lectures* (1924), quoted in Carleton J. H. Hayes, *France: A Nation of Patriots* (New York: Octagon, 1974), p. 366.

[69] Thucydides, *Peloponnesian War*, p. 420.

[70] Quoted in Blainey, *Causes of War*, p. 43.

Africa, "a slap in the face" would bring the Boers around, and at worst "an apology for a fight" would be necessary.[71]

Before World War I, German planners hoped that Britain would send no troops immediately to France even if it joined the war, and that Belgium would confine itself to a cosmetic show of force against German invaders.[72] A Japanese general explained that "we thought China would soon throw up its hands and quit" when Japan invaded China in 1937.[73] Soviet leaders thought Finland would quickly submit in 1939, believing that "we could fire one shot and the Finns would put up their hands and surrender."[74] Hitler underestimated Britain's steely resolve in World War II, even hoping in 1939–40 that Britain would ask for terms.[75] In 1941 Japan's leaders hoped a demoralized United States would settle with Japan after early defeats.[76] During the Vietnam War, U.S. planners had "a confidence—it was never bragged about, it was just there— . . . that when the chips were really down the other people would fold."[77] North Vietnam had parallel illusions: in late 1963 Hanoi thought the United States would not offer much military response if Hanoi committed troops to South Vietnam.[78]

Kuwait doubted that Iraq would attack before its 1990 invasion, dismissing Iraqi threats as bluff.[79] Iraq then thought the United States would abandon its effort to free Kuwait as it had Vietnam, a view that Norman Cigar attributes in part to "an Iraqi perception of American society as decadent and lacking staying power." Before the 1991 U.S. attack, the Iraqi press described the United States as a nation of "highway robbers, criminals, and unwanted people" and claimed that the "will to fight of the U.S. military has declined steadily" over the years. As the attack began, Saddam Hussein predicted a "revolt" by antiwar Americans that would reverse U.S. policy.[80]

---

[71] Quoted in A. J. P. Taylor, *Rumours of War* (London: Hamilton Hamish, 1952), p. 156.

[72] John A. Moses, *The Politics of Illusion: The Fischer Controversy in German Historiography* (London: George Prior, 1975), p. 95; Fischer, *Germany's Aims*, p. 37; Tuchman, *Guns of August*, p. 147.

[73] General Shimomura Sadamu, quoted in Ienaga, *Pacific War*, p. 85.

[74] Khrushchev, *Khrushchev Remembers*, p. 152.

[75] Bell, *Origins of the Second World War*, pp. 275–76. See also Norman Rich, *Hitler's War Aims: Ideology, the Nazi State, and the Course of Expansion* (New York: Norton, 1973), p. 9.

[76] In September 1941 Japanese military planners thought a U.S.-Japan war "may end because of a great change in American public opinion, which may result from . . . the remarkable success of our military operations." Nobutaka Ike, ed., *Japan's Decision for War: Records of the 1941 Policy Conferences* (Stanford: Stanford University Press, 1967), p. 153.

[77] Bill Moyers, quoted in Leslie H. Gelb with Richard K. Betts, *The Irony of Vietnam: The System Worked* (Washington, D.C.: Brookings, 1979), p. 342.

[78] James J. Wirtz, *The Tet Offensive: Intelligence Failure in War* (Ithaca: Cornell University Press, 1991), p. 26. Hanoi considered but dismissed the possibility that the United States would deploy up to a hundred thousand troops to Vietnam (ibid.); in fact the United States eventually committed over half a million men.

[79] Lawrence Freedman and Efraim Karsh, *The Gulf Conflict 1990–1991* (Princeton: Princeton University Press, 1993), p. 49.

[80] Cigar, "Iraq's Strategic Mindset," pp. 4, 7.

Illusions about the balance of power feed illusions about the balance of will. Governments infer that if their opponents are weak they will see the writing on the wall and fold. Hence governments that exaggerate their relative power will also exaggerate their relative will.

Chauvinist nationalism is a prime source of false optimism about the balance of will. Nationalist propaganda often inflates the bravery of one's own people and denigrates the opponents' toughness and character. Carleton Hayes has noted the "exaggerated notion of the bravery and worth of their own countrymen and an equally exaggerated notion of the viciousness and cowardice of foreigners" that pervaded many Western schoolbooks after World War I.[81] Such propaganda is bound to foster illusions about one's own fortitude and that of others.

Nationalist mythology exaggerates the righteousness of the national cause, leading groups to misread the balance of legitimacy between their own and their adversary's claims. The balance of legitimacy, in turn, helps shape the balance of will. Those in the wrong can concede more easily because their concessions set smaller precedents, casting doubt only on their will to defend illegitimate claims; those in the right find concessions harder because they set a broader precedent, casting doubt on their will to defend many interests, both illegitimate and legitimate. Thus, a misreading of the balance of legitimacy will likely lead to a misreading of the balance of will. Those who conclude that "our side is right" will deduce that "our adversaries know we are right, they are testing us to see if we know it too, and they will back down if we stand firm." Adversaries will back down because "once they learn we know we are right, they will realize that we have more will than they do and that we can outlast them; so they will fold if we stand firm." These chains of misperception rest on a false chauvinist-nationalist definition of the situation.

False theories of state motivation can foster illusions about the balance of will. For example, leaders can embrace "bandwagon" beliefs, wrongly assuming that states more often align with than against threatening states.[82] This leads them to exaggerate their ability to cow opponents into submis-

---

[81] Carlton J. H. Hayes, *Essays on Nationalism* (New York: Macmillan, 1926), pp. 88–89. The sentiments Hayes records echo ideas that abound in cultures in conflict. In examples that could be repeated many times, Thucydides records the Corinthians declaring that "there can be little doubt about our superiority so far as courage is concerned" before the Peloponnesian War, and Fujiwara Akira argues that before 1941 the Japanese Army was permeated with the belief that "the American people, because of their liberalism and individualism, would not be able to endure a protracted war." Thucydides, *Peloponnesian War*, p. 105; Fujiwara Akira, "The Role of the Japanese Army," in Dorothy Borg and Shumpei Okamoto with David K. A. Finlayson, eds., *Pearl Harbor as History: Japanese-American Relations 1931–1941* (New York: Columbia University Press, 1973), pp. 189–96 at 194.

[82] On balancing, bandwagoning, and the general prevalence of the former over the latter, see Stephen M. Walt, *The Origins of Alliances* (Ithaca: Cornell University Press, 1987), pp. 17–33, 147–80, 263–66, 276–80.

sion with displays of power, and to wrongly assume that their acts of intimidation have reduced the opponents' will to resist.

States will misread the balance of will if they underestimate the propensity of war to stiffen others' resolve. War can beget war by causing each side to harden its views of the other, leading each side to pursue wider aims with greater tenacity.[83] Elites can underestimate their opponent's will if they disregard this effect, overlooking the energizing effect of their own use of force on the opponent. Japan's main error in 1941 lay in overlooking the impact of the Pearl Harbor attack on American will. Japanese leaders thought a display of Japanese military prowess would cow the Americans; in fact it aroused and enraged them. Likewise, Hitler was blind to the ways his violence and aggression energized others against him.

The relative strength and commitment of allies

Leaders can misjudge relative power because they misjudge the relative loyalty and strength of both sides' allies. Such misjudgments are a common and often key element in decisions for war. Corinth attacked Corcyra, triggering the Peloponnesian War, in the false expectation that Athens would not intervene against it.[84] Frederick the Great falsely expected Britain or the Bourbon powers (France and Spain) to join his 1740 attack on Austria.[85] France declared war on Austria in 1792, wrongly expecting that Britain would stand neutral and that Prussia would more likely side with France rather than against it.[86] U.S. leaders failed to foresee Napoleon's sudden collapse when they declared war on Britain in 1812, assuming instead that he would keep Britain occupied.[87] Russian leaders stirred the Crimean War in 1853 without foreseeing that Austria would stand against them; had they anticipated this, they might well have drawn back.[88] Denmark resisted Prussian and Austrian demands in 1864 partly because it vainly hoped for British help if they attacked.[89] Austria exaggerated the power of its probable allies among the lesser German states before the 1866 Austro-Prussian War.[90] France had false hopes of assistance from Austria-Hungary and Italy when

[83] Noting this possibility is Eric J. Labs, "Fighting for More: The Sources of Expanding War Aims" (Ph.D. diss., MIT, 1994), pp. 65–67, 354.

[84] Donald Kagan, *The Outbreak of the Peloponnesian War* (Ithaca: Cornell University Press, 1969), pp. 351–52, 354.

[85] Reed Browning, *The War of the Austrian Succession* (New York: St. Martin's, 1993), p. 39.

[86] Blanning, *Origins of the French Revolutionary Wars*, pp. 109–10, 118, 135.

[87] Bradford Perkins, *Prologue to War: The United States and England, 1805–1812* (Berkeley: University of California Press, 1961), p. 405.

[88] Smoke, *War*, pp. 188–89.

[89] Ludwig Reiners, *The Lamps Went Out in Europe* (New York: Pantheon, 1955), p. 3.

[90] Smoke, *War*, p. 98.

it sparked the 1870–71 Franco-Prussian War.[91] The Boers vainly hoped for European intervention against Britain in 1899.[92]

Many Germans vainly hoped that Britain would remain neutral in 1914,[93] and that Switzerland, Sweden, Norway, Greece, Bulgaria, and Romania might join the German side.[94]

Hitler hoped Britain and France would not fight for Poland in 1939, despite their many warnings. On August 14 he declared: "While England may talk big, even recall her ambassador, perhaps put a complete embargo on trade, she is sure not to resort to armed intervention in the conflict."[95] On August 22 he told his generals: "Now the probability is great that the West will not intervene."[96] An aide records that Hitler still thought Britain and France would not intervene on August 31, the day before his armies struck and three days before Britain and France declared war on Germany.[97]

Norway resisted German attack in 1940 on the assumption of prompt British aid, but that aid proved too little, too late.[98]

Mussolini joined World War II on the Axis side in 1940, believing the United States would never join on the other side.[99] Japan predicted German behavior correctly but exaggerated German power: in mid-1941 Japan's foreign minister thought Germany would defeat both Britain and the Soviet Union by the end of the year[100]—an assumption that emboldened Japan against the United States. In 1950 China's Mao Zedong approved the North Korean plan to attack South Korea, saying that "the USA would not intervene" since Korea was "such a small territory."[101] In 1956 British and French

---

[91] William Carr, *The Origins of the Wars of German Unification* (London: Longman, 1991), p. 189.

[92] Taylor, *Rumours of War*, p. 156.

[93] See Chapter 7 at notes 20, 21, 40, and 132.

[94] Moses, *Politics of Illusion*, p. 96.

[95] Quoted in Raymond J. Sontag, *A Broken World, 1919–1939* (New York: Harper & Row, 1971), p. 374.

[96] Quoted in A. J. P. Taylor, *The Origins of the Second World War*, 2d ed. (Greenwich: Fawcett, 1961), p. 254.

[97] Rich, *Hitler's War Aims*, p. 130; see also Jeremy Noakes and Geoffrey Pridham, eds., *Nazism 1919–1945: A History in Documents and Eyewitness Accounts*, 2 vols. (New York: Schocken Books, 1988), 2:749. The Poles oppositely expected more help than they got from Britain and France in 1939. The French assured the Poles they would launch a major offensive against Germany in the third week of war; the Poles realized their deceit only after war began. Donald Cameron Watt, *Too Serious a Business: European Armed Forces and the Approach to the Second World War* (Berkeley: University of California Press, 1975), p. 121.

[98] J. Andenaes, O. Riste, and M. Skodvin, *Norway and the Second World War* (Oslo: Johan Grundt Tanum Forlag, 1974), p. 50.

[99] Smith, *Mussolini's Roman Empire*, p. 202.

[100] Ike, *Japan's Decision for War*, pp. 64–65.

[101] Rosemary Foot, *The Wrong War: American Policy and the Dimensions of the Korean Conflict, 1950–1953* (Ithaca: Cornell University Press, 1985), p. 58; Kathryn Weathersby, "The Soviet Role in the Early Phase of the Korean War: New Documentary Evidence," *Journal of*

leaders wrongly thought the United States might support their attack on Egypt, and at worst would remain benevolently neutral.[102] Before the 1967 war, Nasser wrongly expected the world to press Israel to withdraw from any lands it seized if war broke out, and Israel won.[103] Pakistan's dictator Mohammad Yahya Khan wrongly thought China and the United States would protect him if he provoked war with India in 1971.[104] Argentina failed to foresee that the United States would support Britain in the 1982 Falklands War, instead expecting U.S. neutrality.[105] Iraq was wrongly confident that the United States would acquiesce before it invaded Kuwait in 1990.[106] Later it wrongly expected the U.S.-led coalition against Iraq would splinter under the pressure of war: an Iraqi newspaper forecast that "the fragile alliance of the enemies will fall apart and divide into two camps," with the Arabs and other Muslims joining Iraq.[107] Iraq also mistakenly thought the Soviet Union would support it against the United States.[108]

States can misread both the current international political balance and the way their use of force transforms this balance. Aggressors usually frighten neutral states into the enemy camp by their aggressions. Yet aggressors often fail to anticipate this, and underestimate their future opposition as a result. For example, Hitler perceived a real isolationist climate in the United States in the mid-1930s but failed to anticipate how his own aggressions would dissolve it.

ILLUSIONS OF CHEAP WAR

The more costly that governments believe war will be, the more carefully they avoid it.[109] Hence the illusion of cheap wars invites leaders to risk or to launch wars they would otherwise avoid.[110] These illusions of cheapness do

American-East Asian Relations 2 (Winter 1993): 423–58 at 442. Stalin also believed that the United States would not intervene. Ibid., pp. 433–34, 439.

[102] Christer Jöhnsson, "The Suez War of 1956: Communication in Crisis Management," in George, *Avoiding War*, pp. 160–90 at 163–64.

[103] Safran, *Israel*, p. 425.

[104] David K. Hall, "The Indo-Pakistani War of 1971," in Barry M. Blechman and Stephen S. Kaplan, eds., *Force Without War: U.S. Armed Forces as a Political Instrument* (Washington, D.C.: Brookings, 1978), p. 208.

[105] Lebow, "Miscalculation in the South Atlantic," p. 24.

[106] Freeman and Karsh, *Gulf Conflict*, p. 31.

[107] Editorial from *Al-Qadisiyya*, January 12, 1991, quoted in Cigar, "Iraq's Strategic Mindset," p. 11; see also pp. 9–14.

[108] Ibid., pp. 12–14.

[109] Offering empirical support is Jack S. Levy and T. Clifton Morgan, "The Frequency and Seriousness of War: An Inverse Relationship?" *Journal of Conflict Resolution* 28 (December 1984): 731–49. See also Greg Cashman, *What Causes War? An Introduction to Theories of International Conflict* (New York: Lexington Books, 1993), pp. 67–68.

[110] Developing this hypothesis is Lebow, *Between Peace and War*, pp. 247–54.

not precede every war, and belligerents sometimes even exaggerate the costs of a war they face.[111] Overall, however, underestimates of the price of war are a common companion—and often a pivotal element—to decisions for war.

The Greek leaders who launched the Peloponnesian War were blind to its ultimate cost. Historian Donald Kagan writes that "all expected a short war. . . . They all failed to foresee the evil consequences that such a war would have for everyone, victors and vanquished alike, that it would bring economic ruin, class warfare, brutality, [and] erosion of moral standards. . . . Had they done so they would scarcely have risked a war for the relatively minor disputes that brought it on."[112]

Britain expected only a local fight in North America as it launched war with France in 1756.[113] The war spread worldwide, with fighting in the Ohio Valley and Canada, the Caribbean, Europe, and the Indian Ocean. Russia thought the Crimean War would be short and glorious, while Britain and France thought the Sebastopol campaign could be accomplished easily, cheaply, and quickly.[114] War deaths numbered 45,000 British, 180,000 French, and 450,000 Russian, far above all combatants' expectations.[115]

Before the U.S. Civil War, southerners forecast that "a lady's thimble will hold all the blood that will be shed" in the coming conflict.[116] In fact, more Americans died than in all other wars in history combined, including the two world wars, Korea, and Vietnam.

Britain expected an easy victory against the Boers in 1899. On the eve of war, Britain's governor of the Cape Colony quizzically asked the British military commander: "Surely these mere farmers cannot stand for a moment against regular troops?" But the ensuing war killed twenty-two thousand British troops.[117]

Before World War I, most Europeans were blind to the costs of the coming war. Historian James Joll notes that across Europe "very few people inside or outside government circles expected a long and destructive world

[111] U.S. overestimates of expected losses in the 1991 Gulf War offer a striking example. Published prewar assessments almost universally forecast at least 1,000 and perhaps as many as 10,000 U.S. fatalities, while in fact the United States suffered only 146 battle deaths. Joel Achenbach, "The Experts, In Retreat: After-the-Fact Explanations for the Gloomy Predictions," *Washington Post*, February 28, 1991, p. D1; Jacob Weisberg, "Gulfballs: How the Experts Blew It—Big-Time," *New Republic*, March 25, 1991, pp. 17–19; Mike Royko, "Most Experts Really Blew It This Time," *Chicago Tribune*, February 28, 1991. A rare correct forecast, predicting under five hundred U.S. fatalities, was John J. Mearsheimer, "A War the U.S. Can Win—Decisively," *Chicago Tribune*, January 15, 1991.

[112] Kagan, *Outbreak of the Peloponnesian War*, p. 356.

[113] Smoke, *War*, p. 201.

[114] Blainey, *Causes of War*, p. 44; Smoke, *War*, p. 191.

[115] J. A. S. Grenville, *Europe Reshaped* (Great Britain: Fontana, 1976), p. 203.

[116] James M. McPherson, *Battle Cry of Freedom: The Civil War Era* (New York: Ballantine, 1988), p. 238.

[117] Blainey, *Causes of War*, pp. 46–47.

war."[118] German Chancellor Theobald von Bethmann-Hollweg expected a "brief storm."[119] British Foreign Secretary Edward Grey assured the House of Commons in August, 1914: "If we engage in war, we shall suffer little more than we shall suffer even if we stand aside."[120]

Mao Zedong misread the coming clash with the United States in Korea, predicting in October 1950 that "the scope of this war will probably not be great, and the duration will not be long."[121] China lost nine hundred thousand dead, including Mao's son, in what was the bloodiest civil or international conflict on earth since World War II.[122]

States can underestimate the costs of war because they misunderstand new technology or tactics. For example, U.S. Defense Secretary James Schlesinger once suggested that a major Soviet-American nuclear exchange might kill fewer than two million Americans, and perhaps as few as fifteen to twenty-five thousand.[123] A prominent military commentator declared in 1946 that the effect of the atomic bombs dropped on Hiroshima and Nagasaki "had been wildly exaggerated" and that the same bombs dropped on New York or Chicago might have produced property damage limited to "broken window glass over a wide area."[124]

Alternately, leaders may underestimate an adversary's will, as the British underestimated Boer will; or they may fail to understand that "war begets

---

[118] James Joll, *The Origins of the First World War* (London: Longman, 1984), p. 88.

[119] Quoted in L. L. Farrar, Jr., "The Short War Illusion: The Syndrome of German Strategy, August–December, 1914," *Militärgeschichtliche Mitteilungen* 2 (1972): 40. Bethmann-Hollweg sounded more sober at other times; see Lebow, *Between Peace and War*, p. 252. But see also Chapter 7 at notes 38–39 for more German false optimism.

[120] On August 4, quoted in Zara S. Steiner, *Britain and the Origins of the First World War* (New York: St. Martin's, 1977), p. 210. Grey's prediction was wrong by a ghastly measure: Britain suffered 1,031,000 military and civilian deaths in World War I, more than twice its loss in any other war in history. Ruth Leger Sivard, *World Military and Social Expenditures 1991* (Washington, D.C.: World Priorities, 1991), p. 23. Grey's private view of the coming war was gloomier, however. As war began he remarked that "the lamps are going out all over Europe. We shall not see them lit again in our lifetime." Joll, *Origins of the First World War*, p. 31.

[121] Thomas J. Christensen, *Useful Adversaries: Grand Strategy, Domestic Mobilization, and Sino-American Conflict, 1947–1958* (Princeton: Princeton University Press, 1996), p. 272.

[122] Chinese casualties are from J. David Singer and Melvin Small, *The Wages of War, 1816–1965: A Statistical Handbook* (New York: Wiley, 1972), p. 127. Comparison to other wars is with data from Sivard, *World Military and Social Expenditures 1991*, pp. 22–25. Sivard estimates total deaths in Korea at three million.

[123] Schlesinger first estimated U.S. casualties from various Soviet counterforce attacks at fifteen to twenty-five thousand, and later at one to two million, in congressional appearances in 1974. John Duffield and Frank von Hippel, "The Short-Term Consequences of Nuclear War for Civilians," in Julius London and Gilbert F. White, eds., *The Environmental Effects of Nuclear War* (Boulder: Westview, 1984), pp. 26–50 at 30, 32, 36, 47; Desmond Ball, review of *The Effects of Nuclear War*, *Survival* 22 (September/October 1980): 233–34 at 233. For a contrasting estimate see William Daugherty, Barbara Levi, and Frank von Hippel, "The Consequences of 'Limited' Nuclear Attacks on the United States," *International Security* 10 (Spring 1986): 3–45 at 40–41. They forecast at least 13–34 million U.S. deaths.

[124] Major Alexander de Seversky, quoted in Scott D. Sagan, *Moving Targets: Nuclear Strategy and National Security* (Princeton: Princeton University Press, 1989), pp. 13–14.

war"—that the use of force can expand the other's interests and make war harder to end. For example, Alcibiades thought the Athenians could simply "come home again" if their attack on Syracuse went badly,[125] Japan thought it could negotiate peace with the United States after striking Pearl Harbor, and Hitler hoped he could make peace with Britain after fighting a "sham war" in 1939.[126]

Leaders can underestimate the domestic political price that war will exact. Before 1914 many European conservatives failed to see that a great war would destroy Europe's old order, instead hoping that war would bolster the conservative regimes. Russian leaders hoped war would arouse patriotic sentiments that would dampen the fires of revolution,[127] and many German conservatives thought war would weaken the Social Democrats. One conservative German newspaper held in 1911 that war would ensure the "restoration to health of many political and social institutions." A second argued that "the domestic situation would benefit from a bold passage at arms even if it brought tears and anguish to individual families."[128]

Societies can trivialize war by persuading themselves that war is glorious, healthy, romantic, or masculine. Alcibiades recommended Athens's ruinous war with Syracuse in 415 B.C.E. by noting war's benefits: in war Athens "will constantly be gaining new experience," and "a city which is active by nature will soon ruin itself if it changes its nature and becomes idle."[129] Before World War I, many Europeans likewise believed a great war would be a beneficial, healthy exercise for society. A British publicist wrote that wars are "bracing tonics to the national health"; and a British leader declared that war brought benefit by "strengthening the moral fibre of a nation."[130] German publicists stressed "the inevitableness, the idealism, and the blessing of war,"[131] and declared that war was a "savior and a healer," "the periodically indispensable solution" to national problems, which brought "uprise and adventure, heroism and excesses, cold deliberation and glowing idealism."[132] A German newspaper called for a "brisk and merry war," as if this

[125] Thucydides, *Peloponnesian War*, p. 422.

[126] Halder recorded on August 25, 1939: "Fuerher would not take it amiss if England were to wage a sham war." Shirer, *Rise and Fall*, p. 549n.

[127] Lebow, *Between Peace and War*, pp. 248–49. Russia's reactionary minister of the interior V. K. Plehve likewise allegedly confided before the Russo-Japanese War of 1904–5 that "what this country needs is a short victorious war to stem the tide of revolution." Ibid., p. 248.

[128] Fritz Fischer, *War of Illusions: German Policies from 1911 to 1914*, trans. Marian Jackson (New York: Norton, 1975), p. 83, quoting the Berlin *Post* and the *Deutsches Armeeblatt*.

[129] Thucydides, *Peloponnesian War*, p. 422.

[130] Sidney Low in 1898, quoted in Bernard Porter, *The Lion's Share: A Short History of British Imperialism, 1850–1983*, 2d ed. (London: Longman, 1984), p. 129; Lord Lansdowne, quoted in Bernard Brodie, *War and Politics* (New York: Macmillan, 1973), p. 266.

[131] Bernhardi, *Germany and the Next War*, p. 37.

[132] Louis L. Snyder, *German Nationalism: The Tragedy of a People* (Port Washington: Kennikat Press, 1969), pp. 233, 241, quoting unnamed publicists. German historian Heinrich von Treitschke likewise praised "the moral majesty of war" and "the sublimity of war," and

were possible. A leading German historian wrote of "the grandeur of war." German youths were told that "war is beautiful."[133] A German officer argued that war is a "powerful promoter of civilization" and is "fought in the interest of biological, social, and moral progress."[134] When war broke out, the German crown prince summoned his compatriots to a "bright and jolly war."[135] A euphoric Belgian officer exclaimed, "War, what an exalting thing!" when Germany presented its ultimatum.[136]

To Prevent War, Promote Transparency

The historical record suggests that false optimism is a potent and pervasive cause of war. False expectations of victory widely coincide with the outbreak of war.[137] This suggests that false optimism is a strong and common cause of war.

If so, the control or abatement of false optimism would prevent many wars. It follows that the risk of war is reduced when relative power is clear and the nature and costs of war are known. States seldom fight when both sides know the winner and the price. Hence anything that makes the world more transparent will reduce the risk of war. Policies of deception and secrecy are bad; policies of open disclosure are good.

---

scorned the notion of perpetual peace as "not only impossible but immoral as well." Quoted in Blanning, *Origins of the French Revolutionary Wars*, p. 1.

[133] The *Ostpreussische Zeitung* in December 1912, quoted in Lebow, *Between Peace and War*, p. 251; Heinrich von Treitschke in 1899–1900, quoted in Joll, *Origins of the First World War*, p. 187; and the *Jungdeutschland Post* in 1913, quoted in ibid., p. 193.

[134] General Friedrich von Bernhardi in 1912, quoted in Wallace Notestein and Elmer E. Stoll, eds., *Conquest and Kultur: Aims of the Germans in Their Own Words* (Washington, D.C.: U.S. Government Printing Office, 1917), p. 43.

[135] James Joll, *Europe since 1870: An International History* (Harmondsworth: Penguin, 1976), p. 193.

[136] Quoted in M. S. Anderson, *The Ascendancy of Europe: Aspects of European History, 1815– 1914* (London: Longmans, 1972), p. 69.

[137] Concurring are Geoffrey Blainey, who notes "the optimism with which most wars were commenced" during the past three centuries; Alfred Vagts, who notes that "with only a few exceptions, the wars of the century from 1815 to 1914 were undertaken with each side believing that it would win the war"; and John Stoessinger, who notes "a remarkable consistency in the self-images of most national leaders on the brink of war. Each confidently expects victory after a brief and triumphant campaign." Blainey, *Causes of War*, p. 35; Vagts, *Defense and Diplomacy*, p. 284; John G. Stoessinger, *Why Nations Go to War*, 6th ed. (New York: St. Martin's, 1993), p. 214.

[3]

Jumping the Gun: First-Move Advantage and Crisis Instability

Hypothesis 2. War is more likely when the advantage lies with the first side to mobilize or attack.

Strategists have warned since the late 1950s that the risk of war rises with the size of the advantage that accrues to the first side to mobilize or attack.[1] This warning, embodied in what became known as "stability theory,"[2] emerged as a staple argument in U.S. defense and arms control policy debates during the 1960s, 1970s, and 1980s.[3] Its most striking and debated im-

[1] The benefits of surprising others, and the dangers of being surprised, have been familiar since the first rock was thrown. The more general notion that the risk of war rises with the size of the first-strike or first-mobilization advantage is new with the modern era. Jonathan Griffin mentioned it in passing in 1938, but it was first developed by Albert Wohlstetter, Fred Hoffman, and Thomas Schelling in a series of papers appearing during 1954–60. See Albert Wohlstetter and Fred Hoffman, "Defending a Strategic Force after 1960" (Santa Monica: unpublished RAND working paper, February 1, 1954), p. 18; Albert Wohlstetter, "The Delicate Balance of Terror," *Foreign Affairs* 37 (January 1959): 211–34 at 230; Thomas C. Schelling, "Surprise Attack and Disarmament," *Bulletin of the Atomic Scientists* 15 (December 1959): 413–18; idem, "Meteors, Mischief, and War," *Bulletin of the Atomic Scientists* 16 (September 1960): 292–96; and idem, *The Strategy of Conflict* (Cambridge: Harvard University Press, 1960), pp. 207–54. See also Thomas C. Schelling, *Arms and Influence* (New Haven: Yale University Press, 1966), pp. 221–59. Griffin is quoted in George H. Quester, *Deterrence before Hiroshima: The Airpower Background of Modern Strategy* (New York: Wiley, 1966), pp. 88–89. A short history of the idea is Marc Trachtenberg, *History and Strategy* (Princeton: Princeton University Press, 1991), pp. 17–25.

[2] Theorists suggested that the outbreak of crises under conditions of first-strike advantage might trigger "reciprocal fear of surprise attack" (see below), leading to war. This fear of "crisis instability" led many to use the term "stability theory" to refer to all hypotheses framing risks posed by first-strike or first-mobilization advantages. I follow that convention. Many also use "stability theory" to refer to ideas on arms racing ("arms race instability"), but those ideas are not considered here.

[3] Prominent early works elaborating stability theory include Hedley Bull, *The Control of the Arms Race*, 2d ed. (New York: Praeger, 1965), pp. 158–74; Glenn H. Snyder, *Deterrence and Defense: Toward a Theory of National Security* (Princeton: Princeton University Press, 1961),

plication was that states should forego the ability to stage surprise attacks on adversaries because possessing this ability could cause unwanted war. Its proponents believed with Thomas Schelling that "the likelihood of war is determined by how great a reward attaches to jumping the gun."[4] Hence they thought the United States should move to reduce this reward for both superpowers by securing U.S. forces from surprise attack and by foregoing the capacity to make a surprise attack on Soviet forces. Hence they urged greater effort to secure vulnerable U.S. strategic bomber forces in the 1950s, and from the 1960s to the 1980s they opposed a range of counterforce strategic nuclear weapons programs, including hard-target-killing intercontinental ballistic missiles (ICBMs) and area ballistic missile defenses. These counterforce forces, they argued, conferred a surprise-attack capability that the United States should forswear for its own safety.[5]

Stability theorists never offered empirical evidence to support their theory, however, and many critics were unpersuaded. One critic argued that instability has been "inconsequential" in history and that "it is difficult to find even one war caused by 'instability.'"[6] Two other critics complained that stability theory "can appeal only to ambiguous evidence and to abstract deductive logic for its support"; one of these branded the concept of stability "the principal intellectual culprit in our pantheon of false strategic gods."[7] A fourth critic has claimed that preemptive war, the prime danger identified by stability theory, "almost never happens" and that "the significance of preemption has been exaggerated as a path to war."[8]

---

pp. 97–114; and Thomas C. Schelling and Morton H. Halperin with Donald G. Brennan, *Strategy and Arms Control* (New York: Twentieth Century Fund, 1961), pp. 9–17. A survey of the role of stability theory in U.S. arms control policy is Steven E. Miller, "The Limits of Mutual Restraint: Arms Control and the Strategic Balance" (Ph.D. diss., Fletcher School of Law and Diplomacy, 1988), chap. 3.

[4] Schelling, *Arms and Influence*, p. 235.

[5] An example of this school is Charles Glaser, *Analyzing Strategic Nuclear Weapons Policy* (Princeton: Princeton University Press, 1990), pp. 141–45.

[6] Stephen Peter Rosen, "Nuclear Arms and Strategic Defense," *Washington Quarterly* 4 (Spring 1981): 82–99 at 83, 86. Rosen's reference is to both crisis instability and arms race instability (see note 2). He further decries an American "obsession with abstract notions of stability" that has "paralyzed our thinking about nuclear war" (p. 83). Rosen's skepticism is echoed by others. See, for example, Richard K. Betts, "Surprise Attack and Preemption," in Graham T. Allison, Albert Carnesale, and Joseph S. Nye, Jr., eds., *Hawks, Doves and Owls: An Agenda for Avoiding Nuclear War* (New York: Norton, 1985), pp. 54–79, who quotes Rosen approvingly (p. 70). Most diplomatic historians have also dismissed stability theory, as Marc Trachtenberg notes. *History and Strategy*, p. viii.

[7] Colin S. Gray and Keith B. Payne, "Nuclear Strategy: Is There a Future?" *Washington Quarterly* 6 (Summer 1983): 55–66 at 57; Colin S. Gray, "Nuclear Strategy: A Case for a Theory of Victory," *International Security* 4 (Summer 1979): 54–79 at 82. Gray concludes that theories of stability are "obsolescent." Colin S. Gray, "Strategic Stability Reconsidered," *Daedalus* 109 (Fall 1980): 135–54 at 136.

[8] Dan Reiter, "Exploding the Powderkeg Myth: Preemptive Wars Almost Never Happen," *International Security* 20 (Fall 1995): 5–34 at 33.

This chapter argues that stability theorists were right, but largely for the wrong reasons. First-strike and first-mobilization advantages markedly raise the risk of war. However, the specific hazard that stability theorists most often warned against—preemptive war stemming from "reciprocal fear of surprise attack"—is very rare. Other dangers raised by first-move advantages are far more potent and have caused major trouble in the past.

Thus critics of stability theory were correct to doubt the version of the theory advanced by its proponents, but they were wrong to dismiss the theory entirely. Even traditional stability theory has some power, and a repaired version fashioned by adding elements to the traditional version is markedly stronger. (See Diagram 1 for a summary of both versions.)

FIRST-STRIKE, FIRST-MOBILIZATION, AND FIRST-MOVE ADVANTAGES

A *first-strike advantage* obtains when an advantage accrues to the first of two adversaries to use force. A *first-mobilization advantage* obtains when an advantage accrues to the first of two adversaries to mobilize its forces or otherwise prepare for war. I use "first-move advantage" to refer to both first-strike and first-mobilization advantages. A common label fits because they have similar effects.

A first-strike advantage creates a direct temptation to use force (for example, Israel's 1967 attack on Egypt). A first-mobilization advantage causes war indirectly, by tempting states to mobilize their military forces (for example, Russia's 1914 military mobilization). Such mobilization can trigger war through its secondary effects—specifically, through the preventive or preemptive incentives to attack that it can create. (On preventive incentives see Chapter 4.) For example, if the mobilizer's adversary knows that it cannot keep pace with the mobilizer, the adversary may strike before the mobilizer gets mobilization underway.[9] If the mobilizer finishes mobilizing first, it may strike its lagging adversary to consolidate its advantage.[10] If both sides mobilize without war, the side whose forces will degrade faster may strike before degradation begins; or the poorer side may strike to forestall

---

[9] For example, in the 1920s German officers favored a strategy of prompt attack on France at the outset of any French mobilization, since France had more reserves and hence could expand its forces more than Germany during a mobilization race. On this *attaque brusquée* strategy see Barry R. Posen, *The Sources of Military Doctrine: France, Britain, and Germany between the Wars* (Ithaca: Cornell University Press, 1984), p. 185.

[10] Clausewitz sketched the problem: "When one side takes the field before the other, it is usually for reasons that have nothing to do with the intention of attack or defense. They are not the motives, but frequently the result of an early appearance. The side that is ready first and sees a significant advantage in a surprise attack, will for *that* reason take the offense." Carl von Clausewitz, *On War*, ed. and trans. Michael Howard and Peter Paret (Princeton: Princeton University Press, 1976), p. 371.

Diagram 1. Stability theory old and new

Bold lines (——) are strong proposed causal paths
Light lines (——) are very weak proposed causal paths

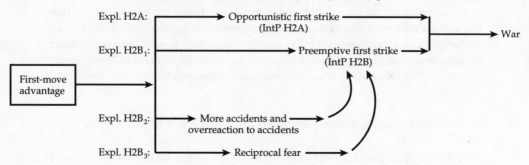

H2, Version 1: Traditional stability theory (Schelling)

H2, Version 2: Repaired stability theory
Changes from Version 1: Reciprocal fear (H2B₃) downgraded to "very weak";
Concealed grievances/capabilities/plans/perceptions (H2C),
Hasty/truncated diplomacy (H2D), Offensive advantage (H2E) added.

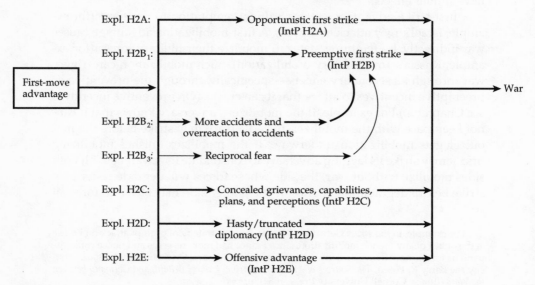

Key:

H2:   Hypothesis 2
Expl.:   Explanation
IntP: Intervening phenomenon

the costs of a prolonged confrontation.[11] Finally, a mobilization can spur another's attack if the other thinks the mobilization is a harbinger of war and that the side striking first will have an advantage. These secondary effects can be potent causes of war; hence a first-mobilization advantage is often nearly as dangerous as a first-strike advantage.

I also use "first-move advantage" broadly in a second sense: to include first strikes and mobilizations against one's *opponent* (for example, Israel's 1967 attack on Egypt) and first strikes against *neutral third parties* launched to forestall an enemy attack on the third party (for example, Germany's 1940 attack on Norway). Both incentives raise the risk of conflict. The first generates conflict between two prime adversaries, the second widens a conflict to engulf neutrals.

Hypotheses on the Effects of First-Move Advantages

First-move advantages have five dangerous effects. Of these, the danger of preemptive war (explanation H2B) is the best known. This danger explains a significant amount of war. Its most famous variant, "reciprocal fear of surprise attack," is very weak, however. Reciprocal fear has been much discussed but rarely occurs.

The strongest danger—the concealment of grievances, capabilities, plans, and perceptions (explanation H2C)—has been overlooked so far. It holds that first-move advantages cause war by crippling diplomacy. Critics have complained that stability theory posits a mechanistic, apolitical interaction. The "concealment" hypothesis frames a danger that stems from the corrosive effect of first-move advantages on the diplomatic process, and shows diplomacy shaped and confined by military factors.

Opportunistic attack (explanation H2A)

A first-move advantage improves an attacker's prospects for victory, since the attacker claims the first move and enjoys the benefits that come with it. This causes war by tempting states to play the attacker. Starting wars carries smaller risks and pays larger rewards; hence states are quicker to start them.

Such opportunistic logic has figured in many decisions for war. Japan at-

---

[11] Israeli strategists have long held that Israel must attack soon after mobilizing because mobilization would drain Israeli economic resources, and Israel has a smaller resource base than its Arab opponents, hence it would lose a prolonged mobilized confrontation. See Edward Luttwak and Dan Horowitz, *The Israeli Army* (New York: Harper & Row, 1975), p. 212.

tacked Russia in 1904 partly because it saw that it could seize the advantage of the initiative.[12] Russian leaders thought Russia could steal a march on Germany in July 1914 by secretly mobilizing first;[13] one historian suggests that this hope helped crystallize Russia's fateful July 30 decision to mobilize.[14] Similar hopes drew Japan toward war in 1941. Admiral Isoroku Yamamoto saw the opportunity to "decide the fate of the war on the very first day" and "at the outset of the war to give a fatal blow to the enemy fleet" in his planned surprise attack on the U.S. fleet at Pearl Harbor, and he conditioned his support for the war on approval of that attack.[15] Israeli Air Force commanders advised war in June 1967 from confidence that they could accomplish their planned surprise smashing of Egypt's air force.[16]

Preemptive mobilization or attack (explanation H2B)

A first-move advantage raises the military cost of letting an opponent move first. It also raises the odds that the opponent will move first unless forestalled by preemptive action, since the opponent is enticed to jump the gun by the temptations outlined in explanation H2A.[17] Therefore, restraint in a crisis is more dangerous. An opponent's first blow is more damaging and more likely, hence a preemptive move to forestall that blow is more expedient.[18]

[12] Patrick Morgan, "Examples of Strategic Surprise in the Far East," in Klaus Knorr and Patrick Morgan, eds., *Strategic Military Surprise: Incentives and Opportunities* (New Brunswick, N.J.: Transaction Books, 1983), pp. 43–76 at 56.

[13] Russian Foreign Minister Sergei Sazonov falsely hoped that Russia could secretly mobilize without being quickly detected. See Luigi Albertini, *The Origins of the War of 1914*, 3 vols., trans. and ed. Isabella M. Massey (1952–57; Westport, Conn.: Greenwood, 1980), 2:573, 584, 624.

[14] Luigi Albertini in ibid., 2:573.

[15] Gordon W. Prange with Donald M. Goldstein and Katherine V. Dillon, *At Dawn We Slept: The Untold Story of Pearl Harbor* (Harmondsworth: Penguin, 1982), pp. 15, 16; Roberta Wohlstetter, *Pearl Harbor: Warning and Decision* (Stanford: Stanford University Press, 1962), p. 368.

[16] Luttwak and Horowitz, *Israeli Army*, p. 219.

[17] The attacker also loses less by breaking the peace, because peace is less likely to endure in any case. The choice is less "war or peace" than "war now or war later"—a choice less of war itself than of its timing and character.

[18] A preemptive mobilization or attack is mounted to seize the initiative, in the belief that the first mover gains an important advantage and a first move by the opponent is imminent. A preventive attack, in contrast, is mounted to engage an opponent before it gains relative strength. The incentive to preempt is two-sided: both adversaries gain by forestalling the other. The incentive to prevent is one-sided: the declining state wants immediate war, while the rising state wants to avert war. My definition accords with Richard K. Betts, *Surprise Attack: Lessons for Defense Planning* (Washington, D.C.: Brookings, 1982), p. 145. Others distinguish preemptive from preventive war temporally: a preemptive war forestalls an immediate attack, a preventive war forestalls a more remote attack. For example, see Reiter, "Powderkeg Myth," pp. 6–7. This usage leaves it unclear whether a first-move advantage or an impending power shift motivates an attack. The answer matters; it decides our choice of remedies. For example, improved warning can reduce the risk of conflict arising from first-move advantage but does not lower the risk of war driven by impending power shifts.

Preemptive motives of this sort are not commonplace, but they are potent catalysts of war when they appear, and they helped catalyze several important wars of the past.[19] In 1914 Russian leaders ordered general mobilization partly from fear that Germany would steal a march on Russia if Russia did not steal a march on Germany by mobilizing first. The Russians "decided that in view of the small probability of avoiding a war with Germany it was indispensable to prepare for it in every way in good time" by promptly mobilizing.[20] Otherwise, they feared, Germany might "gain time to complete her preparations in secret."[21]

In April 1940 Hitler attacked Norway largely to forestall a feared British seizure of Norway. He explained his sudden decision on February 20: "I am informed that the English intend to land [in Norway], and I want to be there before them."[22] In May 1940 Hitler attacked Belgium during his strike

[19] For a contrary view see Reiter, "Powderkeg Myth." He concludes that preemptive wars "almost never happen" after finding that only three of sixty-seven wars since 1815 were preemptive: World War I (reflecting a preemptive German mobilization), the 1967 Arab-Israeli War, and the 1950–53 U.S.-China conflict. Our difference is partly one of historical interpretation, partly one of definition, partly one of language—that is, over what "almost never" means—and partly one of standards of judgment for theories: how strongly must a cause operate before we accord it importance? Reiter argues that Russian mobilizations in 1914 and French mobilization in 1870 were not preemptive (ibid., pp. 14n, 19–20). I see ambiguities in the record of both cases, but I think the bulk of available evidence indicates that preemptive motives operated in both—clearly in 1914, less clearly but probably in 1870. Reiter defines preemptive wars to exclude attacks by states at war on neutrals; hence he omits Hitler's 1940 attacks on Norway and the Low Countries. His definition is reasonable but has no clear heuristic advantage over mine. Reiter argues that three preemptive wars among sixty-seven translates to preemption "almost never" happening. I set a lower standard: a phenomenon that causes three major wars in 180 years happens more than "almost never" and merits fear and respect. Finally, Reiter notes that preemptive motives have never been sufficient to cause war alone, even in the three cases of preemption he identifies. This judges theories of war by standards that are too severe. Wars almost never have a single cause. If we dismiss war causes that cannot cause wars alone, we will dismiss nearly every cause. We should be interested in any cause that contributes significantly to any war. Most of the important contributing causes of war are neither necessary nor sufficient to war, but they are nevertheless important.

Reiter and I also disagree on whether the 1950 U.S.-China war and the 1914 German mobilization were preemptive. I list the 1950 U.S.-China war as an opportunistic first strike but not a preemption. Our difference stems from our use of different definitions, outlined in note 18 above. I regard Russia's 1914 mobilization and Germany's 1914 attack on Belgium as preemptive, but not Germany's 1914 mobilization. Reiter takes an opposite view of all three actions. (Thus we agree that World War I was preemptive but disagree on why.) On the other hand, I concur with Reiter (ibid., p. 14n) that Poland's 1920 attack on Russia and Japan's 1941 attack on Pearl Harbor were not preemptive, although an early draft of this chapter said otherwise. My list of modern preemptive wars is: World War I, the 1967 Arab-Israeli War, Hitler's 1940 attacks on Norway and the Low Countries, and probably the 1870 Franco-Prussian War.

[20] Baron M. F. Schilling's summary of results of a meeting on July 29 between Sazonov, Minister of War V. A. Sukhomlinov, and Chief of General Staff Nicholas Janushkevich, quoted in Albertini, *Origins*, 2:555.

[21] Sazonov's view, recorded by French Ambassador Maurice Paléologue, quoted in Albertini, *Origins*, 2:619.

[22] B. H. Liddell Hart, *History of the Second World War*, 2 vols. (New York: G. P. Putnam's Sons, 1972), 1:56.

against France in part to forestall a feared Anglo-French seizure of Belgium. Germany had to attack, he argued, because if "the French Army enters Belgium in order to attack us, it will be too late for us. We must anticipate them. . . . If we don't violate [Belgian and Dutch] neutrality, England and France will do it."[23]

In June 1967 Israel attacked Egypt in part to forestall what it feared would be a damaging Egyptian first strike.[24] On the eve of war, Israeli Defense Minister Moshe Dayan made a textbook argument for preemptive attack, advising Prime Minister Levi Eshkol that the Egyptians were "anxious to get in the first blow," but "it would be fatal for us to allow them to launch their attack," hence Israel should "strike the first blow."[25] Israel attacked the next day.

Three types of preemptive war can be distinguished: generic, accidental war, and war stemming from reciprocal fear of surprise attack. The first is the most common.

Generic preemptive war (explanation H2B₁)

States mobilize or attack because they see a first-move advantage and they fear they will soon be attacked. Their fears of attack could stem from any cause other than accidents or reciprocal fear. For example, they could fear that an opponent will strike to gain expansionist aims, or will strike preventively to forestall its own relative decline, or will strike to exploit the benefits of holding the initiative.

Accidental war (explanation H2B₂)

States mobilize or attack because they see a first-move advantage and they misread an accident as a signal of an impending attack by an opponent.

Three types of accidents are possible triggers for accidental war.[26] First, misinformation or misinterpretation of evidence could create false warning of attack, sparking preemption of a nonexistent threat. Such misjudgment could arise from human reporting error (for example, an agent falsely reports an adversary mobilization), technical error (a radar mistakes a moon-

---

[23] In late 1939, quoted in Alfred Vagts, *Defense and Diplomacy: The Soldier and the Conduct of Foreign Relations* (New York: Kings Crown, 1956), p. 317.
[24] Michael Handel, "Crisis and Surprise in Three Arab-Israeli Wars," in Knorr and Morgan, *Strategic Military Surprise*, pp. 111–46 at 126–27, 133; Moshe Dayan, *Story of My Life: An Autobiography* (New York: Warner Books, 1976), pp. 409–12; Luttwak and Horowitz, *Israeli Army*, pp. 221–23; Janice Gross Stein, "The Arab-Israeli War of 1967: Inadvertent War through Miscalculated Escalation," in Alexander L. George, ed., *Avoiding War: Problems of Crisis Management* (Boulder: Westview, 1991), pp. 126–59 at 139.
[25] Dayan, *Story*, pp. 410, 412.
[26] Noting these possibilities is Herman Kahn, *On Thermonuclear War*, 2d ed. (New York: Free Press, 1969), p. 228.

rise for incoming missiles), or human misreading of evidence (innocent acts by another are mistaken for preparations to attack, or catalytic acts by a third party are mistaken for enemy action). Second, weapons could be fired by technical error, sparking counterattack. Third, weapons could be deployed or fired without authorization, again sparking counterattack.[27]

Such accidents are more dangerous and more common when states believe that it pays to move first.[28] They are more dangerous because states are quicker to "shoot first and ask questions later." Governments grow more anxious to hold the initiative than to avoid war. Hence they can overreact to a small accident that they falsely believe portends a larger attack.

Accidents are more common because to enable a fast military response to attack, governments keep forces on high alert and disperse the authority to use force. This raises the risk of accidental or unauthorized launch, and of overreaction to false warning by local commanders. For example, during the Cold War both the United States and the Soviet Union secretly adopted risky strategies of launch-on-warning for their nuclear forces, each from fear that the other might smash its force by surprise. No disaster ensued, but the risk of disaster was raised by these policies.[29]

Examples of accidents contributing to the outbreak of war are very rare but not wholly unknown.[30] Carthage launched the second Punic War (218 B.C.E.) in part to forestall a Roman attack that it mistakenly expected.[31] The French decision for mobilization that hastened the slide toward war in 1870 was informed by false warning of Prussian mobilization.[32] Russia's

[27] My definition of accidental war follows Scott D. Sagan, *The Limits of Safety: Organizations, Accidents, and Nuclear Weapons* (Princeton: Princeton University Press, 1993), p. 263. Accidental war should be distinguished from the broader category of "inadvertent war"—wars that grew from decisions taken without the expectation or desire that they would cause war. Inadvertent war includes accidental war and also wars that emerge from a range of other causes, e.g., from overcommitment arising from underestimates of others' resolve, or from deliberate military moves that have unforeseen military effects or trigger unexpected military responses.

[28] Schelling, "Meteors, Mischief, and War," p. 294.

[29] Bruce G. Blair, *The Logic of Accidental Nuclear War* (Washington, D.C.: Brookings, 1993), pp. 8–9, 46–52, 168–218. For more on delegations of authority and difficulties in maintaining central control of military operations in Cold War crises see Scott D. Sagan, "Nuclear Alerts and Crisis Management," *International Security* 9 (Spring 1985): 99–139.

[30] Noting the rarity of accidental wars in history are Sagan, *Limits of Safety*, pp. 262–63; Geoffrey Blainey, *The Causes of War*, 3d ed. (New York: Free Press, 1988) pp. 141–45; and Michael Howard, *The Causes of War and Other Essays*, 2d ed. (London: Temple Smith, 1983), p. 12. Howard argues that accidental war is nonexistent: "If history shows any record of 'accidental' wars, I have yet to find them." The initiation of war "is almost by definition a deliberate and carefully considered act."

[31] R. M. Errington, *The Dawn of Empire: Rome's Rise to World Power* (Ithaca: Cornell University Press, 1972), pp. 55–61.

[32] Deduced from Vagts, *Defense and Diplomacy*, p. 394, and Michael Howard, *The Franco-Prussian War: The German Invasion of France, 1870–1871* (New York: Granada, 1961), p. 58. For other hints at preemptive French motivation see ibid., pp. 45, 52.

general mobilization in 1914 was triggered in part by erroneous reports of German mobilization.[33] In each case, false warning triggered a quick response partly because a perceived first-move advantage made response seem urgent.[34]

Reciprocal fear of surprise attack (explanation H2B$_3$)

States mobilize or attack because they see a first-move advantage, and they fear attack by another *because they think the other fears their own attack and may move to forestall it*.[35] In this view, the incentive to preempt is self-expanding: it generates a reciprocal spiral of fear in the attacker's mind, compounding the primary incentive to preempt. This spiral is driven by awareness that the opponent may fear one's own preemptive attack. Thus Thomas Schelling suggests that under conditions of first-strike advantage governments would fear that the opponent "thinks we think he'll attack; so he thinks we shall; so he will; so we must."[36] A state caught in this mental loop attacks an opponent to preempt the opponent's preemption of its own preemption.

This is the standard version of stability theory. Its logic is compelling, but supporting evidence is scarce. Reciprocal fear is very rare in the real world: my survey of history uncovers only one weak instance of it.[37] States some-

[33] For Russia's exaggerated perceptions of German mobilization measures see Albertini, *Origins*, 2:499, 566–67, 570, 576, 614; 3:2–3, 8–12; and Bernadotte E. Schmitt, *The Coming of the War, 1914*, 2 vols. (New York: Scribner's, 1930), 2:225, 237–38. Schmitt concludes that the Russian general staff "greatly exaggerated the picture which it drew" of German mobilization measures (2:238). For French perceptions of German mobilization measures see Albertini, *Origins*, 2:191, 647; Schmitt, *Coming*, 2:17–18. For actual German mobilization measures taken before 1:00 P.M. on July 31, when preliminary mobilization (*Kriegsgefahrzustand*) was ordered, see Schmitt, *Coming*, 2:18n, 66, 130, 135, 144, 148–49, 225n; Albertini, *Origins*, 2:491, 496. See also Richard Ned Lebow, *Between Peace and War: The Nature of International Crisis* (Baltimore: Johns Hopkins University Press, 1981), pp. 238–42, who notes that Russian, German, and French leaders each exaggerated their adversary's mobilizations and overreacted accordingly.

[34] For more clashes arising from false warning see Schelling, *Arms and Influence*, p. 95n (the 1775 battle of Concord); and Sagan, *Limits of Safety*, p. 263n (the battle of Wounded Knee).

[35] See Schelling, *Strategy of Conflict*, pp. 207–29.

[36] Schelling, *Strategy of Conflict*, p. 207. For another formulation, positing that reciprocation occurs between states, not just in the attacker's mind, see Snyder, *Deterrence and Defense*, p. 104.

[37] During the 1967 Mideast crisis, two Israeli officials, Defense Minister Moshe Dayan and military intelligence chief General Aharon Yariv, mentioned concerns that Egypt might be driven to strike by its fear of an Israeli strike. On May 25, Yariv warned that Egypt might attack that night if Soviet intelligence gave it warning of Israel's planned first strike on Egypt's air force. Handel, "Crisis and Surprise," p. 129. In Israel's last prewar cabinet meeting on June 4, Dayan argued that the Egyptians were "anxious to get in the first blow," and "if they thought that was our intention too, they would not hesitate to beat us to it and launch their attack the day before we did." Stein, "Arab-Israeli War of 1967," pp. 156–57. These arguments were not developed, however, and have the flavor of points that were not strongly believed but were made for effect. Also, the theory of reciprocal fear was well known by 1967 and might have been causing its own echoes in Israeli discussions.

times strike to forestall an adversary's strike. However, the imagined reasons for the adversary's strike seldom lie in the adversary's fear of the attacker's first strike. States often expect sudden violence from others, but they rarely understand that violence as growing from other states' fear of their own sudden violence.[38]

Concealment of grievances, military capabilities, military plans, and national misperceptions (explanation H2C)

When it pays to move first, states conceal their grievances because honesty could trigger an opponent's preemptive attack. States also conceal their military capabilities, their military plans, and their political plans and ideas in order to avoid rousing opponents to take countermeasures that negate their capacity to strike a telling first blow. These concealments cause war by impeding diplomacy, by raising the risk of military missteps in crisis, by leading opponents into military overconfidence, and by preventing others from correcting dangerous national misconceptions.

Hidden interests and grievances

States cannot safely spell out their casus belli in a world of first-move advantage because this tells an opponent when to preempt if it decides to ignore the warning. As Herman Kahn explained, in a first-strike world "real ultimatums of the 'you must back down by 12:00 noon!' type are vastly too dangerous to give because if they are unequivocal they are likely to touch off a pre-emptive strike at 11:00 A.M."[39] As a result, ultimata that might be accepted are not delivered before force is used. Interests that might be respected if declared are inadvertently trampled by others. In this way, conflicts that have peaceful solutions acceptable to both sides can still end in war.

Prussia's Frederick the Great attacked Austria in 1740 without first exploring Vienna's willingness to concede peacefully because, as he later explained, "we would have been potting our own ball if we had tried to negotiate with Vienna."[40] His advisors thought Austria might accept his demands,[41] but Frederick could not probe Austria's feelings without tipping

---

[38] Why is reciprocal fear rare? Robert Jervis argues that states chronically underestimate the threat they pose to others. Robert Jervis, *Perception and Misperception in International Politics* (Princeton: Princeton University Press, 1976), pp. 67–76, 352–55. If so, this misperception should dampen reciprocal fear by blinding states to the possibility that others might fear them enough to strike them defensively. Misperceptions usually raise dangers, but here a misperception is risk reducing.

[39] Kahn, *On Thermonuclear War*, p. 211.

[40] Pierre Gaxotte, *Frederick the Great*, trans. R. A. Bell (New Haven: Yale University Press, 1942), p. 194.

[41] Gaxotte, *Frederick the Great*, p. 193; Ludwig Reiners, *Frederick the Great: A Biography*, trans. Lawrence P. R. Wilson (New York: G. P. Putnam's Sons, 1960), pp. 93–94.

his hand, warning it to prepare for war if it chose to refuse his demands. Hence he attacked without warning, foregoing a chance for a peaceful triumph to gain a more certain military victory.

China faced the same dilemma in the fall of 1950. U.S. forces under UN command were fast approaching China's Yalu River border with North Korea. China's armies could not defeat the U.S.-UN forces unless they gained surprise. They could not gain surprise if UN commanders expected a Chinese attack.[42] Had China clearly warned that it would attack if U.S. forces approached the Yalu, this would have reduced its chance for surprise. What if the United States was bent on gaining the Yalu, whatever China did? China's warning would spur the United States to secure its forces against surprise or even to strike China preemptively. In short, had China clearly told the United States what it planned to do, it might have become unable to do it.[43] China's threat to fight would have reduced its ability to fight. Hence China chose a lulling strategy over a warning strategy. After October 13, China published only one oblique warning and issued no ultimatum before its massive November 26 attack.[44] As a result, U.S. officials were uncertain of China's entry up to the last moment.

For similar reasons, Egyptian president Anwar Sadat lulled Israel by feigning interest in a new U.S. peace effort before the 1973 Arab-Israeli War.[45] Egypt's war plan required surprise. Surprise, in turn, required that Israel believe that Egypt was in a docile mood. Had Israel known that Egypt would fight to regain lost lands, it might have been more willing to return

---

[42] By late November 1950, China had secretly moved 300,000 troops into North Korea, where they joined 83,000 North Korean troops to face 440,000 UN troops of superior firepower. But UN commander Douglas MacArthur estimated Chinese forces at only 40,000–71,000, so he failed to prepare to meet their attack. He was defeated chiefly because his force was poorly deployed when China struck on November 26. For force estimates see Alan Whiting, *China Crosses the Yalu* (Stanford: Stanford University Press, 1960), pp. 122–24; and Peter Lowe, *The Origins of the Korean War* (London: Longman, 1986), p. 200.

[43] Making this point are Alexander George and Richard Smoke, *Deterrence in American Foreign Policy* (New York: Columbia University Press, 1974), p. 189.

[44] China issued a series of six warnings during late September and early October (on September 25 and 30, and October 1, 3, 9, and 13). See Lebow, *Between Peace and War*, pp. 172–73; and Burton I. Kaufman, *The Korean War: Challenges in Crisis, Credibility, and Command* (Philadelphia: Temple University Press, 1986), p. 93. Only the October 3 warning framed an explicit threat, however. The others were couched in negative terms ("we cannot stand idly by") that left unstated what China threatened to do, and all six warnings left the U.S. government unconvinced that China would intervene. Moreover, with one minor exception the warnings stopped after mid-October, once the UN's vulnerable deployment in North Korea became clear and Mao recognized the possibility of surprising the UN force. On this recognition, and Mao's shift to a strategy of surprise attack, see Jian Chen, "China's Changing Aims during the Korean War, 1950–1951," *Journal of American-East Asian Relations* 1 (Spring 1992): 8–41 at 24. On the exception see note 86 below.

[45] Mohamed Heikal, *The Road to Ramadan* (New York: Quadrangle, 1975), p. 17; Trevor N. Dupuy, *Elusive Victory: The Arab-Israeli Wars, 1947–1974* (New York: Harper & Row, 1978), pp. 391–92.

land; but it also could have made Egypt unable to fight by striking Egyptian forces at the first sign of Arab attack. The advantage of moving first forced Sadat to choose between using his military power for coercive diplomacy or for war.[46] He could not do both.

In short, when it pays to move first, governments reduce their ability to execute threats by spelling them out, so they mute their grievances. This hampers negotiation to resolve conflicts. Conversely, when moving first pays no reward, states pay no penalty for framing their interests clearly. Negotiators can be candid, negotiations bear more fruit, and fewer "lines in the dust" are crossed by mistake.

Hidden military capabilities

In a world of first-move advantage, states conceal their military capabilities to preserve their capacity to strike by surprise. At a minimum they conceal their strengths; at a maximum they actively feign weakness. Their object is to avoid scaring the opponent into a preemptive attack, and to lull the opponent into letting down its guard, ripening it for surprise attack. But feigned weakness can also cause wars of false optimism by feeding opponents' military overconfidence, thereby leading them to start wars they cannot win. And it can lead opponents to underestimate one's will to fight— "They won't stand up to us because they know they'll lose"—leading them to inadvertently push crises over the brink to war.

Before Egypt's 1973 attack on Israel, Egyptian officials planted stories in the Western press that their forces were unready for war, their surface-to-air missiles (SAMs) were almost inoperable, and Syrian pilots disliked their Soviet aircraft.[47] Egypt could not defeat Israel unless it gained surprise. To achieve surprise, Egypt sought to appear inept.

Egypt's deception succeeded. Israeli officials thought an Egyptian attack would be suicidal, hence implausible. This ripened Israel for the Arabs' October 6 surprise.[48] But it also meant that in the meantime Israel had less rea-

---

[46] Israel pursued a similar lulling strategy before it attacked in 1967, as noted below at note 122. Japan likewise issued no ultimatum (instead giving a general warning with no deadline) before launching its 1904 surprise attack on Russia. As a result, many Russian officials thought Japan would never fight. Ian Nish, *The Origins of the Russo-Japanese War* (London: Longman, 1985), pp. 206, 211–12, 216, 249. Russia began its premobilization on July 24–25, 1914, without first warning Austria and Germany that it would premobilize unless they backed off. And the United States concealed the fact that it was nearing a decision for war against Britain during the run-up to the War of 1812, to avoid sparking a British preemption. David Nickles, "International Crises, Telecommunications, and the Atlantic Ocean, 1812–1917" (Ph.D. diss., Harvard University, 1999), chap. 1.

[47] Chaim Herzog, *The War of Atonement* (Boston: Little, Brown, 1975), pp. 33–34; Zeev Schiff, *October Earthquake*, trans. Louis Williams (n.p.: University Publishing Projects, 1974), p. 24; Dupuy, *Elusive Victory*, p. 392; Donald Neff, *Warriors against Israel* (Brattleboro, Vt.: Amana Books, 1988), pp. 121–22.

[48] Israeli military intelligence thought the Arabs could be crushed as easily as in 1967. See Insight Team of the London Sunday Times, *The Yom Kippur War* (Garden City: Doubleday,

son to make concessions.[49] Negotiations were probably doomed in any case, but Egypt's deception made certain they went nowhere.

During the fall of 1950, China likewise took elaborate steps to conceal the strength of its growing Korean force from the United States. Chinese troops were given gross underestimates of their own force size, then ordered to surrender in hopes that their U.S. interrogators would believe these underestimates, as in fact they did.[50] On the battlefield the Chinese theater commander pursued a strategy of purposely showing weakness, to encourage the United States to rush unwarily into China's military trap.[51] Mao was overjoyed when his intelligence learned that General Douglas MacArthur, the UN commander, had swallowed the deception.[52] This made MacArthur easier to surprise,[53] but it also fed the growth of U.S. war aims: U.S. leaders soon embraced the goal of conquering North Korea, which seemed an easy prize.

Hidden military plans

In a world of first-move advantage, states more carefully conceal their military plans and capabilities to preserve their capacity to strike by surprise. Otherwise, targets are forewarned and tactical surprise is lost. But such secrecy raises the risk that leaders will issue orders that have unforeseen military effects, which raises the danger of inadvertent war. For example, in July 1914 Russian civilians authorized preliminary mobilization

1974), p. 65. Reflecting this confidence, Israeli Deputy Prime Minister Yigael Allon declared during the summer of 1973 that "Egypt has no military option at all." Donald Neff, *Warriors for Jerusalem: The Six Days That Changed the Middle East* (New York: Simon & Schuster, 1984), pp. 6–7. Israeli Prime Minister Golda Meir declared the Arab attack "suicidal" when she announced the attack to Israel's public. Nadav Safran, *Israel: The Embattled Ally* (Cambridge: Harvard University Press, 1978), p. 477.

[49] The same logic infected the U.S. government. U.S. Secretary of State Henry Kissinger brushed off Egyptian feelers of interest in U.S. mediation in 1972 and early 1973, on the assumption that Egypt had no military option and hence did not need to be placated. Alexander L. George, "The Arab-Israeli War of October 1973: Origins and Impact," in Alexander L. George, ed., *Managing U.S.-Soviet Rivalry: Problems in Crisis Prevention* (Boulder: Westview, 1983), pp. 139–54 at 145–46.

[50] Martin Lichterman, "To the Yalu and Back," in Harold Stein, ed., *American Civil-Military Decisions: A Book of Case Studies* (Birmingham: University of Alabama Press, 1963), pp. 569–642 at 599–600.

[51] Chen, "China's Changing Aims," p. 25.

[52] Thomas J. Christensen, "Threats, Assurances, and the Last Chance for Peace," *International Security* 17 (Summer 1992): 122–54 at 141.

[53] In mid-October MacArthur assured President Truman that there was "very little" chance of Chinese intervention, because China would surely lose: "If the Chinese tried to get down to Pyongyang there would be the greatest slaughter." Michael Doyle, "Endemic Surprise? Strategic Surprises in First World–Third World Relations," in Knorr and Morgan, *Strategic Military Surprise*, pp. 77–110 at 93. See also Lowe, *Origins of the Korean War*, p. 192; George and Smoke, *Deterrence*, pp. 228–30.

on July 24–25 without grasping that if this provoked German mobilization, war would promptly result. Their error grew from their ignorance that the German mobilization plan melded mobilization and attack. The German plan included a darkly secret surprise strike on Belgium by German standing forces at the outset of mobilization.[54] Not knowing this, the Russians could not know that German mobilization inexorably meant immediate war.[55] Hence they triggered the landslide of mobilizations without grasping the cosmic implications of their actions. The secrecy that confused them grew from Germany's effort to gain surprise against Belgium.

A state's military planning secrecy can also lead its adversaries to overconfidence if they underestimate their opponent's cleverness. Thus Japan's secret planning for its Pearl Harbor attack left Americans confident that Japan could not perform it. U.S. commentators declared that "Japanese attack upon Hawaii is a strategical impossibility" and "there is no danger of Japan attacking Hawaii in any force so long as it harbors the battle fleet."[56] The attack depended on closely held Japanese innovations—for example, shallow-water torpedoes—that U.S. planners had never seen and hence assumed away.[57] Americans would not believe without being shown, but could not be surprised if they were, so Japan had to leave their illusions undispelled.

Hidden misperceptions

War-causing misperceptions are self-sustaining in a world of first-move advantages. States planning surprise attacks keep their plans and ideas secret. As a result, the logic and premises that produced these plans are invis-

---

[54] Germany's planned strike on Belgium was a secret even from German leaders, including the naval chief, Admiral Tirpitz, and perhaps even the kaiser. Albertini, *Origins*, 2:581.

[55] Perhaps Russian leaders realized that mobilization meant war by the time they ordered full mobilization on July 30, but they did not know it when they ordered preliminary mobilization on July 24–25. See Chapter 7, note 135. Russian civilians were also unaware that their own forces had to be mobilized on both the German and Austrian frontiers—a partial mobilization against Austria alone was impossible—hence any Russian mobilization was certain to provoke a German mobilization, and war. Albertini, *Origins*, 2:292–94. They learned this crucial detail only when the Russian quartermaster-general returned from travel on July 26. By then partial mobilization was approved in principle (on July 24–25) and preliminary mobilization was already underway. Schmitt, *Coming of the War*, 1:505–6, 2:94–96; D. C. B. Lieven, *Russia and the Origins of the First World War* (New York: St. Martin's, 1983), pp. 144–45. This error stemmed from Russian military secrecy, and shows that secrecy can confuse one's own government as well as others.

[56] George Fielding Eliot in 1938 and W. D. Puleston in 1941, quoted in David Kahn, "United States Views of Germany and Japan in 1941," in Ernest R. May, ed., *Knowing One's Enemies: Intelligence Assessment Before the Two World Wars* (Princeton: Princeton University Press, 1986), pp. 476–502 at 497.

[57] Noting U.S. ignorance of these torpedoes is Ronald H. Spector, *Eagle against the Sun: The American War with Japan* (New York: Random House, 1985), p. 97.

ible to outsiders. This protects them from evaluation, saving false premises from correction by critics.

Frederick the Great launched the War of the Austrian Succession in 1740 in the false hope that other states would help Prussia carve up Austria.[58] Others could not correct his misconception because he concealed his planned attack and the logic behind it.

Kim Il Sung, Mao Zedong, and Stalin launched the Korean War in 1950 in the false hope that the United States would not intervene against a Northern attack on the South.[59] Their error was sustained by the North's decision to seek the advantage of military surprise, which led it to enshroud its planned attack in secrecy. The U.S. government, unaware that plans for war were afoot, could not correct the three leaders' misconception.[60]

The folly-filled 1956 Suez War had similar roots. Israel, France, and Britain planned the war in dark secrecy, partly because Israel thought operational surprise was important.[61] As a result they underestimated worldwide opposition to their scheme, especially U.S. opposition. The U.S. government could not correct this false belief because it was hidden from the United States, along with the rest of the secret Israeli-French-British scheme.[62]

Such secrecy prevents evaluation from within as well as without. The Japanese Navy's disastrous decision to launch the Pacific War by striking Pearl Harbor was so secret that even the top government decision-making body, the Liaison Conference Group, was never told of it.[63] Unaware of the planned attack, other Japanese officials could hardly criticize it. After the war, deceived officials claimed that they would have opposed the attack had they known of it.[64]

The French-British-Israeli decision to attack in 1956 was confined to a very small group that excluded the top diplomats of those countries—an exclusion bound to produce miscalculation of the worldwide reaction.[65]

---

[58] Reiners, *Frederick the Great*, p. 97; Gerhard Ritter, *Frederick the Great*, trans. Peter Paret (Berkeley: University of California Press, 1974), p. 83.

[59] Nikita Khrushchev, *Khrushchev Remembers*, trans. and ed. Strobe Talbott (Boston: Little, Brown, 1970), p. 368; Doyle, "Endemic Surprise," pp. 84–89.

[60] U.S. intelligence was oblivious to the coming Northern attack even on the eve of the war. Douglas Jehl, "C.I.A. Releases Files on Korea and Cold War," *New York Times*, October 1, 1993, p. A7.

[61] Moshe Dayan, *Diary of the Sinai Campaign* (London: Weidenfeld & Nicolson, 1966), pp. 34, 77.

[62] See Christer Jöhnsson, "The Suez War of 1956: Communication in Crisis Management," in George, *Avoiding War*, pp. 160–90 at 161–64, 173–75; Dayan, *Diary*, p. 74; Townsend Hoopes, *The Devil and John Foster Dulles* (Boston: Little, Brown, 1973), passim, especially pp. 350 ff.

[63] Scott D. Sagan, "Origins of the Pacific War," *Journal of Interdisciplinary Studies* 18 (Spring 1988): 893–922 at 916–17.

[64] Morgan, "Examples of Strategic Surprise," p. 52.

[65] Handel, "Crisis and Surprise," p. 116.

To preserve military surprise, U.S. officials concealed the 1961 Bay of Pigs Cuban invasion project even from the State Department Cuban desk and the CIA assessment branch, excluding analysts who might have identified its many preposterous assumptions.[66]

In short, the search for surprise leads states to partition their analytic functions. This impedes analysis.

Hasty or truncated diplomacy (explanation H2D)

All causes of war create incentives to use force, but many (for example, false optimism, commercial motives for war, or nationalist motives for war) create no incentive for war now rather than later. First-move advantage is doubly dangerous in creating incentives to use force and to use it *now*. States must conduct diplomacy under a deadline: conflicts must be resolved before someone preempts. This imposes a corrosive haste on decision making, a haste that hampers diplomacy and magnifies the risk of war-causing errors. Moreover, if preemption follows, it truncates diplomacy that otherwise might bear fruit.

Haste raises two main risks. First, governments may overlook formulas that could bridge their differences because they lack time to explore all options. When the 1914 July crisis exploded in war, diplomats were exploring a "Halt in Belgrade" proposal that seemed to bridge the gap between the two alliances. By July 29 both the British government and the German kaiser had endorsed it, and on July 30 the Russian foreign minister endorsed something similar. But diplomacy was cut short when Russia mobilized preemptively, driving Germany to mobilize and attack.[67] Luigi Albertini argues that "had Russia waited longer before mobilizing, probably if not certainly, some agreement could have been found on a formula in the nature of the *Halt in Belgrade*."[68]

Second, states in crises have less time to verify their assumptions and to cure others' misconceptions. German and Russian bellicosity in July 1914 was fueled by misconceptions that survived until after mobilizations began and the crisis was out of control. German leaders had false hopes that Britain would not enter a continental war against them, a misconception that encouraged their belligerence.[69] Russian leaders wrongly doubted Serbia's

---

[66] Doyle, "Endemic Surprise," pp. 101, 104.

[67] A discussion is Jack Levy, "Crisis Management and World War I," in George, *Avoiding War*, pp. 62–102 at 80–82. On Russia's acceptance see Albertini, *Origins*, 2:562–63.

[68] Albertini, *Origins*, 2:578. Hence Sazonov "bears a heavy responsibility and committed a terrible mistake in resorting to mobilization before diplomacy had irreparably failed to compose the dispute." Albertini in ibid., 2:539.

[69] Jack S. Levy, "Preferences, Constraints, and Choices in July 1914," *International Security* 15 (Winter 1990/91): 151–86 at 163–70.

role in the June assassination of Archduke Francis Ferdinand, a misconception that stiffened their resistance to Austria's demands on Serbia. The Austrian government prepared a dossier showing Serb complicity, but this dossier reached Russia only after war began.[70] The Russians also wrongly assumed that Austria intended large annexations of Serbian territory.[71] Had the crisis developed slowly, these German and Russian fallacies could have been cured before irrevocable steps were taken, but the landslide of mobilizations foreclosed discussion.

The 1967 Mideast crisis likewise exploded before Nasser realized that the United States would not help Egypt recover any lands it lost in a new war. He blithely expected the United States to force Israel to return any conquests, as it had in 1956–57. As a result, he thought he could risk war safely. Israel struck before the United States could dispel his illusions.[72]

Offensive military force postures and capabilities (explanation H2E)

A first-strike advantage invites states to adopt offensive force postures, since striking first requires operating on the tactical offensive. As a result forces grow more offensive, raising the risks of offense dominance (see Chapter 6).

States fearing attack are also slower to mobilize for self-defense in a crisis, since military moves are more likely to trigger preemption by the other side. In trying to avoid provoking war, however, states may do too little to deter it, leaving themselves exposed to an opportunistic strike that mobilization might deter.[73] The acuteness of this dilemma grows in direct proportion to the size of the advantage accruing to the side striking first.

Russia has experienced both sides of the dilemma. Russia began preliminary mobilization in 1914 partly to "take all the steps which would enable us to face an attack," but in so doing triggered a perhaps avoidable war.[74] Twenty-seven years later, as Hitler readied his Barbarossa attack, Stalin re-

---

[70] On Russia's ignorance of Serbia's role see Lieven, *Russia and the Origins of the First World War*, pp. 139–40; M. F. Schilling, *How the War Began in 1914*, trans. W. Cyprian Bridge (London: George Allen & Unwin, 1925), p. 58; and, on the Austrian dossier, Albertini, *Origins*, 2:291.

[71] Sidney B. Fay, *The Origins of the World War*, 2 vols., 2d ed. rev. (New York: Free Press, 1966), 2:325–29; Eugenia V. Nomikos and Robert C. North, *International Crisis: The Outbreak of World War I* (Montreal: McGill-Queen's University Press, 1976), pp. 58, 88–89. On July 24 Germany's ambassador to Russia, Friedrich von Pourtalès, told Sazonov that Austrian aims were limited but Sazonov disbelieved him. Ibid., p. 89. Sazonov's concerns about Austria's aims were eased by assurances from Austria on July 26, but by then Russian preliminary mobilization was already underway. Fay, *Origins*, 2:329.

[72] David Kimche and Dan Bawley, *The Six-Day War* (New York: Stein & Day, 1971), p. 283; Walter Laqueur, *The Road to War 1967* (London: Weidenfeld and Nicolson, 1968), p. 163.

[73] Noting this dilemma is Betts, *Surprise Attack*, p. 18.

[74] Lieven, *Russia and the Origins of the First World War*, p. 143, quoting Minister of Agriculture A. V. Krivoshein.

frained from manning Soviet border fortifications to avoided giving Germany any provocation, easing the way for Hitler's armies.[75]

These, then, are the dangers raised by first-move advantages. The same dangers arise when there is no first-move advantage but governments perceive one. They then act as if one existed, with comparable effects.

Antecedent conditions and counterpossibilities

Under some conditions a first-move advantage raises no risk of war, or even bolsters peace. The dangers outlined above require some level of underlying suspicion or hostility to emerge. For example, a first-move advantage between the United States and Canada would pose few risks. Moreover, a first-move advantage lowers the risk of war if it leads a state to conceal a grievance that, if aired, would produce war; but left unaired, the grievance fades and war is avoided. A first-move advantage could also frighten states that fear war into acting so cautiously that they avert wars that otherwise might occur. Finally, under some conditions states that accept the status quo can use a first-strike advantage to bolster their defenses, thereby strengthening peace. Specifically, a status quo state can arrange a first-strike advantage that deters aggression by ensuring that any war the aggressor starts will escalate. If the aggressor would be deterred by total war but not by limited war, a first-strike advantage serves peace. Thus NATO Cold War doctrine for defending Western Europe rested on the threat of a U.S. strategic nuclear first strike if NATO conventional defenses crumbled. To be credible, this threat in turn required some first-strike advantage at the strategic level, to bolster the U.S. incentive to strike. Strategic instability in this instance made central war more likely if local war broke out, which reduced the risk of local war to begin with.

Examples of states being hypercautious or concealing grievances until they fade in response to first-move advantages are hard to come up with, however. The use of first-strike advantage to bolster defense is also very rare—there are no examples aside from NATO's European Cold War strategy. This suggests that the conditions needed for first-move advantages to produce these pacifying effects are very rare and that first-move advantages raise the risk of war far more often than they reduce it.

TESTS OF STABILITY THEORY

What predictions (that is, observable implications) can be inferred from repaired stability theory (hereafter simply "stability theory")? How can

---

[75] Betts, *Surprise Attack*, pp. 34, 39.

these predictions be tested? What do tests indicate? How much history can stability theory explain?

This section frames four predictions from stability theory and tests them with three case studies. These tests support stability theory and indicate that it explains a fair amount of history. First-move advantage—or perceptions of it—played a significant role in causing more than a few wars.

Theories can include two types of hypotheses, prime and explanatory. A prime hypothesis frames a theory's claim that its independent phenomenon causes its dependent phenomenon. For example, the prime hypothesis of stability theory claims that first-move advantages cause war ("war is more likely when the advantage lies with the first side to mobilize or attack"). Explanatory hypotheses explain how the theory's independent phenomenon causes its dependent phenomenon. For example, stability theory's "concealment" explanation (H2C) includes two explanatory hypotheses: one claims that first-move advantages cause states to conceal their grievances, capabilities, military plans, and misperceptions; another claims that the concealment of grievances, capabilities, military plans, and misperceptions causes war.

Predictions are likewise of two types, prime and explanatory. A theory's prime predictions are inferred from its prime hypothesis. Tests of prime predictions shed light on whether the prime hypothesis operates—in this case, on whether first-move advantages cause war. Explanatory predictions are inferred from a theory's explanatory hypotheses. Testing them tells us if explanatory hypotheses operate and thereby sheds light on both whether and how the prime hypothesis operates. Stability theory's explanatory predictions derive from the hypotheses that comprise its five explanations (H2A–H2E).

Predictions of stability theory

A major prime prediction from stability theory is that war will be more common in times and places of greater real and perceived first-move advantage. Another prime prediction is that states facing larger real or perceived first-move advantages should fight more wars than other states.[76] Unfortunately, testing these predictions would be very hard. Tests would require assembling data on the size of real and perceived first-move advantages

---

[76] These and following predictions frame expectations about the correlates of perceived as well as real first-move advantages because, as noted in Chapter 1, the correlates of perceptions of power are a sound guide to the impact of actual power realities. The effects of power realities are translated into outcomes through their effect on perceptions. Hence perceptions will correlate with phenomena that realities cause. Therefore, even a purely objective version of stability theory makes predictions about the correlates of both actual and perceived first-move advantages, and is tested by data on both reality and perceptions. The same is true of window theory, cumulativity theory, and offense-defense theory, discussed below.

through the ages and across the world, a task of many years. Fortunately, tests of explanatory predictions can also serve well. They give us a good picture of the strength of stability theory, since testing enough parts of a theory also tests the whole.

Four explanatory predictions are tested.

1. Intervening phenomena H2A–H2E (opportunistic first moves; preemptive first moves; concealment of grievances, capabilities, plans, and perceptions; hasty or truncated diplomacy; offensive force postures and fear of taking needed defensive steps in crises) will be more common among states or groups of states that face large real or perceived first-move advantages than among other states.
2. For a given state or group of states, intervening phenomena H2A–H2E will be more common in periods when first-move advantages (real or perceived) are large than in other periods. Elites will more often and actively consider opportunistic or preemptive first strikes. They will more carefully conceal grievances, military capabilities, military plans, and national perceptions. They will more often consider uses of force before verifying facts and finishing negotiations, and they will display more ignorance of their own and other's military arrangements (due to greater secrecy). They will be drawn to offensive force postures, while fearing to deploy forces for deterrence in crises.

In other words, comparisons across states (prediction 1) and comparisons among the same states in different periods (prediction 2) should find that intervening phenomena H2A–H2E correlate with real and perceived first-move advantages.

3. Elites that see large first-move advantages will explain policies that embody intervening phenomena H2A–H2E as required by the need to gain surprise or by the risk of being surprised. For example, officials might explain that "we must attack to forestall our opponents' attack" or "we must fool our adversaries into underestimating our military strength, to ripen them for surprise."
4. Decisions to use force, or that cause others to use force, should embody or respond to one or more of phenomena H2A–H2E, or should reflect misperceptions arising from these phenomena, when taken by states that perceive a first-move advantage. For example, we should observe states starting wars in the thrall of false optimism that stems from an opponent's concealment of its capabilities, or unwittingly triggering war by harming interests that the other never stated.

Tests

These predictions are tested in three cases: the U.S.-China conflict of 1950, World War I, and the 1967 Israel-Egypt War. I chose these cases for three reasons. First, they are well recorded. Second, in each case large real or perceived first-move advantages obtained or emerged. This creates a good setting for tests that contrast conditions in these cases to more average times and places. Third, in two cases the size of the real or perceived first-move advantage varied sharply across time or space. In the 1950 U.S.-China case, the size of the first-move advantage grew markedly over time. This allows fruitful within-case comparisons across time. The 1950 case and the 1967 case saw marked variance in estimates of the size of the first-move advantage among states included in the case, allowing within-case comparisons across states.[77]

Evidence from these cases largely fits the forecasts of stability theory. When the appearance of its intervening phenomena is predicted, at least some are observed. Thus stability theory passes the tests these cases pose. Moreover, the passed tests are fairly strong. Tested predictions are often quite singular—no other theory predicts the observed result—hence their fulfillment lends the theory strong support.

U.S.-China, 1950

The Korean War began on June 25, 1950, when North Korea launched a massive surprise invasion of South Korea. China's new communist government had approved the North's attack, expecting that the United States would not intervene to save the weaker South. But the United States quickly intervened, with powerful effect. U.S. forces deployed to South Korea under UN command in July. By early August these U.S. forces had stemmed the North Korean advance.

Then, on September 15, UN commander General Douglas MacArthur launched a stunning amphibious counterattack at Inchon, in the rear of North Korea's armies. The Northern forces quickly crumbled and fled back into North Korea. MacArthur charged after them in hot pursuit. His armies crossed into North Korea on October 7 and rushed north toward the China–North Korea border.

MacArthur's northward charge soon produced a large first-strike advantage between U.S. and Chinese forces. U.S. leaders were blind to this growing first-strike advantage, but Chinese officials were acutely aware of it. They responded by dropping efforts to deter America's rush to the Yalu, instead muffling their complaints against this rush and concealing China's growing military capabilities in Korea. These Chinese deceptions encouraged America's unwitting rush to an unwanted war.

Eager to destroy the routed Northern armies before they regrouped, MacArthur moved his army northward so fast that its command and communications came unraveled. MacArthur also divided his army, sending one force up each North Korean coast. The two forces were separated by the spine of mountains that runs down the peninsula. Both forces were strung

---

[77] I say more about the logic of these tests in *Guide to Methods for Students of Political Science* (Ithaca: Cornell University Press, 1997), pp. 58–63. On case selection criteria see pp. 77–88.

out over vulnerable mountain roads.[78] These maneuvers exposed Mac-
Arthur's force to devastating Chinese attack, if Chinese forces could steal
down the mountain spine unobserved and then strike its exposed flanks by
surprise. MacArthur's reckless advance had created a first-strike advantage
of historic proportions.

Chinese officials saw this opportunity and seized it. Mao Zedong decided
to intervene in Korea during October 2–13,[79] but at first he had planned a
positional defense against U.S.-UN forces in mid-North Korea.[80] A Chinese
buildup would follow, then an attack on U.S. forces from these positions in
perhaps six months. Shortly after October 15, as the opportunity for surprise
emerged with MacArthur's exposed advance, Mao abruptly switched to a
strategy of drawing the U.S. force northward and then smashing it in a surprise strike.[81] This switch grew from a mix of constraint and temptation: the
rapid U.S. drive north precluded Mao's planned positional defense by over-
running China's planned defensive positions, and the exposed nature of the
U.S. drive created a new opportunity for victory by surprise.[82]

Mao's switch in strategy coincided with a marked change in China's political conduct. China now moved from a strategy of open deterrence to one
of lulling the United States by concealing Chinese capabilities and grievances. Beijing had openly moved large forces close to the China–North
Korea border during the summer and early fall.[83] Beijing had also directly
warned the United States not to send U.S. forces into North Korea on October 3, and issued other veiled warnings during September 25–October 13.[84]
After mid-October, Beijing suddenly fell silent. Mao told other Chinese leaders on October 19 that "in the coming months, we will *only act, not talk.*"[85]

---

[78] On the U.S.-UN deployment see Whiting, *China Crosses the Yalu*, pp. 123, 130.

[79] Hao Yufan and Zhai Zhihai, "China's Decision to Enter the Korean War: History Revisited," *China Quarterly* 121 (March 1990): 94–115 at 108, 111. Chen Jian shows that well before
the Inchon landing, China's leaders anticipated MacArthur's breakout from Pusan and rush
to the Yalu, and during July–September they already leaned toward intervention to forestall
or thwart this rush. Chen Jian, *China's Road to the Korean War: The Making of the Sino-American
Confrontation* (New York: Columbia University Press, 1994), pp. 125–57. However, China's
final decision to intervene came only in mid-October.

[80] On October 14, Mao told Zhou Enlai that he had ordered Marshall Peng Dehuai, the
commander of his Korean deployment, to "build two or three defensive fronts in the region
north of the Pyongyang–Wonsan Railroad and south of the Tokchon–Yongwon Road," and
defend them aggressively. The line he described traverses the narrow neck of North Korea,
roughly midway between the Yalu and the 38th parallel. Christensen, "Threats, Assurances,"
pp. 124, 153.

[81] Chen, "China's Changing Aims," p. 24; Hao and Zhai, "China's Decision," pp. 112–13.

[82] Chen, "China's Changing Aims," p. 24.

[83] Lebow, *Between Peace and War*, p. 173.

[84] Ibid., pp. 172–73; Kaufman, *Korean War*, p. 93. China also issued more oblique warnings
during August 20–September 23. William Stueck, Jr., *The Road to Confrontation: American Policy toward China and Korea, 1947–1950* (Chapel Hill: University of North Carolina Press, 1981),
pp. 208–9, 229.

[85] Shuguang Zhang and Jian Chen, eds., *Chinese Communist Foreign Policy and the New Cold
War in Asia: New Documentary Evidence, 1944–1950* (Chicago: Imprint, 1996), p. 179.

Beijing issued only one more oblique warning and no ultimatum before it attacked on November 26.[86] Instead, on November 10 Beijing soothingly implied an interest in discussing a Korean settlement.[87]

Chinese detachments briefly engaged U.S. forces from October 25 through November 7, then broke off action and vanished. In his memoirs, Marshall Peng Dehuai, China's military commander in Korea, explained that he did this to feign weakness and lack of resolve, in hopes of luring MacArthur into the jaws of his trap.[88] Chinese forces released twenty-seven wounded U.S. prisoners of war with a friendly good-bye wave on November 21, just five days before China's big attack; Peng later explained that this was done to "give the enemy an impression that we are in short supply and are retreating," even as his forces secretly poured into North Korea.[89] These actions reflected a general Chinese policy of deception, summarized later by Peng as "purposely showing ourselves to be weak, increasing the arrogance of the enemies, letting them run amuck, and luring them deep into our areas."[90]

China's silence reinforced U.S. officials in their false hope that China's September 23–October 13 warnings were a bluff.[91] China's military disengagement also had its intended effect. U.S. officials concluded that Chinese forces in Korea were feeble and China would offer only token resistance to the U.S. advance.[92] Emboldened, MacArthur continued his northward lunge into Mao's waiting snare.[93] China's surprise strike on November 26 inflicted the worst ground defeat in U.S. military history.

These events fit stability theory's forecasts. Chinese behavior changed markedly—toward preparations for surprise attack and the concealment of grievances and capabilities—as Chinese leaders watched the first-strike advantage appear and expand in October 1950 (prediction 2). China then

---

[86] On November 1, a leading Chinese publication, *Hsueh Hsi*, warned that "we can under no circumstances allow American imperialism . . . to occupy Korea," but it did not directly threaten force. Quoted in Barton J. Bernstein, "The Policy of Risk: Crossing the 38th Parallel and Marching to the Yalu," *Foreign Service Journal*, March 1977, pp. 16–29 at 20.

[87] Rosemary Foot, *The Wrong War: American Policy and the Dimensions of the Korean Conflict, 1950–1953* (Ithaca: Cornell University Press, 1985), p. 96.

[88] Christensen, "Threats, Assurances," pp. 140–41.

[89] Foot, *Wrong War*, p. 94; and Peng Dehuai quoted in Hao and Zhai, "China's Decision," p. 114. On Peng's thinking see also Zhang and Chen, *Chinese Communist Foreign Policy*, p. 205.

[90] Quoted in Chen, "China's Changing Aims," p. 25.

[91] See Allen S. Whiting, "The U.S.-China War in Korea," in George, *Avoiding War*, pp. 103–5 at 113; Kaufman, *Korean War*, pp. 88–89, 91, 95; Lowe, *Origins of the Korean War*, pp. 192, 199.

[92] George and Smoke, *Deterrence*, pp. 228–30. In mid-November MacArthur falsely believed that China had only 60,000–70,000 troops in Korea, when the real number was at least 260,000. Through intelligence Mao learned of MacArthur's error, and on November 18 sent a celebratory telegram to Marshall Peng telling him this was to China's advantage. Thomas J. Christensen, *Useful Adversaries: Grand Strategy, Domestic Mobilization, and Sino-American Conflict, 1947–1958* (Princeton: Princeton University Press, 1996), p. 171.

[93] Hao and Zhai conclude that China gained surprise "both because of [MacArthur's] miscalculation of China's intention to intervene and the well-disguised Chinese force deployment." "China's Decision," p. 112.

made striking use of strategies of surprise attack and concealment (prediction 1). U.S. leaders saw no first-strike advantage. Accordingly, their conduct showed no change during October (there was no U.S. consideration of preemptive war or greater policy concealment), creating a clear difference between Chinese and U.S. conduct (also prediction 1). Chinese records indicate that Chinese policymakers acted as they did to gain the advantage of surprise (prediction 3). Evidence also indicates that the U.S. rush to the Yalu, which set the stage for war, was encouraged by these Chinese actions (prediction 4).

The U.S.-China case corroborates stability theory, but how strongly? We judge the significance of a passed test by asking whether the successful predictions are unique.[94] In this case, two of stability theory's successful predictions are so. No competing theory predicts either the Chinese switch to a lulling strategy in October 1950[95] or the Chinese testimony that China lulled to gain surprise. The U.S. rush to the Yalu has other possible explanations (for example, "McCarthyite U.S. domestic politics compelled aggressive risk taking by President Truman in Korea in disregard of China's warnings"). The sharp difference observed between Chinese and U.S. behavior also has other plausible causes (for example, "China acted more secretly because totalitarian states are reflexively more secretive than democracies"). Hence these events only weakly corroborate stability theory. But China's switch to lulling and its explanation for the switch strongly support stability theory because other explanations for these events are hard to imagine.

How much importance does this evidence assign to stability theory? That is, how large is the indicated impact of first-move advantages on states' ideas and behavior? This depends on how greatly state behavior varies with shifts in the size of the first-move advantage. Here we see large variance. China's conduct changed markedly as the first-move advantage appeared in October 1950, and Chinese conduct differed sharply from normal international conduct and from U.S. conduct.

Finally, did China's October–November lulling strategy cause an otherwise avoidable war? This seems quite plausible. Recent research has shown that Mao's decision to enter the war in force was crystallized not by the U.S. approach to the Yalu River but by the earlier entry of U.S. forces into North

---

[94] Unique predictions are those made by the tested theory and no other. The more unique the prediction, the more strongly its fulfillment corroborates the theory, since competing explanations for the observed phenomena are less plausible.

We judge the significance of a flunked test by asking how definite were the failed predictions. Definite predictions are those that the theory makes with certainty. The more definite the prediction, the more badly its failure damages the theory.

[95] Window theory (see Chapter 4) posits that windows can lead states to adopt lulling strategies, but it predicts that rising states should do the lulling. The relative position of U.S. forces improved as they approached the Yalu, so window theory predicts that the United States, not China, should do the lulling here.

Table 1. Testing stability theory: The 1950 U.S.-China conflict, World War I, and the 1967 Arab-Israeli War

Case	Prediction 1: Were intervening phenomena H2A–H2E present in above-normal amounts among states that faced or perceived a first-move advantage?	Prediction 2: Were intervening phenomena H2A–H2E more common in periods when states faced or perceived larger first-move advantages?	Prediction 3: Did elites explain policies that embodied intervening phenomena H2A–H2E as required by the need to gain the initiative?	Prediction 4: Does evidence indicate that decisions to use force, or that triggered others' uses of force, stemmed from effects of intervening phenomena H2A–H2E?
U.S.-China, 1950	Yes: China concealed its grievances and capabilities, and struck by surprise.	Yes: China adopted a lulling strategy toward the U.S. only after a first-move advantage appeared.	Yes: Chinese leaders later said that they lulled the U.S. to gain surprise.	Yes: China's lulling encouraged the U.S. rush to the Yalu.
World War I	Yes: Europe's continental powers mobilized in secrecy or attacked by surprise without first issuing warnings or ultimata; and they moved in haste, before facts were verified or diplomacy completed.		Yes: Russian and German leaders said they moved first to gain the advantage of the initiative.	Yes: war-causing British and Russian errors reflected misperceptions that arose from the secrecy of Germany's first-strike military plan.
Israel-Egypt, 1967	Yes: Israel lulled Egypt, then struck by surprise, before the illusions of Egypt's leaders could be dispelled.		Yes: Israeli leaders said they struck first to gain the advantage of the initiative.	

NOTE: Cells are left blank if the case did not offer a good opportunity to test the prediction.

Korea. This research also suggests that Mao aimed at expelling the United States from the whole of Korea, not just from North Korea.[96] If this is correct, a U.S. halt in North Korea short of the Yalu would not have prevented war; hence any Chinese deterrence that gained such a halt would have been insufficient to prevent war. It seems likely, however, that Mao would have reconsidered his decision for war had the United States offered to fully withdraw from the North.[97] It also seems possible that President Truman would have found a way to withdraw from the North, despite the political embarrassment, had he known the huge costs that trying to reunify Korea would involve.[98] The problem was that China could not persuade Truman that he would pay these costs without making itself unable to inflict them. If so, the pernicious effects of first-strike advantage were a necessary cause of the U.S.-China collision.[99]

World War I

The crisis that spawned World War I erupted among European powers that widely (although wrongly) believed that the side moving first would have a large advantage. Russia, France, and Germany were the strongest be-

[96] Christensen, "Threats, Assurances," pp. 128, 138–40, 142–46, 151–53.

[97] Two speculations and one piece of evidence suggest this. First, U.S. willingness to withdraw from the North might have appeased or reassured Mao enough to persuade him drop his plan for war to expel the United States from the South. Second, the Soviets probably would have balked at backing a Chinese attack on a force that the United States had already offered to withdraw from the North, and China probably would not have attacked without Soviet support. See Christensen, *Useful Adversaries*, p. 158, who notes the importance of Soviet support for a Chinese attack, and likely Soviet reluctance to back a Chinese attack on U.S. forces that merely restored the prewar status quo in Korea. Finally, Zhou Enlai told the Chinese People's Political Consultative Conference on October 24 that China would seek a settlement with the United States if it pulled back from its advance into North Korea: "If the enemy does retreat, the issue can be settled through negotiations. . . . We want peace, not war." Zhang and Chen, *Chinese Communist Foreign Policy*, pp. 189–90.

[98] Truman was anxious to avoid conflict with China, as his original September decision to enter North Korea reveals. He conditioned MacArthur's authority to move north on Chinese noninvolvement: on September 26, the Joint Chiefs of Staff authorized the move "provided . . . there has been no entry into North Korea by major Soviet or Chinese Communist forces, no announcement of intended entry, nor a threat to counter our operations." *Foreign Relations of the United States, 1950*, vol. 7, *Korea* (Washington, D.C.: U.S. Government Printing Office, 1976), p. 781. U.S. officials also hedged on making a clear commitment to Korean unification during the fall of 1950, leaving a backtrack on unification politically alive. In November 1950, Secretary of State Dean Acheson told the National Security Council (NSC) that "we have tried to keep the military conquest of all of Korea from being a war aim. . . . Politically we are not committed to the conquest of all of Korea if something short of that can be worked out that is satisfactory." Christensen, *Useful Adversaries*, p. 175.

[99] In explaining the war, stability theory also explains the puzzle of Chinese conduct in the autumn crisis. As Thomas Schelling noted, "It is not easy to explain why the Chinese entered North Korea so secretly. . . . A conspicuous entry in force might have found the U.N. content with its accomplishments." Schelling, *Arms and Influence*, p. 55. The "concealment" explanation (H2C) offers a plausible answer.

lievers in the value of moving first, and all three tailored their conduct to this belief.

Russian military leaders had long seen a first-mobilization advantage between Russia and Germany. They wrongly thought that both Germany and Russia could mobilize in secret. They further thought that a small mobilization lead would provide a large military payoff.[100] When Austria triggered the crisis on July 23 with a stern ultimatum to Serbia, Russia reacted by immediately and secretly ordering preliminary military mobilization measures. Russia's first orders for preliminary mobilization were issued at 4:10 P.M. on July 25,[101] even before Austria's 6:00 P.M. deadline for Serbia's reply had passed. Then, on July 30, Russia drove the crisis over the brink by secretly launching general mobilization, thereby truncating promising British efforts to mediate the crisis[102] and belated German efforts to restrain Austria-Hungary. Thus Russia jumped the gun in a mad rush to mobilize at early signs of war. These Russian actions made the 1914 July crisis the fastest-exploding major international crisis in history: only nine days elapsed between its July 23 eruption and Germany's August 1 declaration of war on Russia. By August 4, seven European states were at war.

Statements by Russian officials suggest that Russia's rash acts arose from its belief that war was inevitable and that the first side to mobilize would have the upper hand in the coming struggle. Serge Sazonov, Russian minister for foreign affairs, exclaimed, "C'est la guerre européenne!" (It is the European war!) when he first learned of the Austrian ultimatum on July 24.[103] He then urged the July 30 mobilization partly from fear that otherwise Germany would "gain time to complete her preparations in secret,"[104] and partly from false hope that Russia could mobilize without German detection. Albertini writes that Sazonov thought that "Russia could mobilize without Germany's knowing of it immediately" and that Sazonov's belief that secret mobilization was possible "may well have made Sazonov more inclined to order it."[105]

Russia began its preliminary and full mobilizations without issuing a clear ultimatum and before checking important facts, some of which it misconstrued. As noted above, Russia wrongly doubted Serbia's role in the

---

[100] See Chapter 7 at notes 57–88.

[101] Fay, *Origins*, 2:309–10.

[102] As noted above at notes 67 and 68, the "Halt in Belgrade" proposal was emerging as a plausible way out of the crisis when Russia mobilized.

[103] Albertini, *Origins*, 2:290. Albertini notes that these words "cast a searchlight into Sazonov's mind and explain much of what was later to happen." Ibid., 2:291.

[104] French Ambassador to Russia Maurice Paléologue's account of Sazonov's explanation for Russian mobilization, quoted in Albertini, *Origins*, 2:619. For more evidence see Chapter 7 at notes 70–72.

[105] Albertini, *Origins*, 2:624, 573. For more evidence see Chapter 7 at notes 74–76.

June assassination of Archduke Francis Ferdinand, and it exaggerated the scope of Austrian aims toward Serbia.[106] It approved partial mobilization against Austria unaware that this was technically infeasible and would have to be abandoned or converted to full mobilization.[107] It launched full mobilization partly in response to false or exaggerated reports of German mobilization.[108]

German leaders saw no first-mobilization advantage, but they did see a large first-strike advantage between Germany and Belgium, embodied in the possibility and necessity of seizing the Belgian fortresses at Liège by surprise. These fortresses controlled a key choke point for Germany's advance into France. They were poorly defended in peacetime. Germany could gain a vast advantage if it could seize them before Belgium could prepare their defense and destroy the tunnels and bridges they guarded. Hence German military planners embedded a top-secret surprise attack on Liège in Germany's mobilization plan, to commence promptly with German mobilization. Mobilization and war were thereby melded in one motion.[109] In essence, Germany had committed itself to striking first if it were compelled to mobilize in a future crisis. German planners made clear that they felt this commitment was compelled by the advantage of the initiative. General Helmuth von Moltke, chief of the German general staff, argued that "the possession of Liège is the *sine qua non* of our advance" through Belgium, and seizing Liège would require "meticulous preparation and surprise."[110]

The Liège attack plan was so secret that top German civilians and other governments were unaware of it and blundered accordingly. German civilian leaders pursued a diplomatic strategy of fait accompli that assumed they had time for crisis bargaining and maneuver. They were unaware that the Liège attack made this impossible because they were unaware of the Liège attack itself.[111] Russia launched mobilization measures unaware that these

---

[106] See above at notes 70 and 71.

[107] See note 55 above.

[108] As noted above. For sources see note 33.

[109] The surprise attack on the Liège fortress was decided in April 1913, and required a strike on the third day of mobilization. Gerhard Ritter, *The Sword and the Scepter: The Problem of Militarism in Germany*, 4 vols. (Coral Gables: University of Miami Press, 1972), 2:266. It was in fact launched on the night of August 4–5, 1914, just over three days after German mobilization was ordered (at 5:00 P.M. on August 1), and two days after it began. James Joll, *The Origins of the First World War* (London: Longman, 1984), pp. 83–84; Schmitt, *Coming of the War*, 2:323. An account of the attack is Barbara Tuchman, *The Guns of August* (New York: Dell, 1962), pp. 188–207, 215–20.

[110] Gerhard Ritter, *The Schlieffen Plan: Critique of a Myth* (1958; reprint, Westport, Conn.: Greenwood, 1979), p. 166.

[111] Albertini, *Origins*, 2:581; 3:195, 250, 391; Ritter, *Sword and Scepter*, 2:266, 271; Fay, *Origins*, 1:41–42; L. C. F. Turner, "The Significance of the Schlieffen Plan," in Paul M. Kennedy, ed., *The War Plans of the Great Powers, 1880–1914* (London: George Allen and Unwin, 1979), pp. 199–221 at 213.

measures would certainly trigger war if they triggered German mobilization.[112] Britain failed to restrain Russia from these measures partly because British leaders, like Russia's leaders, were unaware that Germany's secret plans guaranteed that mobilization meant war.[113] British Foreign Secretary Edward Grey later explained that he had believed "neither Russian nor French mobilization was an unreasonable or unnecessary precaution," as he believed "French and Russian mobilizations to be preparation, but not war."[114]

These events fit stability theory's predictions 1, 3, and 4. Europe's major continental powers saw a large first-move advantage in 1914. Accordingly, they made opportunistic and preemptive military moves; concealed their grievances, military plans, and perceptions; and used force before they knew all the facts or before negotiation had run its course—all in above-average amounts (prediction 1). Testimonial evidence shows that they took these steps to gain the advantage of surprise or to deny it to others (prediction 3), and that other actions that set the stage for war—most importantly, Germany's adoption of a strategy of fait accompli, Russia's decisions for mobilization, and Britain's failure to restrain Russia—were fostered by this conduct (prediction 4).

How strongly does the 1914 case support stability theory? Some fulfilled stability theory predictions are not unique. For example, the concealments of 1914 have other possible explanations (for example, "militarized governments like that of Wilhelmine Germany are quite secretive"). These other causes could explain the dark secrecy of 1914 and the disasters that flowed from it. Blunders in the July crisis also have possible causes other than haste or secrecy induced by a first-move advantage (for example, "the corrosive psychology of high-stress decisionmaking caused the blunders of July 1914," or "the striking incompetence of many European leaders— Nicholas II, Sergei Sazonov, Kaiser Wilhelm II, Edward Grey, Leopold Berchtold—caused the blunders of July 1914"). Hence the observation of these phenomena supplies only weak support for stability theory. Other fulfilled predictions are unique, however. Russia's pre-mobilization of July 24–25—a sudden preemption by a fairly temperate power at the start of a crisis begun by others—is a bizarre event. No plausible competing theory predicts it, hence it strongly corroborates stability theory. The testimony of policymakers affirming that their war-causing acts were driven by perceptions of first-move advantage or by misperceptions arising from others'

---

[112] As noted above, Russian leaders were unaware at the outset of the crisis, and perhaps throughout, that for Germany mobilization inexorably meant immediate war.

[113] See Chapter 7 at note 129.

[114] Schmitt, *Coming of the War*, 2:41n. Albertini concludes that Grey "never made any attempt to prevent the various mobilizations, in fact regarded them as inevitable." Albertini, *Origins*, 2:393.

responses to first-move advantages is likewise quite singular, unpredicted by other theories, and hence strong evidence for stability theory.

How large is the indicated impact of first-move advantages on states' ideas and behavior? The extreme hair-trigger policies that Russia and Germany pursued were a sharp deviation from normal conduct by most powers through history. The marked degree of this deviation is a measure of stability theory's importance.

Was perceived first-move advantage a necessary cause of the war of 1914? The answer depends on whether removing the dangers raised by perceptions of first-move advantages would have reduced the crisis danger level below that required to produce war. This seems quite likely. Absent a perceived first-mobilization advantage, Russia probably would have deferred its military moves a few days until diplomatic solutions were fully explored. It also seems likely that with more time a diplomatic solution based on the Halt in Belgrade proposal would have resolved the crisis. Moreover, had Germany not seen a first-strike advantage, it would have dropped its surprise attack on Liège from its war plan, or concealed the attack less carefully. In the former instance, the automatic link between mobilization and war would have been cut, allowing more time for diplomacy after Russian mobilization. In the latter instance, Russia would have realized that it was unleashing war with its first steps to mobilization,[115] and considered them more carefully. Also, Britain would have realized the danger posed by Russian mobilization and done more to restrain Russia. In short, we can easily

[115] The Russian preliminary mobilization, decided on July 24–25 and ordered on July 25–26, had three effects that helped drive the 1914 July crisis over the brink. First, it spurred Germany to abandon its belated peace effort and opt for mobilization and war. During July 29–30 Chancellor Bethmann-Hollweg and Kaiser Wilhelm finally moved to pull Austria back from the brink and settle the crisis. Albertini, *Origins*, 3:1–24. On July 30, however, Germany received further news of Russian preliminary mobilization measures in districts opposite Germany. Schmitt, *Coming of the War*, 2:207. This news alarmed the German military, which successfully pressed for German mobilization (to occur the next day) and for abandonment of Bethmann-Hollweg's last-minute efforts to restrain Austria. Ibid., 2:205–8; Albertini, *Origins*, 3:12–13, 23. Late on the 30th, Bethmann-Hollweg explained why he canceled his restraint of Austria: "General Staff just tells me that military preparations of our neighbors, especially on the east, compel speedy decision if we do not wish to expose ourselves to surprises." Ibid., 3:13.

Second, Russia's preliminary mobilization probably helped stir the Germans to their first steps toward mobilization during July 27–29. Then Russia's exaggeration of these first German steps helped drive Russia's decision for full mobilization on July 30. For sources see note 33.

Third, it spurred Germany to issue threats to Russia that spurred Russian full mobilization. On July 29, Germany sternly warned Russia that if Russia continued its preliminary measures, Germany would mobilize and war would follow. Ibid., 2:553. See also ibid., 2:498–99, for data clarifying that Germany's threat reacted to Russian preliminary mobilization, not to Russia's partial mobilization against Austria. This German threat helped convince Russian leaders that Germany was bent on war and spurred the Russian general mobilization that sparked war. Ibid., 2:555–56, 565. See also ibid., 2:309, for Albertini's general view of the effects of preliminary mobilization.

[65]

imagine the July crisis ending peacefully in the absence of a perceived first-move payoff.[116]

Israel-Egypt 1967

On May 14, 1967, Egypt sent forces across the Suez canal and into the Sinai desert, triggering a crisis with Israel that ended in war on June 5. During this crisis Israeli officials feared an imminent Arab attack,[117] and they correctly thought the side striking first would have a large advantage. These perceptions fueled an urge to preempt that shaped Israel's conduct in the crisis.[118]

As the May–June crisis intensified, Israeli military leaders pressed for war on grounds that Israel could strike a decisive blow if it hit first and risked a damaging Arab first strike if it waited.[119] In arguing for war, Israeli Defense Minister Dayan forecast that Israel "would knock at least one hundred of their warplanes out of action" if it struck first, and he also warned that "it would be fatal for us" if the Arabs struck first. In his view "the first shot would determine which side would suffer the heaviest casualties, and would assuredly change the balance of forces. . . . Our best chance of victory was to strike the first blow. The course of the campaign would then follow our dictates."[120] Chief of Staff Yitzhak Rabin likewise emphasized that gaining the initiative was "of decisive importance" to the length and results of the war, and to limiting Israeli losses.[121]

After reaching a provisional decision for war, Israel adopted a studied nonchalance to lull Egypt into unwatchfulness. Israeli troops were released on leave, and two days before Israel struck, Dayan told the press that "it is too late for a spontaneous military reaction to Egypt's blockade. . . . We must give [diplomacy] a chance."[122] Israel also covered its plans for surprise attack in dark secrecy, leaving Egypt blind to the devastating blow Israel would strike. Ignorant of Israel's brilliant war plan, Egyptian air force officers expected Israel could destroy at most 20 percent of the Egyptian air force

---

[116] Also suggesting that first-move advantages helped cause the war are Lebow, *Between Peace and War*, pp. 137, 238–42; and Kahn, *On Thermonuclear War*, pp. 350–75. For a contrary view, see Rosen, "Nuclear Arms and Strategic Defense," p. 84. He blames the war on "ambition, not 'instability.'"

[117] Stein, "Arab-Israeli War of 1967," pp. 140–42.

[118] For a contrary view see Alexander L. George, "Findings and Recommendations," in George, *Avoiding War*, pp. 545–66, who argues (citing Janice Stein) that the 1967 war "resembles but does not really meet the exacting standards of preemptive war" (p. 548). However, the facts and sources cited here indicate that the 1967 war meets these standards.

[119] Luttwak and Horowitz, *Israeli Army*, pp. 219, 221, 223.

[120] Handel, "Crisis and Surprise," pp. 127, 133; Dayan, *Story*, pp. 411–12.

[121] Stein, "The Arab-Israeli War of 1967," p. 139.

[122] Handel, "Crisis and Surprise," p. 132. See also Neff, *Warriors for Jerusalem*, pp. 193–94; Laqueur, *Road to War*, p. 156.

in a first strike.[123] In fact, Israel destroyed 66 percent at a cost of only 10 percent of its own smaller force.[124] Egypt also went to war under a second misconception—that other powers would again intervene to restore Egypt's losses if Israel defeated it, as the United States had in 1956.[125] This illusion was alive when Israel struck on June 5, reflecting the short time for discussions that might have dispelled it.

These events satisfy stability theory predictions 1 and 3. During the May–June 1967 crisis, Israel saw a large first-strike advantage, and it adopted policies to match. It lulled and then attacked Egypt (prediction 1). This attack ended diplomacy and discussion before important Egyptian illusions could be dispelled (also prediction 1). Egypt saw less first-move advantage, and accordingly refrained from attack or other first-move-related policies (also prediction 1). Israeli leaders testified that they acted as they did to gain the advantage of surprise (prediction 3).

How strongly does this evidence support stability theory? Israel's attack on Egypt is only weak evidence because it has plausible alternative explanations (for example, "Israel struck to forestall the gathering of Arab armies then underway on Israel's borders," or—Arabs would say—"Israel struck because it sought to seize and colonize Arab territories"). Plausible competing explanations for Israel's policy of lulling Egypt, and for Israeli elites' testimony that they attacked to forestall an Egyptian strike, are harder to find. Some might argue that Israelis invented this testimony to conceal Israel's expansionist aims, but this seems farfetched. Accordingly, these phenomena—Israeli lulling and the testimony by Israeli policymakers—strongly support stability theory.

How large is the indicated impact of first-move advantages on states' ideas and behavior? As in the 1914 case we see policies—this time by Israel—that depart from typical conduct by typical powers through history. Israeli policy was less unusual than the policies of the powers in 1914. Most important, Israel reached a far slower decision to preempt (striking three weeks after the outbreak of the crisis) than did Russia in 1914. Israel even took an extra week to seek U.S. approval as the crisis culminated, despite fears of an Egyptian first strike. Thus the shadow of the first-strike advantage did not dominate every Israeli act or drive it to the furthest extreme. Nevertheless, Israeli conduct was a marked departure from typical conduct, according to which states allow confrontations to smolder for months as in, for example, the Eastern crises of 1832–33, 1839–40, and 1875–78, the Fashoda crisis of 1898, the Moroccan crises of 1905 and 1911, the Bosnian cri-

[123] Safran, *Israel*, p. 241. See also Stein, "Arab-Israeli War of 1967," p. 135.
[124] Calculated from Luttwak and Horowitz, *Israeli Army*, pp. 218, 222, 229. Israel destroyed 254 of Egypt's 385 combat aircraft on the first day, while losing 19 of its 197 combat aircraft.
[125] Kimche and Bawley, *Six-Day War*, p. 283.

sis of 1908, the European crises of 1938–39, the Pacific crisis of 1940–41, the Taiwan Straits crises of 1954–55 and 1958, and the Berlin crises of 1948 and 1958–62. The size of this deviation—not enormous but significant—is a measure of stability theory's importance.

Was first-move advantage a necessary cause the 1967 war? Egypt and Israel had many reasons for war in June 1967 and probably would have come to blows absent a first-strike advantage. With more time, however, Nasser might have realized the world's unwillingness to save him from defeat and might have backtracked accordingly. It also seems remotely possible that with more time for reflection the United States would have intervened more forcefully to prevent war.

Assessing stability theory

Stability theory passes a number of strong tests. Several unique predictions from stability theory are fulfilled. State behavior and elite ideas vary both regularly and markedly with the size of real and perceived first-move advantages. The regularity of this variance gives stability theory a good deal of credibility. The marked size of this variance—that is, the large shifts in government behavior and elite ideas that accompany variance in first-move advantage—indicates that first-move advantage is an important (that is, strong) cause of war.

If we grant that stability theory is valid and important, counterfactual speculation suggests that it also explains a fair amount of history, especially if we frame it to cover the dangers of perceived as well as actual first-move advantages. I argued above that first-move advantages, or perceptions of them, may have been necessary to the chemistry that brought on the three wars analyzed above.[126] In one of these cases (1914) this seems very likely; in another (1950) it seems quite possible; in a third (1967) it seems unlikely but plausible. Perception of first-move advantage also seems plausibly necessary to the outbreak of four other wars mentioned in this chapter: the 1740 War of Austrian Succession, Hitler's 1940 attack on Norway, and the 1956 and 1973 Mideast wars. Frederick might well have hesitated to attack Austria in 1740 had he known that he would stand alone against Austria, and he could have learned this through discussion with others had he not feared

---

[126] Counterfactual analysis is necessary before concluding that cases that confirm a theory are also explained by it. Such analysis involves asking: Given our knowledge of the causes of war, were there enough other causes present to bring about war, absent the impetus to war provided by the dangers raised by the actual or perceived first-move advantage? If the case outcome is overdetermined, first-move advantage gets little or no blame for it. We also ask: did the effects produced by first-move advantage in this case feed the causal stream that produced the case outcome? A theory can operate in a given case but still have no effect on case outcomes, if its effects have no continuing downstream consequences in the case. Analysis can verify when this is so.

that tipping his hand would cost him the advantage of the first move. Hitler preferred to keep Norway neutral, and he decided to attack it only when he saw signs that the allies planned to seize it first.[127] The French-British-Israel coalition of 1956 surely would not have opted for war had it foreseen the strong opposition of the United States. The United States probably would have declared this opposition had it known of the coalition's plans; and the coalition might well have informed the United States in advance, and thereby discovered the U.S. opposition, had it not feared losing military surprise. The 1973 case is less clear. It seems unlikely that Israeli foreknowledge of Egypt's attack and a better Israeli appraisal of Egypt's strength would have persuaded Israel to reach a peace settlement with Egypt. If so, Egypt's concealment of its grievances and strength corroborate stability theory but do not explain the outbreak of war. It seems at least plausible, however, that Egypt would not have attacked had it not seen a fair likelihood of catching Israel by surprise, and had it not foreseen that surprise would provide a large advantage.

Overall, then, seven major wars plausibly required a first-move advantage, or perceptions of a first-move advantage, for their outbreak. Each had a range of other causes, but these might have been insufficient to trigger war without some help from first-move advantages. If so, the critics' claim that instability has been "inconsequential" in history is wide of the mark.[128]

CAUSES OF AND CURES FOR FIRST-MOVE ADVANTAGE

First-move advantages can be large, absent, or negative (when the side moving second has the advantage). What causes produce first-move advantages? How can they be reduced or prevented? I discuss first-strike and first-mobilization advantages in turn.

The size of a first-strike advantage is a function of four factors:

1. *The feasibility of gaining surprise.* Can an attacker prepare and mount an attack without being detected? This is a function of two factors: the speed of the attacker's attack and the speed of the target's warning of attack. The faster the attacker's attack, and the slower the target's warning, the more feasible a surprise strike.[129] If attacks are fast and warning is slow, the attack

---

[127] Liddell Hart, *History of the Second World War*, 1:52–58.
[128] Rosen, "Nuclear Arms and Strategic Defense," p. 86.
[129] The feasibility of surprise is assessed by considering these factors jointly. If preparation and attack are slow, the first-move advantage may nevertheless be large if warning is very sluggish. For example, China took weeks to ready its 1950 attack but U.S. warning was even slower, so the attack succeeded. If preparation and attack are fast, the first-move advantage may nevertheless be small if warning is still faster and quick countermeasures are possible. For example, during the Cold War, Soviet ICBMs could have struck U.S. bomber bases in half an hour, but U.S. warning was still fast enough to allow U.S. bombers to escape.

finds the victim unprepared. If attacks are slow and warning is fast, attacked states can take offsetting countermeasures before the attack arrives.

2. *The effect of a surprise strike on the force ratio between the two sides.* If surprise is achieved, does the attack shift the balance of forces in the attacker's favor? If so, by how much? This is a function of the lethality of the attacker's attack force, the vulnerability of the target's force, and the quality of the target's active defense of the target force. If the target force is vulnerable and poorly defended, a lethally armed surprise attacker may destroy far more forces than it expends. But if the attacker's force lacks punch, or if the target force is invulnerable or well defended, an attacker may expend more forces than it destroys even if it gains complete surprise.

3. *The offense-defense balance.* If surprise is achieved, and if the attack shifts the balance of forces in the attacker's favor, is the attacker now better able to conquer others or to defend itself? This is a function of the offense-defense balance—that is, the balance of forces required for an aggressor state to conquer a defender.

If the offense is strong, a successful surprise pays large dividends because large territories can be defended or overrun by exploiting the material advantage gained by striking first. If the defense is strong, conversely, even a successful surprise confers little reward because little territory can be defended or overrun by exploiting any material gains made by striking first. A first strike that reverses the attacker:defender force ratio from 1:2 to 2:1 is very profitable if an aggressor needs less than 2:1 material superiority to conquer a defender. The attacker escapes insecurity and gains the capacity to conquer. But if an aggressor needs 3:1 superiority to conquer a defender, a first strike that converts 1:2 inferiority to 2:1 superiority means little. Both sides can defend and neither can conquer both before and after the strike.

4. *The size of the political penalty on first strikers.* First strikers usually pay a political penalty for seizing the initiative. By striking first they often brand themselves the aggressor, stirring neutral states to align against them. They also inflame and energize the opponent's public for war.[130] If this political penalty is small, a military first-strike advantage still provides a general first-strike advantage. However, a large political penalty can outweigh even a large military first-strike advantage, converting a military success into a general political-military failure. This is usually the case: the military gains won in surprise strikes are usually offset by the attack's self-encircling international impact and its energizing effect on the opposing society.

The size of a first-mobilization advantage is a function of the same four factors as those governing a first-strike advantage, adjusted to address the

---

[130] For example, Japan's Pearl Harbor attack was a tactical success but a strategic disaster because it energized the American public for war against Japan. See, for example, John Mueller, "Pearl Harbor: Military Inconvenience, Political Disaster," *International Security* 16 (Winter 1991/92): 172–203 at 191–93.

issue of mobilization. (1) The feasibility of mobilizing by surprise. Can forces be mobilized without detection? This is a function of the speed of mobilization and the speed of others' warning of such mobilization. (2) The size of the mobilization. The greater the strength of mobilized forces relative to unmobilized forces, the greater the shift in force ratios caused by an unanswered mobilization. (3) The offense-defense balance. A stealthy mobilization that markedly shifts a force balance is worthless unless this shift confers or removes the capacity to conquer or defend.[131] (4) The size of the political penalty for mobilizing first.

Each of these four factors is necessary to a first-move advantage. Absent any of them there is no first-move payoff. Moving first pays no reward if the defender immediately sees and responds to the attacker's moves. Moving first pays no reward if force ratios are unchanged by a successful surprise. Moving first pays no reward if shifts in force ratios cause no shifts in the power to conquer or defend. And moving first pays no reward if the political backlash that it provokes outweighs the material rewards it provides.

How can first-move advantages be minimized? Gaining surprise is harder if states maintain strong intelligence capabilities, pursue open military policies, and deploy forces that are slow to mobilize and slow to target. The effect of surprise attack on force ratios is limited if states deploy forces that can survive surprise attack and exact a large price from attackers, while not deploying forces that might be used for surprise attack. The effect of surprise mobilization on force ratios is limited by relying more on standing than reserve forces. The strength of the offense is limited by adopting defensive military force postures.

How common is first-move advantage? The record indicates that real first-move advantage is rare while the illusion of first-move advantage is common. Hence measures to curb actual first-move advantages are less important than measures to curb their mirages. A substantial first-move advantage appeared in perhaps four wars mentioned above (the 1904 Russo-Japanese, 1950 U.S.-China, 1967 Mideast, and 1973 Mideast wars). Other well-known surprise attacks produced only meager short-term results, an offsetting long-term backlash, or both. Carthage forestalled an imaginary Roman strike in 218 B.C.E. but lost the war it began. Britain gained little by

---

[131] Thus the belief that it paid to mobilize first in 1914 rested on the assumption that the offense was relatively strong. Demanding mobilization, General Joffre warned French civilians that France would lose fifteen to twenty kilometers of French territory for each day mobilization was delayed. In Germany General Moltke warned delay "might have fatal consequences." Vagts, *Defense and Diplomacy*, pp. 408, 410. Both men believed that small material advantages could be used to make large territorial gains, hence they were anxious to move early to seize that advantage. Had they recognized the power of the defense, their impulse to mobilize early would have waned. Joffre might have warned the French of the less scary danger of losing 1.5–2 kilometers per day of delay; Moltke could have warned that delay would cause problems, but not "fatal consequences." Both sides could have postponed mobilization more easily and negotiated longer.

its surprise naval strike at the outset of the Seven Years' War in 1756, capturing only two French ships.[132] A U.S. attempt to surprise Britain at sea in 1812 produced modest results and launched a futile war.[133] France's first move in 1870 could not compensate for its woeful military preparations or prevent its spectacular defeat. No one argues that Russia's first move in 1914 gave it much advantage, but it did give German propagandists a telling argument that helped persuade German socialists to back the German war effort. Hitler's surprise strikes in 1940 paid short-run rewards but aroused other neutrals against him, expanding the global encirclement that defeated him. His 1941 attack on the Soviet Union was a spectacular tactical success, but the Soviet Union won the war. Japan's Pearl Harbor attack was a tactical success and a political disaster, energizing the United States for war against it. North Korea's first strike in 1950 triggered a ruinous U.S. response. The tripartite Suez attack in 1956 aroused global opposition that cost it political victory.

The problem of first-move advantage, then, lies more in perception than reality. Solutions should address these illusions.

---

[132] Richard Smoke, *War: Controlling Escalation* (Cambridge: Harvard University Press, 1977), p. 203.
[133] J. F. Maurice, *Hostilities without Declaration of War from 1700 to 1870* (London: Her Majesty's Stationery Office, 1883), p. 45.

[4]

Power Shifts: Windows of
Opportunity and Vulnerability

Hypothesis 3. War is more likely when the relative power of states fluctuates sharply.

This chapter and Chapter 3 both argue that war is more likely when states expect better results from a war begun now than a war begun later. Such incentives can arise two ways: from a first-move advantage (see Chapter 3), and from an impending shift in the balance of power between contending states or alliances. A first-move advantage creates a two-sided incentive for war: either side gains by moving first. An impending power shift (or "window") creates a one-sided incentive: the declining state wants an early war, while the rising state wants to avoid war until after the power shift. Specifically, the declining state strikes "preventively," launching war now to prevent later conflict under worse circumstances.[1]

Before the 1980s preventive war was seen as a *kind* of war—historians classified many wars as "preventive"[2]—but the windows that produce preventive incentives were not proposed as *causes* of war. In the 1980s scholars began discussing windows as a war cause,[3] but the hypothesis remained unexplicated and controversial. Do windows cause war? Some observers

---

[1] Thus with a first-move advantage, both sides prefer to move first rather than second in the event of war, regardless of whether the war occurs now or later. With a window, the declining state prefers war now to war later regardless of who moves first (but holding it constant). We have a first-move advantage but no window if the relative power of two competitors is stable over time and both do better moving first than second. We have a window but no first-move advantage if relative power fluctuates but neither side would do better moving first than second at any specific time.

[2] A historical survey of preventive wars is Alfred Vagts, *Defense and Diplomacy: The Soldier and the Conduct of Foreign Relations* (New York: Kings Crown, 1956), pp. 263–350.

[3] Jack S. Levy, "Declining Power and the Preventive Motivation for War," *World Politics* 40 (October 1987): 82–107, was the first published discussion.

remained skeptical.[4] How do they cause war? How much war have they caused in the past? These questions were not addressed.

Windows, I argue, are a potent cause of war. They create incentives for war and for war-risking belligerence by declining states. They also create offsetting incentives for peace among rising states. These peaceful incentives are not fully offsetting, however, because windows also impede peaceful cooperation to resolve conflict. Cooperation requires faith in agreements, but windows corrode declining states' faith that rising states will comply with today's agreement once they grow stronger. As a result, agreements can be impossible, even between two states that could otherwise reach a settlement. Cooperation requires time for diplomacy, while windows impose haste. Cooperation is undercut by expectations of war, which windows create. Cooperation requires candid framing and discussion of goals and grievances, but windows foster concealment of grievances. Finally, once a power shift has occurred, the risen and fallen states often clash over the distribution of privileges. These hypotheses are supported by three case studies: Japanese policy in 1940 and 1941, German policy from 1933 to 1945, and U.S. policy from 1950 to 1954.

TYPES OF WINDOWS

The use of "window" as a term for power shift dates from the 1970s. It refers to a period when a state's relative strength is about to decline, or is in decline.[5] Windows can be distinguished on three dimensions.

Window of opportunity vs. window of vulnerability. The former is a fading offensive opportunity, the latter is a growing defensive vulnerability. A single window can be a window of both opportunity and vulnerability, if the declining state expects to fall all the way from dominance to helpless incapacity.

---

[4] Marc Trachtenberg notes that diplomatic historians have generally dismissed window theory. "Purely military factors, such as the desire to strike . . . before the military balance became unfavorable, were seen [by diplomatic historians] as playing at best a very marginal role" in causing war. Marc Trachtenberg, *History and Strategy* (Princeton: Princeton University Press, 1991), p. viii. Also skeptical, and suggesting that during power shifts rising states are more likely to initiate war than declining states, are A. F. K. Organski and Jacek Kugler, *The War Ledger* (Chicago: University of Chicago Press, 1980), pp. 19–20, 28. Another somewhat skeptical view of the dangers raised by windows is Richard Ned Lebow, "Windows of Opportunity: Do States Jump Through Them?" *International Security* 9 (Summer 1984): 147–86. A skeptical discussion of the specific danger of windows produced by arms races is Stephen Peter Rosen, "Nuclear Arms and Strategic Defense," *Washington Quarterly* 4 (Spring 1981): 82–99 at 83–87.

[5] The term is attributed to James Wade, a U.S. Defense Department official. Peter Pringle and William Arkin, *SIOP: The Secret U.S. Plan for Nuclear War* (New York: Norton, 1983), p. 196.

Diagram 2. Window theory

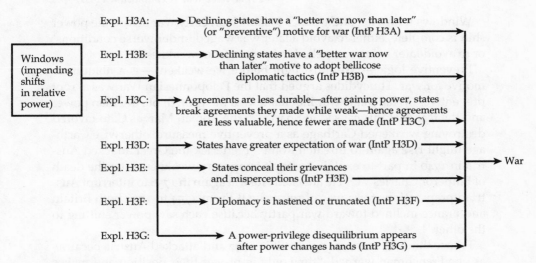

Expl.: Explanation
IntP: Intervening phenomenon

Long-term vs. short-term windows. Long-term windows arise from slow trends in the balance of power, stemming from different rates of economic growth or military buildup. Short-term windows arise from actions that quickly change the balance of power, including military mobilizations and deployments. For example, the Russian military buildup planned for 1914–17 caused German visions of a long-term (three-year) window in 1914. The rapid German mobilization in August 1914—a month faster than Russia—created a short-term window for Germany that it had to exploit or lose when Russia finished mobilizing in several weeks.

Internal (military and economic) vs. external (diplomatic) windows. Windows can stem from changes within states (for example, from different rates of long-term economic growth, long-term military buildup, or short-term military mobilization), or from diplomatic change (for example, a state briefly gathers more allies than it normally enjoys). Both types of windows can trigger "now is better than later" thinking.

HYPOTHESES ON THE EFFECTS OF WINDOWS

Windows have seven effects on the risk of war. (See Diagram 2.) These effects are somewhat interdependent. The first two effects need others to operate.

Preventive war (explanation H3A)

Windows tempt declining states to launch an early war before the power shift is complete, either to avoid a later war waged under worse conditions[6] or to avoid later being compelled to bargain from weakness.[7]

Preventive logic—"We must fight before we weaken"—is a ubiquitous motive for war. Thucydides argued that the Peloponnesian War was at root preventive: "What made war inevitable was the growth of Athenian power and the fear that this caused in Sparta."[8] The Roman Marcus Cato favored destroying weakened Carthage as a preventive measure: otherwise Carthage might rise again to threaten Rome.[9] Frederick the Great attacked Austria in 1740 in part to exploit Austria's temporary weakness after the death of Emperor Charles VI.[10] He attacked Austria again in 1756 to interrupt Austrian preparations for a war of revanche.[11] From 1754 to 1756 both Britain and France inclined toward war partly because each saw power shifting to the other.[12]

France thought time was against it in 1792 and attacked Austria because, as one Frenchman warned, "time only improves their position and makes ours deteriorate."[13] By attacking, France was "making the stormcloud burst instead of letting it grow."[14] James Madison led the United States to war

[6] Machiavelli outlined this logic: "You do not want to be subjugated? Then promptly proceed to subjugate the neighbor as long as his weakness offers you the occasion; for if you let it pass, fugitive opportunity will move over into the enemy's camp; and he will subjugate you." Quoted in Vagts, *Defense and Diplomacy*, p. 269.

[7] Preventive war is sometimes defined as driven by two fears: of declining relative power, and of later attack by the opponent. Hence it is a war fought now to prevent a war begun by others later under worse circumstances (thus the term "preventive"). See, for example, Vagts, *Defense and Diplomacy*, p. 263. I use a broader definition: preventive war is driven by fear of declining relative power and fear of later disputes with the opponent. The attacker's purpose is to halt its own relative decline in power or to create a fait accompli on the issue in dispute. Its goal is to avoid a war waged later under worse conditions, or to avoid being later compelled to bargain from weakness. My definition accords with Levy, "Declining Power": Preventive war "arises from the perception that one's military power and potential are declining relative to that of a rising adversary, and from the fear of the consequences of that decline" (p. 87).

[8] Thucydides, *History of the Peloponnesian War*, trans. Rex Warner (Harmondsworth: Penguin, 1954), p. 49.

[9] Klaus Knorr, "Threat Perception," in Klaus Knorr, ed., *Historical Dimensions of National Security Problems* (Lawrence: University Press of Kansas, 1976), pp. 78–119 at 99.

[10] Pierre Gaxotte, *Frederick the Great*, trans. R. A. Bell (New Haven: Yale University Press, 1942), p. 193.

[11] Gerhard Ritter, *Frederick the Great*, trans. Peter Paret (Berkeley: University of California Press, 1974), p. 109. Frederick explained his attack as preventive: "It is necessary to break up the conspiracy before it becomes too strong." Vagts, *Defense and Diplomacy*, p. 277.

[12] Britain observed a steady French naval buildup; France saw growing British influence in the Ohio Valley and on the European continent. Richard Smoke, *War: Controlling Escalation* (Cambridge: Harvard University Press, 1977), pp. 202, 217–18. For other preventive temptations in the crisis see ibid., pp. 224–25, 231.

[13] Jacques Brissot, quoted in Vagts, *Defense and Diplomacy*, p. 280.

[14] Charles Dumouriez, quoted in Vagts, *Defense and Diplomacy*, p. 281.

with Britain in 1812 partly because Napoleon's rampage in Europe opened a U.S. window of opportunity by tying down British power.[15] Turkey attacked Russia in 1853 partly to exploit the window of opportunity opened by momentary Franco-British backing for Turkey against Russia.[16] The Confederacy seceded in 1861 partly because it feared that the North would outgrow it in the long run.[17]

In 1866 Bismarck was drawn to war against Austria by the unfinished state of Austrian military reforms and by a fleeting opportunity to attack Austria without opposition from other powers.[18] In 1870 leaders in both France and Prussia advised war for preventive reasons: Prussia's army chief of staff favored war before French military reforms took effect, and France's war minister favored war before Prussia improved its rifles and copied the French *mitrailleuse*.[19]

Japan felt compelled to attack Russia in 1904 by the daily growth of Russian military power in the Far East.[20] Japan's general staff advised war because "the present is the most favorable time for this purpose. . . . If we let today's favorable opportunity slip by, it will never come again."[21]

German hawks offered preventive arguments for war in 1914. General Moltke declared during the July crisis that "we shall never hit it again so well as we do now with France's and Russia's expansion of their armies incomplete."[22] Reflecting on the war's origins in early 1918, Bethmann-Hollweg, the German chancellor, explained that "Lord yes, in a certain sense it was a preventive war," motivated by "the constant threat of attack . . . and by the military's claim: today war is still possible without defeat, but not in two years!"[23]

On the eve of war in 1939, Hitler told his generals that Germany should fight to exploit "favorable circumstances [that] will no longer prevail in two or three year's time"; Germany would suffer "certain annihilation sooner or

[15] Bradford Perkins, *Prologue to War: England and the United States, 1805–1812* (Berkeley: University of California Press, 1961), pp. 405–6.

[16] Smoke, *War*, p. 181.

[17] William Barney, *The Road to Secession: A New Perspective on the Old South* (New York: Praeger, 1972), p. 165.

[18] Vagts, *Defense and Diplomacy*, pp. 284–85; Smoke, *War*, pp. 87–91.

[19] Michael Howard, *The Franco-Prussian War: The German Invasion of France, 1870–1871* (New York: Granada, 1961), pp. 54, 56; see also 40–42. As in 1866, Bismarck also engineered and exploited a fleeting favorable diplomatic constellation. Smoke, *War*, pp. 125–34.

[20] Vagts, *Defense and Diplomacy*, p. 296.

[21] In 1903, quoted in Ian Nish, *The Origins of the Russo-Japanese War* (London: Longman, 1985) p. 157; see also pp. 18, 154.

[22] Volker R. Berghahn, *Germany and the Approach of War in 1914* (London: Macmillan, 1973), p. 203, quoting the Saxon military plenipotentiary's paraphrase. Moltke likewise declared on June 1: "We are ready, and the sooner it comes, the better for us." Fritz Fischer, *Germany's Aims in the First World War* (New York: Norton, 1967), p. 50.

[23] Konrad H. Jarausch, "The Illusion of Limited War: Bethmann Hollweg's Calculated Risk, July 1914," *Central European History* 2 (March 1969): 48–76 at 48. For more on perceptions of windows in 1914 see Chapter 7 at notes 91–115.

later" if it failed to seize this promising opportunity to attack.[24] Later in 1939, Stalin hurried to seize Baltic bases from Finland while Hitler was tied down in the West, triggering the Soviet-Finnish Winter War.[25]

During 1941 Japanese leaders were obsessed with windows, and their arguments for war were dominated by preventive logic. Japan's naval chief of staff, Admiral Osami Nagano, declared on September 3: "I am confident that at the present time we have a chance to win a war," but "we are getting weaker. By contrast, the enemy is getting stronger. With the passage of time we will get increasingly weaker, and we won't be able to survive." [26]

Israel struck Egypt in 1956 to forestall a leap in Egypt's military strength following a large 1955 Czech-Egyptian arms deal, and to exploit a rare and fleeting opportunity to fight with Britain and France as allies.[27] Israel struck Egypt again in 1967 in part to forestall the gathering of Arab armies on its borders. The assembling Arab forces would have doubled Arab strength over time, and Israeli officers estimated that each passing day would cost Israel an extra two hundred casualties in event of war.[28] Egypt struck Israel in 1973 in part to exploit a peaking of Egyptian military capacity.[29] The United States attacked Iraq in 1991 in part to forestall Saddam Hussein's emerging nuclear arsenal.[30]

[24] From notes by Admiral Canaris, quoted in Jeremy Noakes and Geoffrey Pridham, eds., *Nazism 1919–1945: A History in Documents and Eyewitness Accounts*, 2 vols. (New York: Schocken Books, 1988), 2:740–41; see also 2:731–32. France also saw preventive reasons for war in 1939: Chief of Staff General Maurice Gamelin argued on August 23 that "even if we would be stronger in a few months Germany would also be much more so because she would dispose of Polish and Rumanian resources. Consequently France has no choice" other than war. Anthony P. Adamthwaite, *The Making of the Second World War* (London: George Allen & Unwin, 1977), p. 222.

[25] Max Jakobson, *The Diplomacy of the Winter War* (Cambridge: Harvard University Press, 1961), pp. 143–44.

[26] Nobutaka Ike, *Japan's Decision for War: Records of the 1941 Policy Conferences* (Stanford: Stanford University Press, 1967), pp. 130–31.

[27] Nadav Safran, *Israel: The Embattled Ally* (Cambridge: Harvard University Press, 1979), pp. 226, 238, 352, 356; Michael Handel, "Crisis and Surprise in Three Arab-Israeli Wars," in Klaus Knorr and Patrick Morgan, eds., *Strategic Military Surprise* (New Brunswick: Transaction Books, 1983), pp. 111–46 at 115; Michael Handel, *Israel's Political-Military Doctrine* (Cambridge: Harvard University, Center for International Affairs, Occasional Papers no. 30, July 1973), p. 32; Ernest Stock, *Israel on the Road to Sinai, 1949–1956* (Ithaca: Cornell University Press, 1967), pp. 147–48, 154–55, 191–93. Noting that Israel's window was largely illusory is ibid., pp. 212–14.

[28] Edward Luttwak and Dan Horowitz, *The Israeli Army* (New York: Harper & Row, 1975), p. 222; Yoav Ben-Horin and Barry Posen, *Israel's Strategic Doctrine* (Santa Monica: RAND Corporation, report R-2845-NA, 1981), p. 37. Some Arabs also saw preventive reasons for war in 1967, arguing that Israel's emerging nuclear capability would later preclude the recovery of Palestine. Walter Laqueur, *The Road to War 1967* (London: Weidenfeld and Nicolson, 1968), p. 81.

[29] Sadat made these arguments for war in prewar discussions. Mohamed Heikal, *The Road to Ramadan* (New York: Quadrangle, 1975), p. 20.

[30] U.S. News and World Report, *Triumph without Victory: The History of the Persian Gulf War* (New York: Times Books, 1992), pp. 140, 179.

A. J. P. Taylor concluded a famous survey of European diplomacy by noting that "every war between Great Powers [in the 1848–1918 period] started out as a preventive war." Paul Schroeder likewise concludes that preventive wars are "normal, even common, tools of statecraft."[31] Preventive motives were evident in most wars surveyed for this book.

Bellicose diplomacy (explanation H3B)

Windows lead declining states to risk war more willingly. They regard even unwanted wars as less calamitous because their coming decline makes standing pat look relatively worse. As a result they adopt more risky policies.[32]

This was the mind-set of top German civilians in 1914. Bethmann-Hollweg favored a sudden smashing of Serbia despite the risk that this would trigger war with the Entente powers, saying, "If war must break out, better now than in one or two years' time when the Entente will be stronger."[33] Bethmann-Hollweg thought Germany's window was too small to support a decision for war against the Entente, but large enough to justify risking such a war to subdue Serbia. America's impending loss of military superiority triggered similar thoughts in the United States during the 1950s. In 1953 a presidential study group argued that "time has been working against us. This trend will continue unless it is arrested and reversed by positive action." Hence the United States should "prosecute relentlessly a forward and aggressive political strategy in all fields," a policy that the group admitted would entail "a substantial risk of general war."[34] Peace was preferred, but it was worth risking war to stem U.S. relative decline.[35]

Windows also foster "touchstone" arguments for bellicose diplomacy. Advocates for bellicosity argue that crises have the benefit of testing the

[31] A. J. P. Taylor, *The Struggle for Mastery in Europe, 1848–1918* (New York: Oxford University Press, 1954), p. 166; and Shroeder quoted in Levy, "Declining Power," p. 84.

[32] For more evidence see Richard Ned Lebow, *Between Peace and War: The Nature of International Crisis* (Baltimore: Johns Hopkins University Press, 1981). Lebow found that impending relative decline played a major role in motivating the instigators of a number of international brinkmanship crises (p. 62).

[33] On July 6, 1914, quoted in Lebow, *Between Peace and War*, p. 28. Jagow likewise declared on July 18: "I have no wish for a preventive war, but if the fight offers itself, we dare not flinch." Luigi Albertini, *The Origins of the War of 1914*, 3 vols., trans. and ed. Isabella M. Massey (1952–57; Westport, Conn.: Greenwood, 1980), 2:158.

[34] Group C of the Solarium exercise, quoted in H. W. Brands, "The Age of Vulnerability: Eisenhower and the National Security State," *American Historical Review* 94 (October 1989): 963–89 at 967–68.

[35] In 1955, Vice President Nixon likewise suggested that the United States should take "forceful diplomatic steps . . . to take advantage of its opportunity" before U.S. military superiority faded after 1958. *Foreign Relations of the United States, 1955–1957*, vol. 19, *National Security Policy* (Washington, D.C.: U.S. Government Printing Office, 1990), p. 149. The Gaither committee made a similar suggestion in 1957. See ibid., p. 651.

opponent's intentions. If the opponent takes the bait and fights today, this shows that it would also have fought tomorrow. If war results, nothing is lost (war was inevitable) but much is gained (war is fought at a time of strength, not weakness). This argument surfaced in Germany in 1914: Russia's response to a German-Austrian strike on Serbia would be a "touchstone whether Russia meant war or not" in the future.[36] If Russia would fight now it would surely fight later, and Germany was better off to learn this early. Japan's leaders likewise favored a tough negotiating stance with the United States during 1941, saying, "If they do not accede to the conditions that we propose, we must regard it as disclosing their true intention, which is to bring Japan to her knees."[37]

In sum, the "preventive war" and "bellicose diplomacy" explanations (H3A and H3B) suggest that windows incline states toward both preventive attack and toward bellicosity that can produce unwanted war.

However, windows also create countervailing pressures toward peace. They give declining powers reason to fight, but give ascending powers equal reason to avert war for now. Why do these two pressures not balance out? The next four explanations together argue that windows make cooperation more difficult. They thereby make states less able to defuse "now or never" pressures for preventive war and bellicose conduct through diplomacy.

Less credible threats and offers, hence fewer
peaceful settlements (explanation H3C)

Windows reduce the credibility of states' threats and offers. As a result, states are less able to resolve disputes peacefully. Even states that could agree on substance may fight because the other's compliance with the agreement is less certain, hence an agreement is less valuable, hence a forceful solution is relatively more attractive. Declining states wonder: "Will they keep their word after we decline? We will lose our ability to compel their compliance once we weaken; hence our threats to enforce their promises are empty; hence their promises are also empty." Ascending states think: "We cannot persuade them to believe even a sincere offer, because we cannot guarantee our own future conduct and they cannot enforce it. So why try to bargain?"

In short, declining powers cannot trust rising powers' offers, because rising powers know the declining power cannot enforce the agreement later.[38]

---

[36] German publicist Viktor Naumann, on July 1, 1914, quoted by Austro-Hungarian Chief of Cabinet Alexander von Hoyos, quoted in Albertini, *Origins*, 2:130.

[37] Liaison committee "Reference Materials," September 6, 1941, in Ike, *Japan's Decision*, p. 161.

[38] Framing this problem is James Fearon, "Rationalist Explanations for War," *International Organization* 49 (Summer 1995): 379–414 at 381, 385–86, 401–2, 404–8. Fearon notes that agreements are difficult when states will later have incentives to renege on the terms, and that

Agreements are easy in worlds of windows only if they freeze the two sides' relative power, thus shutting the window. But windows are usually created by forces that diplomacy cannot control, so this is rarely an option.

For example, a settlement between Palestinian Arabs and Zionists proved impossible in the 1930s partly because Arab leaders feared the Zionists would break the accord after Jewish numbers and power in Palestine grew.[39] Japan's leaders likewise doubted the value of an agreement with the United States in 1941 because they feared the United States would break it after Japan's relative power waned.[40]

As Bismarck noted, all treaties carry the implied proviso *rebus sic stantibus*: "as long as conditions remain the same."[41] Fluctuations in relative power lead states to break agreements by changing the conditions they were premised upon. Windows also reduce the value of new agreements because leaders expect they will have a short useful life. Both sides look ahead, one hoping for the day when it need not abide by what it just signed, the other fearing the day it cannot enforce the rights it was promised.

As a result, war can make sense even for declining powers whose adversaries will settle on generous terms. Rising powers that want to trade their privileges for peace often cannot because they cannot bind themselves to their promises.[42]

Greater expectation of war (explanation H3D)

Windows raise the risk of war. In so doing they magnify the risk posed by war causes that are catalyzed by expectations of war—including first-move advantages and windows themselves.

Windows cause rising states to fear preventive attack. This can spur them to strike preemptively if they see a first-move advantage.[43] Russia mobilized

---

windows raise this problem. Also relevant is Robert Axelrod, *The Evolution of Cooperation* (New York: Basic Books, 1984), pp. 126–32. Axelrod argues that cooperation is easier the longer the "shadow of the future"—the greater the relative importance of later to current interactions. Windows shorten the shadow of the future by reducing the impact of later retaliation that enforces today's agreement.

[39] See David Ben-Gurion, *My Talks with Arab Leaders*, trans. Aryeh Rubinstein and Misha Louvish (Jerusalem: Keter, 1972), pp. 20, 31, on the views of Auni Abdul Hadi and Musa Alami. Ben-Gurion later concurred with their argument; see ibid., p. 61.

[40] Akira Iriye, *The Origins of the Second World War in Asia and the Pacific* (London: Longman, 1987), p. 162. For another example see Jakobson, *Diplomacy of the Winter War*, p. 133.

[41] James Joll, *The Origins of the First World War* (London: Longman, 1984), p. 35.

[42] Not all want to make the trade. Some rising states avoid negotiation until after their rise, despite the risk of preventive attack in the meantime by their opponent, since they can then strike a better bargain if they rise without war. For example, Nasser rejected the Rogers Plan in 1969 partly because he did not want to negotiate from an inferior position. Yaacov Bar-Siman-Tov, "The War of Attrition, 1969–1970," in Alexander L. George, ed., *Avoiding War* (Boulder: Westview, 1991), pp. 320–41 at 325.

[43] Noting this danger are Thomas C. Schelling and Morton H. Halperin with Donald G. Brennan, *Strategy and Arms Control* (New York: Twentieth Century Fund, 1961), p. 14.

against Germany preemptively in 1914 partly because Russian leaders knew Germany was considering a preventive war against Russia. This heightened Russian fears of a German strike, which magnified Russia's impulse to preempt once a crisis erupted. Russia's General Nicholas Janushkevich later explained that Russia had mobilized because Russian leaders "knew well that Germany was . . . longing for [war] at that moment, because our big armaments programme was not yet completed (was to be completed only by 1917) and because our war potential was not as great as it might be." Hence "we knew that war [with Germany] was inevitable," hence failure to mobilize early "might have brought about a disaster." [44]

Windows can also cause declining states to fear preventive attack by the rising state if power trends will later reverse direction—that is, if today's descending power will later rise, and today's ascender will later fall, shifting the preventive impulse from one to the other. This fear arises if power relations are generally unstable. Rousseau sketched the problem: "Everyone, having no guarantee that he can avoid war, is anxious to begin it at the moment that suits his own interest, and so forestall a neighbor who would not fail to forestall the attack in his turn at any moment favorable to himself." [45]

For example, Germany attacked France in 1914 partly from fear that France would attack Germany to regain Alsace-Lorraine if German troops were ever tied down in a war against Russia. Such a war would open a French window of opportunity, triggering a French preventive war that Germany felt compelled to forestall by preventive attack of its own. [46]

Later Hitler justified many of his aggressions as preventive strikes to forestall other states' preventive strikes. In August 1939 he told his generals that he had to attack Poland because Poland would attack Germany if Germany ever moved against France. [47] In November 1939 he justified his attack on France by explaining that "we can oppose Russia only when we are free in the West." [48] German soldiers accepted the June 1941 attack on the Soviet Union because, in the words of one, "the Soviet Union was a great potential threat even in 1940, and it would have become an active one as soon as we tied down our forces against Britain." [49]

---

[44] Albertini, *Origins*, 2:559. See also D. C. B. Lieven, *Russia and the Origins of the First World War* (New York: St. Martin's, 1983), p. 49.

[45] Quoted in Kenneth N. Waltz, *Man, the State, and War* (New York: Columbia University Press, 1959), p. 180.

[46] The German declaration of war against France explained that France might suddenly attack from behind if Germany fought Russia; hence "Germany cannot leave to France the choice of the moment" at which to attack. Albertini, *Origins*, 3:194. Such thinking in Germany went back to Bismarck: see Gerhard Ritter, *The Sword and the Scepter: The Problem of Militarism in Germany*, 4 vols. (Coral Gables: University of Miami Press, 1972), 1:231.

[47] Norman Rich, *Hitler's War Aims: Ideology, the Nazi State, and the Course of Expansion* (New York: Norton, 1973), p. 128. See also Noakes and Pridham, *Nazism*, 2:737, 739.

[48] Noakes and Pridham, *Nazism*, 2:764; also 617.

[49] General Erich von Manstein, quoted in Vagts, *Defense and Diplomacy*, p. 319.

Concealment of grievances and misperceptions (explanation H3E)

Rising states conceal their grievances against others from fear of triggering preventive attack. This causes war by impeding diplomacy and deterrence. Conflicts are not resolved because they are not acknowledged. If the rising state intends aggression after its rise, its lulled targets may form a defending coalition too late to deter it. If its grievances rest on misperceptions, these cannot be addressed because they are not declared.

The coalition to contain Nazi aggression formed late, and Hitler underestimated its eventual scope, in part because he concealed his aggressive plans in the early 1930s to avoid triggering an allied preventive strike during Germany's early rearmament. Instead he conveyed a docile image, declaring in May 1933 that the "one great task" for himself and the German leadership was "to secure peace in the world."[50] This concealment lulled Britain and France into delayed rearmament. Paul Goebbels, the Nazi minister of propaganda, later noted that France should have waged preventive war on Germany while it was weak, but instead Germany "got through the danger zone" because "[we] managed . . . to keep our opponents guessing as to Germany's real aims."[51] Germany also lulled the United States, which awoke to the Nazi threat only after Hitler was firmly embarked on his course of aggression. Germany might have curbed its aims had it known from the start that it faced war with the United States, but German elites were oblivious partly because they hid the aggressive schemes that eventually provoked the United States.[52]

Hastened or truncated diplomacy (explanation H3F)

Like first-move advantages, windows force states to hurry diplomacy or to end it before it bears fruit. Declining states rush to secure agreement before their bargaining power vanishes, or to use force while they can still win on the battlefield. This haste raises the risk that workable diplomatic solu-

[50] Ian Kershaw, *The 'Hitler Myth': Image and Reality in the Third Reich* (New York: Oxford University Press, 1987), p. 125. See also Noakes and Pridham, *Nazism*, 2:653–58, 721; and Wolfram Wette, "Ideology, Propaganda, and Internal Politics as Preconditions of the War Policy of the Third Reich," in Wilhelm Deist et al., *Germany and the Second World War*, vol. 1, *The Buildup of German Aggression*, trans. P. S. Falla, Dean S. McMurray, and Ewald Osers (New York: Oxford University Press, 1990), pp. 9–155 at 96–104, 115.

[51] In 1940, quoted in Wette, "Ideology, Propaganda, and Internal Politics," pp. 96–97. In 1895 Baron Hayashi advised that rising Japan do likewise: "What Japan has now to do is to keep perfectly quiet, to lull the suspicions that have arisen against her, and to wait, meanwhile strengthening . . . her national power, watching and waiting for the opportunity which must one day surely come in the Orient." John Albert White, *The Diplomacy of the Russo-Japanese War* (Princeton: Princeton University Press, 1964), p. 135.

[52] For more examples of window-induced concealment of aims see Marc Trachtenberg, "A 'Wasting Asset': American Strategy and the Shifting Nuclear Balance, 1949–1954," *International Security* 13 (Winter 1988/89): 17–18, 18n.

tions will be overlooked, that deterrence will be attempted too late, and that decisions will be made under the sway of unexamined assumptions.

For example, as the Anglo-French Ohio Valley negotiations of 1755 neared success they were interrupted by window jumping by both sides. The Ohio dispute grew largely from misconceptions sown by false intelligence. French leaders were just discovering this when short-term windows triggered military action.[53] Fearing war, France hurried to move troops to North America before Britain used its superior navy to close the Atlantic. France shipped these troops on a fleet of warships stripped of guns; Britain then leapt at the rare and passing opportunity to smash this fleet while it sailed disarmed.[54] With more time, leaders on both sides might have uncovered the misconceptions that fueled their collision, but these window-driven military moves halted discussion.

The United States hurried to war in 1812 in part to exploit the fleeting chance to fight Britain while Napoleon engaged British energies. Britain was about to concede the key U.S. demand as the war erupted. As one historian summarizes, "Ironically, Britain surrendered [to U.S. demands] just a few weeks too late to preserve peace, while America . . . embarked upon war just too soon to enjoy the fruits of British surrender."[55]

Russia's preliminary mobilization in 1914 led Germany's General Moltke to argue for ending negotiations to resolve the July crisis. Russia's growing military advantage left no more time for talk, he argued on July 30. Instead, Germany now had to mobilize and attack. If Germany delayed mobilizing to pursue talks, "the result will be that if, as is to be anticipated, these parleys fail, Germany will enter the war in the most unfavorable conditions."[56]

Moscow halted negotiations with Finland in 1939 and attacked before the Finns even realized that they faced war if they stood firm.[57] Stalin, desperate to gain bases in Finland before Germany turned eastward, abruptly launched war soon after discussions began. With more time, Finland probably would have realized that concessions were needed to avert war, and would have given enough to preserve peace.

Window-imposed haste fostered Japan's blunders in 1941. In its blind rush to choose a policy before its oil ran out, the government failed to ask key questions. Even the crucial question of Japan's chances of winning a war

[53] Patrice Higgonet, "The Origins of the Seven Years' War," *Journal of Modern History* 40 (March 1968): 57–90 at 82.

[54] Smoke, *War*, pp. 217–18, 224–25, 231.

[55] Bradford Perkins, *Prologue to War: The United States and England, 1805–1812* (Berkeley: University of California Press, 1961), pp. 300, 405.

[56] Albertini, *Origins*, 3:25.

[57] D. W. Spring, "The Soviet Decision for War against Finland, 30 November 1939," *Soviet Studies* 38 (April 1986): 207–26 at 220; John H. Wourinen, *Finland and World War II, 1939–1944* (Westport, Conn.: Greenwood, 1983), p. 61; Jakobson, *Diplomacy of the Winter War*, pp. 100, 131–32, 140–42.

against the United States and Britain was never seriously discussed by the top policy group.[58]

In the autumn of 1950, China failed to deter the United States from crossing into North Korea partly because windows hurried the Sino-American crisis. The United States faced a large but fast-shutting window of opportunity after U.S. forces routed North Korean forces following the September 15 Inchon landing. The United States had a golden chance to destroy North Korea's shattered armies, but only if they had no time to regroup. This required pursuing them north, which swiftly brought U.S. forces up to the North Korean border and forced Truman to quickly decide whether to cross. He decided between September 24 and 27, a scant nine to twelve days after Inchon, and before China could convey a clear warning against crossing. Actions outran diplomacy partly because the post-Inchon U.S. window required rapid exploitation.[59]

In 1962 it took a tense week for the U.S. and Soviet governments to devise a settlement to the Cuban missile crisis, and a faster pace might have led the United States to use force before that settlement emerged. Robert Kennedy later wrote that if the United States had been compelled to make decisions on the first day of the crisis, U.S. policies might have been "quite different and filled with far greater risks." The days of quiet planning were "essential in choosing our ultimate course."[60] During the first three days of the crisis, October 16–18, the case for a U.S. air attack on the Soviet missiles in Cuba seemed compelling to most U.S. policymakers, and the consensus swung away from it only on October 19–20.[61] The concept of a quarantine, which President Kennedy finally adopted, was not developed until October 19,[62] and pressure to take faster action would have left it undiscovered. President Kennedy's advisors did not recognize the promise of the no-invasion-pledge formula that resolved the crisis until October 26—twelve days into the crisis.[63]

---

[58] Ike, *Japan's Decision*, p. 130; see also 186, 188, 196.

[59] Richard Neustadt, *Presidential Power* (New York: Wiley, 1960), pp. 131–34; Thomas J. Christensen, "Threats, Assurances, and the Last Chance for Peace," *International Security* 17 (Summer 1992): 122–54, at 130–32. The U.S. rush to the Yalu then created a Chinese window of vulnerability that hurried things further. At first China planned to move forces into North Korea, build them up, and attack after six months. The rapid U.S. rush northward forced China to act faster or not at all. Hence China shortened its timetable for war from six months to six weeks, attacking on November 26, less than two months after it decided in principle to intervene. This cut the chance for discussions that might have cured misperceptions that fed the crisis. On China's change of strategy see Jian Chen, "China's Changing Aims during the Korean War," *Journal of American-East-Asian Relations* 1 (Spring 1992): 8–41 at 24.

[60] Robert F. Kennedy, *Thirteen Days* (New York: Norton, 1971), p. 89.

[61] Raymond L. Garthoff, *Reflections on the Cuban Missile Crisis*, rev. ed. (Washington, D.C.: Brookings, 1989), p. 165.

[62] McGeorge Bundy, *Danger and Survival: Choices about the Bomb in the First Fifty Years* (New York: Random House, 1988), p. 401.

[63] Garthoff, *Cuban Missile Crisis*, pp. 72–73.

Power-privilege disequilibrium (explanation H3G)

Even power shifts that pass without war leave danger in their wake. The powers and privileges of states are now in disequilibrium, and the process of restoring equilibrium may trigger war.[64] States demand privileges in proportion to their power. Their sense of entitlement expands when their power grows. But declined states cannot concede without inviting blackmail from others. They fear a slippery slope—today's concessions will feed tomorrow's demands. Concessions also require hard judgments on what interest to sacrifice, forcing traumatic decisions that are too hard for some governments to make. As a net result, risen states demand their "place in the sun" but declined states often refuse to yield it.[65] This causes collisions between risen and fallen.

For example, before World War I Germans argued that Germany deserved a wider empire to match its increased power. The other powers refused to concede, setting the stage for war.

These are the dangers that arise when windows of opportunity and vulnerability appear. False perceptions of windows raise the same dangers. Governments that wrongly believe they face windows will respond as to real windows, with the same effects.

Antecedent conditions: When windows
cause war, when windows cause peace

Under some conditions, windows raise little risk of war or even bolster peace. Windows are less dangerous when declining states can offset their relative decline by finding new allies or building up their economic or military might.[66] They are less dangerous between states with few conflicts of interest. Decliners then have less fear that war will erupt later, hence less reason to jump through today's window.[67]

Windows can avert war if they cause rising states to defer war until after the dispute fades. Windows can also avert war if declining states decide to settle disputes before they lose bargaining leverage, despite the risk that the

---

[64] Offering this argument is Robert Gilpin, *War and Change in World Politics* (Princeton: Princeton University Press, 1981), chap. 5; also, less explicitly, E. H. Carr, *The Twenty Years' Crisis, 1919–1939* (New York: Harper & Row, 1964), chap. 13.

[65] Robert Gilpin argues that no risen state has ever accepted the old status quo, and no formerly dominant declined power has ever willingly conceded its dominance. *War and Change*, pp. 208–9.

[66] A catalogue of states that addressed their own relative decline by seeking more allies rather than by war is in Randall L. Schweller, "Domestic Structure and Preventive War: Are Democracies More Peaceful?" *World Politics* 44 (January 1992): 235–69 at 256.

[67] On the role of expectations of war in fueling preventive war see Lebow, *Between Peace and War*, pp. 254–63.

other state will later violate the agreement. This can avert wars that might occur if the dispute festered unsettled.

However, the conditions that make windows dangerous are common, and those making them benign seem rare. We do find examples of rising states actively working to defer war. For example, in 1941 some U.S. officials sought to defer the conflict with Japan until U.S. forces were stronger.[68] We also find instances of more generous bargaining by declining states.[69] But these examples are far outnumbered by instances where windows are associated with war-risking policies.

TESTS OF WINDOW THEORY

What predictions can be inferred from window theory? How could these predictions be tested? What do tests indicate? How much history can window theory explain? This section tests predictions from window theory with three case studies. These tests corroborate window theory and suggest that it explains a good deal of history.

Predictions of window theory

Window theory makes both prime predictions and explanatory predictions. As noted in Chapter 3, a theory's prime predictions derive from its prime hypothesis—in this case, that "war is more likely when the relative power of states fluctuates sharply." Tests of window theory's prime predictions shed light on whether windows cause war. The theory's explanatory predictions derive from hypotheses that comprise its seven explanations, H3A–H3G. Tests of these predictions shed light on both whether and how windows cause war.

An obvious prime prediction from window theory is that across history, war will be more common in places and eras where real or perceived windows are larger and more numerous. Another is that states that face, or believe they face, more and larger windows should fight more wars than other states. Testing these predictions, however, would require a massive effort to collect data on the size of windows through history and around the world. So I omit a test of prime predictions and instead test explanatory predic-

---

[68] Thomas A. Bailey, *A Diplomatic History of the American People*, 9th ed. (Englewood Cliffs, N.J.: Prentice-Hall, 1974), pp. 735–36.

[69] Thus the Killian and Gaither panels advised Eisenhower to reach a settlement with the Soviets while the United States held nuclear superiority. Bundy, *Danger and Survival*, pp. 349–50. See also John Lewis Gaddis, *The Long Peace: Inquiries into the History of the Cold War* (New York: Oxford University Press, 1987), p. 152; *Foreign Relations of the United States, 1955–1957*, 5:211, 237.

tions. These tests suffice to give us a good picture of the strength of window theory.

Four explanatory predictions are tested.

1. Intervening phenomena H3A–H3F (preventive attack, belligerent diplomacy, mistrust of agreements, expectation of war, concealment of grievances and misperceptions, and truncation of diplomacy) will be more common among states that face, or believe they face, large shifts in their relative power than among other states. Intervening phenomenon H3G (demands to align privileges with power) will be more common among states that recently gained power than among other states.

2. For a given state or group of states, intervening phenomena H3A–H3G will be more common in periods when windows are large and numerous, or seem large and numerous, than in other periods. Governments will conceal their grievances and misperceptions as their power grows. At their zenith they will consider preventive war and belligerent diplomacy, will mistrust agreements, and will rush diplomacy. Demands that privileges be realigned with power will be heard after power shifts are complete.

In other words, comparisons across states (prediction 1) and comparisons among the same states in different periods (prediction 2) should find that intervening phenomena H3A–H3G correlate with real and perceived shifts in relative power.

3. Elites that expect large shifts in their state's relative power will explain policies that embody intervening phenomena H3A–H3G as invited or required by impending or recent power shifts. For example, officials should explain that "we should attack now because otherwise they will attack later when we are relatively weaker" or that "we cannot trust agreements because our opponents will break them after they grow stronger."

4. Policymakers who believe windows are large will more strongly advocate policies embodying intervening phenomena H3A–H3G than those who see smaller windows.

Tests

These predictions are tested in three cases: Japan's policies in 1940–41, Germany's policies from 1933 to 1945, and the global policies of the United States from 1950 to 1954. These cases have four positive characteristics. First, they are well recorded. Second, in the cases of Germany and Japan very large real or perceived windows emerged. This creates a good setting for tests that contrast conditions in these cases to more average times and places. Third, the size of perceived windows varies sharply over time in all three cases, and

[88]

varies sharply across states in the case of Germany. This allows fruitful comparison of different periods and different states in the same case. Fourth, competing theories make divergent predictions of the German case. Specifically, ideological explanations of German foreign policy make predictions that diverge sharply from those of window theory. This lets us compare the relative strength of window theory and ideology.

Window theory does well in these tests. When the appearance of its intervening phenomena is predicted, at least some phenomena are observed. The tested predictions are often unique—no other theory predicts the observed result—hence these tests give window theory strong support.

Japan, 1940–1941

In 1941 Japan perceived a window of enormous size. The caprice of world politics had raised Japan momentarily to a historic pinnacle of power. Ahead, Japan's leaders believed, lay a rapid descent to helpless weakness unless Japan acted. Four factors combined to create Japan's window.[70]

First, in 1941 Japan briefly gained a fleeting military advantage over the United States. Japan secretly began a major naval buildup in 1937. The U.S. response lagged; it began in earnest only after the fall of France in May 1940.[71] As a result, Japan achieved a brief Pacific naval superiority in 1941–42. Japan's leaders knew that this superiority would be swept away in 1942–44 by the vastly larger U.S. naval building program.[72] A U.S. military buildup in the Philippines, scheduled for completion in early 1942, would also shift the balance of power against Japan.[73]

Second, the war in Europe created a huge diplomatic opportunity for Japan. The outbreak of war in 1939 pinned down British and French forces against Germany, leaving their Asian colonies unprotected. The fall of France and the Netherlands in 1940 left the Dutch East Indies and French Indochina with no protecting metropole, wide open to invasion. The European war led the United States to redeploy one-quarter of its fleet to the

[70] A summary of this window's elements is Arthur J. Marder, Mark Jacobsen, and John Horsfield, *Old Friends, New Enemies: The Royal Navy and the Imperial Japanese Navy*, 2 vols. (Oxford: Clarendon Press, 1990), 2:548–53.

[71] Stephen E. Pelz, *Race to Pearl Harbor: The Failure of the London Naval Conference and the Onset of World War II* (Cambridge: Harvard University Press, 1974), pp. 196, 204–5, 210–11, 217–18, 221.

[72] Japanese naval planners estimated that Japan had a chance for victory if it maintained at least an overall 5:10 naval ratio with the U.S. Navy. They felt 5:10 would be sufficient because large U.S. forces were pinned down in the Atlantic, and because Japan would have the advantage of standing on the defensive against a U.S. cross-Pacific assault. They predicted that this ratio would be 7:10 in late 1941, 5:10 in 1943, and 3:10 in 1944. They further estimated that in 1941 Japan had 320,000 tons of warships under construction, to 900,000 tons for the United States. Ibid., p. 224.

[73] John Mueller, "Pearl Harbor: Military Inconvenience, Political Disaster," *International Security* 16 (Winter 1991/92): 172–203 at 185.

Atlantic in the spring of 1941, leaving it weaker in the Pacific.[74] Finally, the June 1941 German attack on the Soviet Union reduced the danger that the Soviets would attack Japan in the north if Japan moved south. These events gave Japan a golden, never-to-be-repeated chance to conquer an Asian empire.[75]

Third, the United States imposed an oil embargo on Japan in July 1941. This embargo created a huge Japanese window of vulnerability. Japan would exhaust its oil stocks in two years at most under the embargo, leaving its oil-dependent navy helpless.[76]

Fourth, Japanese planners believed that any strike to the south should be launched in the winter months, when the Soviet Union could not exploit Japan's distraction to strike in the north. This imposed a deadline as Japan considered war in the fall of 1941.[77]

Moreover, Japan's elite believed that the Americans would launch war later if Japan did not forestall them. Hence Japan believed it faced both decline and a likely post-decline war.[78]

These windows dominated Japanese thought and behavior in 1940–41. They led Japan to abandon its policy of limited regional aggression and to embark on a reckless global war, including war against a United States that possessed many times Japan's latent war potential.

Japan's hawks argued for preventive war, resting their arguments heavily on the size of Japan's current opportunity and on the danger of later vulnerability if Japan failed to act. In 1940 they had visions of opportunities. The July 1940 grand strategic plan of the army general staff argued that Japan should act before the European conflict ended, when "British and American pressure against Japan will be greatly increased," and that Japan "should not miss the opportunity to establish a self-sufficient economic sphere. . . .

[74] Pelz, *Race to Pearl Harbor*, p. 221.

[75] See Ike, *Japan's Decision*, p. xix, who notes that there was "much talk in Japanese circles of a 'never-to-be-repeated' opportunity to build a great empire." Japan also feared that a German-British settlement could quickly erase this opportunity. Robert J. C. Butow, *Tojo and the Coming of the War* (Stanford: Stanford University Press, 1969), p. 180. And it feared the consolidation of a British-American-Soviet alliance, and sought to move before it formed. Iriye, *Origins of the Second World War*, p. 142.

[76] On the U.S. embargo see Jonathan G. Utley, *Going to War with Japan, 1937–1941* (Knoxville: University of Tennessee Press, 1985), pp. 151–56. On Japan's reaction see Michael A. Barnhart, *Japan Prepares for Total War: The Search for Economic Security, 1919–1941* (Ithaca: Cornell University Press, 1987), pp. 237–41, 268.

[77] Iriye, *Origins of the Second World War*, p. 162; Ike, *Japan's Decision*, p. 142.

[78] Japan's top planners thought it "historically inevitable that the conflict between [the United States and Japan] . . . will ultimately lead to war." "Reference Materials" compiled by secretaries of the Liaison Conferences, September 6, 1941, quoted in Ike, *Japan's Decision*, p. 152. On November 1, Admiral Nagano saw the chance of a U.S. attack on Japan as a "50-50" likelihood if Japan did not move first, and Army Vice-Chief of Staff Ko Tsukada thought "war cannot be avoided," although some civilians (Finance Minister Okinori Kaya and Foreign Minister Shigenori Togo) disagreed and opposed war for this reason. Ibid., pp. 201–2, 207.

We should grasp the favorable opportunity that now presents itself."[79] After the U.S. naval buildup began and the United States imposed its oil embargo, Japan's hawks had visions of vulnerability. Prime Minister Hideki Tojo summarized the common view on November 12, 1941: "Two years from now we will have no petroleum for military use. Ships will stop moving. When I think about the strengthening of American defenses in the Southwest Pacific, the expansion of the American fleet, the unfinished China Incident, and so on, I see no end of difficulties. . . . I fear that we would become a third-class nation after two or three years if we just sat tight."[80]

The Japanese government considered its decision in great window-imposed haste. In early September, the governing Liaison Conference set a deadline of October 10 for a decision for war.[81] Although that deadline slipped, later Liaison Conferences met under intense time pressure. At the conferences of September 3 and September 6, military officers warned that "our Empire's national power is declining day by day," hence "it is essential that we make up our minds quickly."[82] At the October 23 Liaison Conference, General Gen Sugiyama, the army chief of staff, opposed further analysis: "We can't devote four or five days to study," he said.[83] The October 30 Liaison meeting found two cabinet members asking for a single extra day to think before deciding on war; Prime Minister Tojo then insisted on a decision in two days "even if we have to meet all night."[84] This hasty deliberation produced slovenly analysis and slapdash decisions. For example, it seems that the Liaison Conferences never even seriously studied or discussed Japan's prospects for winning a war against the United States and Britain.[85]

Haste also hampered Japan's efforts to reach a settlement with the United

---

[79] Jun Tsunoda, "The Navy's Role in the Southern Strategy," in James William Morley, ed., *The Fateful Choice: Japan's Advance into Southeast Asia, 1939–1941* (New York: Columbia University Press, 1980), pp. 241–95 at 247–48. In July 1941, the Japanese navy chief of staff argued that "there is now a chance of achieving victory" against the United States, although "the chances will diminish as time goes on." Ike, *Japan's Decision*, p. 106. On the day the war in Europe began (September 1, 1939), the navy vice-chief of staff declared that "finally the time has come . . . [Japan] should today commence its advance to the Bay of Bengal." Ibid., p. 242.

[80] Ike, *Japan's Decision*, p. 238. Stephen Pelz likewise notes that Japan's prowar admirals often contended that "Japan had to strike before the Americans tipped the naval balance back against the empire." Pelz, *Race to Pearl Harbor*, p. 212. For other examples see ibid., p. 223; and Ike, *Japan's Decision*, pp. xix, 106, 130–31, 139, 142, 148, 200, 207.

[81] Scott D. Sagan, "Origins of the Pacific War," *Journal of Interdisciplinary Studies* 18 (Spring 1988): 893–922 at 909.

[82] General Suzuki and Admiral Nagano, quoted in Ike, *Japan's Decision*, pp. 131, 148.

[83] Ibid., p. 186. At the same meeting Admiral Nagano implored: "The Navy is consuming 400 tons of oil an hour. The situation is urgent. We want it decided one way or the other quickly."

[84] Ibid., pp. 196, 198; see also p. 193.

[85] Ibid., p. 130. Jun Tsunoda notes that "no careful study was ever made of Japan's material ability to carry out a comprehensive policy of southern expansion." Tsunoda, "Navy's Role," p. 249.

States. On October 15 Prime Minister Fumimaro Konoye thought a compromise with the United States possible, but General Tojo opposed exploring a deal because it would take too much time to arrange.[86] Shigenori Togo, the foreign minister, complained on November 12 that negotiations with the United States were in difficulty "because of the need to conclude them in a short time."[87]

Japan's leaders doubted the value of any diplomatic settlement with the United States. General Tojo voiced fears in September 1941 that the United States would exploit an agreement to gain strength and then would attack Japan once the balance of power shifted.[88]

These events fit three of window theory's predictions. Japan saw a huge and growing window in 1940–41. Accordingly, Japan considered and then executed a military attack, doubted the value of a negotiated settlement, and deliberated and negotiated in great haste (prediction 1). These behaviors intensified as Japan's window opened wider (prediction 2). Japanese policymakers justified these policies as required by Japan's impending relative decline (prediction 3).

Thus the 1941 Japan case corroborates window theory, but how strongly? As I noted in Chapter 3, we judge the significance of passed tests by asking if successful predictions are unique—that is, not made by other theories. The predictions tested here are fairly unique. Competing explanations for Japan's attack on the United States seem too weak to explain it by themselves.[89] It seems implausible that Japan would attack a state with ten times its industrial power, absent the fleeting military advantage and the impending ruinous decline that Japan perceived in 1941. Likewise, window theory has no competitors that plausibly explain Japan's haste in deciding to attack the United States,[90] or the statements by Japan's leaders explaining that Japan's relative decline compelled these actions.

How much importance does this evidence assign to window theory? That is, how large is the indicated impact of windows on states' ideas and behavior? The opening of the window of 1940–41 saw large change in Japan's behavior, most clearly in its dramatic switch from a policy of limited regional aggression to one of global war against the United States and Britain. This suggests that windows have large effects when they appear.

Did the 1941 Pacific window cause the Pacific War? If the U.S.-Japan war

---

[86] Barnhart, *Japan Prepares*, p. 251.

[87] Ike, *Japan's Decision*, p. 242.

[88] Iriye, *Origins of the Second World War*, p. 162.

[89] Other factors that propelled Japan's attack on the United States include Japan's rabid hypernationalism, its perception of a first-move advantage (as mentioned in Chapter 3), and its underestimate of the U.S. will to fight (as mentioned in Chapter 2).

[90] Stability theory also predicts hasty decision making, but only among states that fear an early first move by the other side. Japan saw a first-move advantage but did not fear an early U.S. first move, hence stability theory does not predict hasty Japanese decision making.

Table 2. Testing window theory: Japan, 1940–1941; Germany, 1933–1945; and the United States, 1950–1954

Case	Prediction 1: Were intervening phenomena H3A–H3G present in above-normal amounts among states that faced or perceived large windows?	Prediction 2: Were intervening phenomena H3A–H3G more common in periods when windows were large and numerous, or were believed to be large and numerous?	Prediction 3: Did elites explain policies that embodied intervening phenomena H3A–H3G as invited or required by windows?	Prediction 4: Did policymakers who thought windows were large more strongly advocate policies that embodied intervening phenomena H3A–H3G than other policymakers?
Japan, 1940–41	Yes: Japan's leaders deliberated and negotiated in great haste, doubted the value of a negotiated settlement, and launched war.	Yes: Japan's leaders deliberated in haste, expressed mistrust of agreements, and decided for war against the U.S. only after a large window opened for Japan.	Yes: Japan's leaders explained that windows required quick decisions, mistrust of diplomacy, and preventive war.	
Germany, 1933–45	Yes: Germany concealed grievances during its rise, then eschewed diplomacy and launched several wars after it rose.	Yes: Hitler moved to war against his neighbors only after Germany's window opened.	Yes: Hitler explained his concealment of German grievances, dismissal of diplomacy, and aggressive wars as required by windows.	
United States, 1950–54	Yes: the U.S. adopted fairly bellicose policies. But also no: the U.S. did not launch a war against the Soviet Union.	Yes: the U.S. adopted bellicose policies at a relative high-point of U.S. power. Also, the Soviet Union was less bellicose when the U.S. window was open than at other times.	Yes: U.S. officials said these bellicose policies were chosen to exploit the U.S. window before it shut.	Yes: Americans who saw a larger U.S. window favored more bellicose U.S. policies.

NOTE: Cells are left blank if the case did not offer a good opportunity to test the prediction.

had been averted until the spring of 1942, it might well have never occurred, because by then German victory looked more doubtful, and the assumption of German victory was a linchpin of Japan's plan for war.[91] If so, the windows that pushed Japan to quick action were a necessary element in the chemistry that caused the war.

Germany, 1933–1945

The case of Germany 1933–45 sets up a "three-cornered fight" that competes window theory against both the null hypothesis and a major competitor: ideology.[92]

A test against the null hypothesis is performed by asking only if observed facts confirm predictions inferred from the test theory. Such tests support or infirm a theory, but shed no direct light on its power relative to competing theories. A test against a competing theory asks which theory best predicts outcomes in situations where the two theories make divergent predictions. Such a test indicates the relative power of the two theories. If the competitor's power is known though other tests, such a test can also indicate a test theory's absolute power by comparing it to the metric of power that the competing theory provides. A "three-cornered fight" allows both types of test—against the null and against a competing theory—in one setting.

Germany from 1933 to 1945 is a good site for testing window theory against the null hypothesis, since the case includes large and numerous windows whose size varies over time. It also lets us test window theory against ideology, because the two theories make clear and differing predictions about the case.

Adolf Hitler dominated German foreign policymaking from 1933 to 1945. He took all major foreign policy decisions and held far tighter control of foreign than domestic policy.[93] Thus German policies expressed his person and ideas. The main elements of his ideology are clear: he stated them in two books and many speeches.[94] Though its details are sometimes incoherent, three general overlapping philosophic tenets stand out in this ideology:

---

[91] Utley, *Going to War with Japan*, makes this argument (p. 180).

[92] Imre Lakatos distinguishes "a two-cornered fight between theory and experiment" and "three-cornered fights between rival theories and experiment." His "two-cornered fights" are tests against the null hypothesis; his "three-cornered fights" include a test against the null and a theory-against-theory test. Imre Lakatos, "Falsification and the Methodology of Scientific Research Programmes," in Imre Lakatos and Alan Musgrave, eds., *Criticism and the Growth of Knowledge* (Cambridge: Cambridge University Press, 1970), pp. 91–196 at 115.

[93] Ian Kershaw, *The Nazi Dictatorship*, 2d ed. (London: Edward Arnold, 1989), p. 115.

[94] Good overviews of Hitler's ideas are Eberhard Jäckel, *Hitler's World View* (Cambridge: Harvard University Press, 1982); P. M. H. Bell, *The Origins of the Second World War in Europe* (London: Longman, 1986), pp. 74–85; Sebastian Haffner, *The Meaning of Hitler* (Cambridge: Harvard University Press, 1979), pp. 78–95. A survey of scholarship on Hitler's foreign policy is Kershaw, *Nazi Dictatorship*, chap. 6.

social Darwinism (the inevitability of a struggle for survival among the world's peoples), anti-Bolshevism, and racism, expressed especially as anti-Semitism and anti-Slavism. These tenets gave rise to three general overlapping programmatic goals: the destruction of Bolshevism, the destruction of European Jewry, and the seizure of living space in the East for German settlement. Expansion to the west and north were not prime goals.[95] Hitler viewed the British more as Aryan cousins than as enemies. He had no short-term wish to conquer them; instead he sought British (and Italian) partnership in carving up other parts of the world.[96] Nor was the conquest of France a prime goal. He believed conflict with France was inevitable, but wrote that "the long and in itself fruitless struggle between ourselves and France" was meaningful only "provided, Germany really regards the destruction of France solely as a means for . . . expansion elsewhere" ("elsewhere" being the Soviet Union).[97]

This was Hitler's long-term strategic worldview. His tactical worldview was filled with windows. Five distinct windows—a Franco-British window against Germany in the early to mid-1930s, followed by four German widows against a range of opponents from 1938 to 1941—shaped his policies. These windows led him away from the eastern war that his ideology prescribed and toward a wholly different war in the West. In the end the windows prevailed: Hitler shaped the direction and sequence of his expansion more to the contours of window-created dangers and opportunities than to the contours of his ideology.

Britain and France held a fast-waning military superiority over Germany during the early phase of German rearmament (1933–35). This Franco-British window framed a valley of danger that Hitler had to transit carefully. After leading Germany safely through it he saw a second window, this one a large window of opportunity opening for Germany against France and Britain from 1938 to 1943.

Defense spending data portray these two windows nicely. Britain and France together outspent Germany on defense by roughly 6:1 in 1930 and

---

[95] In *Mein Kampf* Hitler wrote, "We are putting an end to the perpetual German march towards the South and West of Europe and turning our eyes towards the lands in the East. . . . When we speak of new land in Europe today we must principally bear in mind *Russia* and the border states subject to her. Destiny itself seems to wish to point the way for us here." Noakes and Pridham, *Nazism*, 2:615.

[96] Jäckel, *Hitler's World View*, pp. 32–35. Hitler entertained the idea of an alliance with Britain even in 1942. Klaus Hildebrand, *The Foreign Policy of the Third Reich*, trans. Anthony Fothergill (Berkeley: University of California Press, 1973), p. 117.

[97] Jäckel, *Hitler's World View*, pp. 37–38. Hitler distinguished his ends and means in a 1939 statement: "Everything that I undertake is directed against Russia. If those in the West are too stupid and too blind to understand this, then I shall be forced to come to an understanding with the Russians to beat the West, and then, after its defeat, turn with all my concerted force against the Soviet Union." Hildebrand, *Foreign Policy of the Third Reich*, p. 88.

2:1 in 1933. After 1933 German military spending grew rapidly, bringing Germany from inferiority through parity to a fleeting superiority. In 1935 Germany passed France and Britain (combined), and in 1937 and 1938 Germany outspent them by roughly 2:1.[98] In 1939 Britain and France were closing the spending gap but had not yet caught Germany. Overall, from March 1933 to March 1939 Germany spent about half again as much on arms as Britain and France together,[99] and it held a corresponding material advantage in 1939. However, Britain and France together had greater industrial capacity than Germany (17 percent of world manufacturing output in 1929 compared to 11.1 percent for Germany, a 1.5:1 ratio);[100] hence Germany would again lose the lead in military material to France and Britain once they fully mobilized their economies for war.

Before German power overtook Franco-British power, Hitler concealed Germany's aggressive plans and soothed Europe with repeated assurance of his peaceful intentions. In 1933 he proclaimed that Germany wished "from its innermost heart to live in peace and friendship" with other nations, and in 1935 he declared that Nazi Germany "desires peace from its innermost ideological convictions. . . . Germany needs and desires peace."[101]

Once Germany's window opened, Hitler changed to a menacing bellicosity toward Europe. He also repeatedly argued in private that Germany should jump through its window before it closed. In late 1937 he rested arguments for an aggressive policy largely on fear that German military superiority was a fading asset.[102] On August 22, 1939, he explained to his generals that windows compelled the coming war: "The present moment is more favorable than in two or three years' time. . . . We are faced with the harsh alternatives of striking or of certain annihilation sooner or later."[103] Ten days later he launched his lightning war on Poland, triggering World War II.

---

[98] Paul Kennedy, *The Rise and Fall of the Great Powers: Economic Change and Military Conflict from 1500 to 2000* (New York: Random House, 1987), p. 296, using the Hillman estimate for 1930 and averaging the Hillman and Correlates of War estimates for other years. These figures show the following Germany: Britain-plus-France military spending ratios: 1:6.2 (1930); 1:2.0 (1933); 1.2:1 (1935); 2.1:1 (1937 and 1938 combined). Britain and France were hardly standing still during this period: the share of British national income spent on defense nearly tripled, from 3 percent in 1933 to 8 percent in 1938. However, German military spending grew even faster, from 3 percent of GNP in 1933 to 17 percent in 1938. Adamthwaite, *Making of the Second World War*, p. 73.

[99] Tim Mason, "Some Origins of the Second World War," *Past and Present*, no. 29 (December 1964), pp. 67–87 at 80.

[100] Kennedy, *Rise and Fall*, p. 330.

[101] Kershaw, '*Hitler Myth*,' p. 125.

[102] William Carr, *Arms, Autarky and Aggression: A Study in German Foreign Policy, 1933–1939* (London: Edward Arnold, 1972), p. 106; Noakes and Pridham, *Nazism*, 2:684–85.

[103] Noakes and Pridham, *Nazism*, 2:740–41, quoting notes by Admiral Canaris. See also p. 732.

After he crushed Poland, the same window, enlarged by fleeting Soviet weakness, drew Hitler west in his high-risk May 1940 attack on France and the Low Countries. Germany's military advantage over the Franco-British alliance was waning fast. "The moment is favorable now: in six months it may not be so any more. . . . Time is working for our adversaries. Now there is a relationship of forces which can never be more propitious."[104] So now was the time for decisive battle with France and Britain, if there was to be one. Hitler argued that such a battle was necessary because France would seize the opportunity of a future German-Soviet war to launch a preventive strike on Germany; hence Germany had to forestall this strike by smashing France before turning east. He also argued that such a battle was timely because Germany could safely move west without fearing a Soviet stab in the back: "Russia is at present not dangerous. It is now weakened by many developments . . . at the present time the Russian army is of little account."[105] But this Soviet weakness would soon pass, and with it the chance to strike west safely. (The Soviets had signed a nonaggression pact with Germany in 1939, but Hitler assumed that a recovered Soviet Union would break it if Germany was ever enmeshed in a western war.)

A third window led Hitler to press the war against Britain after the fall of France in 1940. Britain's strength was at low ebb after it lost its expeditionary army's equipment at Dunkirk. Hitler was anxious to defeat Britain before it recovered from this loss and from its late start at rearmament.[106] His chief of naval staff, Erich Raeder, also urged him to press Britain hard "before the USA could intervene effectively."[107] This logic led to the battle of Britain.

In June 1941 a fourth window helped convinced Hitler that the time was finally right for war with the Soviet Union. In late 1940 he argued that "in the Spring [of 1941] we will be at a discernable high in leadership, material, and troops, and the Russians will be at an unmistakable low."[108] The Red Army was still reeling from Stalin's 1937–38 purges, which killed roughly half the Soviet officer corps.[109] Stalin's massacre created a beckoning opportunity to crush the Soviet forces while they stood leaderless. Hitler's officers

---

[104] Hitler on November 23, 1939, quoted in Noakes and Pridham, *Nazism*, 2:764. See also ibid., 2:760–62; Rich, *Hitler's War Aims*, pp. 147–48.

[105] Noakes and Pridham, *Nazism*, 2:764.

[106] Barry R. Posen, *The Sources of Military Doctrine: France, Britain, and Germany between the Wars* (Ithaca: Cornell University Press, 1984), p. 99.

[107] Rich, *Hitler's War Aims*, p. 169. See also Noakes and Pridham, *Nazism*, 2:794.

[108] Earl F. Ziemke and Magna E. Bauer, *Moscow to Stalingrad: Decision in the East* (Washington, D.C.: United States Army Center of Military History, 1987), p. 15. See also Noakes and Pridham, *Nazism*, 2:764.

[109] Stalin murdered 3 of the Soviet Union's 5 marshals, 13 of 15 army commanders, 51 of 85 corps commanders, and 110 of 195 divisional commanders. In all, 90 percent of all Soviet generals, 80 percent of all colonels, and roughly half the entire officer corps were killed. John Gooch, *Armies in Europe* (London: Routledge & Kegan Paul, 1980), p. 204.

also feared that if Germany let the opportunity pass, the Soviets would launch a preventive strike on Germany once Germany committed its forces more deeply against Britain.[110] In addition, Hitler feared the United States would enter the European war by 1942 at the latest, and he sought to finish off the Soviet Union before the United States arrived in force.[111]

Visions of a fifth window underlay Hitler's seemingly bizarre declaration of war on the United States on December 11, 1941. Hitler expected the United States would soon enter the war anyhow, and he thought an early declaration would allow his forces to strike U.S. shipping before U.S. defenses were ready.[112]

These events satisfy three predictions of window theory. As its power grew, Germany concealed its grievances and ambitions, walking meekly before the other powers. Then, at its zenith, Germany spurned agreements and launched a number of wars (predictions 1 and 2). German policymakers justified these policies as invited or required by windows facing Germany (prediction 3).[113] There is no obvious contending explanation that competes with window theory to explain this evidence.

Moreover, the German policy shifts that accompany opening windows are quite substantial. Germany moves all the way from passivity to open war as Germany's window opens, and Germany's violent attentions leap around Europe and the world as windows jump from place to place. This supports the inference that windows have a large impact on state conduct.

Thus window theory does well when tested against the null hypothesis. It also does well when tested against ideology, predicting the structure of the war better than ideology when their predictions differ. Admittedly, ideology predicts Hitler's war against the Jews and window theory does not. Both theories predict the German-Soviet war. But window theory predicts the western wars on France and the Low Countries, Britain, and the United States, while ideology does not.[114] Thus window theory sometimes loses to

110 See General Manstein, quoted above at note 49.

111 Kershaw, *Nazi Dictatorship*, p. 128, quoting Andreas Hillgruber.

112 Rich, *Hitler's War Aims*, pp. 245–46.

113 Not every window of 1933–45 produced behavior that window theory predicts. Specifically, the British and French governments did not wage or even consider preventive war during 1933–35. This does window theory little damage, however, because conditions needed for window theory's operation arguably were absent during this window. Britain and France vastly underestimated German aggressiveness, so they did not expect war with a recovered Germany. This error calmed their anxiety at early German military growth. Britain also underestimated the window's size as it opened because British intelligence underestimated the German defense effort. Bell, *Origins of the Second World War*, p. 180; Wesley K. Wark, *The Ultimate Enemy: British Intelligence and Nazi Germany, 1933–1939* (Ithaca: Cornell University Press, 1985), pp. 35–51, 80–86, 228, 235, 245–47. This dampened Britain's response.

114 Others have observed that Hitler fought a misshapen war that ill-suited his ideological obsessions. Thus Jeremy Noakes and Geoffrey Pridham note that "the foreign policy which Hitler carried out between 1933 and 1939 . . . culminated in a pact with the Soviet Union, the

ideology when their predictions differ, but it wins most of the time. More-over, Hitler strongly believed in his ideology, and used it as a lodestar for policy.[115] This means that window theory beats a strong competitor here, and suggests that windows have large effects on policy.

United States, 1950–1954

From 1950 to 1954 the United States pursued a military buildup that raised it to a position of great but temporary superiority over the Soviet Union. U.S. policies during this period are a good laboratory for testing window theory because the buildup opened a sizable U.S. window of opportunity. As we know, window theory's main predicted outcome—preventive war—failed to materialize. Are its other predictions also unfulfilled?

Marc Trachtenberg, a diplomatic historian, studied the Cold War windows of 1950–54 with this question in mind.[116] He found that U.S. officials shaped policy to fit predicted shifts in the military balance, and often justified their policies on window grounds. When U.S. officials thought the United States was weak but gaining strength, they advised caution; when they thought U.S. strength had peaked, they advised belligerent policies and considered preventive war. This pattern is observed across periods, regions, and individuals. Thus window theory's predictions are largely fulfilled.

The U.S. buildup of 1950–54 was the largest peacetime military buildup in U.S. history. It was spurred by NSC-68, a secret 1950 State Department study that painted an ominous Soviet threat, and by the outbreak of the Korean War, which U.S. officials thought Stalin had ordered, and which they feared was a precursor to wider Soviet aggression. During the buildup, U.S. defense spending more than tripled, rising from \$13.1 billion (4.6 percent of U.S. GNP) in 1950 to \$46.6 billion (12.8 percent of GNP) in 1954. The buildup hit full stride in 1952, when spending reached \$44.0 billion (12.7 percent of GNP), almost double U.S. defense spending in 1951 (\$22.5 billion, or 6.9 percent of GNP). After 1954, U.S. defense spending dropped back to an average level of \$41.9 billion and an average of 9.8 percent of GNP in 1955–58.[117]

This massive buildup shifted the East-West military balance toward the

---

very power which he had claimed to wish to destroy, and in a war with Britain, whom he had originally envisaged as an ally." Noakes and Pridham, *Nazism*, 2:750. Neither ideology nor windows predicts Hitler's 1940 northern strike against Norway. It is, however, predicted by stability theory. See Chapter 3 at note 22.

[115] The influence of Hitler's ideology is suggested by his needless shift, on taking power in 1933, from Germany's previous businesslike relations with the Soviet Union to a policy of "natural antagonism"; and by his relentless murder of the Jews despite that policy's great political and military cost to Germany and himself. Neither policy has an obvious explanation aside from ideology. Kershaw, *Nazi Dictatorship*, pp. 117, 123; Haffner, *Meaning of Hitler*, pp. 101–6.

[116] Trachtenberg, "Wasting Asset."

[117] John Lewis Gaddis, *Strategies of Containment* (New York: Oxford University Press, 1982), p. 359.

United States and caused a marked shift in U.S. perceptions of the military balance. In 1950, U.S. officials saw the United States in a period of vulnerability and weakness. For example, in December 1950 the State Department policy planning staff spoke of "our present position of military weakness," and General Omar Bradley guessed that if global war occurred in November 1950, "we might be in danger of losing."[118] Later official estimates are far more optimistic: in 1953, Secretary of State John Foster Dulles spoke of "our much greater power and the Soviet Union's much greater weakness currently."[119]

U.S. policy fits the contours of this power shift. The United States pursued a cautious policy in 1950–51 during the perceived valley of U.S. weakness, then a much tougher policy in 1952–54, after crossing the valley.[120] U.S. policymakers explained their policies as responses to impending power shifts. Officials who advised the cautious 1950–51 policy argued that the United States should avoid provoking war until the military balance improved.[121] Later advocates of toughness argued that the United States should exploit its fleeting superiority. For example, the joint chiefs of staff argued in June 1954 that the United States should press its demands on the Soviet Union while the United States still held atomic superiority,[122] and President Eisenhower briefly considered preventive war, wondering to Dulles in September 1953 "whether or not our duty to future generations did not require us to *initiate* war at the most propitious moment we could designate."[123]

---

[118] *Foreign Relations of the United States, 1950,* vol. 1, *National Security Affairs; Foreign Economic Policy* (Washington, D.C.: U.S. Government Printing Office, 1977), p. 464; Trachtenberg, "Wasting Asset," pp. 15, 21. Were these assumptions of U.S. weakness correct? I think they were overdrawn: if World War III had started in 1950, the United States probably could have parlayed its atomic near-monopoly and vastly superior industry into a clear victory, and the buildup of 1950–54 only put the United States in a position to win more quickly at lesser cost. Nevertheless the question deserves further study. If U.S. officials underestimated U.S. strength, this also presents a mystery that deserves study.

[119] Trachtenberg, "Wasting Asset," p. 31.

[120] On early caution, see ibid., pp. 16–18, 21, 27; on later toughness, ibid., 32–37, 39, 41–42, 44.

[121] Charles Bohlen in 1951 warned that during "a period of danger" such as the United States faced, its diplomacy should seek to "minimize . . . the danger of general war." Ibid., p. 17. In 1952, the Policy Planning Staff likewise advised that talk of rollback was ill advised during the period of U.S. weakness. Ibid., pp. 17–18. See also General Omar Bradley in ibid., p. 27.

[122] Gaddis, *Long Peace,* p. 132. For more examples see above at notes 34–35.

[123] Gaddis, *Strategies of Containment,* p. 149. Many other U.S. officials and observers—far more than we now remember—also called for preventive war at early Cold War moments when they saw U.S. superiority. For details see Trachtenberg, "Wasting Asset," pp. 5, 7–11, 20–21, 35–42, 44–47; George E. Lowe, *The Age of Deterrence* (Boston: Little, Brown, 1964), pp. 52–59; Scott D. Sagan, "The Perils of Proliferation: Organization Theory, Deterrence Theory, and the Spread of Nuclear Weapons," *International Security* 18 (Spring 1994): 66–107 at 87–90; Stephen E. Ambrose, *Eisenhower,* 2 vols. (New York: Simon & Schuster, 1984), 2:229; Burton I. Kaufman, *The Korean War: Challenges in Crisis, Credibility, and Command* (Philadelphia: Temple University Press, 1986), pp. 56–57. Examples of calls by prominent commentators include Major George Fielding Eliot, *If Russia Strikes* (Indianapolis: Bobbs-Merrill, 1949),

This trend from caution to toughness in U.S. policy occurred across the globe. From Berlin to Korea to Indochina the United States was cautious during 1950–51, then much more aggressive during 1952 and later. In Europe the United States planned a mild response if Western access corridors to Berlin were cut or if Berlin were attacked during 1950–51. There would be no military probe to reopen corridors or general war to defend the city. In 1952 the United States switched to a much tougher policy, including plans for probes to open closed corridors and the launching of general war if Berlin were attacked.[124] In Korea, restraint was observed in 1950–51, largely for window reasons: in February 1951, Secretary of State Dean Acheson opposed a general advance north of 38th parallel because of the "risk of extending the Korean war . . . into a general war at a time when we are not yet ready to risk general war."[125] Beginning in August 1951, the restraints came off U.S. Korea policy.[126] Regarding Indochina, in 1950 the U.S. military opposed U.S. counter-intervention if China intervened in Indochina; in 1952 the United States planned to counter-intervene and to attack the Chinese homeland.[127]

The policy preferences of officials and commentators matched and varied with their perceptions of power balances and trends. Government insiders were pessimistic about the 1950 balance but saw an upward trend. They accordingly advised caution in 1950 while favoring belligerent policies later. Those outside government were more optimistic about the 1950 balance and accordingly favored more aggressive policies at that time.[128]

Meanwhile, Soviet policy moved in the opposite direction from U.S. policy. The Soviets were quite belligerent in 1950–51 (for example, endorsing Kim Il Sung's attack in Korea), but they adopted a policy of caution during their period of weakness, beginning in 1952.[129] Thus each superpower was more belligerent when its power was at peak and more cautious during times of lesser strength.

These events satisfy four window theory predictions. The United States adopted quite belligerent policies after its military buildup gained momentum, and Soviet policy grew tamer at the same time (predictions 1 and 2). U.S. policymakers explained this U.S. shift as a response to the opening U.S.

---

pp. 13, 21–22; and James Burnham, *The Coming Defeat of Communism* (London: Jonathan Cape, 1950), p. 156.

[124] Trachtenberg, "Wasting Asset," p. 31.

[125] Ibid., p. 27. In December 1950 General Omar Bradley spoke of war with China as the "wrong war . . . at the wrong time," implying there was a right time. Ibid. On U.S. restraint see also pp. 6, 21, 24, 46.

[126] Ibid., pp. 6, 28–31, 46.

[127] Ibid., p. 32.

[128] Ibid., pp. 24–25.

[129] This caution was embodied in Soviet acquiescence with West German rearmament in 1952 and in the March 10, 1952, Soviet offer to settle the German question on the basis of reunification and neutralization. Ibid., pp. 47–49.

window of opportunity (prediction 3). Observers who believed that the U.S. window was large favored more belligerent policies than those who believed it smaller (prediction 4).

The observed shifts in U.S. policy are substantial, suggesting that window theory has substantial importance. U.S. conduct changes markedly, although not overwhelmingly, with the opening of the U.S. window. The United States does not move all the way from peace to war, but across the globe it does move by marked degrees toward belligerence.

Does the failure of preventive war to occur in 1952–54 count as a flunked test? Yes, and it shows the limits of window theory. The window of 1952–54 was only middle-sized, and the costs of war seemed large to U.S. leaders. They had little fear that U.S. sovereignty would later be threatened if they let Soviet power grow, since U.S. superiority would fade into parity, not inferiority. The post-Stalin softening of Soviet policy reassured some that war was not inevitable. U.S. officials also thought a preventive war would be costly, and U.S. allies would be disapproving.[130] Thus U.S. leaders saw a fading window of opportunity, but the opportunity was not very attractive; it would not be followed by vulnerability; and it probably would not be followed by a war. The case indicates that windows lose some of their potency under such conditions. They can bring states to risk war, but not to start it.

Assessing Window Theory

Many of window theory's predictions are borne out. Official ideas and national policies shift both regularly and markedly with the appearance and disappearance of windows. The regularity of these shifts, and the weakness of competing explanations for them, give window theory substantial credibility. The large size of these shifts indicates that windows have a sizable impact. Window theory's success against ideology in the Germany 1933–45 case also supports an inference that it has large importance, although the U.S. 1950–54 case shows the limits of its strength.

If we grant that window theory has validity and importance, counterfactual speculation suggests that it also explains a substantial amount of international history, especially if we expand it to include the effects of perceived as well as actual windows. A plausible argument can be made that perhaps ten wars mentioned above in this chapter needed windows, or perceptions of windows, to get started. Thucydides argues that "what made war inevitable" between Athens and Sparta was a Spartan window of vulnerability. The French and British might have sorted out their mutual misperceptions and avoided war in 1756 had windows not ended talks by triggering mili-

---

[130] Ibid., pp. 39–42. Eisenhower at one point remarked that "the only thing worse than losing a global war is winning one." Ibid., p. 40.

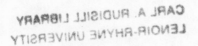

tary moves during the prewar crisis. The Confederates might have deferred secession in 1861, absent the impulse to rush provided by their window; and with waiting they might have realized that the North really did intend to fight their secession, and did not intend to destroy the South's social order (as the North's postwar acceptance of Southern white supremacy later revealed). "Now-or-never" arguments were a central and perhaps necessary element in Japan's decision for war in 1904, and in Germany's decision to launch the 1914 July crisis. Hitler largely relied on window arguments to sell his skeptical and potentially rebellious generals on war in 1939; absent these arguments they might have plotted to prevent war, as they did in 1938. Window arguments formed the core of the case for war in Japan in 1941; a decision for war is hard to imagine without them. With more time for discussion in the fall of 1939, the Finns probably would have realized that peace required large concessions and made those needed to appease Stalin. With more time for decision in the fall of 1950, the United States might have appraised the risk of Chinese intervention more accurately and proceeded more carefully. Window arguments were prominent in the Israeli deliberations that led to war in 1956, and without them Israel might have decided differently.

CAUSES AND CURES OF WINDOWS

Two factors govern the size and number of windows: the frequency and degree of fluctuations in the balance of power, and the offense-defense balance. Phenomena that affect these factors affect the size and number of windows.

1. *Fluctuation in relative power.* Any factor that affects states' relative strength can open windows. Arms racing causes shifts in the relative power of states unless they race in perfect synchrony; hence anything that causes arms racing also causes windows. Poor intelligence leads arms-racing states to lag in responding to each other; hence anything that promotes secrecy and retards transparency also causes windows. Military strategies that rely more heavily on mobilized than standing forces cause power fluctuations as states mobilize in crisis, especially if one side gains a jump on the other; hence mobilization systems cause preventive war. Factors that affect rates of national economic growth can cause power fluctuations if they have a differential impact on national economies.[131] Diplomatic alignments and realignments cause power fluctuations by shifting the relative strength of opposing alliances. Wars cause power fluctuation by causing states to focus forces on one border, creating momentary opportunities for others to attack on empty

---

[131] A discussion of these factors is Gilpin, *War and Change*.

borders. Wars also cause power fluctuations by leaving the losers or battle-damaged winners temporarily weakened.

2. *The offense-defense balance.* Windows are larger when conquest is easy. If the offense dominates, a small relative military decline can spell descent from dominance to vulnerability. If the defense dominates, shifts in force ratios produce smaller shifts in the capacity to overrun territory, hence they produce smaller shifts in meaningful political power. If the defense is very strong, neither side can conquer the other within a wide range of force ratios, so only very wide gyrations in force ratios have political meaning. A fluctuation that reverses the force ratio between two states from 1:2 to 2:1 creates a large window if an attacker can conquer a defender with less than 2:1 superiority. But if the attacker needs 3:1 superiority, a reversal from 1:2 to 2:1 leaves the balance of power unchanged. Both can defend and neither can conquer both before and after the shift. Hence there is no window, and thus no impulse to jump through a window, despite the shift in relative force size.

The risk of window-caused war is reduced by reducing the size of windows; it is also reduced by limiting the expectation of war, since preventive attack makes more sense when war is expected later. However, even more war can be prevented by controlling illusions of windows. Windows have been far more common in the minds of leaders than in reality. Many, perhaps most, preventive wars in history were disasters for the initiator: the windows were nonexistent or too small to exploit with success. In retrospect, the window that beckoned Germany in 1914 was unreal. Japan's 1941 window, while large, was not large enough to reward the use of force. The same was true of the German windows of 1939, 1940, and 1941, the Israeli window of 1956, the French windows of 1792 and 1870, the U.S. window of 1812, and the Confederate window of 1861. Preventive war can succeed and pay rewards, as it did for Israel in 1967, Japan in 1904, and the United States against Iraq in 1991. More often, preventive attack brings on the ruin it aims to avert. As Bismarck remarked, it is "suicide for fear of death."[132] The cause of false visions of windows poses an important puzzle.

---

[132] Quoted in Berghahn, *Germany and the Approach of War,* p. 167.

[5]

Cumulative Resources

Hypothesis 4. War is more likely when the control of resources enables the protection or acquisition of other resources.

A resource is cumulative if its possession helps its possessor to protect or acquire other resources.[1] The more its possession eases the protection or seizure of other resources, the more cumulative the resource.

Robert Dahl notes that inequalities in the distribution of political resources—wealth, education, land, votes, military power, the right to make laws—can be cumulative or dispersed within societies. If they are cumulative, inequalities in the distribution of one resource cause inequalities in the distribution of other resources. If they are wholly dispersed, or noncumulative, inequalities in the distribution of one resource have no effect on the distribution of other resources.[2]

As Dahl observes, the cumulativity of inequalities varies across social and political orders. In traditional societies, inequalities in the distribution of land and political power are highly cumulative. Landed oligarchs can

---

[1] "Cumulative" is defined as "increasing or enlarging by successive additions." *American Heritage Dictionary of the English Language*, 3d ed.

[2] See Robert A. Dahl, *Modern Political Analysis*, 3d ed. (Englewood Cliffs, N.J.: Prentice-Hall, 1976), pp. 37, 56–59, 74–76, 95–96; also Robert A. Dahl, *Who Governs? Democracy and Power in an American City* (New Haven: Yale University Press, 1961), pp. 7, 16–24, 85–86. Political resource are "means by which one person can influence the behavior of other persons," and include "money, information, food, the threat of force, jobs, friendship, social standing, the right to make laws, vote." *Modern Political Analysis*, p. 37. When inequalities are cumulative, "the more of one resource an individual had, the more he would have of the rest." Ibid., p. 75. When inequalities are perfectly cumulative, individuals would have the same relative standing in a rank ordering of their possession of all resources. When inequalities are perfectly dispersed, there is no correlation in ranking from one resource to the other. Ibid.

threaten eviction to coerce landless rural workers. This confers political power on the oligarchs; they use it to maintain or expand their control of land.[3] Inequalities in land and political power are less cumulative in industrial societies, where urban workers have no coercing landlords. Inequities in the distributions of land and power are also more cumulative in democracies with open ballots, since landlords can coerce landless voters more easily if ballots are not secret.[4] Likewise, inequities in the distribution of literacy and political power are more cumulative in democracies with a literacy requirement for voting. Literacy then confers votes, conferring political power, which confers control of other resources.

When inequalities are more cumulative, conflict for the control of each resource is more intense, since each resource decides control of others. As a result, the overall level of political conflict is more intense, since each conflict decides the outcome of others.

Dahl applies the concept of cumulativity to inequalities and to domestic politics. The concept also applies to resources themselves and to international affairs.[5] A resource is cumulative if its possession eases the retention or acquisition of other resources. A resource can be cumulative, noncumulative, or negative-cumulative. The control of cumulative resources allows the protection or control of other resources. The control of noncumulative resources has no effect on the capacity to protect or control other resources. The control of negative-cumulative resources lowers one's capacity to control other resources.

The cumulativity of a given resource is a function of two factors: the utility of the resource for acquiring or protecting other resources, and the cost of extracting the resource from its territory, including the cost of policing and administering the territory. If the utility exceeds the extraction cost, cumulativity is positive. If they are equal, cumulativity is zero. If extraction cost exceeds utility, cumulativity is negative—the resource is a millstone that drains its possessor's power.

The utility and extraction cost of resources vary sharply from one resource to another and from one place to another; hence cumulativity varies sharply as well. For example, Germany's defense industry is more useful for acquiring or retaining other resources than Cuba's tobacco surplus, and a conqueror could extract Kuwaiti oil at less police cost than Vietnam's agricultural surplus.

The net utility of a resource is a function of the power that it confers on

[3] Dahl, *Modern Political Analysis*, pp. 58, 76.
[4] Dahl, *Who Governs?* pp. 16–17.
[5] The best discussion of cumulativity in international affairs, focused specifically on the cumulativity of industrial resources in the twentieth century, is Peter Liberman, *Does Conquest Pay? The Exploitation of Occupied Industrial Societies* (Princeton: Princeton University Press, 1996).

its current owner and the power it would confer on a conqueror. The most cumulative resources empower both; the least cumulative resources empower neither. Often resources empower their current owners but not a conqueror, or they empower the conqueror at a discount, conferring less power on the new owner than the old. Sometimes the opposite is the case—the resource confers more power on the new owner than the old—but such cases are rare.[6]

The cumulativity of the same resource can rise and fall over time as technology and military doctrine change. For example, naval stores—timber for masts, pitch for sealing—were cumulative in the age of sail but lost utility in the steam age. Coal supplies and coaling stations then became more cumulative. Overseas air bases were more useful for the United States in the early Cold War, when the United States relied on medium-range bombers that needed forward bases to reach the Soviet Union. After the United States deployed intercontinental bombers and missiles, these overseas bases lost value. Uranium ore was a noncumulative resource before the nuclear age but has become more cumulative. Agricultural land was more cumulative before the age of nationalism; nationalism devalued it by raising the cost of policing conquered land (unless conquerors had the same nationality as the conquered population). And nuclear weapons reduce the cumulativity of many resources (see below).

Cumulative resources can ease their owner's control of core resources (the national home economy) or of other power resources that protect the core. The regress of empowerment is unlimited: a resource can secure control of a resource that secures a resource . . . that secures control of the national core. For example, in the Cold War U.S. defense planners feared that the Soviets could use Caribbean military bases to interdict U.S. shipment of reinforcements to Europe, easing a Soviet seizure of Western Europe, which in turn would ease Soviet expansion in North America. The direct effects of Soviet Caribbean bases were less feared than the remote effects.

Cumulativity varies with the relative ease of conquering and defending territory—that is, with the offense-defense balance. If conquest is difficult, the cumulativity of resources is lowered because a resource advantage then cannot be used either to seize very much of an opponent's resources; nor can it be used to forestall the seizure of much by an opponent (since the opponent cannot seize much to begin with). If conquest is easy, cumulativity is greater because even a small resource advantage might be parlayed into large gains or used to forestall large gains by an opponent.

Cumulativity further varies with the size of the transfer discount, that

---

[6] For example, India's Kashmir State might empower Pakistan more than India if Pakistan conquered it, since the Muslim-majority region would probably cost Pakistan less than India to administer.

is, the gap between the power that a resource confers on its current owner and the power it gives a conquering state. A transfer discount appears, for example, if conquerors are less able to squeeze industrial production from conquered industry than the original owners, due to resistance by conquered workers. Most conquerors also face extra administrative costs stemming from resistance by conquered populations. Cumulativity is dampened when the transfer discount for a resource is high; only current owners derive full empowerment from the resource, while conquerors derive less or no power. (In such cases conquerors still gain relative power by conquering their enemy's territory, but they gain only by weakening their enemy, not by strengthening themselves.) The cumulativity of a resource is greatest when there is no transfer discount.

The size of the transfer discount varies with the conquered people's will to resist the conqueror, their capacity for passive and military resistance, the efficiency of the conqueror's police tactics, and the degree of local cooperation that conquerors require to extract the resource successfully.[7] If the conquered people's will to resist is strong, if their resistance capacity is large, if the conqueror uses ineffective strategies of control, and if extraction requires extensive local cooperation, then the discount is high. If not, the discount is low or zero.

CUMULATIVITY AND CONFLICT

International politics is more competitive, hence more violent, when resources are more cumulative. When many resources are highly cumulative, states more fiercely defend what they have, seek more for themselves, and seek to prevent others from gaining more. Each struggle decides the outcome of the next, so states strive harder to win each encounter. Every dispute becomes a potential trigger for all-out conflict. If cumulativity is low, states are less expansionist and less worried by other states' expansionism. If resources are wholly noncumulative, states can lose today's quarrel without hurting their chance of winning tomorrow's, so they can pursue more relaxed policies.

High cumulativity fuels both expansionism and resistance to expansionism, causing intense conflict.[8] For example, both German and Japanese expansionism in the 1930s were driven by beliefs that many conquerable

[7] On factors governing the transfer discount see Liberman, *Does Conquest Pay?* pp. 18–31.
[8] E. H. Carr notes that "the most serious wars are fought in order to make one's own country militarily stronger or, more often, to prevent another country from becoming militarily stronger"—an argument that assumes the resources for which states contend are cumulative. Edward Hallett Carr, *The Twenty Years' Crisis 1919–1939* (New York: Harper & Row, 1964), p. 111.

resources were highly cumulative. Germany and Japan each believed its economy could be strangled by an enemy blockade unless it achieved economic independence. Each believed a wider empire could provide economic independence. Hence each sought empires.[9] U.S. resistance to their expansion was likewise premised on the assumed cumulativity of West European and East Asian resources: Americans feared that Axis control of these resources would allow the Axis powers to threaten the United States.[10] The same logic later led the United States to contain Soviet expansion.[11] High cumulativity also leads states to destroy resources they cannot control. Examples include allied strategic bombing of German and Japanese industry in World War II and scorched-earth policies by many retreating armies. This magnifies war's violence.

A parable explains that "for want of a nail the shoe was lost; for want of a shoe the horse was lost; for want of a horse the rider was lost; for want of a rider the battle was lost; and for loss of a battle the kingdom was lost." Peace is frail in a "want of a nail" world where many resources ease the seizure or defense of other resources. Things are safer when lost nails cannot decide battles or when nails become millstones for their conquerors.

Peace is most frail if many resources are highly cumulative and lie exposed near national frontiers. Small territorial gains can then be more easily parlayed into larger gains, and small territorial losses can spell disaster.

[9] Germany sought self-sufficiency in food; Hitler explained in August 1939 that "I need Ukraine so they can't starve us out like in the last war." Jeremy Noakes and Geoffrey Pridham, eds., *Nazism 1919–1945: A History in Documents and Eyewitness Accounts*, 2 vols. (New York: Schocken Books, 1988), 2:739. Earlier Hitler justified German expansion by declaring that a nation must be "sustained by its own soil"; dependence on others would "lead to the decline or even annihilation of the nation concerned." Ibid., 2:614. Hitler also sought German energy independence and attacked the Soviet Union in 1941 in part to secure Germany's Rumanian oil fields and gain new oil from the Caucasus. Joel Hayward, "Hitler's Quest for Oil: The Impact of Economic Considerations on Military Strategy, 1941–42," *Journal of Strategic Studies* 18 (December 1995): 94–135 at 94–99. In July 1940, the Japanese army likewise urged that Japan expand to "free itself from its dependence upon Britain and the United States . . . through the establishment of a self-sufficient economic sphere." Jun Tsunoda, "The Navy's Role in the Southern Strategy," in James William Morley, ed., *The Fateful Choice: Japan's Advance into Southeast Asia, 1939–1941* (New York: Columbia University Press, 1980), pp. 241–95 at 247.

[10] On Franklin Roosevelt's prewar thought see G. R. Sloan, *Geopolitics in United States Strategic Policy, 1890–1987* (New York: St. Martin's, 1988), pp. 113–16. On others see John A. Thompson, "The Exaggeration of American Vulnerability: The Anatomy of a Tradition," *Diplomatic History* 16 (Winter 1992): 23–44 at 35–37; and Walter Lippmann, *U.S. Foreign Policy: Shield of the Republic* (Boston: Little, Brown, 1943), pp. 108–13, 162–64. A general survey and assessment of U.S. geopolitical thought is Robert J. Art, "A Defensible Defense: America's Grand Strategy after the Cold War," *International Security* 15 (Spring 1991): 5–53 at 10–23.

[11] See Melvyn P. Leffler, "The American Conception of National Security and the Beginnings of the Cold War," *American Historical Review* 89 (April 1984): 346–81 at 356–8, 370, 374, 377; and John Lewis Gaddis, *Strategies of Containment: A Critical Appraisal of Postwar American National Security Policy* (New York: Oxford University Press, 1982), pp. 29–30, 57, 201.

[109]

Things are least dangerous if few resources are cumulative and if those that are cumulative lie far from national borders in defensible redoubts. Best of all are conditions where cumulative resources lie entirely beyond reach of attackers, as did the U.S. ballistic missile submarine force during the Cold War.

TYPES OF CUMULATIVITY

Several types of resources can be cumulative in international affairs. In modern times *industrial capacity* is widely recognized as by far the most cumulative.[12] Modern military power is distilled from industrial capacity; states cannot remain front-rank military powers without a large industrial base. Much twentieth-century warfare grew from the struggle for control of the world's great industrial regions, which conferred control of other areas or eased control of homelands.[13] Those who won these struggles harvested handsome power-profits.

Nazi Germany, for example, vastly expanded its war production by conquering and harnessing vassal economies. It achieved an average net extract rate—that is, the value of extracted material minus the costs of occupation—of 33 percent of prewar GNP from its major Central and Western European conquests (the Netherlands, Belgium, France, Norway, Bohemia-Moravia, and Denmark).[14] This is less net extract than the ousted former regimes could have gained, but it is nevertheless a very large surplus. As points of comparison, Germany and Britain mobilized an average of 52 percent and 50 percent of their prewar GNPs for war production during their first four full years at war (1940–43), respectively, and the United States mobilized 67 percent of its prewar GNP for war production during its first two full

[12] For example, in 1904 Halford Mackinder argued that "the successful powers will be those who have the greatest industrial base.... Those people who have the industrial power and the power of invention and science will be able to defeat all others." Quoted in Paul Kennedy, *Strategy and Diplomacy 1870–1945* (Aylesbury: Fontana, 1983), p. 47. Likewise George Kennan argued that modern military power could be produced in quantity only in the world's five major industrial regions—the United States, the United Kingdom, the Rhine Valley with adjacent industrial areas, the Soviet Union, and Japan. George F. Kennan, *Memoirs 1925–1950* (Boston: Little, Brown, 1967), p. 359.

[13] See notes 9–11 above on the origins of World War II and the Cold War. Many struggles within World War II also arose from both sides' efforts to control or destroy industrial capacity. For example, Hitler struck west in 1940 partly to remove the Franco-British threat to Germany's Ruhr industrial region. The Ruhr's production, he explained in October 1939 was "the precondition for the successful conduct of the war ... any serious loss of production in this area cannot be compensated for elsewhere. It must lead sooner or later to the collapse of the German war economy and thereby to our powers of defense." Noakes and Pridham, *Nazism*, 2:761.

[14] Liberman, *Does Conquest Pay?*, p. 43. Extraction rates ranged from 44 percent for the Netherlands and Belgium down to 19 percent for Denmark. Figures represent extraction rates from the time of their surrender to Germany through March 1944.

years at war (1942–43).[15] Thus Germany's net rate of extraction in its empire was quite high—more than half the rate achieved by Germany and Britain in their homelands, and about half the rate achieved by the United States in its homeland. This supports arguments that the conquest of industrial areas could tilt the balance of power sharply in favor of their conquerors, at least in the 1940s.[16]

Various other resources can also prove cumulative under the right conditions. *Raw material inputs* to industrial economies are a cumulative resource if their loss will substantially reduce a state's industrial output, especially its output of war material. For example, both Germany and Japan saw food and energy inputs as highly cumulative resources that they had to control to avoid strangulation by their enemies. Likewise, U.S. interventionists often warned that hostile control of Third World raw materials could injure U.S. security during the Cold War. President Eisenhower explained that Indochina's tin and tungsten made it a crucial prize,[17] and *Newsweek* once warned that Indochina's raw materials were "essential to Western industrial civilization."[18]

Military bases and *strategic depth* are cumulative resources if they provide military strength that cannot be cheaply replaced. Accordingly, contests for bases and strategic depth have often sparked conflict.[19] For example, Israel saw the territories that it occupied in the 1967 war as highly cumulative resources because they offered valuable strategic depth.[20] Over the centuries Britain has often fought to keep continental hegemons out of Belgium and Holland, hence off the English Channel and the North Sea, hence further from Britain.[21] The Soviet Union attacked Finland in 1939 to gain military bases in Finland for the coming war with Germany.[22] The United States intervened repeatedly in the Caribbean after 1898 to avert the establishment of European military bases there.

[15] Ibid., p. 33.

[16] Whether a Eurasian hegemon could harvest enough strength from its empire to threaten the United States is another issue. An assessment, concluding in the negative for the Cold War, is Art, "Defensible Defense," pp. 19–23.

[17] See William Appleman Williams, Thomas McCormick, Lloyd Gardner and Walter LaFeber, eds., *America in Vietnam: A Documentary History* (Garden City: Anchor Press, 1985), p. 156; see also pp. 111–13, 122.

[18] On April 12, 1954, quoted in Leslie H. Gelb with Richard K. Betts, *The Irony of Vietnam: The System Worked* (Washington, D.C.: Brookings, 1979), p. 205.

[19] An overview of the value of military bases is Michael C. Desch, "The Keys That Lock Up the World," *International Security* 14 (Summer 1989): 86–121.

[20] Postwar discussions of Israel's situation include Dan Horowitz, *Israel's Concept of Defensible Borders* (Jerusalem: Jerusalem Post, 1975); and Aharon Yariv, "Strategic Depth," *Jerusalem Quarterly*, no. 17 (Fall 1980), pp. 3–12.

[21] See, for example, on this motive 1793, T. C. W. Blanning, *The Origins of the French Revolutionary Wars* (London: Longman, 1986), p. 138, 157.

[22] D. W. Spring, "The Soviet Decision for War against Finland, 30 November 1939," *Soviet Studies* 38 (April 1986): 207–26 at 207–8; Max Jakobson, *The Diplomacy of the Winter War* (Cambridge: Harvard University Press, 1961), pp. 8, 15–16, 117–18.

Military forces themselves are cumulative resources, and are most cumulative if conquerors can easily convert them to their own use. For example, three of the ten Panzer divisions that keyed Germany's 1940 conquest of France were equipped with combat vehicles looted from Czechoslovakia.[23] *Labor*, including military and civilian labor, is a cumulative resource, especially if conquerors can convert it to their own use. For example, Nazi Germany bolstered its production with more than seven million foreign workers during World War II.[24] (Conquered labor is often hard to exploit in the age of nationalism, however.) *Tax base* and *currency* have been cumulative resources in the past. In the mercantile era of the eighteenth century, international competition revolved largely around contests for the control of specie, needed especially to pay mercenary armies.[25]

The *credibility of one's threats* is a cumulative resource, since states concede more quickly to threats they believe. Most evidence suggests that little credibility is gained by using force, however.[26] States put small weight on another state's past propensity to fight when assessing its willingness to carry out threats in the future. Hence there is little temptation to use force to gain credibility, as long as policymakers understand this. The cumulativity of threat credibility is thus less dangerous than the cumulativity of resources that can be gained by force (for example, buffer room, military bases, and other physical resources).

Territories that provide cumulative resources may not be cumulative themselves. If extraction rates are low and costs of governance are high, they can be reverse-cumulative millstones, as noted above. Conquests can also become millstones if they trigger balancing behavior by other states, or if the costs of defending them against outsiders is high.

BELIEFS ABOUT CUMULATIVITY AND THEIR IMPLICATIONS

Debates about cumulativity have recurrently divided hawks and doves in the United States and elsewhere.[27] Two major questions have recurred: How

[23] P. M. H. Bell, *The Origins of the Second World War in Europe* (London: Longmans, 1986), p. 172.
[24] David Kaiser, *Politics and War: European Conflict from Philip II to Hitler* (Cambridge: Harvard University Press, 1990), pp. 380, 384.
[25] A summary of mercantilist principals is David Baldwin, *Economic Statecraft* (Princeton: Princeton University Press, 1985), pp. 72–74.
[26] See Ted Hopf, *Peripheral Visions: Deterrence Theory and American Foreign Policy in the Third World, 1965–1990* (Ann Arbor: University of Michigan Press, 1994); Jonathan Mercer, *Reputations and International Politics* (Ithaca: Cornell University Press, 1996); and Robert Jervis, *The Meaning of the Nuclear Revolution: Statecraft and the Prospect of Armageddon* (Ithaca: Cornell University Press, 1989), pp. 38–39, and works cited therein.
[27] The cumulativity of resources also emerges as a central question in debates over foreign economic policy. The long debate between nationalist and liberal views of international trade turns in essence on a dispute over the size and cumulativity of gains from restrictive trade

cumulative are conquerable territorial resources? Which resources and regions are more cumulative and which are less?

Hawks in aggressor states (Nazi Germany and imperial Japan) and in more satisfied powers (the United States) have often rested hard-line arguments on claims that conquerable resources are highly cumulative, while doves have argued that these resources are less cumulative. For example, in the early Cold War, U.S. hard-liners argued that Eurasia's resources were highly cumulative, hence the threat posed to U.S. security by potential Soviet expansion was great, hence the United States should adopt an aggressive rollback strategy toward the Soviet Union.[28] In contrast, those favoring more restraint often doubted that resource cumulativity was high. For example, State Department policy planning chief George Kennan favored a more temperate policy partly because he saw a large owner-to-conqueror transfer discount, endorsing Gibbon's view that "there is nothing more contrary to nature than the attempt to hold in obedience distant provinces."[29]

Disagreements on cumulativity underlay the long debate over U.S. Cold War intervention in the Third World. Domino theorists held that the capture of one Third World state would allow the capture of the next, and the next. In other words, they believed Third World states were highly cumulative assets. Domino theory doubters thought Third World states were less cumulative, hence intervention to prevent domino effects from starting was less necessary.[30]

---

policies. Nationalists see large cumulativities, liberals see few or none. On this debate see Robert Gilpin, *The Political Economy of International Relations* (Princeton: Princeton University Press, 1987), pp. 172–90. The more recent debate over the importance of relative gains in foreign policymaking also turns on the assumed cumulativity of gains. Those who argue for the dominance of relative gains concerns in policymaking believe that gains are cumulative, since such concerns arise only in a world of cumulative resources. On this debate see David A. Baldwin, ed., *Neorealism and Neoliberalism: The Contemporary Debate* (New York: Columbia University Press, 1993).

[28] See, for example, NSC 7, which warned in March 1948 that noncommunist Europe and Asia had "areas of great potential power which if added to the existing strength of the Soviet world would enable the latter to become so superior in manpower, resources and territory that the prospect for the survival of the United States as a free nation would be slight." The authors concluded that the United States should "take the lead in organizing a world-wide counter-offensive aimed at . . . undermining the strength of communist forces in the Soviet world." Quoted in Thomas H. Etzold, eds., *Containment: Documents on American Policy and Strategy, 1945–1950* (New York: Columbia University Press, 1978), pp. 165, 167; see also 169. Likewise, in 1950 the hard-line NSC 68 warned that "any substantial further extension of the area under the combination of the Kremlin would raise the possibility that no coalition adequate to confront the Kremlin with greater strength could be assembled," the operative word "any" suggesting that every resource and region was essential to the defense of every other. Ibid., p. 386.

[29] Kennan, *Memoirs 1925–1950*, pp. 129–30. Kennan concluded that "no one people is great enough to establish a world hegemony," hence "one must not be too frightened of those who aspire to world domination." Ibid., p. 130.

[30] Assessments of the domino theory include Jerome Slater, "Dominos in Central America: Will They Fall? Does It Matter?" *International Security* 12 (Fall 1987): 105–34; Jerome Slater, "The Domino Theory and International Politics: The Case of Vietnam," *Security Studies* 3

Which view was right? Because the disagreement over cumulativity has been a muted contest of buried assumptions rather than an open debate, the question of cumulativity has received little scholarly attention;[31] hence answers are uncertain. Moreover, answers depend on which cumulativity argument is addressed. The cumulativity of industrial sources was believed high in the mid-twentieth century, and it was in fact high, as shown by the large power gains that Nazi Germany realized from its empire. On the other hand, good evidence indicates that Americans overstated the cumulativity of Third World resources during the Cold War.[32] Some also argue persuasively that Americans exaggerated the cumulativity of industrial resources in the nuclear age,[33] and that great powers have a general propensity to exaggerate the cumulativity of resources.[34] Overall, it appears that cumulativity has been overstated more often than not.

THE FUTURE OF CUMULATIVITY

Seven developments have reduced the cumulativity of many resources over the past few decades. First, the nuclear revolution has reduced the cumulativity of many material resources. Great powers can now build nuclear forces that can destroy an attacker's society several times over, even after absorbing an all-out attack. Even with few resources, they can still annihilate an attacker; with more resources they can only bounce the rubble. A gain or loss of resources has little effect on their capabilities.

Nuclear forces are also impervious to distance. Their lightness and small size, together with ballistic missile technology, allow their delivery across continents. Far-flung bases and strategic buffer room on national borders do little to ease or prevent their delivery. This further lowers the cumulativity of military bases and strategic depth. For example, strategic depth was valuable to a conventionally armed Israel but grew less essential once Israel developed a nuclear deterrent.[35]

(Winter 1993/94): 186–224; and Robert Jervis and Jack Snyder, eds., *Dominoes and Bandwagons: Strategic Beliefs and Great Power Competition in the Eurasian Rimland* (New York: Oxford University Press, 1991), especially pp. 3–50, 276–90.

[31] The first study of the cumulativity of industrial regions was Liberman, *Does Conquest Pay?* published in 1996.

[32] Slater, "Dominos in Central America"; Slater, "Domino Theory and International Politics"; Robert Johnson, "Exaggerating America's Stakes in Third World Conflicts," *International Security* 10 (Winter 1985/86): 32–68; and Stephen Van Evera, "Why Europe Matters, Why the Third World Doesn't: American Grand Strategy After the Cold War," *Journal of Strategic Studies* 13 (June 1990): 1–51 at 18–25.

[33] Art, "Defensible Defense," pp. 18–21.

[34] Jack Snyder, *Myths of Empire: Domestic Politics and International Ambition* (Ithaca: Cornell University Press, 1991), pp. 3–4 and passim.

[35] Arguing this is Shai Feldman, *Israeli Nuclear Deterrence* (New York: Columbia University Press, 1982), p. 49 and passim.

Second, the evolution of Western industrial economies from smokestack to knowledge-based high-technology production since 1945 has reduced the cumulativity of industrial base. Knowledge-based economies are harder to operate at gunpoint than smokestack economies, because the police methods required to gain workers' obedience also ruin their productivity. The workforce must be denied information to inhibit organized resistance; hence it must be denied information technologies such as computers, photocopiers, scientific journals, and international contact and travel. A smokestack economy can operate under these strictures, but a computer-age industrial economy cannot. Hence the conqueror of the modern industrial economy must wreck it to control it. Hitler could harness the heavy industry of the French and Benelux economies to serve his war machine, but today his Gestapo would have to strip those societies of the very information technologies that make them productive. The Soviet Union also faced this dilemma in the 1980s. Its strictures on information left it at a growing disadvantage against the West, and this disadvantage helped motivate Gorbachev's reforms. Any modern conqueror of industry would face the same dilemma.

Third, the increasing flexibility of modern industrial economies, and the increased capacity of the modern state to redirect the economy in an emergency, have reduced economic interdependence. Volumes of trade remain large, but the economic impact of supply interruptions are smaller because states have a wider range of effective responses.[36] The notorious weakness of international materials cartels—all except OPEC have failed, and OPEC's success has been limited—illustrate the effectiveness of these responses. As a result, states need smaller spheres of influence to operate independent economies. The opposite argument, that wide empires are needed to insure against wartime strangulation, is weaker.[37]

Fourth, the rise of nationalism—fueled by the spread of literacy—and, fifth, the global spread of lethal small arms and land mines have both vastly increased the police costs of empires. Nationalism guarantees popular resistance to conquest, and the spread of small arms and land mines ensures

[36] Noting the decline in the importance of raw material inputs to industrial economies over the past few decades, and the widespread availability of substitutes and alternative sources of supply, is Carl Kaysen, "Is War Obsolete? A Review Essay," *International Security* 14 (Spring 1990): 42–64 at 56–57. Concurring is Klaus Knorr, *On the Uses of Military Power in the Nuclear Age* (Princeton: Princeton University Press, 1966), pp. 24–25. A more general assessment of global trends in interdependence is Janice E. Thomson and Stephen D. Krasner, "Global Transactions and the Consolidation of Sovereignty," in Ernst-Otto Czempiel and James N. Rosenau, eds., *Global Changes and Theoretical Challenges: Approaches to World Politics for the 1990s* (Lexington, Mass.: Lexington Books, 1989), pp. 195–219. On the measurement of dependence and interdependence is Kenneth N. Waltz, "The Myth of National Interdependence," in Charles P. Kindleberger, ed., *The International Corporation* (Cambridge: MIT Press, 1970), pp. 205–23.

[37] Many scholars argue that interdependence promotes peace by raising the cost of war and by promoting communication and the growth of transnational institutions, but interdependence also sharpens international competition by making gains and losses more additive.

that this resistance, in the form of guerrilla war, will be effective. Also, the rise of human rights norms now restrains many conquerors from using the police methods needed to subdue guerrilla resistance. Many societies would shrink from the ruthless means of control that Hitler used so effectively.[38]

Sixth, the development of high-technology warfare, combined with the rise of nationalism, has reduced the cumulativity of military manpower. Military manpower remains cumulative for its conqueror only if the dominant style of war allows the exploitation of disloyal soldiers, as in eighteenth-century mercenary warfare or in the ancient naval war of slave-driven galleys. Modern armored war requires individual initiative and cannot be waged with disloyal troops.

Finally, the rise of balancing diplomacy distinguishes the modern era from the ancient. Rome's expansion was eased by its victims' inability to forge a counterbalancing coalition. The communication revolution now allows the targets of aggressors to better coordinate their efforts, raising the likelihood that expansion will generate an offsetting balancing reaction. Resources are less cumulative because military gains more quickly trigger countervailing diplomatic losses.

Two trends cut the other way. The urbanization of industrial societies has made them easier to police, since counterinsurgency is far more effective in an urban than a rural setting. More important, the nuclear revolution has increased the cumulativity of threat credibility. In a nuclear world the balance of capabilities loses importance; disputes are decided more by the balance of will to use force, as seen by the parties in conflict. This perceived balance depends in part on the credibility that adversaries attach to each other's threats.

However, the overall trend is toward less cumulativity. The imperial stakes for which states struggled in the past are now far less important than they once were. This reduces a root cause of international conflict.

In recent decades, unfortunately, strategists and governments have widely misread these trends and, as a result, have exaggerated the cumulativity of resources. This error has caused a fair amount of avoidable international conflict.

[38] Stressing the importance of efficient means of repression to the successful exploitation of empire is Liberman, *Does Conquest Pay?* pp. 5, 21–25 and passim.

[6]

Offense, Defense, and the Security Dilemma

Hypothesis 5. War is more likely when conquest is easy.

The hypothesis that war is more likely when conquest is easy drew little attention before the 1980s. It then gained a following in Europe and the United States, but it remains undeveloped, untested, and—I would argue—underappreciated. Though slighted or ignored by many Realists, offense-defense theory is the most powerful and useful Realist theory on the causes of war.[1] If recast as the theory of perception—"war is more likely when governments believe conquest is easy"—it becomes even stronger and offers a potent explanation for much modern war. Its strength comes from its role as a master theory; it helps explain other important causes of war, including causes framed in Chapters 2–5.

---

[1] I use "offense-defense theory" for the hypothesis that war is more likely when conquest is easy, plus explanatory hypotheses that define how this causation operates. Another label for these ideas, "security dilemma theory," is a misnomer because the security dilemma—a situation where the means that states use to increase their security decrease the security of others—is not the only possible cause of offense dominance. States may also develop offensive capabilities because they have aggressive aims unrelated to their security requirements. These capabilities raise the risk of war by enabling conquest by their possessor and making others insecure, but the wars they cause do not stem from the security dilemma.

An overview of offense-defense theory is Sean M. Lynn-Jones, "Offense-Defense Theory and Its Critics," *Security Studies* 4 (Summer 1995): 660–91. Defining the security dilemma is Robert Jervis, "Cooperation under the Security Dilemma," *World Politics* 30 (January 1978): 167–214 at 169: "Many of the means by which a state tries to increase its security decrease the security of others."

The offense-defense hypothesis is unmentioned in classical Realism's core works. See Hans J. Morgenthau, *Politics Among Nations*, 5th ed. (New York: Knopf, 1973), and Edward Hallett Carr, *The Twenty Years' Crisis, 1919–1939: An Introduction to the Study of International Relations* (New York: Harper and Row, 1964). The prime Neorealist text, Kenneth N. Waltz's *Theory of International Politics* (Reading, Mass.: Addison-Wesley, 1979), makes passing reference to the security dilemma (pp. 186–87) but no reference to the greater dangers of an offense-dominant world, although Waltz notes the idea in later works.

Before the twentieth century, several observers briefly remarked on the prudence of defensive policies and the greater peacefulness of a defense-dominant world,[2] but none developed these ideas.[3] Peace groups focused instead on quantitative arms reductions as a route to peace.

A flurry of interest in offense-defense theory arose in 1932. This flurry had no roots in scholarship on the causes of war and seemed to come from nowhere. It inspired an effort to limit offensive arms at the 1932 World Disarmament Conference, but interest in the idea waned after the conference failed.[4] Academics left the idea unexplored until the late 1970s.[5] A major

---

[2] In this book "offense dominant" means that conquest is fairly easy, "defense dominant" means that conquest is very difficult. It is almost never easier to conquer than to defend, so I use "offense dominant" broadly, to denote that offense is easier than usual. I use "offense-defense balance" to denote the relative ease of aggression and defense against aggression. As noted below, this balance is shaped by both military and diplomatic-political factors. Two measures of the overall offense-defense balance work well: (1) the probability that a determined aggressor could conquer and subjugate a target state with comparable resources; or (2) the resource advantage that an aggressor requires to gain a given chance of conquering a target state. I use "offense" to refer to strategic offensive action—the taking and holding of territory—as opposed to tactical offensive action that involves the attack but not the seizing and holding of territory. The two are usually congruent—tactical defense dominance usually bolsters strategic defense dominance, and tactical offense dominance bolsters strategic offense dominance—but not always. For example, tactical defense dominance can ease limited seize-and-hold aggressions by helping the attacker hold territory seized by surprise. But such cases of incongruity are the exception.

[3] I find two brief allusions to these ideas in older writings. In the eighteenth century, Rousseau argued that war would diminish in a world of self-sufficient states that were insulated from each other and armed only for self-defense. Robert E. Osgood and Robert C. Tucker, *Force, Order, and Justice* (Baltimore: Johns Hopkins University Press, 1967), p. 12n. In 1899 Ivan Bloch argued at length that the defense had the advantage in modern war, and mentioned that this fact should discourage war if leaders grasped it. Ivan S. Bloch, *The Future of War*, trans. R. C. Long (New York: Doubleday and McClure, 1899), pp. xxx–xxxi, lxxix.

[4] On the ideas that shaped the 1932 conference, see Marlies ter Borg, "Reducing Offensive Capabilities—the Attempt of 1932," *Journal of Peace Research* 29, no. 2 (1992): 145–60 at 147–50; Harry B. Hollins, Averill L. Powers, and Mark Sommer, *The Conquest of War: Alternative Strategies for Global Security* (Boulder: Westview, 1989), pp. 64–68; Marion Boggs, *Attempts to Define and Limit "Aggressive" Armament in Diplomacy and Strategy* (Columbia: University of Missouri Studies 16, no. 1, 1941), pp. 14, 21, 30–31, 94; League of Nations, *Conference for the Reduction and Limitation of Armaments: Records of the Conference*, Series B, Minutes of the General Commission (Geneva: League of Nations, 1932–36), pp. 38–39; and *An American Foreign Policy toward International Stability* (Chicago: University of Chicago Press, 1934), pp. 16–22. Borg gives B. H. Liddell Hart and Robert Cecil prime credit for advancing the offense-defense hypothesis before 1932. Liddell Hart's views are found in Basil Liddell Hart, "Aggression and the Problem of Weapons," *English Review* 55 (July 1932), pp. 71–78.

[5] The idea got brief mention in Quincy Wright, *The Causes of War and the Conditions of Peace* (London: Longmans, Greene, 1935), p. 58; General Omar Bradley, "This Way Lies Peace," *Saturday Evening Post*, October 15, 1949, pp. 33, 168–70 at 33, 168; John Herz, "Idealist Internationalism and the Security Dilemma," *World Politics* 2 (January 1950): 157–80 at 157–58, 163 (discussing the security dilemma, but omitting the effects of defense or offense dominance); John Herz, *Political Realism and Political Idealism: A Study in Theories and Realities* (Chicago: University of Chicago Press, 1951), pp. 3–4, 12–15 (repeating the omissions of Herz, "Idealist Internationalism"); and, very indirectly, Herbert Butterfield, *History and Human Relations* (London: Collins, 1950), pp. 19–20. However, like miners who content themselves with a few nuggets after striking the mother lode, these writers dropped the idea after a few words.

wave of writing on deterrence and war appeared during 1954–66, but it focused on stability theory and left offense-defense theory undiscussed.

A developed version of offense-defense theory was first offered by Robert Jervis in a path-breaking 1978 article, "Cooperation under the Security Dilemma."[6] Jervis developed the cryptic arguments of others and added important ideas of his own. Soon after this article appeared, but apparently independently, offense-defense theory gained a following in Western Europe, inspiring a peace movement that endorsed nonoffensive military postures as a way to ease East-West tensions.[7] Mikhail Gorbachev's Soviet regime also absorbed offense-defense theory, and between 1985 and 1991 shifted toward a defensive military doctrine partly because of it. Nevertheless, the theory remained controversial and undeveloped. Its European adherents applied it widely but developed it little. In the United States, offense-defense theory was sometimes applied to current problems,[8] but it was left untested and was not further developed. This chapter outlines, qualifies, and tests the hypotheses that Jervis and others proposed, and it suggests and tests new hypotheses.

I argue that eleven war-causing effects (summarized in Diagram 3) arise when conquest is easy. First, states more often pursue opportunistic expansion, because attempts at expansion succeed more often and so pay greater rewards (see explanation H5A in Diagram 3). Second, states more often pursue defensive expansion, because they feel less secure. Being more vulner-

---

Herz's article is especially striking: he featured the security dilemma in his title but said almost nothing about it in the text.

[6] Jervis, "Cooperation," pp. 186–214. Another discussion was George H. Quester, *Offense and Defense in the International System* (New York: John Wiley and Sons, 1977), pp. 7–11, 208. Unaware of these works and of each other, Jack Snyder (then at Columbia) and Shai Feldman (then at Berkeley) also independently developed large elements of offense-defense theory during the late 1970s, although their work appeared later. See Jack Snyder, *The Ideology of the Offensive: Military Decision Making and the Disasters of 1914* (Ithaca: Cornell University Press, 1984); and Shai Feldman, *Israeli Nuclear Deterrence* (New York: Columbia University Press, 1982), pp. 45–49. Influenced by Feldman and unaware of Jervis, I also did a primitive paper on the topic: "Nuclear Weapons, Nuclear Proliferation and the Causes of War" (January 1978, typescript), pp. 31–38, 70–71, 74–80.

[7] Late Cold War surveys of the nonoffensive defense concept include Stephen J. Flanagan, "Nonprovocative and Civilian-Based Defenses," in Joseph S. Nye, Jr., Graham T. Allison, and Albert Carnesale, *Fateful Visions: Avoiding Nuclear Catastrophe* (Cambridge: Ballinger, 1988), pp. 93–109; Jonathan Dean, "Alternative Defense: Answer to NATO's Central Front Problems?" *International Affairs* 64 (Winter 1987/88): 61–82; Hollins, Powers, and Sommer, *Conquest of War*, pp. 78–88; Marlies ter Borg and Wim Smit, eds., *Non-Provocative Defense as a Principle of Arms Reduction* (Amsterdam: Free University Press, 1989).

[8] Applying offense-defense theory to U.S. military problems were, for example, Barry R. Posen, *Inadvertent Escalation: Conventional War and Nuclear Risks* (Ithaca: Cornell University Press, 1991), pp. 28–67, 129–58; and Charles Glaser, *Analyzing Strategic Nuclear Weapons Policy* (Princeton: Princeton University Press, 1990). Applying the theory to other problems were Feldman, *Israeli Nuclear Deterrence*, pp. 45–49; Kenneth N. Waltz, *The Spread of Nuclear Weapons: More May Be Better*, Adelphi Paper no. 171 (London: International Institute for Strategic Studies, 1981), pp. 5–7; and Barry R. Posen, "The Security Dilemma and Ethnic Conflict," *Survival* 35 (Spring 1993): 27–57.

Diagram 3. How offense-defense theory developed: A schematic history

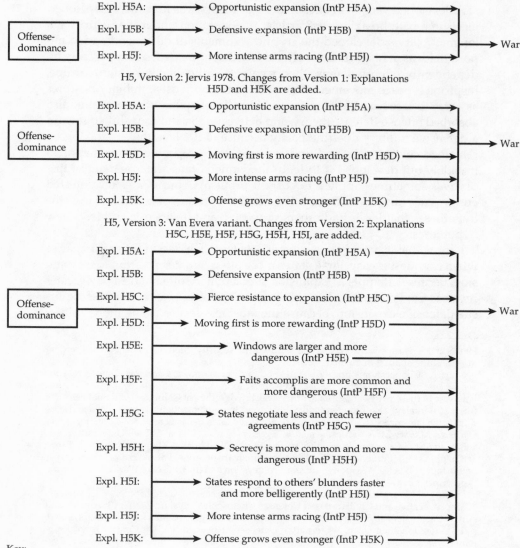

H5, Version 1: From 1750 to 1950: [1]

Expl. H5A: → Opportunistic expansion (IntP H5A)
Expl. H5B: → Defensive expansion (IntP H5B)
Expl. H5J: → More intense arms racing (IntP H5J)

Offense-dominance

→ War

H5, Version 2: Jervis 1978. Changes from Version 1: Explanations H5D and H5K are added.

Expl. H5A: → Opportunistic expansion (IntP H5A)
Expl. H5B: → Defensive expansion (IntP H5B)
Expl. H5D: → Moving first is more rewarding (IntP H5D)
Expl. H5J: → More intense arms racing (IntP H5J)
Expl. H5K: → Offense grows even stronger (IntP H5K)

Offense-dominance

→ War

H5, Version 3: Van Evera variant. Changes from Version 2: Explanations H5C, H5E, H5F, H5G, H5H, H5I, are added.

Expl. H5A: → Opportunistic expansion (IntP H5A)
Expl. H5B: → Defensive expansion (IntP H5B)
Expl. H5C: → Fierce resistance to expansion (IntP H5C)
Expl. H5D: → Moving first is more rewarding (IntP H5D)
Expl. H5E: → Windows are larger and more dangerous (IntP H5E)
Expl. H5F: → Faits accomplis are more common and more dangerous (IntP H5F)
Expl. H5G: → States negotiate less and reach fewer agreements (IntP H5G)
Expl. H5H: → Secrecy is more common and more dangerous (IntP H5H)
Expl. H5I: → States respond to others' blunders faster and more belligerently (IntP H5I)
Expl. H5J: → More intense arms racing (IntP H5J)
Expl. H5K: → Offense grows even stronger (IntP H5K)

Offense-dominance

→ War

Key:

H5:   Hypothesis 5
Expl.: Explanation
IntP: Intervening phenomenon

---

[1] Version 1 is an amalgam of the ideas of J.-J. Rousseau, Ivan Bloch, Hugh Gibson, B. H. Liddell Hart, Omar Bradley, and John Herz. Each proposed or implied one or two of the three hypotheses presented, none offered all three. Their separate views are recorded in this chapter's footnotes.

able to conquest, they are more anxious to extend their borders to more defensible lines, and to cut strong neighbors down to size (explanation H5B). Third, their greater insecurity also drives states to resist others' expansion more fiercely. Power gains by others raise larger threats to national security; hence their expansion prompts a more violent response (explanation H5C). Fourth, first-move advantages are larger, creating the risk of preemptive war and other dangers (explanation H5D). Fifth, windows of opportunity and vulnerability are larger, creating the risk of preventive war and other dangers (explanation H5E). Sixth, states more often adopt fait accompli diplomatic tactics, and such tactics more often trigger war (explanation H5F). Seventh, states negotiate less readily and cooperatively; hence negotiations fail more often, and disputes fester unresolved (explanation H5G). Eighth, states enshroud foreign and defense policy in tighter secrecy, raising the risk of military miscalculations and political blunders (explanation H5H). Ninth, states react faster and more belligerently to others' blunders, making blunders more dangerous (explanation H5I). Tenth, arms racing is faster and harder to control, raising the risk of preventive wars and wars of false optimism (explanation H5J). Finally, offense dominance is self-feeding. As conquest grows easier, states adopt policies (for example, more offensive military doctrines) that make conquest still easier. This magnifies the first ten effects (explanation H5K).[9]

False perceptions of offense dominance raise these same eleven dangers. If states think the offense is strong, they will act as if it were, creating the same risks that appear when conquest is in fact easy.

Are offensive capabilities always dangerous? The one-sided possession of offensive capabilities by status quo powers that face aggressors can lower rather than raise the risk of war under some conditions. For example, status quo powers may need offensive capabilities to defend other states against aggressors (France, for instance, required some offensive capability to defend Czechoslovakia and Poland from Germany in 1938–39). If so, deterrence of the aggressor can be stronger if the status quo power has some offensive capacity. Offensive capabilities in the hands of a status quo power also may cause more peace than war if the aggressor state knows that it provoked the status quo power's hostility; if the aggressor knows that the sta-

---

[9] Some of these explanations (H5A–H5E) posit that offense dominance causes war directly by lowering the costs and raising the benefits of using force. Some (explanations H5D–H5K) posit that offense dominance causes war indirectly, by raising the benefits of war-risking policies that fall short of force. Explanations H5D and H5E frame both direct and indirect ways in which offense dominance causes war.

Jervis offers five of these explanations (H5A, H5B, H5D, H5J, H5K). I add six more (H5C, H5E, H5F, H5G, H5H, H5I). My six are variations on Jervis's prime theme, that states are more competitive when conquest is or appears to be easy.

tus quo power has no bedrock aggressive intentions; if the offensive force can succeed only against an enemy in the act of attacking; if the aggressor cannot remove the status quo power's offensive capability by force; if the aggressor cannot be dissuaded from aggression by any punishment less than its own conquest; if it cannot be pacified by measures short of replacing its regime; and if a war has gained such momentum that it cannot be stopped except by the total defeat of one side. These conditions are rare but not unknown, and they pose an important qualification to offense-defense theory.

What causes offense and defense dominance? Military technology and doctrine, geography, national social structure, and diplomatic arrangements (specifically, defensive alliances and balancing behavior by offshore powers) all matter. The net offense-defense balance is an aggregate of these military, geographic, social, and diplomatic factors.

How does offense-defense theory perform in tests? Four case studies are presented in this and the next chapter. They corroborate offense-defense theory and indicate that it has great importance: shifts in the offense-defense balance have large effects on the risk of war.

Offense-defense theory also has broad applicability. Offense-dominance is rather rare in history; hence it explains only middling amounts of war. However, perceptions of offense dominance are common, and they explain much warfare. The abatement of offense-dominance would prevent nontrivial amounts of war; the abatement of perceptions of offense-dominance would prevent a great deal of war.

On balance, how does offense-defense theory measure up? It has the attributes of a good theory. As just noted, it has importance and broad applicability. It also has wide explanatory range and prescriptive richness. It explains an array of important war causes—expansionism, fierce resistance to expansion, first-move advantages, windows of opportunity and vulnerability, faits accomplis, negotiation failure, secrecy, fierce reactions to others' blunders, arms races, and offense dominance itself—that were once thought to be independent of one another. In so doing offense-defense theory explains the dangers that these phenomena produce and the wars they cause. This simplifies the problem of power and war: a number of disparate dangers are shown to stem from a common source. Moreover, both the reality and the perception of easy conquest can be shaped by human action; hence prescriptions for controlling the dangers framed by offense-defense theory can be found.

The next section frames dangers that arise when conquest is easy or is believed easy. The following section qualifies these arguments, framing conditions when offensive capabilities can be benign or pacifying. Later sections outline causes of offense and defense dominance, discuss three single-case-study tests of offense-defense theory, assess the ability of offense-defense theory to explain history, and consider the general value of offense-defense theory in light of evidence offered in this and the next chapter.

HYPOTHESES ON THE EFFECTS OF OFFENSE DOMINANCE

A host of dangers arise when conquest is easy. Some are obvious and some more subtle, some are direct and some indirect. Together they make war very likely when the offense dominates.

Opportunistic expansionism (explanation H5A)

When conquest is hard, states are deterred from aggression by fear that victory will prove costly or unattainable. When conquest is easy, cheap gains can be had by war, so states go to war. Aggression brings larger rewards at lower cost, so states are drawn to try it.[10] Aggressors can also move with less fear of reprisal because they win their wars more decisively, leaving their victims less able to retaliate later. Thus even aggressive states are dissuaded from attacking if the defense is strong, and even temperate powers are tempted to attack if the offense is strong.

Hitler refrained from invading France during the fall and winter of 1939–40 because he lacked a plausible theory of victory. He attacked in May 1940 after his generals developed the promising—and successful—Manstein invasion plan.[11] North Korean dictator Kim Il Sung refrained from invading South Korea while U.S. troops remained there (1945–49); after U.S. troops withdrew he attacked in hopes of a quick victory.[12] Conversely, Communist China's ambitions toward Taiwan shrank after the United States interposed its Seventh Fleet in the Taiwan Strait in June 1950, making Beijing's planned invasion impossible.[13]

Early in the Mideast crisis of May–June 1967, Israel's leaders thought a decisive victory over Egypt would be difficult or impossible, hence they shrank

---

[10] Suggesting this hypothesis are Bloch, *Future of War*, pp. xxx–xxxi, lxxix; Liddell Hart, "Aggression and the Problem of Weapons," pp. 72–73; Hugh Gibson, leader of the U.S. delegation to the 1932 World Disarmament Conference (whose arguments are paraphrased in Boggs, *Attempts to Define*, pp. 30, 94); Wright, *Causes of War*, p. 58; Quester, *Offense and Defense*, p. 9 ("the risk of war emerges whenever offensive campaigns become tempting"); and, obliquely, Jervis, "Cooperation," pp. 187, 189. A corroborating test is John J. Mearsheimer, *Conventional Deterrence* (Ithaca: Cornell University Press, 1983).

[11] Mearsheimer, *Conventional Deterrence*, pp. 99–133.

[12] Sergei N. Goncharov, John W. Lewis, and Xue Litai, *Uncertain Partners: Stalin, Mao, and the Korean War* (Stanford: Stanford University Press, 1993), pp. 134–37, 141–46, 152, 155.

[13] Chen Jian, *China's Road to the Korean War: The Making of the Sino-American Confrontation* (New York: Columbia University Press, 1994), p. 131.

from war. They attacked after Egypt deployed its army in vulnerable dis-
array in the Sinai, and after Moshe Dayan, who was more optimistic about
Israel's chance of attacking successfully than other Israeli leaders, was ap-
pointed defense minister.[14]

Defensive expansionism and fierce resistance
to expansion (explanations H5B and H5C)

When conquest is hard, states are blessed with secure borders; hence they
are less aggressive and more willing to accept the status quo. They have less
need for more territory because their current territory is already defensible.
They are less anxious to cut neighbors down to size because even strong
neighbors cannot conquer them. They have less urge to intervene in other
states' internal affairs because hostile governments can do them less harm.

Conversely, when conquest is easy, states are more expansionist because
their present borders are less defensible.[15] They seek wider territories to
gain resources that would bolster their defenses. They find strong neighbors
more frightening; hence they are quicker to use force to destroy their neighbor's power. They worry more when hostile regimes arise nearby because
such neighbors are harder to defend against; hence they are quicker to intervene in their neighbors' domestic politics. These motives drive states to become aggressors and foreign intervenors.[16]

States also resist others' expansion more fiercely when conquest is easy.
Adversaries can parlay smaller gains into larger conquests; hence stronger
steps to prevent gains by others are more appropriate. This attitude makes
disputes more intractable.

Both dangers—defensive expansion and strong resistance to expansion—

[14] Mearsheimer, *Conventional Deterrence*, pp. 143–55; and on the opportunity presented by
Egypt's deployment, Donald Neff, *Warriors for Jerusalem: The Six Days That Changed the Middle
East* (New York: Simon and Schuster, 1984), pp. 141, 168.

[15] As Robert Jervis notes, "when the offense has the advantage over the defense, attacking
is the best route to protecting what you have . . . and it will be hard for any state to maintain
its size and influence without trying to increase them." "Cooperation," p. 211; see also
pp. 168–69, 173, 187–99. Making this argument more obliquely are Hugh Gibson and his U.S.
delegation to the 1932 World Disarmament Conference, paraphrased by Boggs, *Attempts to
Define*, pp. 21, 30; and Herz, *Political Realism*, p. 14.

[16] It also seems possible that states should be more careful to avoid war when conquest is
easy, because war then brings greater risk of total defeat. If so, offense dominance should
cause more caution than belligerence among states, and should lower the risk of war. Advancing this argument are Marc Trachtenberg, *History and Strategy* (Princeton: Princeton University Press, 1991), p. 72; and James Fearon, "The Offense-Defense Balance and War since
1648" (paper prepared for the annual meeting of the International Studies Association, Chicago, February 1995), pp. 18–24. Their argument seems deductively sound, but history offers very few examples of elites who argued that offense dominance was a reason for caution. This is one of many cases where deduction and the historical record point in opposite
directions.

stem from the same basic problem: resources are more cumulative when conquest is easy. One's ability to conquer others and to defend oneself is more elastic to one's control over strategic areas and resources. As a result, gains are more additive—states can convert small conquests into larger ones—and losses are less reversible. Hence small losses can spell disaster, and small gains can open the way to hegemonic dominance. States therefore compete harder to control any assets that confer power, seeking wider spheres for themselves while fiercely resisting others' efforts to expand.

This problem is compounded by its malignant effect on states' expectations about one other's conduct. When conquest is hard, states are blessed with neighbors made benign by their own security and by the high cost of attacking others. Hence states have less reason to expect attack. This leaves all states even more secure and therefore more willing to pursue pacific policies. Conversely, when the offense dominates, states are cursed with neighbors made aggressive by both temptation and fear. These neighbors see easy gains from aggression, and danger in standing pat. Plagued with such aggressive neighbors, all states face greater risk of attack. This drives them to compete still harder to control resources and create conditions that provide security.

Thus states become aggressors because their neighbors are aggressors. This can proceed reciprocally until no state accepts the status quo.

The expansionism of ancient Athens and ancient Rome was driven by their feelings of insecurity, and their hopes of gaining security by conquest. Athenian expansionists stressed security arguments: one typically warned that "we ourselves may fall under the power of others unless others are in our power."[17] In Rome things were similar: R. M. Errington concludes that Roman imperialism "aimed to achieve, first and foremost, merely the security of Rome."[18]

Most of modern Europe's great wars were fueled by security-driven expansionism. Fear of invasion and subversion fed French revolutionary expansionism in 1792. French Foreign Minister Charles Dumouriez explained that "we carry the war into the states of the House of Austria in order to avoid our own ruin by wreaking hers."[19] Russia triggered the Crimean War of 1854–56 by demands on Turkey that it made to secure its southern flank.[20]

[17] Alcibiades, quoted in Thucydides, *History of the Peloponnesian War*, trans. Rex Warner (Harmondsworth: Penguin, 1954), p. 421.

[18] R. M. Errington, *Dawn of Empire: Rome's Rise to World Power* (Ithaca: Cornell University Press, 1972), p. 3.

[19] Alfred Vagts, *Defense and Diplomacy: The Soldier and the Conduct of Foreign Relations* (New York: Kings Crown, 1956), p. 280. See also T. C. W. Blanning, *The Origins of the French Revolutionary Wars* (London: Longman, 1986), pp. 76, 80–81, 99–101, 111, 123.

[20] See Richard Smoke, *War: Controlling Escalation* (Cambridge: Harvard University Press, 1977), pp. 148–49, 158–59; also J. A. S. Grenville, *Europe Reshaped, 1848–1878* (North Brighton: Fontana, 1976), p. 184.

Prussia sparked the wars of 1864, 1866, and 1870 in part to gain its ancient goal of more defensible frontiers.[21]

In 1914 Austria attacked Serbia because Austrian leaders thought Serb subversion threatened Austria's existence,[22] and Germany pursued expansion in its continued search for secure borders. The German crown prince complained in 1913 that Germany was "badly protected by its unfavorable geographic frontiers, situated at the heart of Europe," hence it must make gains by "trusting in our reliable sword."[23] German Chancellor Bethmann-Hollweg explained in 1914 that Germany fought to gain "security for the German Reich in west and east."[24]

Poland attacked the Soviet Union in 1920 largely to bolster Polish security, its Supreme Command arguing that the "reduction of Russia to her historical frontiers is a condition of [Poland's] existence."[25] Later, Japanese expansionists argued that "our Empire, to save its very life, must take measures to secure the raw materials of the South Seas."[26]

Hitler claimed that all his aggressions were required by national security. He complained in *Mein Kampf* of "the extremely unfavorable situation of the Reich from the viewpoint of military geography," and on the eve of war he told his generals: "The alternative is either for us to strike now or ourselves be destroyed sooner or later."[27] He justified his 1939 attack on Poland as required by defensive necessity, explaining that "we [Germans] are faced with the harsh alternatives of striking or of certain annihilation sooner or later."[28] Once at war, he declared that "the very existence of the nation" was at stake.[29] He attacked the Soviet Union in 1941 in part to lift the threat that

[21] As Joseph Joffe argues, Prussia-Germany's perennial expansionism grew from the need to "overcome the congenital curse of its vulnerable geographic position in the heart of Europe." Quoted in Julian Lider, *Origins and Development of West German Military Thought*, vol. 2, *1866–1986* (Aldershot: Gower, 1988), p. 86.

[22] Austrian Minister for Foreign Affairs Leopold von Berchtold explained during the July crisis that the destruction of Serb propaganda "is a matter of life or death for Austria-Hungary as a Great Power" (as quoted by N. A. Kudachev, Russian chargé in Vienna, July 26, 1914). Quoted in M. F. Schilling, *How the War Began in 1914*, trans. W. Cyprian Bridge (London: George Allen and Unwin, 1925), p. 39. See also James Joll, *The Origins of the First World War* (London: Longman, 1984), pp. 10, 93–94, 201.

[23] Fritz Fischer, *War of Illusions: German Policies from 1911 to 1914*, trans. Marian Jackson (New York: Norton, 1975), p. 254.

[24] In September 1914, quoted in Fritz Fischer, *Germany's Aims in the First World War* (New York: Norton, 1967), p. 103.

[25] Quoted in Piotr Wandycz, *Soviet-Polish Relations, 1917–1921* (Cambridge: Harvard University Press, 1969), p. 198.

[26] Japanese Foreign Minister Tijiro Toyoda, in July 1941, quoted in Daniel Yergin, *The Prize: The Epic Quest for Oil, Money, and Power* (New York: Simon and Schuster, 1992), p. 319.

[27] Adolph Hitler, *Mein Kampf*, trans. Ralph Manheim (Boston: Houghton Mifflin, 1943), p. 617; and in August 1939, quoted in Vagts, *Defense and Diplomacy*, p. 424.

[28] In August 1939, quoted in Jeremy Noakes and Geoffrey Pridham, eds., *Nazism 1919–1945: A History in Documents and Eyewitness Accounts*, 2 vols. (New York: Schocken Books, 1988), 2:741.

[29] On November 23, 1939, in Noakes and Pridham, *Nazism*, 2:765.

looming Soviet armies, deployed in newly seized territories abutting the German empire, posed to vulnerable German economic lifelines.[30]

The Cold War was fueled by Soviet expansion that stemmed in part from Soviet insecurities. George Kennan wrote in 1944 that "behind Russia's stubborn expansion lies only the age-old sense of insecurity of a sedentary people reared on an exposed plain in the neighborhood of fierce nomadic peoples."[31]

After 1967 many Israelis argued that Israel had to retain Arab lands conquered in 1967 because Israel's pre-1967 borders were indefensible. Yigal Allon expressed the common Israeli view: the pre-1967 lines "fail to provide Israel with the essential minimum of strategic depth," hence a return to these lines would create "a concrete and intolerable threat" to Israel's security.[32] This Israeli expansion worsened the conflict between Israel and its Arab neighbors, fueling Israel's 1969–70 Canal War with Egypt, its 1973 October War with Egypt and Syria, and the 1982 Lebanon War.

States also resist others' expansion more strongly in an offense-dominant world, sharpening conflicts between satisfied and dissatisfied powers. They cede their own territory more grudgingly from fear of weakening their defenses. For example, Israel refused limited Arab territorial demands in the 1950s because it felt that concessions would leave it dangerously weakened, enabling the Arabs to destroy it at will.[33] States also defend their allies more strongly and unconditionally, from fear that their ally's demise will spell their own. For example, Russia sprang to defend Serbia in 1914 because Russians believed that "from an Austrian invasion of Serbia to a future partition of Russia was a relatively short step."[34] And Russia leapt to defend France because Russian leaders felt that Russia could not hold alone against Germany and Austria, and that Russian security therefore required French survival.[35] France pledged in 1912 to defend Serbia from Austrian attack because "territorial grabs by Austria affect the general European balance and therefore France's own interests"[36]—a logic that assumed French security

---

[30] Norman Rich, *Hitler's War Aims: Ideology, the Nazi State, and the Course of Expansion* (New York: Norton, 1973), p. 206.

[31] Quoted in Robert Jervis, *Perception and Misperception in International Politics* (Princeton: Princeton University Press, 1976), p. 64.

[32] Yigal Allon, "Israel: The Case for Defensible Borders," *Foreign Affairs* 55 (October 1976): 38–53 at 41, 43. See also Yoav Ben-Horin and Barry Posen, *Israel's Strategic Doctrine* (Santa Monica: RAND Corporation, report R-2845-NA, 1981), pp. 5, 26.

[33] Nadav Safran, *Israel: The Embattled Ally* (Cambridge: Harvard University Press, 1978), p. 225.

[34] D. C. B. Lieven, *Russia and the Origins of the First World War* (New York: St. Martin's, 1983), p. 100, summarizing Prince G. N. Trubetskoy's views. Likewise the Petersburg *Novoye Vremya* warned in 1909 that Russia must sustain the Triple Entente or "German preponderance would at once be established over all the continent of Europe." Quoted in ibid., p. 133.

[35] Bruce W. Menning, *Bayonets before Bullets: The Imperial Russian Army, 1861–1914* (Bloomington: Indiana University Press, 1992), p. 247. See also Snyder, *Ideology of the Offensive*, p. 164.

[36] Russian ambassador to Paris A. P. Izvol'sky's summary of French views, quoted in

was so frail that injury to faraway Serbia could shake it. China aided its communist allies in Vietnam and North Korea in 1950—triggering war with the United States—from fear that otherwise the United States could use those countries as springboards to threaten China.[37]

These arguments assume that conquest is fairly easy. Their logic fails if the defense dominates, because states could then be secure without checking their main opponent at every point.

Moving first is more rewarding (explanation H5D)

When conquest is easy, the benefits of mobilizing or striking first are greater.[38] Hence offense dominance raises the risks that arise when it pays to move first: incentives to mobilize or strike first; concealment of grievances, capabilities, plans, and perceptions; hurried diplomacy; and more offensive force postures (see Chapter 3). Offense dominance is a remote cause of these direct causes of war.[39]

Offense dominance expands the advantage of moving first for four reasons.

- More territory can be overrun or defended with any material advantage that moving first provides when the offense dominates. Conversely, little can be done with a material advantage gained by moving first if the defense dominates. Aggressors can be checked even if they gain the initiative, and defenders can succeed even if they lose the initiative. Early mobilization was tempting in 1914 partly because leaders thought the first army to mobilize could overrun large chunks of enemy territory. Had they known the offense was weak, they would have known that the first army to mobilize could not

---

Lieven, *Russia and the Origins of the First World War*, p. 48. Germans firmly backed German allies for similar reasons. General Friedrich von Bernhardi declared in 1913 that "the numerical superiority of our opponents is so great that we cannot tolerate" the weakening of states friendly to Germany. "It would be a very serious mistake . . . to remain neutral if . . . our allies and friends should seriously be endangered. If Austria and Russia should come to blows, Germany cannot act as a spectator," and "it is of the utmost importance for us to preserve Turkey." General Friedrich von Bernhardi, *Britain as Germany's Vassal*, trans. J. Ellis Barker (New York: George H. Doran, 1914; first published in Germany in 1913), pp. 52, 216–17; see also pp. 231–32.

[37] Shuguang Zhang, "'Preparedness Eliminates Mishaps': The CCP's Security Concerns in 1949–1950 and the Origins of the Sino-American Confrontation," *Journal of American-East Asian Relations* 1 (Spring 1992): 42–72 at 63–66; Thomas J. Christensen, "Threats, Assurances, and the Last Chance for Peace," *International Security* 17 (Summer 1992): 122–54, at 135, 138; Chen Jian, "China's Changing Aims during the Korean War, 1950–1951," *Journal of American-East Asian Relations* 1 (Spring 1992): 8–41 at 18, 21; Jian, *China's Road*, pp. 159, 202, 206.

[38] See Jervis, "Cooperation," pp. 183, 188, 190–93.

[39] Offense dominance is not sufficient to create a first-move advantage, but under most conditions it will increase the advantage of moving first. For other causes of first-move advantages, see "Causes of and Cures for First-Move Advantage" in Chapter 3.

get far into enemy territory, so they would have been less fearful of an enemy first move and less tempted to move first themselves.[40]

- When offense dominates, the side moving first can disrupt the other's mobilization by quickly invading, if the opponent has a military mobilization system.[41] Conversely, if the defense dominates, states can ready their reserve forces behind the protection of their standing forces even if an opponent steals a march on them.

- Offense dominance leads states to tighten military and political secrecy (see the "states are more secretive" explanation, H5H, below). This eases surprise and heightens fears of being surprised.

- Insecure states may compensate for their insecurity by adopting a hair-trigger first-strike military doctrine. For example, before 1967, Israel's lack of strategic depth drove it to take a standing decision to preempt if war seemed imminent.[42] After 1967 it could better afford to absorb a first strike, so it abandoned its hair-trigger stance.[43]

Windows are larger and more dangerous (explanation H5E)

When conquest is easy, windows of opportunity and vulnerability are larger and declining states are more tempted to shut them by force. Hence offense dominance raises the risks that open windows generate (see Chapter 4). States start more preventive wars and adopt other belligerent policies. They reach fewer settlements because offers and agreements are less credible. They conduct diplomacy under window-imposed deadlines, which hampers negotiations and causes decisions to be made before their effects are fully considered and understood. Offense dominance is a remote cause of these direct war causes.

Offense dominance opens windows wider in three ways.

1. A shift in the relative size of national forces causes a larger shift in relative national power when the offense dominates. Such shifts erase larger

---

[40] German armies did get quite far into France during August and September of 1914, but only because French forces began the war by lunging across the Franco-German border, thereby letting German armies move around them into northern France. France could have smashed these German armies at the Franco-Belgian border by dropping its attack on Germany and focusing on frontier defense.

[41] See Jervis, "Cooperation," p. 191.

[42] General Aharon Yariv later framed Israel's logic, noting that "the principle of preemptive strike [is] a defensive measure which may compensate for lack of strategic depth." Quoted in Ariel Levite, *Offense and Defense in Israeli Military Doctrine* (Boulder: Westview, 1989), p. 60.

[43] General Israel Tal, "Israel's Defense Doctrine: Background and Dynamics," *Military Review*, March 1978, pp. 22–37 at 25, 27, 30–31. On preemption in Israeli doctrine see also Ben-Horin and Posen, *Israel's Strategic Doctrine*, pp. 27, 34–37; and Safran, *Israel*, p. 239. Israeli strategists have warned that Israeli withdrawal from the occupied territories could compel a return to the earlier doctrine of first strike. On Tal see, for example, Ben-Horin and Posen, *Israel's Strategic Doctrine*, p. 27n.

offensive opportunities and create larger defensive vulnerabilities. Declining states face a steeper descent from dominion to subordination, so they use more force to forestall their fall.

Conversely, when the defense dominates, shifts in the relative size of forces create few offensive opportunities and defensive vulnerabilities. Declining states have little offensive capability to begin with, so they lose little offensive capability when they decline. And their opponent gains little offensive capability even from a large relative rise. Hence declining states can do nearly as well fighting later as earlier. Preventive war makes less sense because there is less future threat to prevent.

2. When the offense dominates, using force offers a more effective remedy for one's decline, while peaceful buildup is less effective. The enemy resource base can be overrun more easily, hence shutting windows by force is more feasible. At the same time, halting one's relative decline by counter-buildup is harder, because one must build more defense to offset the opponent's military growth.

Things are reversed when the defense dominates. Using force to shut windows is less feasible, while a counter-buildup is cheaper and more effective.

3. Offense dominance fosters secrecy and arms racing (see explanations H5H and H5J). When secrecy is tight, states under- or overreact to an opponent's buildup because they misjudge its size. This opens fleeting gaps favoring overreacting states. Arms races quicken the pace of military change, and this quickening brings more shifts in relative force size.

Hitler saw large windows of opportunity and vulnerability with the Soviet Union in 1941 partly because he thought both Germany and the Soviets could move offensively—Germany today, the Soviets tomorrow.[44] Soviet forces could overrun Germany in a later war, he argued,[45] but Germany could crush the Soviets if it struck while Soviet forces were still building up and were reeling from Stalin's purges. Had he thought either side could defend successfully at its nadir, he would have seen smaller windows or none at all.

Conversely, Bismarck opposed preventive war in the 1880s partly because he thought neither Germany nor its adversaries could move offensively. Even if Germany were "attacked at a less favorable moment, we shall be strong enough to defend ourselves," he declared in 1888. But if Germany launched a preventive war, political factors (what he termed "imponder-

[44] Russia's aggressive war plan in 1914 grew from parallel thoughts. General Iurii Danilov believed that Russia had to fully exploit Germany's temporary weakness in the eastern theater at the beginning of the war because he doubted Russia's ability to stand alone against Germany if France were defeated. See Snyder, *Ideology of the Offensive*, p. 164.

[45] Vagts, *Defense and Diplomacy*, p. 318. On German fears of and vulnerability to Soviet attack see also Rich, *Hitler's War Aims*, pp. 205–8.

ables") would favor the defender: "the full weight of the imponderables— which weigh far heavier in the balance than material factors—will be on the side of the enemies we have attacked."[46] Hence he thought preventive war was imprudent and unnecessary.

Likewise, many U.S. isolationists opposed U.S. involvement in World War II and the Cold War because they thought the United States could defend itself against a Eurasian superstate; hence, they believed, the United States had no need to forestall the rise of German or Soviet hegemonies in Eurasia. Senator Robert Taft opposed U.S. entry in World War II because "my whole idea of foreign policy is based largely on the position that America can successfully defend itself against the rest of the world."[47] Former President Herbert Hoover opposed the U.S. troop deployment to Europe in 1951 because "this Hemisphere can be defended from Communist armies come what will. . . . Communist armies can no more get to Washington than any allied armies can get to Moscow."[48] These relaxed views rested on the implicit assumption that conquest, at least of the United States, was relatively hard.

Faits accomplis are more common and more dangerous (explanation H5F)

When conquest is easy, states adopt more dangerous diplomatic tactics— specifically, fait accompli tactics—and these tactics are more likely to cause war.

A fait accompli is a halfway step to war. It promises greater chance of political victory than quiet consultation, but it also raises a greater risk of violence.[49] The acting side moves without warning, presenting others with an

[46] Gerhard Ritter, *The Sword and the Scepter: The Problem of Militarism in Germany*, 4 vols. (Coral Gables: University of Miami Press, 1972), 1:245.

[47] Quoted in Daniel Yergin, *Shattered Peace: The Origins of the Cold War and the National Security State* (Boston: Houghton Mifflin, 1978), p. 46. See also Vagts, *Defense and Diplomacy*, p. 323.

[48] Quoted in Hugh Ross, ed., *The Cold War: Containment and Its Critics* (Chicago: Rand McNally, 1963), p. 17.

[49] On fait accompli strategies see Alexander L. George, "Strategies for Crisis Management," in Alexander L. George, *Avoiding War: Problems of Crisis Management* (Boulder: Westview, 1991), pp. 377–94 at 382–83; Alexander L. George, "Findings and Recommendations," in George, *Avoiding War*, pp. 545–66 at 549–50, 553–54; R. B. Mowat, *Diplomacy and Peace* (London: Williams and Norgate, 1935), chap. 10 (on "sudden diplomacy"); Richard Ned Lebow, *Between Peace and War: the Nature of International Crisis* (Baltimore: Johns Hopkins University Press, 1981), pp. 57–97 (on "brinkmanship"); Herman Kahn, *Thinking about the Unthinkable* (New York: Avon, 1964), pp. 47–50; Herman Kahn, *On Thermonuclear War*, 2d ed. (New York: Free Press, 1969), pp. 289–95; and Thomas C. Schelling, *Strategy of Conflict* (New York: Oxford University Press, 1963), pp. 22–28, with these last three works discussing "committal strategies" and games of "chicken."

Famous faits accomplis include the sudden German-Austrian move against Serbia in 1914, the secret Soviet movement of nuclear missiles to Cuba in 1962, Argentina's sudden seizure of the Falklands/Malvinas in 1982, and Iraq's 1990 seizure of Kuwait.

accomplished fact. It cannot retreat without losing face, a situation that it exploits to compel its opponents to concede. But if the opponents stand firm, a collision is hard to avoid. Faits accomplis also pose a second danger: because they are planned in secret, the planning circle is small, raising the risk that flawed policies will escape scrutiny because critics cannot expose mistaken premises.

When the offense dominates, states are more drawn to fait accompli diplomacy,[50] and faits accomplis are more likely to cause war. Thus offense dominance increases both the number of faits accomplis and the danger that each raises.

Faits accomplis are more common when the offense dominates because the rewards they promise are more valuable. When security is scarce, winning disputes becomes more important than avoiding war. Leaders become more concerned about how spoils are divided—and relatively less concerned about avoiding violence—because failure to gain their share can spell their doom. This leads to gain-maximizing, war-risking diplomatic strategies—above all, to fait accompli tactics.

Faits accomplis are more dangerous when the offense dominates because a successful fait accompli, if it confers resources, confers more power to threaten the safety of others. Hence faits accomplis evoke a stronger backlash from others. States faced with a fait accompli will shoot more quickly because they are more threatened by it.

The sudden Austro-German assault on Serbia that triggered World War I stemmed from a fait accompli strategy that Germans adopted because they thought German security was precarious.[51] Germany's top leaders hoped the Triple Entente powers would accept the smashing of Serbia, but they knew they were risking war. To them the risk was justified because they thought they lived in a dog-eat-dog world of growth or death—Germany must choose "world power or downfall," as General Bernhardi put it.[52] They also thought that German security required the safety of Austria-Hungary, Germany's only ally, and that Austria-Hungary was gravely threatened and could be secured only by smashing Serbia.[53] Hence they thought the stakes warranted the risk of war they were running.

[50] Arguing that fait accompli tactics arise largely from threats to national security is Lebow, *Between Peace and War*, pp. 61–62.

[51] On Germany's fait accompli strategy see John A. Moses, *The Politics of Illusion: The Fischer Controversy in German Historiography* (London: George Prior, 1975), pp. 31–32, 35–39; and Karl-Heinz Janssen, "Gerhard Ritter: A Patriotic Historian's Justification," in H. W. Koch, ed. *The Origins of the First World War* (London: Macmillan, 1972), pp. 257–85 at 263–64 (both discussing Kurt Riezler's strategy of "bluff diplomacy").

[52] General Friedrich von Bernhardi, *Germany and the Next War*, trans. Allen H. Powles (New York: Longmans, Green, 1914; first published in 1912), p. 85.

[53] See, for example, M. S. Anderson, *The Ascendancy of Europe: Aspects of European History 1815–1914* (London: Longman, 1972), p. 65.

These beliefs rested in turn on the German assumption that the offense was strong and security scarce. Had Germans thought that the defense dominated, risking war over faraway Balkan quarrels would have made less sense. Germans would have known that Balkan events could not shake German security and hence were not worth war.

The Austro-German move on Serbia also led more directly to the war because other Europeans believed the offense was dominant. This belief enlarged the threat that the Austro-German action seemed to pose to their security, hence it stiffened their will to resist. Russian leaders feared that Austria could quickly crush Serbia if it attacked with a free hand.[54] They also thought this would gravely threaten Russia because they believed Serbia added vital power to their alliance, and they feared a domino effect, running to Constantinople and beyond, if Serbia were overrun. Russian Foreign Minister Serge Sazonov highly valued Serbian and Bulgarian military forces: they were "five hundred thousand bayonets to guard the Balkans" that would "bar the road for ever to German penetration, Austrian invasion."[55] If this asset were lost, Sazonov feared, Russia's defense of its own territories would be jeopardized by the German approach to Constantinople: "First Serbia would be gobbled up; then will come Bulgaria's turn, and then we shall have her on the Black Sea." This would be "the death-warrant of Russia" because in such an event "the whole of southern Russia would be subject to [Germany]."[56]

Similar views were found in France,[57] and they spurred Russia and France to react fiercely to Austria's sudden move of July 23. Both launched military preparations on July 25. These preparations moved Germany to threaten war unless they were halted, and to begin its own preparations. These German actions helped trigger Russian general mobilization on July 30, which made German general mobilization and war inevitable. The effects of the original fait accompli rippled outward in ever wider circles because each state's reactions threatened the safety of others, forcing them to react or preempt, and ultimately spurring Germany to launch a world war that even it wished to avoid.

Had Europeans known that the defense dominated, the whole explosion might not have occurred. Germany and Austria would have had less reason to resort to a fait accompli. Instead they might have complained openly against Serbia without framing a sudden ultimatum. The Entente

---

[54] Lieven, *Russia and the Origins of the First World War*, p. 148.

[55] Bernadotte E. Schmitt, *The Coming of the War 1914*, 2 vols. (New York: Scribner's, 1930), 1:131n. See also Lieven, *Russia and the Origins of the First World War*, pp. 40–41, 99–100, 147.

[56] Sidney B. Fay, *The Origins of the World War*, 2 vols., 2d ed. rev. (New York: Free Press, 1966), 2:300; Serge Sazonov, *Fateful Years, 1909–1916* (London: Cape, 1928), p. 179; Schmitt, *Coming of the War*, 1:87.

[57] See, for example, J. Herbette, quoted at note 122 in Chapter 7.

powers then could have warned Germany and Austria-Hungary against overreaching before they became overcommitted.[58] Moreover, any Austro-German fait accompli would have alarmed the Entente powers less, and their reactions (if any) would have triggered a less violent Austro-German response.[59]

The Soviet Union used similar tactics for similar reasons when it secretly moved medium-range missiles to Cuba in 1962; and it nearly got similar results. The Soviets deployed missiles to Cuba mainly to redress their precarious military weakness.[60] The United States held massive nuclear superiority over the Soviets in 1961–62, perhaps possessing a first-strike capability.[61] The Soviets, anxious to escape their inferiority,[62] responded by secretly moving some of their many medium-range missiles to Cuba, in range of U.S. targets. Such a fait accompli was dangerous, but in Soviet eyes the military sta-

[58] The lack of Entente warning was a key to the outbreak of the war. Had the Entente clearly warned the Central Powers of war before the Austrian ultimatum on July 23, or perhaps even later in the crisis, Germany probably would have pressured Austria-Hungary to stand down, and war would have been prevented. Concurring is Jack S. Levy, "Preferences, Constraints, and Choices in July 1914," *International Security* 15 (Winter 1990/91): 151–86 at 170. But the Entente could not warn because the Central Powers themselves moved without warning, even concealing their impending move.

[59] The effects of the sudden German seizure of Austria in March 1938 offer an interesting contrast. The European powers widely assumed that the defense dominated, and their response to the *Anschluss* was very relaxed. P. M. H. Bell notes that among them "no one even thought of going to war" to reverse the German action; the risk of war arising from the Austrian crisis was "almost nil." *The Origins of the Second World War in Europe* (London: Longmans, 1986), pp. 226, 229; see also pp. 209–10 for another example.

[60] On Soviet motives see Raymond L. Garthoff, *Reflections on the Cuban Missile Crisis*, rev. ed. (Washington, D.C.: Brookings, 1989) p. 21, also pp. 23, 24, 188; Bruce J. Allyn, James G. Blight, and David A. Welch, "Essence of Revision: Moscow, Havana, and the Cuban Missile Crisis," *International Security* 14 (Winter 1989/90): 136–72 at 138–43; McGeorge Bundy, *Danger and Survival: Choices about the Bomb in the First Fifty Years* (New York: Random House, 1988), pp. 416–17; and Richard Ned Lebow, "Deterrence: A Political and Psychological Critique," in Paul C. Stern, Robert Axelrod, Robert Jervis, and Roy Radner, *Perspectives on Deterrence* (New York: Oxford University Press, 1989), pp. 25–51 at 43–44.

The Cuban missile deployment added substantially to Soviet first-strike capability, but added little to its second-strike capability. Hence the deployment did not solve the Soviets' most serious military weakness, its lack of a secure second-strike deterrent. However, it is in character for the Soviet military to address a nuclear weakness with a first-strike-bolstering deployment, because Soviet nuclear doctrine emphasized first strike. An assessment of the deployment's military impact is Garthoff, *Cuban Missile Crisis*, pp. 202–11.

[61] Outlining the weakness of Soviet strategic nuclear forces in the early 1960s is Robert Weinland, "The Evolution of Soviet Requirements for Naval Forces: Solving the Problems of the Early 1960s," *Survival* 26 (January/February 1984): 16–25 at 17–20. See also Fred Kaplan, *The Wizards of Armageddon* (New York: Simon and Schuster, 1983), pp. 289, 294–95.

[62] Until 1961 the Soviets had hoped to hide their weakness from the United States by tight secrecy and false boasts of large strategic programs. On this Soviet deception campaign see Arnold L. Horelick and Myron Rush, *Strategic Power and Soviet Foreign Policy* (Chicago: University of Chicago Press, 1966), chaps. 3–5. They learned that the United States knew it held superiority in October 1961. Bundy, *Danger and Survival*, pp. 381–82; for background see also Kaplan, *Wizards*, pp. 286–90.

tus quo was also dangerous. Soviet Premier Nikita Khrushchev underrated the risk of a firm U.S. response partly because he made his policy in dark secrecy, excluding advisors who could have predicted Kennedy's tough reaction.[63] Khrushchev also deceived the United States about his plans; hence it could not signal its response until he was overcommitted.[64]

The 1962 case illustrates two problems: insecure states are more willing to run the risks that faits accomplis entail, and these states tend to miscalculate because they make policy in a secret setting that excludes analysts who might correct their false premises.

States negotiate less and reach fewer agreements (explanation H5G)

When conquest is easy, states have less faith in agreements because others break them more often. They also bargain harder and concede more grudgingly, causing more deadlocks; they find that compliance with agreements is harder to verify; and they insist on better verification and compliance. As a result, states negotiate less often and settle fewer disputes; hence more issues remain unsettled, and misperceptions survive that dialogue might dispel.

States break agreements more quickly when the offense dominates because cheating pays larger rewards. Bad faith and betrayal become the norm. The secure can afford the luxury of negotiating in good faith, but the insecure must worry more about short-term survival. Their worry drives them to deceit and sudden betrayals of all kinds—diplomatic faits accomplis (as just discussed), military surprise attacks, and other breakings of solemn agreements. States also break more agreements because power fluctuates more dramatically when the offense dominates (see the "windows are larger and more dangerous" explanation, H5E, above), so states are less able to en-

---

[63] The only Soviet diplomat aware of the secret deployment was the obtuse Andrey Gromyko. Bundy, *Danger and Survival*, p. 451. Sergo Mikoyan notes that Khrushchev's circle of advisors was confined by the need for secrecy: the missile deployment "was a very secret operation from the very beginning. Not even all members of the Central Committee or the cabinet ministers were involved. It was only possible to discuss it within a circle of about ten or maybe fifteen people, not more." Quoted in Bernd Greiner, "The Cuban Missile Crisis Reconsidered: The Soviet View: An Interview with Sergo Mikoyan," *Diplomatic History* 14 (Spring 1990): 205–21 at 213.

[64] The United States failed to warn Khrushchev against deploying missiles to Cuba until September, when they were already en route. Kennedy finally issued warning statements on September 4 and 13. See Bundy, *Danger and Survival*, p. 393 for texts. U.S. policymakers thought the Soviets were unlikely to put missiles in Cuba, and thus the warnings were crafted to warn against what JFK thought the Soviets would not do. Had U.S. policymakers thought otherwise, they might have raised the goalpost, warning against any deployment above one hundred missiles or some other expected and acceptable level. Garthoff, *Cuban Missile Crisis*, pp. 33–34. As things developed, these warnings tightened the conflict by committing JFK to prevent the Soviets from doing exactly what they were already committed to do.

force each other's compliance (as outlined in Chapter 4). Hence the effective life of agreements is shorter, hence they are seen as less valuable, hence states seek and reach fewer agreements.[65]

For example, diplomacy deteriorated markedly in ancient China when the offense assumed dominance over the defense during the "Spring and Autumn" and "Warring States" periods (722–221 B.C.E.). During the Spring and Autumn period, Chinese diplomacy was fairly well mannered,[66] but rules and norms broke down during the Warring States period. One historian writes that "agreements were made to be broken, and diplomats were experts in treachery and deceit."[67]

When states do negotiate, they bargain harder and concede less when the offense dominates. Agreements must be more finely balanced to gain both sides' agreement, because a relative gain by either side poses greater risks to the other's safety.[68]

Finally, verification of compliance with agreements is both more necessary and more difficult when the offense dominates. States insist on better verification of others' compliance because smaller violations can have larger security implications: an opponent can convert a smaller advantage gained by cheating into a larger offensive capability. At the same time, verification of compliance is harder because states are more secretive when security is scarce (see the "states are more secretive" explanation, H5H, below). As a result, the range of issues that can be negotiated is narrowed to the few where near-certain verification is possible despite tight state secrecy.

As a net result, states negotiate less and let more disputes fester when the offense dominates. This raises the risk of misunderstandings and collisions

---

[65] If experience shows that promises cannot be believed, states will reach fewer settlements. For example, during World War II the British eventually ruled out a settlement with Hitler because, as Foreign Secretary Samuel Hoare later said, the experience of 1936–39 showed that "negotiations and agreements with Hitler were of no permanent value." A. J. P. Taylor, *The Origins of the Second World War*, 2d ed. (Greenwich: Fawcett, 1961), p. 199. Neville Chamberlain likewise dismissed Hitler's peace proposal of October 6, 1939: "The difficulty is that you can't believe anything Hitler says . . . the only chance of peace is the disappearance of Hitler and that is what we are working for." John L. Snell, *Illusion and Necessity: The Diplomacy of Global War, 1939–1945* (Boston: Houghton Mifflin, 1963), p. 51.

[66] Samuel B. Griffiths, "Introduction," in Sun Tzu, *The Art of War* (London: Oxford University Press, 1971), pp. 24, 30.

[67] Dun J. Li, *The Ageless Chinese: A History*, 3d ed. (New York: Charles Scribner's Sons, 1978), p. 56.

[68] States also bargain harder because their interlocutors are more aggressive, and aggressors are more likely to take concessions as a sign of weakness and make further demands. For example, before the Seven Years' War, Britain and France were reluctant to negotiate because both thought the other had aggressive aims that negotiations would only encourage. As a result they were drawn to war by misperceptions that more negotiations might have exposed. Patrice Higgonet, "The Origins of the Seven Years' War," *Journal of Modern History* 40 (March 1968): 57–90 at 78, 81–82.

over small matters, and of wars born of misperceptions that survive because the talks that might expose them never occur.

States are more secretive (explanation H5H)

When conquest is easy, governments cloak their foreign and defense policies in greater secrecy. An information advantage confers more rewards, and a disadvantage raises more dangers: lost secrets could risk a state's existence. Hence states compete for information advantage by concealing their foreign policy strategies and their military plans and forces.

Openness with military and foreign policy information has benefits. States can better deter enemies by displaying their power. They can reach more arms control agreements and better avoid arms racing if they keep few secrets. Their policies will be better evaluated if their policymakers consult a wide circle of experts. Other powers are less likely to inadvertently injure national interests that are openly framed and explained.

When the offense dominates, the dangers of openness can outweigh these advantages, driving states back to secrecy. An open policy risks revealing secrets that give an enemy the keys to total victory. States also grow more concerned that agreements to share information be equal, impeding agreement to exchange information or permit mutual reconnaissance. States ask, Who gains more from openness? instead of Do we both gain? So agreements to foster openness must be more nearly equal before the "loser" agrees.

All the European powers enshrouded their policies in dark secrecy during the heyday of the "cult of the offensive" before 1914 (on the cult see Chapter 7). Everywhere, writes Sidney Fay, military plans "were worked out and guarded in such absolute secrecy" that "they were often not even known to the Minister of Foreign Affairs."[69] The German war plan was so secret that German Chancellor Bethmann-Hollweg, Secretary of State Jagow, Admiral Tirpitz, and probably even the kaiser were unaware that it required an immediate surprise attack on Belgium once German mobilization began.[70] In Britain, Foreign Secretary Edward Grey knew nothing of plans for Franco-British military cooperation being evolved by the military staffs during 1906–11.[71] In Austria the army chief of staff, Franz Conrad von Hötzendorff, and his senior military officers shared little intelligence information with other officials. Civilians were allowed fragments of information, but no government agency assessed the information collectively.[72] In Russia, the mili-

---

[69] Fay, *Origins*, 1:41.
[70] See Chapter 3, note 111.
[71] Fay, *Origins*, 1:41.
[72] Samuel R. Williamson, Jr., *Austria-Hungary and the Origins of the First World War* (New York: St. Martin's, 1991), pp. 102–3.

tary held a monopoly of information and withheld crucial data from civilians, leaving the Ministry of Foreign Affairs ignorant of the state of the army.[73] As one historian notes, this secrecy fostered "mutual incomprehension between statesmen and soldiers."[74]

In the Cold War, tight secrecy on both sides during the 1940s and 1950s gave way to far greater openness as a defense-dominant military order emerged and deepened in the 1960s and 1970s. President Truman enforced a policy of secrecy on all nuclear matters.[75] All Atomic Energy Commission reports to President Eisenhower on the arsenal were given verbally, to avoid leaving a paper record.[76] Soviet secrecy was even tighter, also from fear that the United States could wring advantage from any knowledge it gained.

Once both sides developed secure nuclear deterrents, the fear of disclosure diminished. Neither side could possibly conquer the other, with or without access to the other's secrets. Hence both had less to fear from openness. Thus Khrushchev argued in retirement that because the Soviet Union now had a powerful deterrent, it could allow on-site inspection to ease arms control—once an unthinkable policy.[77] The United States likewise eased public access to defense information, especially during the late 1970s. By the 1980s civilians could analyze military questions using unclassified data, something largely impossible before 1975. Both sides also tacitly agreed to allow photo-reconnaissance satellite overflights by the other—a transparency measure that greatly reduced the potential for miscalculation.[78] Either could have instead deployed antisatellite systems to sweep the skies clean of satellites. Their decision not to do so was a conscious choice that reflected the more relaxed conditions of the no-win nuclear stalemate.

The openness of the later Cold War contrasts sharply with the dark secrecy of the more offense-dominant Arab-Israeli competition. Arabs and Israelis both know that their opponents could perhaps translate information into the power to conquer. And each pursues tight secrecy.

Secrecy in turn is a Hydra-headed war cause, and the secrecy that offense dominance fosters has a host of war-causing effects. Nine bear special mention:

[73] William C. Fuller, Jr., "The Russian Empire," in Ernest R. May, ed., *Knowing One's Enemies: Intelligence Assessment before the Two World Wars* (Princeton: Princeton University Press, 1986), pp. 98–126 at 190.

[74] Lieven, *Russia and the Origins of the First World War*, pp. 152–53.

[75] Bundy, *Danger and Survival*, pp. 200–201; see also pp. 172–73, 203, 339. Even George Kennan, when head of the State Department policy planning staff (1947–49) and hence the senior advisor to the Secretary of State on the policy aspects of atomic weapons matters, never knew the size or power of the U.S. atomic arsenal. Ibid., p. 201.

[76] Stephen E. Ambrose, *Eisenhower*, 2 vols. (New York: Simon and Schuster, 1984), 2:92n.

[77] Nikita Khrushchev, *Khrushchev Remembers: The Last Testament*, trans. and ed. Strobe Talbott (New York: Bantam, 1974), p. 613.

[78] On the reconnaissance revolution see John Lewis Gaddis, *The Long Peace: Inquiries into the History of the Cold War* (New York: Oxford University Press, 1987), pp. 195–214, 232–33.

Secrecy causes false optimism; states more often exaggerate their prospects of victory when their opponent's military strength is hidden. For example, Israel's tradition of extreme secrecy in military matters fostered false Arab optimism and, in so doing, helped cause Arab-Israeli wars. Michael Handel has noted an "almost fanatical tradition of secrecy" in military matters in Israel and argued that the 1967 Arab-Israeli War grew in part from Egypt's inability to penetrate Israel's wall of secrecy and accurately estimate Israel's power. This illustrates "the loss of credibility and the weakening of deterrence as a result of too much secrecy."[79] Ian Nish likewise concludes that Russia's false optimism before the Russo-Japanese War of 1904–5 arose from Japan's deliberate policy of secrecy and concealment.[80]

First-move advantages are larger in a more secret world, because the side moving first gains a longer jump on the other.[81] Hence states are more tempted to jump first. For example, Russia mobilized in 1914 partly because its leaders thought that Russia could steal a march on Germany and that otherwise Germany would steal a march on Russia. France launched preliminary mobilization partly because French leaders feared being forestalled by Germany.[82] With less secrecy, both would have behaved more calmly, being more confident that they could quickly detect German mobilization and more certain that Germany would quickly detect and counter their own.

Secrecy delays states' reactions to others' military buildups; this opens windows of opportunity for the building-up state that tempt it to launch preventive war. Japan cloaked its 1937–41 naval buildup in dark secrecy to avoid provoking a U.S. reaction. As a result the U.S. response lagged until 1940, giving Japan a window of opportunity in 1941–42 that helped move it to war.[83] Nazi Germany likewise concealed the buildup it began in the early 1930s. As a result Britain underestimated it. Britain's response therefore lagged into the late 1930s, which created a German window of opportunity during 1938–43.[84] In a more open world, the United States and Britain

---

[79] Michael Handel, *Israel's Political-Military Doctrine*, Harvard University, Center for International Affairs, Occasional Papers, no. 30 (Cambridge, July 1973), pp. 12, 50.

[80] Ian Nish, *The Origins of the Russo-Japanese War* (London: Longman, 1985), p. 241.

[81] Greater openness is not an unmixed blessing. It can give an attacker target information that enables its first strike, and the value of this information could outweigh the value of the earlier warning of attack, leaving the first-strike advantage larger as openness increases. But examples of this result are hard to find. Warning almost always seems more important and in shorter supply than target information.

[82] For details see Chapter 7 at notes 70–80. Russian and French leaders also incorrectly believed that Germany was in fact mobilizing during the July crisis, and they began mobilizing partly in response. See Chapter 3, note 33.

[83] See Chapter 4, note 71.

[84] On the early British underestimate see Bell, *Origins of the Second World War*, p. 180; Wesley K. Wark, *The Ultimate Enemy: British Intelligence and Nazi Germany, 1933–1939* (Ithaca: Cornell University Press, 1985), pp. 35–51, 80–86, 227–28, 235, 245–47. For more on the German window see Chapter 4 at notes 92–115.

would have reacted faster, shrinking the Japanese and German windows and reducing the risk of war.

Secrecy promotes diplomatic faits accomplis. They are more feasible in a secret world, hence more tempting to try. For example, Khrushchev was tempted to move missiles to Cuba in 1962 by the false hope that he could deploy them secretly.[85]

Secrecy causes deterrence failure by causing states to conceal their war plans. This leaves others unaware of their shape until after the state is overcommitted to elements of a plan that are casus belli for the others. Deterrence then fails because deterrent threats are made too late. For example, in 1914 Britain failed to warn Germany early that Britain would fight if Germany attacked westward partly because the German war plan was a dark secret, hence British leaders were unaware that it mandated German conquest of Belgium[86]—a casus belli for Britain. This misconception left British leaders blithely unaware of the urgent need to warn Germany against a westward strike. In a more open world, Britain might have known what Germany planned and deterred it from acting.

Oppositely, *secrecy can lead states to trigger war unwittingly* because they cannot see the hidden tripwires that will spark others' decisions for war. On July 25, 1914, Russian leaders ordered preliminary mobilization, thus starting the general rush to mobilize, without realizing that for Germany mobilization inexorably meant war—and that Russian mobilization therefore meant war if it triggered German mobilization, as it surely would.[87] This was hidden because a key reason why mobilization meant war for Germany—the planned German surprise attack on Liège, which melded German mobilization and attack into a single motion—was a dark secret.

Secrecy can also lead states to trigger war unwittingly by concealing the implications of their military plans and operations from their own national leaders. Some of the German leaders who instigated the 1914 July crisis were unaware of the German army's Liège operation. Hence they, like their Russian counterparts, were unaware that diplomacy would end once mobilization began, even as they took steps that would trigger it.

Secrecy promotes arms racing, causing windows and false optimism. As noted above, secrecy can foster underreaction, opening windows of op-

---

[85] Garthoff, *Cuban Missile Crisis*, pp. 13–17.

[86] See Chapter 7 at note 135.

[87] On July 26, after ordering preliminary mobilization, Sazonov belatedly asked the German ambassador to Russia: "Surely mobilization is not equivalent to war with you, either, is it?" Luigi Albertini, *The Origins of the War of 1914*, 3 vols., trans. and ed. Isabella M. Massey (1952–57; Westport, Conn.: Greenwood, 1980), 2:481. See also citations in Chapter 7, note 135. Belgium also mobilized forces on July 29 without realizing that this would surely cause war if it triggered German mobilization. Jean Stengers, "Belgium," in Keith Wilson, ed., *Decisions for War 1914* (New York: St. Martin's, 1995), pp. 151–74 at 158.

portunity and vulnerability. Secrecy also causes overreaction by fostering worst-case assessments of opponents' military programs. This, too, opens windows and fosters false optimism by quickening the pace of military change.[88]

Soviet secrecy in the 1950s fostered vast U.S. overestimates of Soviet military programs, embodied in the bomber gap and missile gap scares of 1955–60.[89] These overestimates spurred U.S. military overbuilding that opened a large U.S. window of opportunity in the early 1960s. The United States did not seize this opportunity, but some thought it should.[90] Such errors were not repeated—at least not on the same scale—after U.S. intelligence estimates improved with the tacit mutual reconnaissance regime that arose in the early 1960s.[91] Later U.S. overestimates of Soviet forces, and episodes of U.S. responsive overbuilding, were markedly smaller.

Secrecy inhibits arms control agreements by impeding verification measures. This leaves states less able to channel their arms competition by agreement.

Secrecy narrows the circle of experts consulted on national policy. This impedes national policy evaluation, fostering policy blunders and miscalculations.[92]

Germany's blueprint for war in 1914, the Schlieffen plan, was a flawed scheme whose illogic was hidden by secrecy. Its planned surprise attack on Liège made any crisis harder to control by ensuring that mobilization meant war. This clashed with Bethmann-Hollweg's strategy of peaceful victory through brinkmanship. The plan's programmed German conquest of Belgium and France disastrously ensured that Britain and Belgium would be

---

[88] On secrecy and overreaction see Thomas C. Schelling and Morton H. Halperin with Donald G. Brennan, *Strategy and Arms Control* (New York: Twentieth Century Fund, 1961), pp. 34–37, 101.

[89] At the height of bomber gap, U.S. intelligence exaggerated Soviet bomber production by a factor of four. The August 1956 National Intelligence Estimate forecast 470 Soviet heavy bombers for 1958 and 800 for mid-1960; in fact the Soviets had under 200 (perhaps 185) by 1960. John Prados, *The Soviet Estimate: U.S. Intelligence Analysis and Soviet Strategic Forces* (Princeton: Princeton University Press, 1986), p. 45, 48–49. U.S. overestimates of the missile gap were still larger. In late 1959, U.S. public estimates forecast 1,000–1,500 Soviet intercontinental ballistic missiles (ICBMs) by late 1961 or early 1962; this was 250–375 times the actual late-1961 figure of only four (4) Soviet ICBMs. Edgar M. Bottome, *The Balance of Terror: A Guide to the Arms Race* (Boston: Beacon Press, 1971), pp. 55–56; Kaplan, *Wizards*, p. 289. For more on the bomber and missile gaps see Bottome, *Balance of Terror*, pp. 35–73, 156–59.

Poor U.S. intelligence also fed chronic overestimates of Soviet conventional capabilities in Europe in the 1950s. See John S. Duffield, "The Soviet Military Threat to Western Europe: U.S. Estimates in the 1950s and 1960s," *Journal of Strategic Studies* 15 (June 1992): 208–27.

[90] For example, General Curtis LeMay urged general nuclear war during the Cuban Missile Crisis. Garthoff, *Cuban Missile Crisis*, p. 94n.

[91] An assessment of U.S. Cold War intelligence estimates is Les Aspin, "Debate Over U.S. Strategic Forecasts: A Mixed Record," *Strategic Review* 8 (Summer 1980): 29–43 at 40.

[92] As John Gaddis notes, "the accuracy of information tends to decline as the level of its classification rises, if for no other reason than that opportunities for independent verification are diminished thereby." John Lewis Gaddis, *Strategies of Containment: A Critical Appraisal of Postwar American National Security Policy* (New York: Oxford University Press, 1982), p. 257.

ranged against Germany in any war, and that France would be energized for war by German attack.[93] Moltke the Elder's earlier plan for a German defensive in the West and offense in the East was far superior. But Germans could not make these criticisms before 1914 because the Schlieffen plan itself was a state secret. Even the Prussian War Ministry was kept in the dark on Schlieffen's plans until December 1912, six years after Schlieffen retired.[94]

Japan's miscalculations of 1941 grew in part from the concealment of important data from Japan's top decision-making group, the Liaison Conference. The conference tried to assess Japan's war capacity during the fall of 1941 but was starved of data by the military. Foreign Minister Shigenori Togo, a conference member, later remarked that "I was astonished at our lack of statistical data," and noted the "absurdity of our having to base our deliberations on assumptions, since the high command refused to divulge figures on the numbers of our forces, or any facts relating to operations."[95] Even General Teiichi Suzuki, the director of the Japanese Cabinet Planning Board, was denied information about the military's stored petroleum stocks until about October 1941.[96] The conference was also uninformed of the navy's plan to begin the war by striking Pearl Harbor.[97] As a result, a key strategic contradiction in Japan's war plan—it sought to end the war with a negotiated settlement, but to begin it with an inflammatory sneak attack— went unaddressed by top officials.[98]

Blunders have larger and less reversible effects (explanation H5I)

I noted above that blunders are more common when conquest is easy, because states make policy in fear-driven secrecy and in window-driven haste (see explanations H5E and H5H). These blunders also have larger and less

---

[93] An assessment of the Schlieffen plan is Gerhard Ritter, *The Schlieffen Plan: Critique of a Myth*, trans. Andrew and Eva Wilson (London: Oswald Wolff, 1958; reprint, Westport, Conn.: Greenwood Press, 1979). An assessment and explanation is Snyder, *Ideology of the Offensive*, pp. 107–56.

[94] Holger Herwig, "From Tirpitz Plan to Schlieffen Plan: Some Observations on German Military Planning," *Journal of Strategic Studies* 9 (March 1986): 53–63 at 57.

[95] Nobutaka Ike, ed., *Japan's Decision for War: Records of the 1941 Policy Conferences* (Stanford: Stanford University Press, 1967), p. 188.

[96] Ibid.

[97] Scott D. Sagan, "Origins of the Pacific War," *Journal of Interdisciplinary Studies* 18 (Spring 1988): 893–922 at 916–17.

[98] Sagan, "Origins of the Pacific War," pp. 916–17. Even Prime Minster Tojo learned of the Pearl Harbor attack only in November 1941. Hideki Tojo, "The Planning of Japanese Invasion Operations against the Philippines," in Donald S. Detwiler and Charles B. Burdick, eds., *War in Asia and the Pacific 1937–1949*, 15 vols. (New York: Garland, 1980), vol. 2, document 6, pp. 1–2 at 1. Patrick Morgan speculates that the Pearl Harbor attack was authorized only because so few people had to agree to it. Patrick Morgan, "Examples of Strategic Surprise in the Far East," in Klaus Knorr and Patrick Morgan, eds., *Strategic Military Surprise: Incentives and Opportunities* (New Brunswick: Transaction Books, 1983), pp. 43–76 at 52.

reversible effects when conquest is easy. States see larger threats in others' moves, so they respond faster with more violent moves of their own. Hence errors are often irreversible and quickly trigger war.

The blunders of 1914 evoked quick, strong reactions that quickly made them irreversible:

Many Germans thought the Entente powers would peacefully accept Austria's crushing of Serbia,[99] and they pushed Austria to issue its ultimatum with this false hope in mind. Instead, Russia moved toward war almost instantly, and without warning, on hearing of the July 23 Austrian ultimatum. The first Russian orders for preliminary mobilization were issued at 4:10 P.M. on July 25,[100] even before the deadline for Serbia's reply had expired. To recover its mistake, Germany now had to get Russia to promptly halt its military preparations, something it proved unable to do. The German error had large and hard-to-reverse effects almost as soon as it was made.

Russian leaders assumed that mobilized armies could stand peacefully while leaders talked when they launched their preliminary mobilization measures on July 25.[101] In fact, German mobilization plans mandated immediate war, but Russian policymakers had only five days to detect and retrieve their error, a time that proved too short. On July 30 German military officers demanded that Germany answer Russia's preliminary mobilization measures with German mobilization, making war inevitable.[102]

British leaders also failed to understand that mobilization meant immediate war. Hence they failed to take strong measures to restrain Russia from mobilization.[103] This error had very rapid effects—Russian mobilization, German mobilization and war—that Britain was helpless to reverse once they began.

The leaders of 1914 are often criticized for their blundering during the July crisis, but conditions in 1914 also made mistakes easy to make and hard to undo. Leaders appear as blunderers in retrospect partly because the cult of the offensive created a harsh strategic environment that forgave no errors.

---

[99] German Secretary of State Gottlieb von Jagow wrongly predicted on July 18, 1914, that "the more determined Austria shows herself, the more energetically we support her, the more quiet will Russia remain. . . . Russia is not ready to strike at present. Nor will France or England be anxious for war at the present time." The kaiser likewise argued on July 5 that France "would put the brake on Russia, because of France's unfavorable financial position and her shortage of artillery." And Bethmann-Hollweg believed that "England would certainly be neutral." All quoted in Robert C. North, "Perception and Action in the 1914 Crisis," in John C. Farrell and Asa P. Smith, eds., *Image and Reality in World Politics* (New York: Columbia University Press, 1967), pp. 103–22 at 108–9.

[100] Fay, *Origins*, 2:309–10.

[101] On Russian unawareness that mobilization meant war see Chapter 7, note 135.

[102] Albertini, *Origins*, 3:6–16. Russia's decision for full mobilization, taken the same day, also made war inevitable.

[103] Albertini, *Origins*, 2:330–36, 393; Imanuel Geiss, ed., *July 1914: The Outbreak of the First World War: Selected Documents* (New York: Norton, 1967) pp. 198, 212–13, 250–51; Schmitt, *Coming of the War*, 2:41n.

Arms racing intensifies (explanation H5J)

Arms racing is more intense when conquest is easy.[104] Arms racing in turn raises other dangers—of windows of opportunity and vulnerability, false optimism, and militarism. Thus offense dominance is a remote cause of the dangers that arms racing produces.

States have eight incentives to build larger forces when the offense is strong:

- Resources are more cumulative (see the "defensive expansion" and "fierce resistance to expansion" explanations, H5B and H5C, above). Wartime gains and losses matter more: gains provide a greater increase in security, and losses are less reversible. Therefore, the forces that provide these gains and protect against these losses are also worth more.
- Self-defense is more difficult, because other states' forces have more inherent offensive capability. Hence states need more forces to offset deployments by others.
- States are more expectant of war. Their neighbors are more aggressive (see the "opportunistic expansion" and "defensive expansion" explanations, H5A and H5B, above), so they must be better prepared for attack or invasion.[105]
- The early phase of war is more decisive. Lacking time to mobilize their economies and societies in the event of war, states maintain larger standing forces.[106] The possibility of quick victory puts a premium on forces in being.[107]
- States transfer military resources from defense to offense, because offense is more effective (see the "conquest grows still easier" explanation, H5K, below). Others then counter-build because their neighbors' capabilities are more dangerous and so require a larger response. States also infer aggressive intent from their neighbor's offensive buildup, leading them to fear attack, and to build up in anticipation.

[104] See Jervis, "Cooperation," pp. 172, 188–90. Offering similar suggestions are Hugh Gibson, in League of Nations, *Conference*, pp. 38–39; Gibson's U.S. delegation to the 1932 Disarmament Conference, paraphrased in Boggs, *Attempts to Define*, p. 30; and Bradley, "This Way Lies Peace," pp. 33, 168.

[105] Thus the intensifying arms race before 1914 was driven by the general expectation of war, which in turn was rooted in part in the cult of the offensive. On expectations of war as a cause of the pre-1914 arms race see David G. Herrmann, *The Arming of Europe and the Making of the First World War* (Princeton: Princeton University Press, 1996), pp. 165–66, 169–70, 172, 191, 193, 198.

[106] See Jervis, "Cooperation," pp. 172, 189.

[107] For example, General Joseph Joffre argued for a larger French standing force in 1913, because "the affair will already have been settled" by the time reservists were mobilized in 3–4 weeks. Herrmann, *Arming of Europe*, p. 193.

- States hold military secrets more tightly when the offense dominates (see the "states are more secretive" explanation, H5H, above). This causes rational over-arming, as states gauge their defense efforts to worst-case estimates of enemy strength, on grounds that underspending is disastrous while overspending is merely wasteful. It also allows national militaries to monopolize defense information more tightly. This leads to dysfunctional over-arming, because militaries are prone to threat-inflation for organizationally self-serving reasons.
- States reach fewer arms control agreements when the offense dominates, because agreements of all kinds are fewer (see the "states negotiate less and reach fewer agreements" explanation, H5G, above). Hence states are less able to limit arms competition through agreement.
- National militaries have more influence on national perceptions when the offense dominates. Secrecy is tighter, which increases the military's influence on public perceptions of international affairs, as noted above. Militaries also grow in size, prestige, and social influence when states are insecure. Hence societies grow more militarized when the offense dominates. This further fuels arms racing. The pre-1914 European arms race illustrates. Germany's geography left it insecure; hence it maintained a large, prestigious military. This military infused Germany with an international social Darwinist worldview that fueled German aggressiveness and threatened Germany's neighbors. This spurred their military programs, which in turn spurred German military programs.

If the defense dominates, things are reversed. Resources are less cumulative, so the military forces that provide and protect resources are less worth owning. Self-defense is easier, so other states' military deployments pose less threat and call for a smaller responsive deployment. War is less likely, so preparations for war are less urgent. The early phase of a war is less decisive, allowing states to maintain smaller standing forces and to rely more on latent military capabilities. States transfer military resources from offense to defense; hence their military deployments pose less threat to their neighbors, compelling less response. States hold military secrets less closely; hence worst-case estimates are fewer and military control on defense information is looser; hence overreaction to other states' deployments is less common. Arms control agreements are reached more easily. Societies are less prone to militarization, and so less prone to spur their neighbors to arm by threatening their safety.

When the defense dominates, in short, states deploy smaller forces, and less offensive forces. This leads to still smaller and less offensive forces. If information were perfect, arms racing would slow to a crawl. Things would reach equilibrium with minimal defensive forces on both sides.

Offense-defense theory's explanation for arms racing improves on two prominent existing explanations. Arms controllers have argued that the pace of military competition varies inversely with the capacity of both sides to estimate adversary capabilities.[108] They suggest that easier estimation slows competition by inhibiting worst-case analysis and by easing verification of arms control agreements. Lewis Richardson argues rather differently that the pace of competition is largely governed by the strength of each side's impulse to react to the other's military preparations; a stronger impulse causes a more intense competition.[109] Both hypotheses are valid but unsatisfying: what makes force capabilities more or less estimable? What governs the strength of the impulse to react to others' buildups? Offense-defense theory posits that the offense-defense balance is a remote cause of both factors. It helps decide if capabilities are estimable by shaping the degree of international secrecy. It also influences the strength of a state's reaction to an opponent's military program: the more offensive capability those programs generate, the stronger the response.

Does arms racing raise the risk of war? Deduction suggests that arms racing opens windows, promotes false optimism, and feeds militarism. Confirming cases are easy to find.[110] The window that Germany jumped through in 1914 clearly grew from the European land arms race of 1912–14.[111] The French miscalculation of 1870 grew from the rapid pace of military change during 1866–70.[112] The Israeli miscalculations of 1973 grew from the rapid military changes after 1967. Both Wilhelmine German and Imperial Japanese militarism flourished amidst arms races (although causation probably ran both ways—militarism caused the arms race as well as vice versa). The bulk of large-*n* evidence also indicates that arms racing makes war more likely.[113]

---

[108] This depends in turn on the quality of intelligence, and the nature of the forces: Could weapons easily be counted? Could their capability be assessed?

[109] This is one of three causal factors that Richardson identified. The others are the scope of states' grievances against one another and the degree of restraining exhaustion that reaction produces on the reacting state. A summary of Richardson is Michael D. McGinnis, "Richardson, Rationality, and Restrictive Models of Arms Races," *Journal of Conflict Resolution* 35 (September 1991): 443–73 at 445–49.

[110] Case studies that explored the relationship between arms races and the outbreak of war would nevertheless be a useful supplement to the large-*n* studies on the subject.

[111] On this arms race see Herrmann, *Arming of Europe*, pp. 173–237.

[112] The French exaggerated the value of their new *chassepot* rifle and *mitrailleuse* gun, while underestimating Prussia's artillery improvements. See Smoke, *War*, pp. 128–29.

[113] Reviewing the positive case critically is Randolph M. Siverson and Paul F. Diehl, "Arms Race, the Conflict Spiral, and the Onset of War," in Manus I. Midlarsky, ed., *Handbook of War Studies*, (Boston: Unwin, Hyman, 1989), pp. 195–218. Reaching a more positive conclusion is John A. Vasquez, "The Steps to War: Toward a Scientific Explanation of Correlates of War Findings," *World Politics* 40 (October 1987): 108–45 at 135–38. Noting that the evidence generally indicates some association between the occurrence of an arms race and the outbreak of war is Martin Patchen, "When Do Arms Buildups Lead to Deterrence and When to War?" *Peace and Change* 11, no. 3/4 (1986): 25–46 at 26.

This evidence does not suggest a powerful relationship—the dangers of arms racing have probably been exaggerated by the many authors who have identified it as a prime cause of war—but neither does it seem trivial.

Conquest grows still easier (explanation H5K)

Offense dominance and defense dominance are self-reinforcing.[114] This gives an offense-dominant world a self-sustaining character that makes it hard to escape. Once in, states cannot withdraw without swimming against a strong military and political current.

States buy the force that works, hence they buy defensive forces when the defense dominates, and they buy offensive forces when the offense dominates.[115] This bolsters the capability that already dominates. For example, Germany switched from an offensive to a defensive strategy against France in 1879 chiefly because France built new defenses that made a German attack more difficult.[116] France adopted a defensive strategy in the 1920s partly because French leaders thought that the defense had the advantage in land warfare.[117] Conversely, the Eisenhower administration adopted its offensive Massive Retaliation strategy partly because U.S. officials thought a purely defensive strategy was infeasible.[118] Israel has long embraced an offensive military strategy mainly because Israel's tiny size, long and unprotected borders, elongated shape, and incapacity to sustain a long war of attrition made defense too difficult.[119]

Offense is self-exporting as well as self-strengthening. As Jack Snyder writes, "offensive strategies tend to spread in a chain reaction, since one

---

[114] Making this argument is Jervis, "Cooperation," pp. 188, 199, 201.

[115] Thus Clausewitz explained: "If attack were the stronger form [of war], there would be no case for using the defensive, since its purpose is only passive. No one would want to do anything but attack. Defense would be pointless." Carl von Clausewitz, *On War*, ed. and trans. Michael Howard and Peter Paret (Princeton: Princeton University Press, 1976), p. 359.

[116] Snyder, *Ideology of the Offensive*, p. 131; Ritter, *Sword and Scepter*, 1:231–32.

[117] Barry R. Posen, *Sources of Military Doctrine: France, Britain, and Germany between the Wars* (Ithaca: Cornell University Press, 1984), pp. 23–24, 106–9.

[118] Massive Retaliation envisioned a disarming U.S. nuclear first strike in response to local Soviet aggression. In 1954 Secretary of State John Foster Dulles explained it, saying there was "no local defense which alone will contain the mighty landpower of the Communist world," because the Soviet opponent could always "attack in places where his superiority was decisive." Hence the United States would instead "retaliate, instantly, by means and at places of our choosing" with "massive retaliatory power." Kaplan, *Wizards*, p. 175; Bundy, *Danger and Survival*, p. 256; see also p. 248.

Before 1914 Russia was likewise tempted toward offense by the ease of attacking. See Snyder, *Ideology of the Offensive*, pp. 157–59.

[119] Ben-Horin and Posen, *Israel's Strategic Doctrine*, pp. v–vi, 5, 29–34; Dan Horowitz, *Israel's Concept of Defensible Borders* (Jerusalem: Jerusalem Post, 1975), pp. 5–6; Edward Luttwak and Dan Horowitz, *The Israeli Army* (New York: Harper and Row, 1975), pp. 91, 212; Levite, *Offense and Defense*, pp. 28, 35.

state's offensive tends to create impending dangers or fleeting opportunities for other states, who must adopt their own offensives to forestall or exploit them."[120] The allies of a state threatened by an offensively armed opponent often can aid it best by an offensive of their own that threatens the opponent's rear. Opportunity also tempts them to adopt the offensive: when the opponent concentrates forces to attack their ally, it eases their own attack by stripping its forces from their common border. For example, Russia's 1914 offensive against Germany was designed in part to save France by distracting Germany from its attack on France, and in part to exploit German vulnerability in the east created by Germany's western concentration against France.[121]

States adopt more aggressive foreign policy goals when the offense dominates (see the "opportunistic expansion" and "defensive expansion" explanations, H5A and H5B, above), and then buy offensive forces to serve these goals.

Arms control agreements are harder to reach when the offense dominates (see the "arms racing intensifies" explanation, H5J, above). This makes the control of offensive forces by mutual agreement more difficult.

Political factors do less to impede aggressors when the offense dominates. Most important, alliances assume a more offensive character,[122] because aggressors can more easily drag their allies into their wars of aggression.[123] Insecure states can less afford to see allies destroyed, so they must support even bellicose allies who bring war on themselves. Knowing this, the allies feel freer to get into wars. As a net result, even de jure defensive alliances operate as defensive-and-offensive alliances. This largely explains why the European alliance system evolved from the defensive network Bismarck organized during 1879–87 to the defensive-and-offensive network of 1914.[124] By 1914 Britain and France felt they could not let Germany defeat Russia even if Russia triggered the war, since they feared Russia's demise would

---

[120] Jack Snyder, "Civil-Military Relations and the Cult of the Offensive, 1914 and 1984," *International Security* 9 (Summer 1984): 108–46 at 141.

[121] Snyder, *Ideology of the Offensive*, pp. 17, 23, 157, 165, 180. This ripple effect continued to Austria, which attacked Russia in 1914 largely to save Germany from the Russian attack that was spurred by Germany's plan to attack France. See Norman Stone, "Conrad von Hötzendorf," *History Today* 13 (July 1963): 480–89 at 486.

[122] A defensive alliance is conditioned on defensive behavior by the ally; the alliance operates if the ally is attacked but not if it attacks. A defensive-and-offensive alliance operates in the event of war regardless of which side started it. The distinction began with Thucydides, who used "empimachy" to denote defensive alliance, "symmachy" for defensive-and-offensive alliances. G. E. M. de Ste. Croix, *The Origins of the Peloponnesian War* (Ithaca: Cornell University Press, 1972), pp. 60, 72–73, 106–8, 184, 298–302, 328.

[123] Developing this point are Thomas J. Christensen and Jack Snyder, "Chain Gangs and Passed Bucks: Predicting Alliance Patterns in Multipolarity," *International Organization* 44 (Spring 1990): 137–68.

[124] For sources on Bismarck's defensive network see note 195 below.

mean their own.[125] This freed Russia to pursue belligerent policies. Russia and France could not restrain Serbia for similar reasons. They saw their own survival tied to Serbia's, hence they could not abandon Serbia even if it provoked war.[126]

Alliances also become more offensive if the allies adopt purely offensive military doctrines. This hamstrings states that would like to demand that their allies confine themselves to defensive preparations in a crisis, because all preparations are offensive. In July 1914 Britain could not restrain Russia partly because all Russian military preparations were inherently offensive, since Russian war plans were offensive. Hence Britain had to ask Russia to stand unprepared or consent to provocative Russian preparations.[127] Its alliance with Russia could not be defensive because Russia could not fight defensively.

States shrink from taking deterrent military measures when the offense dominates because these measures have larger offensive implications, raising larger risk of provoking the war the state seeks to deter. As a result, states may do too little to defend themselves or their allies in their effort not to do too much. For example, Stalin refused to alert Soviet frontier troops just before Germany's 1941 attack because he feared this would provoke Germany.[128] Some argue that Israel likewise refrained from mobilizing before the 1973 October War from fear of provoking the Arab attack that was already being prepared.[129] This dilemma is less acute in a defense-dominant world, because alert measures pose less threat to others' security, hence are less provocative.[130]

Status quo states may lack time to move to their allies' defense when the

---

[125] See Chapter 7 at notes 157–60.

[126] See above at notes 34, 36, 54–57.

[127] See Chapter 7 at notes 160–62. Either choice can cause war. If the ally is not restrained its belligerence can trigger conflict, but if the ally is not supported others may attack it because its isolation leaves it vulnerable. Britain teetered on both horns of the dilemma in 1914. Early in the crisis Grey hesitated to back Russia from fear of encouraging Russian belligerence and provoking Germany, while later he hesitated to restrain Russia because he could not ask it to stand defenseless. On his early hesitation see Joll, *Origins of the First World War,* pp. 19–20; Levy, "Preferences, Constraints, and Choices," p. 168. This early hesitation contributed to Britain's larger failure to scare Germany into a timely unwinding of the crisis.

[128] Stalin snapped at the generals who requested the alert: "That means war! Do you two understand that or not?" Earl F. Ziemke and Magna E. Bauer, *Moscow to Stalingrad: Decision in the East* (Washington, D.C.: United States Army Center of Military History, 1987), p. 56.

[129] Janice Gross Stein, "Calculation, Miscalculation, and Conventional Deterrence II: The View from Jerusalem," in Robert Jervis, Richard Ned Lebow, and Janice Gross Stein, *Psychology and Deterrence* (Baltimore: Johns Hopkins University Press, 1985), pp. 60–88 at 73, 75–78; Chaim Herzog, *The War of Atonement* (Boston: Little, Brown, 1975), pp. 159–61. Suggesting oppositely that Israeli restraint grew from a wish to avoid scaring the Arabs into canceling a war that some Israelis wanted is Safran, *Israel,* p. 287.

[130] The dilemma is still less acute if offensive and defensive forces and deployments are distinguishable from each other, allowing purely defensive mobilizations. On the importance of distinguishability see Jervis, "Cooperation," pp. 199–210.

offense dominates, because attackers can overrun defenders before help can arrive. If so, defensive alliances have less deterrent effect. For example, in 1914 some Germans dismissed British power because they thought they could overrun France before Britain could intervene effectively.[131] Stalin approved North Korea's 1950 attack on South Korea after Kim Il Sung convinced him that Northern forces could overrun the South before the United States could weigh in. Khrushchev recalled that Stalin "was worried that the Americans would jump in, but we were inclined to think that if the war were fought swiftly—and Kim Il-sung was sure it could be won swiftly—then intervention by the U.S.A. could be avoided."[132] The United States invaded North Korea in October 1950 because U.S. policymakers thought fast-advancing U.S. forces could occupy the North before China could intervene effectively for the North.[133] Many Israelis doubt the value of U.S. security guarantees partly because Israel could lose a war before U.S. power could be brought to bear.[134]

Finally, when the offense dominates, wars more often erupt from interactions so rapid that onlookers cannot tell who to blame for the war. Hence aggressors can escape punishment for their wars by obscuring their responsibility.

For example, Europe's pre-1914 cult of the offensive helped Germany obscure its central role in catalyzing World War I.[135] As war erupted, German Admiral Georg von Müller accurately gloated: "The mood is brilliant. The government has succeeded very well in making us appear as the at-

---

[131] Levy, "Preferences, Constraints, and Choices," pp. 164–65. The same logic tempted the French attack on the Dutch in 1793. One historian writes that France hoped for "a blitzkrieg so rapid that the British would not have time to respond." Blanning, *Origins*, p. 153.

[132] Nikita Khrushchev, *Khrushchev Remembers*, trans. and ed. Strobe Talbott (Boston: Little, Brown, 1970), p. 368.

[133] Martin Lichterman, "To the Yalu and Back," in Harold Stein, ed., *American Civil-Military Decisions: A Book of Case Studies* (Birmingham: University of Alabama Press, 1963), pp. 569–642 at 596. Similarly, Hitler often trusted the speed of his attack to outrun countervailing diplomacy. On Czechoslovakia see Anthony P. Adamthwaite, *The Making of the Second World War* (London: George Allen and Unwin, 1977), p. 187; Hitler counted on quick victory to prevent intervention by other powers if he had to smash Czechoslovakia by force. Later, planning the smashing of Poland, he wrote that "the isolation of Poland will be all the more easily maintained . . . if we succeed in starting the war with sudden, heavy blows and in gaining rapid success." Noakes and Pridham, *Nazism*, 2:736. And in October 1939 he argued that the war would be over before the United States could intervene. Saul Friedländer, *Prelude to Downfall: Hitler and the United States, 1939–1941*, trans. Aline B. Wirth and Alexander Wirth (New York: Knopf, 1967), p. 87.

[134] Levite, *Offense and Defense*, p. 35; Ben-Horin and Posen, *Israel's Strategic Doctrine*, pp. 24–25.

[135] I concur with the Fischer school's argument that Germany deserves primary blame for the war. Germany willfully instigated and sustained the July crisis. In so doing it consciously took a large risk of war, although it preferred the precrisis status quo to a world war. Summaries of the Fischer school's views include Imanuel Geiss, *German Foreign Policy 1871–1914* (Boston: Routledge and Kegan Paul, 1976); and Moses, *Politics of Illusion*.

tacked."[136] During the war even President Woodrow Wilson was unsure who to blame for causing it: he reportedly thought "the causes of the war were enormously complex and obscure."[137] After 1918 historians were confused for decades, quarreling over the meaning of quick interactions that unfolded in a single week. Germany had provoked Russia into moving first militarily, but many criticized Russia's move more than Germany's provocation. Hence many apportioned blame for the war about equally among all the European powers;[138] some even assigned Russia primary blame. Their error reflects the explosive nature of the crisis that led to war, which reflected the explosive military context of the times, which stemmed largely from the cult of the offensive. Whether German leaders foresaw this result is unclear, but before and during the crisis they seemed confident that the public relations aspects of the crisis they instigated, and of any wars growing from it, could somehow be handled. They were proved right; the confusing speed of the crisis masked their responsibility.

In contrast, Hitler's responsibility for World War II is obvious partly because he could not catalyze other states into moving first, a reflection of their belief that the defense dominated.

Military offense dominance has one self-limiting effect: it leads status quo powers to cooperate more closely against aggressors.[139] They jump to aid an aggressor's victims because each knows that its neighbor's demise could lead more directly to its own undoing. Conversely, when states think that the defense dominates, they do less to save others from aggression because each expects it can defend itself alone even if others are overrun. As a result, aggressors can more often attack their victims seriatim, which is far easier than defeating a unified coalition.

This countervailing dynamic has important effects. Perceptions of offense dominance helped motivate the Triple Entente to firmly resist German-Austrian expansion before 1914, and perceptions of defense dominance weakened the same states' resistance to Hitler in the 1930s, easing his aggressions of 1938–41.[140] This countervailing effect seems more than offset by the several ways that offense dominance strengthens itself, however.

These are the dangers raised by offense dominance. As noted above, these dangers also arise when the offense is weak but states think that it dominates. They then act as if it dominates, with the same effects.

---

[136] On August 1, 1914, quoted in J. C. G. Röhl, "Admiral von Müller and the Approach of War, 1911–1914," *Historical Journal* 12 (December 1969): 651–73 at 670.

[137] Arthur S. Link, *Wilson the Diplomatist* (New York: Franklin Watts, 1974), p. 33.

[138] Noting the prevalence of such views among British and American historians in the 1930s is Hans-Ulrich Wehler, *The German Empire 1871–1918*, trans. Kim Traynor (Leamington Spa, England: Berg, 1985), p. 192.

[139] Making this argument are Christensen and Snyder, "Chain Gangs and Passed Bucks."

[140] Developing this point is ibid., pp. 150–67.

QUALIFICATIONS: WHEN OFFENSIVE DOCTRINES
AND CAPABILITIES CAUSE PEACE

Symmetrical offense dominance—a situation where both sides have strong offensive capabilities—is always more dangerous than symmetrical defense dominance, other things being equal. Asymmetrical possession of offensive capabilities by one of two adversaries, however, can sometimes reduce the risk of war. Specifically, the possession of offensive capabilities by a status quo power that faces an aggressor state can lower the risk of war under eight conditions. These conditions are uncommon but not unknown. Together they pose an important qualification to offense-defense theory: in some hands and under some conditions, offensive capabilities promote peace.

Offense can defend allies that cannot be defended by other means

Offensive strategies can be the best means to defend allies from aggressors.[141] When this is the case, offensive power in the hands of status quo states favors peace by making aggression harder and dissuading aggressors from attacking. Many observers argue that France could have deterred German attack on Czechoslovakia in 1938 and Poland in 1939 by threatening to attack Germany in the west if Germany concentrated forces elsewhere.[142] Some likewise argue that France and Russia needed offensive capabilities against Germany in 1914 to prevent Germany from conquering each piecemeal.[143]

The strength of these arguments hinges on the answers to three questions. First, in wartime is it easier for threatened allies to attack the aggressor or to reinforce each other? If an aggressor can cut wartime transport links between allies, it can prevent them from reinforcing each other. This allows the aggressor to destroy the defenders piecemeal if they pursue a defensive strategy. When geography lets allies attack the aggressor, they can pursue mutual defense by offense. If both conditions are present—if, that is, transport links between the allies are vulnerable and the allies can feasibly attack

---

[141] A discussion is Jervis, "Cooperation," pp. 183–84, 202.

[142] Hitler was acutely aware of, and emboldened by, Anglo-French unwillingness to take the offensive if he moved east. In May 1939 he stated that a serious threat from the west would preclude a German move eastward: "There must be no simultaneous conflict with the West [France and England]" when Germany struck Poland. Quoted in Adamthwaite, *Making of the Second World War*, p. 215. Later, confident that Britain and France would not attack, he assured his generals that Germany could safely attack Poland: "Attack in the West from the Maginot Line: I consider this impossible . . . England cannot help Poland . . . We will hold our position in the West until we have conquered Poland." On August 22, 1939, quoted in Noakes and Pridham, *Nazism*, 2:742.

[143] Scott D. Sagan, "1914 Revisited: Allies, Offense, and Instability," *International Security* 11 (Fall 1986): 151–76.

the aggressor—mutual defense may best be achieved by offense. This is most clearly the case when the aggressor lies between the defenders, when defenders abut the aggressor, and when the aggressor's territory is relatively small, so that defenders can project decisive power into the aggressor.

In 1914 Germany lay astride the Baltic sea lane between France and Russia. This hampered French and Russian ability to bolster each other's defenses if Germany attacked the other. France and Russia also abutted German territory, and Germany was small enough to make a decisive Franco-Russian attack on Germany thinkable. This left each ally best able to help the other by threatening Germany with direct attack, not by bolstering each other's defenses. By contrast, in the Cold War the Soviet Union could not sever sea traffic between the United States and Western Europe.[144] Also, the United States lacked ready access to Soviet territory, and the size of Soviet territory made a decisive U.S. conventional attack more difficult. Hence the United States could reinforce its NATO allies far more easily than it could project conventional power into the Soviet Union. Thus for the Franco-Russian alliance reinforcing allies in wartime was harder than attacking the adversary, while for NATO attacking the adversary was harder than reinforcement. Accordingly, offensive strategies were a better choice for the Franco-Russian alliance,[145] defensive strategies were better for NATO.

The second question is, Can defensive power be transplanted? States sometimes bolster threatened allies by transplanting their own defensive forces to the ally's territory. But if this is impossible, an offensive strategy may be the best substitute. The ability to transplant forces is a function of geography (can these forces be reinforced in wartime?) and political factors (will the recipient state accept foreign troops?).

These factors can make the transplant of defense hard or easy. In 1938 the coalition against Hitler could not station forces in Czechoslovakia for political reasons: Poland would not allow Soviet troops to transit Polish territory en route to Czechoslovakia from fear they would never leave Poland. In contrast, the NATO alliance stationed six foreign armies and five thousand theater nuclear weapons in Germany during the Cold War, providing an effective defense arrangement for Europe.

The third question is, Are the threatened states strong enough to stand alone against the aggressor? The offense-defense balance governs the ability of allies both to withstand attack in isolation and to defend by attacking.

---

[144] On the Soviet threat to the NATO sea line of communication (SLOC) see Karl Lautenschläger, "The Submarine in Naval Warfare, 1901–2001," *International Security* 11 (Winter 1986–87): 96–97, 134–38.

[145] This does not always mean that both allies should attack the aggressor, as France and Russia did in 1914. Rather, it recommends that only the unattacked ally should attack. In 1914, both France and Russia would have been better off had France stood on the defensive, as Jack Snyder has argued ("Correspondence," p. 191).

If the defense has a large advantage, even isolated defenders can thwart aggressors alone. This removes the need for allies to rescue each other by offense and opens up the option of defensive wars of attrition. In the late 1880s Germany was dissuaded from attacking anyone because each of its opponents looked individually impregnable.[146] Likewise, in 1914 France probably could have defeated the German attack at the Franco-Belgian border had it fortified and strongly defended that border instead of attacking into Lorraine. A Russian attack in the German rear still would have been helpful, but probably not necessary, given the battlefield dominance of the defense over the offense. Furthermore, even if France could not defend alone, a French attack on Germany was unwise; the dominance of the defense made such an attack infeasible, as France's disastrous defeat in the Battle of the Frontiers demonstrated.

In short, the need to extend deterrence by offense varies widely from alliance to alliance. The Western allies of the 1930s needed offensive capabilities and might have deterred the war had they adopted more offensive strategies. The Entente members of 1914 had less need for offense, but they probably needed some. For Cold War NATO, offense was unnecessary and infeasible.

The aggressor knows it has provoked the hostility of others

An offensive threat can make the target of the threat less aggressive if the threat is clearly contingent on the target's conduct—operating only if the target attacks others—and the target knows this. Such a threat dissuades without provoking. The target faces large punishment if it aggresses and little risk if it behaves well.

Offensive threats seem more clearly contingent, hence are more effective and less dangerous, when they are aimed at aggressors who know they are aggressors. Aggressors often underestimate their own aggressiveness, hence they underestimate their own role in provoking other's hostility.[147] Such aggressors will construe a conditional threat as a sign of unprovoked, unconditional hostility, and respond with more aggression. Thus myth-ridden Wilhelmine Germany provoked the Triple Entente alliance into existence and then failed to realize that it had done so, leading Germans to argue that the ring of "unprovoked" Entente encirclement should be broken by war.

If the aggressor elite knows it is aggressive, however, it is more likely to realize that others' threats are contingent on its belligerence and that it can

---

[146] Christensen and Snyder, "Chain Gangs and Passed Bucks," p. 167.

[147] On the tendency to underestimate one's own role in provoking others' hostility see Jervis, *Perception and Misperception*, 67–76, 343, 349–55.

secure itself by better conduct. Such self-awareness is most common among aggressive authoritarian dictatorships governed by small groups or a single strongman. Such rulers remember their own deeds; hence they know when they have provoked others, and they know that they can diminish the threat they provoked by reducing their own provocation. This is especially true of Orwellian regimes that have provoked conflict with others to excuse domestic repression or gain domestic support. Having purposely provoked others, they know they can persuade others to stand down by behaving better. For example, Stalin and his successors behaved better in the face of fast-growing U.S. power and belligerence, including an offensive military buildup, during 1952–55.[148] Hitler might have behaved better had he faced a credible threat of immediate allied conquest in 1938 or 1939, since he would have known that he created this threat by his own belligerence and could remove it by better conduct. The same may be true of the post-1970 Alawite dictatorship in Syria and the post-1979 fundamentalist Shiite regime in Iran. Both regimes have used conflicts with others to excuse domestic repression and bolster domestic support. Both doubtless knew this and would not have misconstrued others' provoked threats to retaliate as unprovoked.

Thus the response to offense depends in part on the nature of the aggressor. Offensive threats provoke some aggressors and calm others.

The aggressor knows that the status quo power is benign

Offensive threats seem more clearly contingent if the aggressor knows that the threatening power has no aggressive aims. If the threatening power is known for reckless conduct or has aggressive aims of its own, the aggressor may react aggressively even to offensive threats that it knows it provoked, because it cannot be sure that the threat will lift if it changes its ways. Hence status quo powers can wield offensive threats more effectively if they cultivate a reputation for modest aims and restrained behavior.

[148] Khrushchev writes that in the days leading up to Stalin's death "we believed that America would invade the Soviet Union. . . . Stalin trembled at this prospect. He knew that we were weaker than the United States. We had only a handful of nuclear weapons, while America had a large arsenal." Soviet military inferiority "weighed heavily on Stalin. He understood that he had to be careful not to be dragged into a war." Nikita Khrushchev, *Khrushchev Remembers: The Glasnost Tapes*, trans. and ed. Jerrold L. Schecter with Vyacheslav V. Luchow (Boston: Little, Brown, 1990), pp. 100–101; see also 69. The Soviets responded by backtracking during 1952–55. Specifically, they offered a plan to reunify Germany in early 1952, cooperated in ending the Korean War, tolerated German rearmament in 1954 without instigating a new Berlin crisis, forced the communists in Vietnam to make a disadvantageous peace, and agreed to the reunion of a neutralized Austria.

Reagan administration claims that its aggressiveness produced Gorbachev's standdown in the 1980s are more doubtful. See, for example, Georgi Arbatov, *The System: An Insider's Life in Soviet Politics* (New York: Times Books, 1992), pp. 321–22, arguing that this aggressiveness delayed reform and bolstered Soviet hard-liners.

The offensive force can only attack an attacker

Offensive threats seem more clearly contingent if backed by forces that can attack only if the aggressor also attacks. For example, in the late 1930s France had enough offensive punch to invade Germany if Germany stripped its western defenses to concentrate against the Czechs or Poles, but not enough to invade otherwise. (Hitler was still undeterred because he knew France lacked the will to use this offensive punch.) Some U.S. Cold War strategists likewise recommended that the United States develop what Herman Kahn called a "credible first-strike capability"—the ability to launch a first strike that could limit U.S. damage from Soviet retaliation to a level below what the United States would accept to defend Western Europe, but above the level that the United States would accept to conquer the Soviet Union.[149] The Soviets then would risk a disarming U.S. attack if and only if they attacked Western Europe.[150]

Slow-working offensives that require mobilization or lengthy military operations are another type of conditional or retaliatory offensive force. Pre-1945 U.S. military strategy provides an illustration. The United States planned to conquer its opponents, but only after a long military mobilization taking months or years. If this buildup was directed against aggressors, as it was in 1941–45, it threatened them with deferred but certain conquest. Had it been directed at status quo powers, however, its targets could have rallied allies to defeat it, exploiting the general tendency of neutral states to balance against aggressors. Hence it posed little threat to benign states.

In short, offensive forces produce more deterrence with less provocation if they can only attack attackers. Such finely tuned threats are hard to arrange, however. A standing force that can attack an attacker can usually threaten status quo powers as well. A slow-working mobilization offensive is more clearly contingent, but has its own shortcomings. Because it rests on less visible latent power and requires a traumatic national decision to mobilize, it may leave aggressors doubting the status quo power's strength and will, as Germany and Japan disbelieved U.S. strength and will before 1941.

The aggressor cannot "cut the noose"

The safest offensive strategies are those that threaten a target state without leaving it able to remove the threat by force. The worst are those that leave the target state able to cut the noose around its neck by force, since these strategies give the target a motive and a capacity for violence.

The threats that the United States made to Japan in 1940–41 comprised a

[149] Kahn, *On Thermonuclear War*, pp. vii–ix, 27–36.

[150] Some strategists also recommended that the United States pursue only a second-strike counterforce capability, eschewing a first-strike counterforce capacity, so that the Soviets would could be disarmed only if they attacked the United States first. See Sagan, "1914 Revisited," p. 174.

classic cuttable noose. To coerce Japan, the United States moved a large naval force from California to Hawaii in May 1940, began moving a B-17 bomber force to the Philippines in the fall of 1941, and imposed a strangling oil embargo on Japan in August 1941. These moves posed a much increased offensive threat to Japan, but they also presented a ripe target. The fleet and the bombers had moved in range for a surprise Japanese strike. If that strike succeeded, Japan could hope to seize Indonesia, and with it enough oil to counter the U.S. oil embargo. Such a tight but highly cuttable noose presented an irresistible provocation to Japan.[151]

In contrast, the Soviets could not cut the American noose during the Cuban missile crisis. America's virtual strategic first-strike capability posed a grave offensive threat to the Soviets, but the Soviets had no operational escape. No use of force would restore their deterrent.

Offensive threats will better deter weaker than stronger states, because the weak can seldom cut the noose alone, while the strong can more often find a way. During the Cold War, U.S. offensive threats aimed at Sandinista Nicaragua were bound to produce more compliance than offensive threats aimed at the Soviet Union.

The aggressor cannot be deterred by lesser punishment

A few regimes highly value only those assets that can be threatened by offensive action. Purely defensive or deterrent threats may not be enough to keep such regimes peaceful; threat of punishment by offense is also required. This can be true, for example, of Orwellian dictatorships that use international conflict to bolster their domestic power. Small increments of pain are not real pain to them. They enjoy wars of attrition, since these build up their domestic strength. They are truly alarmed only by threats to their hold on domestic power, including challenges to their instruments of social control (such as their armed forces), or by the threat of direct conquest.

During the Korean War, some U.S. policymakers favored the U.S. counteroffensive against North Korea for this reason. Merely thwarting the North's attack on the South, they argued, inflicted too little harm on the North to deter future aggressions.[152] Some Israelis have likewise suggested that Hafez

---

[151] On the Hawaii and Pearl Harbor deployments see Jonathan G. Utley, *Going to War with Japan, 1937–1941* (Knoxville: University of Tennessee Press, 1985), pp. 84, 163–65. On Japan's reaction to the oil embargo, Michael A. Barnhardt, *Japan Prepares for Total War: The Search for Economic Security, 1919–1941* (Ithaca: Cornell University Press, 1987), p. 239: it produced "what Washington hoped to avoid: a firm decision in Tokyo to proceed with the Southward Advance"; also p. 265. On false U.S. expectations that these tough policies would deter war see Utley, *Going to War with Japan*, pp. 156–57.

[152] In July 1950 the State Department's John Allison favored a counteroffensive against North Korea, arguing that "the aggressors should not go unpunished." With a U.S. offensive against the North, "notice would be served on the aggressor [i.e., the Soviet Union] elsewhere . . . that he cannot embark upon acts of aggression with the assurance that he takes only

Assad's Syrian regime highly values only its own survival, which depends on the Syrian army, which in turn can be threatened only by offense. Lesser threats cannot menace the regime with losses that really hurt.[153]

Such regimes are rare, however. Most governments lose legitimacy if they expend lives in warfare without gain; hence they respond to credible threats of denial or of punishment short of offensive action.

Conquest can reform an otherwise incorrigible aggressor state or leave it too weak to make trouble

Offensive strategies can enable the reform of regimes that cannot be tamed except by conquest. Such drastic means of reform obviously have less appeal in the nuclear age, since they could require nuclear war. But they sometimes worked in the past when status quo powers had the means to conquer the aggressor. Revolutionary France, Nazi Germany, and Imperial Japan were finally tamed by a conquest and occupation that uprooted warlike political elements and reshaped national values and perceptions. Such campaigns can bolster peace when nothing short of conquest will tame the aggressor.

This approach requires that occupying powers understand war's causes. The United States, Britain, and France squandered their 1918 victory over Germany because they misconstrued the causes of the war and hence failed to remove them. The Versailles peace is often wrongly criticized for harshness; in fact it failed because the Allies failed to root out warlike elements from German national institutions and perceptions. The 1945 peace was harsher, but Germany has since been much better behaved because allied policies were better designed.

States also might use offensive power to keep aggressors weak by periodically destroying their forces before they develop full strength. The Versailles Treaty was premised on allied enforcement of German disarmament, and many have argued that the allies could have prevented World War II by smashing German strength before it developed. Similarly, Israeli leaders

---

a limited risk—that of being driven back to the line from which the attack commenced." *Foreign Relations of the United States, 1950*, vol. 7, *Korea* (Washington, D.C.: U.S. Government Printing Office, 1976), p. 394. Allison strongly opposed settling the war at the 38th parallel, arguing that this would tell the aggressor "that all he had to fear from aggression was being compelled to start over again." Instead, a move north would "make clear once and for all that aggression does not pay . . . that he who takes the sword will perish by the sword." Peter Lowe, *The Origins of the Korean War* (London: Longman, 1986), p. 182.

[153] During the 1973 Arab-Israeli War, Moshe Dayan favored a counteroffensive against Syria because it could bring the Syrians "to realize that by launching war upon us, not only would they not gain the Golan Heights or defeat the Israeli Army, but their own armies would be routed and their capital . . . endangered." Donald Neff, *Warriors Against Israel* (Brattleboro, Vt.: Amana Books, 1988), p. 206. See also Ben-Horin and Posen, *Israel's Strategic Doctrine*, p. 13.

hoped that their victories in 1967 and 1982 would destroy Egyptian and Syrian military power for many years to come.

Such hopes have seldom been borne out, however. Willful states can seldom be kept from realizing their military potential for long. They can always find allies and external sources of arms. Even pariah states can find enough support (perhaps from other pariahs) to restore their national strength. The domestic political cost of repeated attacks is high for the status quo powers, weakening their will to act. Furthermore, just a few years of nonvigilance can be enough to let the disarmed state escape, as Germany rapidly escaped in the 1930s.

In short, offensive action is often recommended as a means of weakening aggressors, but it seldom proves practical.

Offense can end or limit war

Once begun, some wars continue until one side is decisively defeated, because the belligerent states' war aims grow and harden during the war. In such situations, even costly offensives can save lives by ending the bloodshed when compromise cannot. The United States had to invade far into Mexico during the Mexican War because the Mexican government would not concede even after its defeat was clear.[154] Some argue that the Allies could have ended World War I only by decisive victory over Germany, and the Allied offensives on the western front, despite their cost, were cheaper than any alternative policy. During the Korean War, Dean Acheson favored an offensive to destroy North Korea partly to avert the large cost of supporting South Korea in an indefinite military standoff against the North.[155] Responding to this U.S. offensive, China tried to expel U.S. forces from Korea and reunite the Korean peninsula in order to avert the large cost of supporting North Korea in a long military standoff with the South.[156]

Some observers also argue that disarming offensive actions are needed to limit wars between states armed with weapons of mass destruction. For example, during the Cold War some strategists argued that in wartime the United States should try to destroy Soviet nuclear forces as a war-limitation measure, since these forces would otherwise be used.

These arguments needs three qualifications. First, offensive operations can generate their own war-sustaining opposition by convincing others that

---

[154] T. Harry Williams, *The History of American Wars from 1745 to 1918* (New York: Knopf, 1981), pp. 176–77, 182–85. A Whig senator complained that "Mexico is an ugly enemy. She will not fight—and will not treat." Ibid., p. 176.

[155] In July 1950, quoted in Thomas J. Christensen, *Useful Adversaries: Grand Strategy, Domestic Mobilization, and Sino-American Conflict, 1947–1958* (Princeton: Princeton University Press, 1996), p. 152.

[156] Ibid., pp. 156, 165–66, 170.

one is a dangerous aggressor. The target state then fights harder and more allies join it, making the war harder to end. If so, offensive operations have offsetting effects that both shorten and lengthen war, and may lengthen it overall. Second, many wars never develop such mad momentum that offense is necessary to end them. In fact, most wars end in compromise without a decisive offensive by either side. Third, the threat of retaliation in kind may deter states from using weapons of mass destruction, which makes war limitation by offense unnecessary. The more these qualifications govern the situation, the more they render offensive strategies to limit warfare inappropriate.

CAUSES OF OFFENSE AND DEFENSE DOMINANCE

The feasibility of conquest is shaped by military, geographic, and domestic social and political factors, and by the nature of diplomacy. Discussions of the offense-defense balance often focus on military technology, but technology is only part of the picture.[157]

Military factors

Military technology, doctrine, force posture, and deployments all affect the military offense-defense balance.[158]

Technology and doctrine
Military technology can favor the aggressor or the defender. In past centuries, strong fortification techniques bolstered the defense, and strong methods of siege warfare strengthened the offense. Technologies that favored mass infantry warfare (for example, cheap iron, which allowed mass production of infantry weapons) strengthened the offense because large mass armies could bypass fortifications more easily, and because mass armies fostered more egalitarian polities that could raise loyal popular armies that would not melt away when sent on imperial expeditions. Technologies that favored chariot or cavalry warfare (for example, the stirrup) strengthened the defense because cavalry warfare required smaller forces that were

---

[157] Discussing the causes of offense- and defense-dominance are Jervis, "Cooperation," pp. 176, 194–99; and Charles L. Glaser and Chaim Kaufmann, "What is the Offense-Defense Balance and Can We Measure It?" *International Security* 22 (Spring 1998): 44–82 at 60–72.

[158] Four measures of the military offense-defense balance work well: the material superiority that an attacker needs to have a given probability of defeating a defender; the probability that an attacker's force can overcome a defender's force of equal cost; the relative cost that attackers and defenders must pay for forces that offset incremental improvements by the other; and the loss ratio when an attacker attacks a defending force of equal cost. All capture the relative military difficulty of conquest and defense.

more easily stopped by fortifications;[159] cavalry warfare also fostered hierarchic societies that could not raise armies that would remain loyal if sent on quests for empire.[160] In modern times, technology that gave defenders more lethal firepower (for example, the machine gun) or greater mobility (the railroad) strengthened the defense. When these technologies were neutralized by still newer technologies (motorized armor), the offense grew stronger.

Thus when fortresses and cavalries dominated in the late Middle Ages, the defense held the advantage. Cannons then made fortifications vulnerable and restored the strength of the offense. In the seventeenth and eighteenth centuries, new fortification techniques strengthened the defense. The mercenary armies of the age also remained tightly tied to logistical tails that kept them close to home: one historian writes that an eighteenth-century army "was like a diver in the sea, its movements strictly limited and tied by the long, slender communicating tube which gave it life."[161] Then revolutionary France's mass armies strengthened the offense because they had greater mobility. Their size let them sweep past border forts without leaving the bulk of their manpower behind for siege duty, and their more loyal troops could be trusted to forage without deserting, so they needed less logistical support. After the conservative restoration in France, Europe abandoned the *levée en masse* because it required, and fostered, popular government. The end of the *levée en masse* restored the power of the defense. That power waned somewhat as Europe democratized and large mass armies reappeared in the mid-nineteenth century.[162]

As 1914 approached, the defense gained a large and growing advantage from the combined effects of lethal small arms (accurate fast-firing rifles and machine guns), barbed wire, elaborate entrenchments, and railroads. Lethal small arms, barbed wire, and developed trenches gave defenders a large advantage at any point of attack. Railroads let defenders reinforce points of attack faster than invaders could, because defenders had full use of their own rail lines while attackers were often without rail transport, deprived by the difference in rail gages across states and by defenders who often destroyed rail lines as they retreated.

---

[159] Cavalry warfare was capital intensive, as it was usually waged by small forces of tax-supported specialists—knights in shining (and expensive) armor on expensive horses. Older infantry warfare was more manpower intensive and was usually waged by larger, less capitalized armies.

[160] On the effects of the stirrup on warfare and society in the Middle Ages, see Lynn White, Jr., *Medieval Technology and Social Change* (New York: Oxford University Press, 1964), pp. 1–38. On the general effect of military technology on social stratification, see Stanislav Andreski, *Military Organization and Society* (Berkeley: University of California Press, 1971), pp. 20–74.

[161] Harold Temperley, quoted in Geoffrey Blainey, *The Causes of War*, 3d ed. (New York: Free Press, 1988), p. 188.

[162] Large armies aid the offense only up to a point, however. Once armies grow so big that they can cover an entire frontier (as on the western front in World War I), their size aids the defense because offensive outflanking maneuvers against them become impossible.

During 1919–45 the power of the offense was restored by motorized armor and an offensive doctrine—blitzkrieg—for its employment. This combination overrode machine guns, trenches, railroads, and barbed wire. After 1945 thermonuclear weapons restored the power of the defense, this time giving it an overwhelming advantage.[163]

Technology and doctrine combined to define these tides of offense and defense. Sometimes technology overrode doctrine, as in 1914–18 and in the years since 1945 (when the superpowers embraced offensive doctrines but could not find offensive counters to the nuclear revolution). Sometimes doctrine shaped technology, as in 1939–45, when blitzkrieg doctrine fashioned armor technology into an offensive instrument.[164]

Military force posture, deployment, and wartime operations

States shape the military offense-defense balance by their military posture and force deployments. For example, Stalin eased attack for both himself and Hitler during 1939–41 by moving most of the Red Army out of strong defensive positions on Soviet territory and forward into newly seized territories in Poland, Bessarabia, Finland, and the Baltic States.[165] This left Soviet forces better positioned to attack Germany, and far easier for Germany to attack, as the early success of Hitler's 1941 invasion revealed. The United States eased offense for both itself and Japan in 1941 when it deployed its fleet forward to Pearl Harbor and bombers forward to the Philippines.[166] Egypt eased Israel's attack by its chaotic forward deployment of troops into poorly prepared Sinai positions in the crisis before the 1967 war.[167]

States also can change the offense-defense balance by their wartime military operations. Aggressive operations can corrode key enemy defenses, and reckless operations can expose one's own defenses. Thus the dangers of offense dominance can be conjured up by unthinking wartime policymakers. General Douglas MacArthur's imprudent rush to the Yalu River in 1950 created an offensive threat to China's core territory and, by exposing badly

---

[163] A synoptic history of the military offense-defense balance is Jack S. Levy, "The Offensive/Defensive Balance of Military Technology: A Theoretical and Historical Analysis," *International Studies Quarterly* 28 (June 1984): 219–38 at 230–34. Other discussions include Quester, *Offense and Defense*; and Andreski, *Military Organization and Society*, pp. 75–78. A detailed history is needed.

[164] Arguing that military doctrine can overcome technology is Jonathan Shimshoni, "Technology, Military Advantage, and World War I: A Case for Military Entrepreneurship," *International Security* 15 (Winter 1990/91): 187–215.

[165] Peter Calvocoressi and Guy Wint, *Total War: The Story of World War II* (New York: Pantheon Books, 1972), p. 168.

[166] Utley, *Going to War with Japan*, pp. 84, 163.

[167] Neff, *Warriors for Jerusalem*, p. 141, 168. During the same crisis Jordan eased attack for itself and Israel by dispersing its forces along the Israeli-Jordanian border, instead of concentrating further back in the hills. This blunder helped cause Jordan's quick collapse when Israel struck. David Kimche and Dan Bawley, *The Six-Day War* (New York: Stein and Day, 1971), p. 198.

deployed U.S. forces to attack, eased a Chinese offensive. During the Cold War, some likewise worried that NATO might inadvertently threaten the Soviet Union's strategic nuclear deterrent if it used aggressive means to defend NATO's Atlantic sea lanes during an East-West conventional war.[168]

Geography

Conquest is harder when geography insulates states from invasion or strangulation. Hence conquest is hindered when national borders coincide with oceans, lakes, mountains, wide rivers, dense jungles, trackless deserts, or other natural barriers that impede offensive movement or give defenders natural strong points. Human-made obstacles along borders, such as urban sprawl, can also serve as barriers to armored invasion. Conquest is hindered if foes are separated by wide buffer regions (for example, third states or demilitarized zones) that neither side can enter in peacetime. Conquest is hindered when national territories are mountainous or heavily forested and when populations live mainly in rural settings; guerrilla resistance to invaders is then more effective. Conquest is hindered when states are large and their critical war resources or industries lie far in their interior, where they cannot be quickly overrun. Conquest is hindered when states are invulnerable to economic strangulation: when they are self-sufficient in food, water, energy, and critical raw materials or when their trade routes cannot be severed by land or sea blockade.

The geography of Western Europe, with its mountain ranges and ocean moats, is less favorable to conquest than the exposed plains of Eastern Europe or the open terrain of the Middle East. Israel's geography is especially unfortunate: physically small, its frontiers have few obstacles and much of its industry and population lie on exposed frontiers. Israeli territory is not conducive to guerrilla resistance, and its economy is import dependent. Germany's borders are better but still relatively poor: its eastern frontier is open, its economy is import dependent, and its trade routes are vulnerable. Britain, France, and Italy have formidable frontier barriers that make them relatively defensible. The vast size of the United States, its ocean-moat frontiers, and its independent economy make it highly defensible.

Social and political order

Popular regimes are generally better at both conquest and self-defense than are unpopular regimes, but these effects are not equal. Conquest is probably harder among popular than unpopular regimes today, but in past centuries the reverse was likely true.

---

[168] Posen, *Inadvertent Escalation*, pp. 129–58. On a related danger, see ibid., pp. 28–67.

Popular governments can raise large, loyal armies that can bypass others' border forts and can operate far from home with less logistical support. This gives popular regimes great offensive power. Popular regimes can organize their citizens for guerrilla resistance, making them hard to conquer. Citizen-defense guerrilla strategies are viable for modern Switzerland or China, but not for modern Guatemala or ancient Sparta, because such unpopular governments cannot arm their people without risking revolution. The citizens of unpopular oligarchies may also actively assist advancing invaders. This gives attackers more penetrating power and makes early losses less reversible. For example, Sparta feared that an invading army would gain strength once it entered Spartan territory because slaves and dissident tribes would desert to the enemy.[169]

Unpopular regimes are more vulnerable to subversion or revolution inspired from abroad. Subversion is a form of offense, and it affects international relations in the same way as offensive military capabilities. Frail regimes are more frightened of unfriendly neighbors and are therefore more determined to impose congenial regimes on neighboring states. Both the French revolutionary regime and the oligarchic Austrian regime feared that the other side might subvert them in 1792; both sides consequently became more aggressive.[170] After the Russian revolution, similar fears fueled Soviet-Western conflict, as each side feared subversion by the other.

On balance, popularity of regime probably aided offense before roughly 1800 but aided defense since then. The reversal stems from the appearance of cheap mass-produced weapons useful for guerrilla war—assault rifles and machine guns, light mortars, and mines. The small arms of early times (sword and shield, pike and arquebus, and heavy slow-firing muskets) were poorly adapted for guerrilla resistance. Guerrilla warfare has burgeoned since 1800 partly because the availability of cheap small arms has eased the hit-and-run harassment that characterize guerrilla operations. The defensive power of popular regimes has risen in step with this increase in guerrilla warfare.

Diplomatic factors

Three types of diplomatic phenomena strengthen the defense: collective security systems, defensive alliances, and balancing behavior by neutral states. All three impede conquest by adding allies to the defending side.

States in a collective security system (for example, the League of Nations)

---

[169] Ste. Croix, *Peloponnesian War*, pp. 89–94. Likewise Hannibal hoped to defeat Rome by recruiting dissident tribes as he penetrated the Italian peninsula. See Errington, *Dawn of Empire*, pp. 62–64.

[170] Stephen M. Walt, *Revolution and War* (Ithaca: Cornell University Press, 1996), pp. 123–24; Blanning, *Origins*, pp. 76, 85–86, 99–101, 111.

promise mutual aid against aggression by any system member. Such aggressors will face large defending coalitions if the system operates.[171]

States in a defensive alliance promise mutual aid against outside aggressors, leaving such aggressors outnumbered by resisting defenders. For example, during 1879–87 Bismarck wove a network of defensive alliances that discouraged aggression and helped preserve peace throughout Central and Eastern Europe.[172]

Neutral states act as balancers when they join the weaker of two competing coalitions to restore balance between them. Aggression is self-limiting when neutrals balance, because aggressors generate more opposition as they expand. Britain and the United States have traditionally played the role of balancers to Europe, providing a counterweight to potential continental hegemons.

Balancing behavior is more selective than defensive alliance. Balancers balance to avert regional hegemony; hence pure balancers oppose expansion only by potential regional hegemons. Smaller states are left free to aggress. But balancing does contain hegemons and leaves their potential victims more secure. Conversely, if states bandwagon—that is, join the stronger coalition against the weaker one—conquest is easier because aggressors win more allies as they seize more resources.[173]

Diplomatic arrangements have had a large influence on the offense-defense balance in modern Europe, and shifts in diplomatic arrangements have produced large shifts in the overall offense-defense balance. Collective security was never effective, but defensive alliances came and went, erecting barriers to conquest when they appeared. Balancing behavior rose and fell as the power and activism of the two traditional offshore balancers, Britain and the United States, waxed and waned. When either was strong and willing to intervene against aspiring continental hegemons, conquest on the continent was difficult. To succeed, a hegemon had to defeat both its continental victims and the offshore power. But when Britain and the United

---

[171] An introduction to collective security is Inis L. Claude, Jr., *Swords into Plowshares: The Problems and Progress of International Organizations*, 4th ed. (New York: Random House, 1971), pp. 411–33. An advocacy of collective security is Charles A. Kupchan and Clifford A. Kupchan, "Concerts, Collective Security, and the Future of Europe," *International Security* 16 (Summer 1991): 114–63. A criticism is Richard K. Betts, "Systems for Peace or Causes of War? Collective Security, Arms Control, and the New Europe," *International Security* 17 (Summer 1992): 5–43.

[172] In principle, a security organization could target both aggressive organization members and aggressive outsiders. A hybrid collective-security-cum-defensive-alliance that did this would offer members the most protection.

[173] On balancing, bandwagoning, and other theories of alliances, see Stephen M. Walt, *The Origins of Alliances* (Ithaca: Cornell University Press, 1987). Historians have often suggested that a "breakdown in the balance of power" caused a certain war. They usually mean—and should recast their claim to say—that states failed to engage in balancing behavior, which made aggression easier, causing war. War occurs not when the balance of power breaks down, but when balancers fail to balance, leaving aggressors unchecked, as in the late 1930s.

States were weak or isolationist, continental powers could expand against less resistance, leaving all states less secure.

Predictions and Tests of Offense-Defense Theory

What predictions can be inferred from offense-defense theory? How can they be tested, and what do tests show? How much history does offense-defense theory explain?

Offense-defense theory makes both prime predictions and explanatory predictions. As noted in Chapter 2, a theory's prime predictions are inferred from its prime hypothesis ("war is more likely when conquest is easy"). Tests of offense-defense theory's prime predictions shed light on whether offense dominance cause war.

Offense-defense theory's explanatory predictions are inferred from the hypotheses that comprise its eleven explanations. Tests of these predictions shed light on both whether and how offense dominance causes war.

Prime predictions

Three prime predictions of offense-defense theory are tested here.

1. War will be more common in periods when conquest is easy, or is believed easy, than in other periods.
2. States that have, or believe they have, large offensive opportunities or defensive vulnerabilities will initiate and fight more wars than other states.
3. A given state will initiate and fight more wars in periods when it has, or believes it has, larger offensive opportunities and defensive vulnerabilities.

These predictions are tested below in three case studies: Europe since 1789 (treated as a single regional case study), ancient China during the Spring and Autumn and the Warring States periods, and the United States since 1789. I selected these cases because the offense-defense balance, or the perception of it, varies sharply across time in all three, creating a good setting for tests that contrast different periods in the same case; because the United States is very secure relative to other states, making it fruitful to compare U.S. conduct with the conduct of average states; and because two of these cases are well recorded (Europe and the United States).

The case of Europe since 1789 allows tests of predictions 1 and 2.[174] We

---

[174] In principle, prediction 3 could also be tested with this case. But this would require tracing and describing trends in each individual state's sense of opportunity and vulnerability over time—a large task that would fill many pages.

can make crude indices of Europe's actual and perceived offense-defense balances over the past two centuries and match them with the incidence of war. (See Table 3.) Offense-defense theory predicts more war when conquest is easy or is believed easy. We can also crudely estimate the offensive opportunities and defensive vulnerabilities of individual powers—for example, since 1789 Prussia-Germany has been more vulnerable and has had more offensive opportunity than Spain, Italy, Britain, or the United States—and we can match these estimates with states' rates of war involvement and initiation. Offense-defense theory predicts that states with more defensive vulnerability and offensive opportunity will be more warlike.

The ancient Chinese case allows a test of prediction 1. The offense-defense balance shifted markedly toward the offense during China's Spring and Autumn period and its Warring States period. Offense-defense theory predicts a parallel rise in the incidence of warfare during these periods.

The U.S. case allows testing of predictions 2 and 3. The United States is less vulnerable to foreign military threats than are other great powers. Offense-defense theory therefore predicts that the United States should start and fight fewer wars. Americans have also felt more vulnerable to foreign military threats in some eras than in others. The rates of U.S. war involvement and initiation should co-vary with this sense of vulnerability.

Explanatory predictions

Offense-defense theory posits that offense dominance leads to war through the war-causing action of its eleven intervening phenomena, H5A–H5K: opportunistic expansionism; defensive expansionism; fierce resistance to others' expansion; first-move advantage; windows of opportunity and vulnerability; faits accomplis and belligerent reactions to them; less negotiation and agreement; policies of secrecy; rapid and belligerent reactions to others' blunders that make them irreversible; intense arms racing; and policies that ease conquest, such as offensive force postures and offensive alliances. If offense-defense theory is valid, these intervening phenomena should correlate with the offense-defense balance and with perceptions of it. Also, elites should testify that they adopted policies that embodied these phenomena because they believed conquest was easy, or because they were responding to behavior by others that was driven by this belief.

Accordingly, three explanatory predictions are tested in this and the next chapter:

4. Intervening phenomena H5A–H5K will be more abundant in periods of real or perceived offense dominance than in other periods.
5. States that have, or believe they have, large offensive opportunities or defensive vulnerabilities will more often adopt policies that embody intervening phe-

nomena H5A–H5F and H5H–H5K—that is, all intervening phenomena except "less negotiation and agreement" (H5G)—than will other states. ("Less negotiation and agreement" is an exception because it reflects states' reactions to other states' reaction to offense dominance, hence it should be diffused across both vulnerable and invulnerable states, and across both offense-capable and offense-incapable states.)[175]

In other words, comparisons across time (prediction 4) and comparisons across states (prediction 5) should find that intervening phenomena H5A–H5K correlate with real and perceived offense dominance.

6. Evidence should indicate that elites that adopted policies that embodied intervening phenomena H5A–H5K did so because they believed that the offense dominated. For example, if offense dominance causes opportunistic expansionism (as posited in explanation H5A), elites who believe offense is dominant should be observed arguing that empire should be seized because it could be taken easily. If offense dominance causes defensive expansionism (explanation H5B), elites should argue that "we must expand because we are insecure." And so forth.[176]

Tests of offense-defense theory

The case of Europe in the era of the cult of the offensive, 1890–1914, is a good setting for testing all three predictions. Belief in the power of the offense increased during this era, rising to extreme levels as 1914 approached. Hence intervening phenomena H5A–H5K should be present in above-normal amounts in pre-1914 Europe. These phenomena should be most clearly embodied in the policies of those European states that had (or per-

---

[175] Insecure states more often break their word, causing other states to mistrust their promises. Insecure states are also more secretive, making other states leery of forging agreements with them because their compliance with the agreement is harder to verify. Because these behaviors are reactions to others' reactions to offense dominance, their location will be diffuse, or perhaps even focused in the more secure states.

[176] These four explanatory predictions are inferred from the left side of offense-defense theory—that is, from the hypotheses that frame the claim that offense dominance causes intervening phenomena H5A–H5K (see Diagram 3). Predictions could also be inferred from the hypotheses that comprise the right side of the theory, and frame the claim that intervening phenomena H5A–H5K cause war. For example, we could infer that (7) warfare will be more common in eras and regions where intervening phenomena H5A–H5K are more prevalent, (8) states that embrace policies that embody phenomena H5A–H5K will be involved in more wars and will initiate more wars than other states, and (9) policymakers should testify that they opted for war in response to conditions that phenomena H5A–H5K created. I leave such right-side predictions untested here because the effects of phenomena H5A–H5K are less debated than their causes; most agree that they cause trouble. For elaboration see Chapter 7, note 26.

ceived they had) the largest offensive opportunities and defensive vulnerabilities. European elites should say that they embraced these policies because they thought conquest was easy or because they were responding to acts by others taken under the influence of this belief. I explore this case in Chapter 7.

The case of Europe from 1789 to the 1990s sheds a little light on predictions 4 and 5. Since we have information on only two of offense-defense theory's eleven intervening phenomena for the whole period—opportunistic and defensive expansionism—we can test only the two explanations that include them (H5A and H5B). To do this we will ask if expansionism correlates with periods of real or perceived offense dominance and if states that were (or believed they were) less secure and more able to aggress were more expansionist.

The case of the United States since 1789 also allows a more complete test of prediction 5.

Europe, 1789–1990s

A composite measure of the offense-defense balance in Europe since 1789 can be fashioned by blending the histories of Europe's military and diplomatic offense-defense balances.[177] In sum, the offense-defense balance went through six phases comprising three up-and-down oscillations after 1789. Conquest was never easy in an absolute sense during these two centuries, but it was markedly easier from 1789 to 1815, from 1856 to 1871, and from the 1930s to 1945 than it was from 1815 to 1856, from 1871 to the 1920s, and from 1945 to the 1990s.

Elite perceptions of the offense-defense balance parallel these oscillations quite closely, but not exactly. Elites chronically exaggerated the power of the offense, but did so far more in some periods than in others. Most important, they much exaggerated the power of the offense from 1890 to 1918. The defense was very strong in those years, but elites thought it was very weak.

Tides of expansionism and war correlate loosely with the offense-defense balance during this period, and tightly with the perceived offense-defense balance. Expansionism and war were more common when conquest was

---

[177] My composite index represents my own "author's estimates" based on sources noted above and below. I judged the actual and perceived Europe-wide offense-defense balances by asking: (1) Did military technology, force posture, and doctrine favor the offense or the defense? Did elites and publics believe these factors favored the offense or the defense? (2) Did geography and the domestic social and political order of states favor the offense of the defense? Did elites and publics believe they favored the offense or defense? (3) How numerous and powerful were balancer states, and how strongly did they balance? Did elites believe other states would balance or bandwagon? (4) Did defensive alliances form, and did they operate effectively? Did elites believe they operated effectively? I gave these factors the same rough relative weight they receive in standard historical accounts.

easy than when it was difficult, and were far more common when conquest was believed to be easy than when it was believed difficult. Moreover, states that believed they faced large offensive opportunities and defensive vulner-abilities—especially Prussia-Germany—were the largest troublemakers. They were more expansionist, they were involved in more wars, and they started more wars than other states.

1789–1815. The period after 1789 saw immense interstate violence in Europe, fueled by an extreme expansionism in France and a milder expansion-ism in Prussia.[178] This was also a period when the offense was strong and was believed even stronger. Offense was strong militarily because France adopted the popular mass army (enabled by the popularity of the French revolutionary government).[179] Moreover, European elites widely exagger-ated one another's vulnerability to conquest: at the outset of the War of 1792 all three belligerents (France, Austria, and Prussia) thought their opponents were on the verge of collapse and could be quickly crushed.[180] Defense-enhancing diplomacy was sluggish: Britain, Europe's traditional balancer, issued a formal declaration of neutrality and stood by indifferently during the crisis that produced the War of 1792.[181] Moreover, French leaders under-estimated the power of defense-enhancing diplomacy because they widely believed that other states would bandwagon with French threats instead of balancing against them.[182] In short, military factors helped the offense, and this help was further exaggerated; political factors did little to help defend-ers, and this help was underestimated.

1815–1856. After 1815 expansionism and war abated in Europe for several decades. During this calm, both arms and diplomacy favored defenders.

[178] On Prussia's expansionism, see Blanning, *Origins*, pp. 72–82. On French expansionism see ibid, passim.

[179] A discussion of the military offense-defense balance in this era is Quester, *Offense and Defense*, pp. 66–72.

[180] Blanning, *Origins*, p. 116. Austrian and Prussian leaders were assured that revolution-ary France could be quickly smashed. Ibid., p. 114. Meanwhile, French revolutionaries wrongly expected a pro-French revolutionary uprising of the oppressed peoples of feudal Europe. Ibid., p. 136; R. R. Palmer, *The World of the French Revolution* (New York: Harper & Row, 1971), p. 95; and George Rudé, *Revolutionary Europe, 1783–1815* (Glasgow: Fontana/ Collins, 1964), p. 209. Austria and Britain also feared French offensive capabilities, in the form of revolutionary contagion. Blanning, *Origins*, pp. 85–86 on Austria; 145–46 on Britain.

[181] Blanning, *Origins*, pp. 131–35.

[182] French expansionists of the 1790s thought they could shatter the anti-French coalition by inflicting military defeats on its members. Steven T. Ross, *European Diplomatic History 1789–1815* (Garden City, N.Y.: Anchor Doubleday, 1969), p. 186. Later, Napoleon thought he could compel Britain to make peace by establishing French continental dominion, proclaim-ing after the Peace of Amiens, "with Europe in its present state, England cannot reasonably make war on us unaided." Geoffrey Bruun, *Europe and the French Imperium, 1799–1814* (1938; New York: Harper & Row, 1963), p. 118. See also Blanning, *Origins*, pp. 109.

Table 3. Offense-defense balance among great powers, 1700s–present

Era	(1) Military factors factored:	(2) Military factors were thought to favor:	(3) Diplomatic factors favored:	(4) Diplomatic factors were thought to favor:	(5) Together, military and diplomatic factors favored:	(6) Military and diplomatic factors were both thought to favor:	(7) Amount of warfare among great powers:	(8) Amount of expansionism amont great powers:
Pre-1789	Defs.	Defs.	Med.	Med.	Med.	Med.	Medium	Medium
1789–1815	Aggrs.	Aggrs.	Med.	Aggrs.	Aggrs.	Aggrs.*	High	High
1815–1856	Defs.	Defs.	Defs.	Defs.	Defs.	Defs.	Low	Low
1856–1871	Med.	Med.	Aggrs.	Aggrs.	Aggrs.	Aggrs.*	Medium	Medium
1871–1890	Defs.	Med.	Defs.	Defs.	Defs.	Defs.	Low	Medium
1890–1918	Defs.	Aggrs.	Aggrs.	Aggrs.	Aggrs.	Aggrs.	High	High
1919–1945	Aggrs.	Mixed†	Aggrs.	Aggrs.‡	Aggrs.	Aggrs.§	High	High
1945–1990s	Defs.	Med.	Defs.	Defs.	Defs.	Defs.*	Low	Medium

NOTE: The perceptions entries are an average of the perceptions of the great power elites. In some cases the perceptions of these elites varied sharply across states, for example, perceptions of military realities in the 1930s.

Aggrs.: the factor favors aggressors.

Defs.: the factor favors defenders.

Med.: a medium value: things are somewhere in between, cut both ways.

Mixed: some national elites saw defense dominance, some saw offense dominance.

*Elites exaggerated the strength of the offense during 1789–1815, 1871–90, and 1945–90s, but not by enough to give the realities and perceptions of the offense-defense balance different scores.

†Things varied across states. The German elite recognized the military power of the offensive in the late 1930s; the elites of other great powers thought the defense was dominant.

‡Things varied across states. The German elite (above all Hitler) exaggerated the considerable actual diplomatic weakness of the defense; the elites of other great powers recognized this weakness but did not overstate it. These beliefs average to a perception of substantial diplomatic offense dominance.

§When we aggregate perceptions of the offense-defense balance, the errors of Germany and the other powers cancel each other out. Germany's exaggeration of the diplomatic power of the offense offsets other powers' exaggeration of the military power of the defense, leaving an aggregate perception fairly close to the offense-dominant reality.

Mass armies disappeared.[183] Britain was in a strong-and-active phase. It loomed over the continent, willing and able to thwart any reach for hegemony. The British economy was Europe's strongest, the British navy was almost unopposed from 1805 until the French naval buildup of the 1840s, and Britain often intervened to preserve the continental balance of power. Continental powers expected Britain to maintain the balance, and they widely thought British strength could not be overridden.

This defense-dominant arrangement began weakening before the Crimean War (1853–56). When that war began, military factors still favored defenders, but elites underestimated the power of the defense. Britain and France launched their 1854 Crimean offensive in false expectation of quick and easy victory.[184] In general, diplomatic factors favored defenders—Britain still balanced actively—but during the prewar crisis in 1853 diplomacy favored the offense because Britain and France blundered by giving Turkey unconditional backing that amounted to an offensive alliance. This support encouraged the Turkish aggressions that sparked the war.[185]

1856–1871. After the Crimean War, barriers to conquest fell further. Changes in the military realm cut both ways. Mass armies were appearing (bolstering the offense), but small arms were growing more lethal and railroads were expanding (bolstering the defense). In the diplomatic realm, the power of defenders fell dramatically because defense-enhancing diplomacy largely broke down. Most important, Britain entered an isolationist phase that lasted into the 1870s, and Russia lost interest in maintaining the balance among the Western powers.[186] This removed two outlying balancers from the continental balance-of-power game,[187] leaving Central and Western European aggressors free to conquer without outside opposition. Napoleon III, Bismarck, and their allies seized this opportunity to launch four wars of opportunistic expansion in 1859, 1864, 1866, and 1870. But defense-enhancing diplomacy had not disappeared completely, and it helped keep these wars short and limited.

---

[183] On the post-1815 restoration of pre-Napoleonic warfare, see Quester, *Offense and Defense*, pp. 73–74; and Michael Howard, *War in European History* (London: Oxford University Press, 1976), pp. 94–95.

[184] Smoke, *War*, p. 191.

[185] Smoke, *War*, pp. 167, 179–81, 185; Richard Smoke, "The Crimean War," in George, *Avoiding War*, pp. 36–61 at 48–49, 52.

[186] After the Crimean War, Russia focused on overturning the harsh Crimean War settlement that Britain had imposed upon it. Overthrowing that settlement became Russia's chief aim in European diplomacy, superseding its interest in preserving order to its west. M. S. Anderson, *The Eastern Question, 1774–1923* (London: Macmillan, 1966), pp. 144–46.

[187] Osgood and Tucker, *Force, Order, and Justice*, pp. 80–81; see also W. E. Mosse, *The European Powers and the German Question, 1848–71* (New York: Octagon, 1969).

In 1859 British and Russian neutrality gave France and Sardinia a free hand, which they used to seize Lombardy from Austria.[188] In 1864 British, Russian, and French neutrality allowed Prussia and Austria a free hand to seize Schleswig-Holstein from Denmark.[189] In 1866, British, French, and Russian neutrality gave Prussia carte blanche against Austria, which Prussia used to smash Austria and consolidate its control of North Germany.[190] Even after war broke out, major fighting proceeded for weeks before any outside state even threatened intervention.[191] As A. J. P. Taylor notes, Bismarck's 1866 diplomatic opportunity—a wide-open field for unopposed expansion—was "unique in recent history."[192]

In 1870 Bismarck ensured the neutrality of the other European powers by shifting responsibility for the war to France and convincing Europe that the war stemmed from French expansionism.[193] As a result, Prussia again had a free hand to pursue its expansionist aims—and used it to smash France, seize Alsace-Lorraine, and consolidate control over South Germany.[194]

1871–1890. After the Franco-Prussian War, Europe again calmed down for some twenty years. The European powers pursued colonial expansion in Africa and Asia, but no European power harbored large expansionist aims against its peers, and no major wars erupted.

During these calm years conquest was difficult in Europe, due to Bismarck's new diplomacy and Britain's renewed activism. In the military area, the cult of the offensive had not yet taken hold. In diplomacy, Bismarck wove

[188] A. J. P. Taylor, *The Struggle for Mastery in Europe, 1848–1918* (New York: Oxford University Press, 1954), pp. 108, 110.

[189] Taylor, *Struggle for Mastery*, pp. 146–54. Britain would have backed Denmark had it found a continental ally but none was available. Ibid., pp. 146–48.

[190] Smoke, *War*, pp. 85–92. Britain remained in a semi-isolationist mood in 1866, and Napoleon III thought France would profit from the long, mutually debilitating Austro-Prussian war he expected. Like the Soviets in 1939, Napoleon underestimated the danger of a quick, lopsided victory by either side. Ibid., pp. 87–90.

[191] Smoke, *War*, p. 86.

[192] Taylor, *Struggle for Mastery*, p. 156. Moreover, Bismarck stopped the 1866 war partly because he feared French or Russian intervention if Prussia fought on too long or conquered too much. Smoke, *War*, pp. 101–2. Thus lack of defense-enhancing diplomacy helped cause the war while Prussian fear of such diplomacy shortened and limited the war.

[193] William Carr, *The Origins of the Wars of German Unification* (London: Longman, 1991), p. 202; Michael Howard, *The Franco-Prussian War: The German Invasion of France, 1870–1871* (New York: Granada, 1961), p. 57. Austria also stayed neutral because Hungarian Magyar influence was growing inside the Dual Monarchy, and the Magyars felt that the more Austria was pushed out of Germany the stronger the position of the Magyars within it would be. R. R. Palmer and Joel Colton, *A History of the Modern World*, 4th ed. (New York: Alfred A. Knopf, 1971), p. 574.

[194] On Prussia's free hand, see Smoke, *War*, pp. 133–36; Norman Rich, *The Age of Nationalism and Reform, 1850–1890*, 2d ed. (New York: Norton, 1977), p. 140; W. E. Mosse, *The European Powers and the German Question, 1848–71* (New York: Octagon, 1969), pp. 291, 295.

a web of defensive alliances that deterred aggressors and calmed status quo powers after 1879.[195] British power waned slightly, but this was offset by the recovery of Britain's will to play the balancer. The "war-in-sight" crisis of 1875 illustrates the change: Britain and Russia together deterred a renewed German attack on France by warning that they would not allow a repeat of 1870–71.[196]

1890–1919. The years after 1890 saw a marked rise in expansionism in Europe, as detailed below in Chapter 7. Germany embraced wide imperial aims in Europe and Africa, Austria sought a wider sphere of influence in the Balkans, and Serbia sought to expand against Austria. Expansionism was more muted in Russia and France, but not wholly absent. This expansionism primed Europe to erupt in war in 1914.

During these years military conditions increasingly favored defenders, but elites mistakenly believed the opposite. Diplomatic factors swung toward aggressors, and elites believed that these factors favored aggressors even more than they did.

Europe's militaries were seized by the cult of the offensive. All the European powers adopted offensive military doctrines, culminating with France's adoption of the highly offensive Plan 17 in 1913 and with Russia's adoption of the similarly offensive Plan 20 in 1913–14. More important, militaries persuaded civilian leaders and publics that the offense dominated and conquest was easy. As a result, elites and publics widely believed that a decisive offensive would quickly win the next war.

Bismarck's defensive alliances withered or evolved into defensive-and-offensive alliances after he left office in 1890, largely because the cult of the offensive made defensive alliances hard to maintain. Pacts conditioned on defensive conduct became hard to enforce because states defended by attacking, and states shrank from demanding defensive conduct of allies they felt less able to lose. For example, Britain and France felt unable to enforce defensive conduct on their Russian ally because Russia defended by attacking, and because they could not afford to see it defeated. Elites also thought that aggressors could overrun their victims before allies could intervene to save them, making defensive alliances seem less effective. Specifically, Brit-

---

[195] Bismarck formed defensive alliances with Austria, Italy, and Rumania, and more limited defensive accord with Russia—specifically, a reciprocal agreement not to join a war against the other unless the other attacked France (in the German case) or Austria (in the Russian case). Synopses include Rich, *Age of Nationalism and Reform*, pp. 233–40, 244–50; Paul Kennedy, *The Rise and Fall of the Great Powers: Economic Change and Military Conflict from 1500 to 2000* (New York: Random House, 1987), pp. 249–50; and Osgood and Tucker, *Force, Order, and Justice*, pp. 80–81. A longer account is Taylor, *Struggle for Mastery*, pp. 258–80, 316–19.

[196] Geiss, *German Foreign Policy*, p. 28.

ain seemed less able to save France before Germany overran it, leading Germans to discount British power. Thus conquest seemed politically easier because it seemed militarily easier. Germans also expected to quickly conquer in Europe any resources they needed, leading them to discount the threat of blockade by the Royal Navy. Lastly, German leaders subscribed to a bandwagon theory of diplomacy, which led them to underestimate other states' resistance to German expansion. Overall, perceptions of offense dominance reached an all-time high in the years before 1914.

1919–1945. The interwar years were a mixed situation, but, overall, barriers to conquest were weak by 1939, and the German elite believed they were even weaker than in fact they were. Germany also pursued vast expansionist aims, triggering World War II in the process.

Military doctrine and technology gave the defense the advantage until the late 1930s, when German blitzkrieg doctrine combined armor and infantry in an effective offensive combination. This offensive innovation was unrecognized outside Germany and doubted by many within, but it found a firm believer in the man who counted most, Adolf Hitler. His faith in blitzkrieg reflected his faith in the offense as a general principle, a belief that expressed the international social Darwinism he imbibed in his youth.[197]

More important, the workings of interwar diplomacy opened a vast political opportunity for Nazi expansion. The League of Nations collective security system quickly broke down. British power declined further, and Britain fell into a deep isolationism that left it unwilling to commit this declining power to curb continental aggressors.[198] The United States also with-

---

[197] Hitler often echoed international social Darwinist slogans on the short, precarious lives of states, for example, "Politics is in truth the execution of a nation's struggle for existence," and "Germany will either be a world power or there will be no Germany." Quoted in Bell, *Origins of the Second World War*, p. 81; and in Adamthwaite, *Making of the Second World War*, p. 119.

Hitler's faith in the offensive differed from that of the pre-1914 cultists of the offensive in three ways. First, he saw offensive capabilities arising from a long search for offensive methods, not from permanent properties of war. Germany would discover offensive answers only after a long effort. In contrast, the pre-1914 cultists thought offense inherently easier than defense. There was no need to make it superior, because it already was. Second, Hitler's offensive optimism was based on racism and social prejudice, as well as on assessment of military factors. Specifically, his contempt for Slavs and Jews led him to expect the Soviets would quickly collapse under German attack. Third, Hitler's fears for German security focused on fear of conquest by economic strangulation, not conquest by French or Soviet blitzkrieg. He thought German security was precarious, but for reasons rooted more in the political economy of war than in the nature of doctrine or weaponry.

These differences aside, the logical implications of Hitler's offensive cult were the same as those of the pre-1914 cult. He exaggerated both German insecurity and the feasibility of imperial solutions to redress it.

[198] Chamberlain said in 1937 that Britain would not send another large ground force to the continent, as it had in 1914–18. Bell, *Origins of the Second World War*, p. 177. Britain had only

drew into isolation, removing the counterweight that checked Germany in 1918.[199] The breakup of Austria-Hungary in 1918 created a new diplomatic constellation that further eased German expansion. Austria-Hungary would have balanced against German expansion, but its smaller successor states tended to bandwagon.[200] This let Hitler extend German influence into southeast Europe by intimidation and subversion.

The Soviet Union and the Western powers failed to cooperate against Hitler.[201] Ideological hostility divided them. Britain also feared that a defensive alliance against Hitler would arouse German fears of allied encirclement and spur German aggressiveness. This chilled British enthusiasm for an Anglo-French-Soviet alliance.[202]

Hitler exaggerated the already large advantage that diplomacy gave the offense because he thought bandwagoning prevailed over balancing in international affairs. This false faith led him to vastly underestimate other countries' resistance to his aggressions. Before the war, he failed to foresee that Britain and France would come to Poland's rescue, assuring his generals that "the West will not intervene" to defend Poland.[203] Once the war began, he believed Germany could intimidate Britain into seeking alliance with Germany after Germany crushed France—or, he later held, after Germany smashed the Soviet Union.[204] He thought the United States could be cowed into staying neutral by the 1940 German-Japanese alliance. (The alliance had the opposite effect, spurring U.S. intervention.)[205] In short, Hitler's false theories of diplomacy made three of his most dangerous opponents shrink to insignificance in his mind.

These realities and beliefs faced Hitler with temptations like those facing

---

two divisions available to send to the continent during the 1938 Munich crisis, and the four-division force it actually sent in 1939 was smaller and less well trained than its small expeditionary force of 1914. These four divisions were a drop in the bucket relative to the 84 French and 103 German divisions then deployed. Ibid., p. 175.

[199] The United States also proclaimed this isolationism in four neutrality laws passed during 1935–39, giving Hitler a clear if misleading signal of U.S. indifference to his aggression. On these laws a synopsis is Thomas A. Bailey, *A Diplomatic History of the American People*, 9th ed. (Englewood Cliffs, N.J.: Prentice-Hall, 1974), pp. 701–2, 715.

[200] Explaining why weaker states are more prone to bandwagon than stronger states is Walt, *Origins of Alliances*, pp. 29–30.

[201] Bell, *Origins of the Second World War*, pp. 172, 224, 260; and Adamthwaite, *Making of the Second World War*, pp. 60, 69. This failure greatly eased Hitler's aggressions, since geography made Britain's 1939 guarantees to Poland and Rumania unenforceable without a Soviet alliance. Ibid., pp. 86, 91.

[202] Raymond J. Sontag, *A Broken World 1919–1939* (New York: Harper and Row, 1971), p. 361.

[203] On August 22, 1939, quoted in Noakes and Pridham, *Nazism*, 2:741.

[204] See Jack Snyder, *Myths of Empire: Domestic Politics and International Ambition* (Ithaca: Cornell University Press, 1991), p. 94.

[205] Noakes and Pridham, *Nazism*, 2:797. Some German leaders also hoped that Germany could win decisively in Europe before the United States could bring its power to bear. See, for example, Admiral Raeder in September, 1940, in ibid., 2:794.

Bismarck in 1866 and 1870. Hitler thought he could conquer his victims seriatim. He also thought his conquests would arouse little countervailing opposition from distant neutral powers. As a result he thought he faced a wide opportunity for aggression.

Unlike 1914, the late 1930s were not a pure case of perceived offense dominance. Hitler thought the offense strong and even exaggerated its strength, but other powers—the Soviet Union, Britain, and France—underestimated its strength. Their perceptions of defense dominance relaxed their urge to jump the gun at early signs of threat, as Russia had in 1914. This made things safer. But their perceptions also relaxed their will to balance Germany, because they found German expansion less frightening. This weakened the coalition against Hitler and left him wide running room.[206] Thus the status quo powers' perceptions of defense dominance created real offensive opportunities for Germany.

1945–1990s. After 1945 an uneasy peace returned to Europe. The Soviet Union harbored expansionist aims but pursued them cautiously, never pushing things to the point of war. Germany and Italy abandoned their previous expansionism.

Meanwhile, two changes had swung the European offense-defense balance back toward the defense. First, the end of American isolationism transformed European political affairs. The United States replaced Britain as continental balancer, bringing far more power to bear in Europe than Britain ever had. As a result, Europe in the years after 1945 was unusually defense-dominant from a diplomatic standpoint.

Second, the nuclear revolution gave defenders a large military advantage—so large that conquest among great powers became virtually impossible. Conquest now required a nuclear first-strike capability (the capacity to launch a nuclear strike that leaves the defender unable to inflict unacceptable damage in retaliation). Defenders could secure themselves merely by maintaining a second-strike capability (the capacity to inflict unacceptable damage on the attacker's society after absorbing an all-out surprise attack). The characteristics of nuclear weapons—their vast power, small size, light

---

[206] Would the risk of war have fallen had all powers believed the offense was dominant in the late 1930s? This seems unlikely. The status quo powers would have balanced harder against Hitler, offering him more discouragement, but they also would have been jumpier, making early crises more dangerous. One of these crises—Hitler's remilitarization of the Rhineland, the Spanish civil war, or the German seizure of Austria or Czechoslovakia—probably would have served as the "Sarajevo" for World War II, with the Allies moving first as Russia did in 1914.

The implication is that war is more likely if any state believes that conquest is easy. If all states think conquest is easy, war will erupt from a confrontation between two belligerent alliances, as in 1914. If only one state thinks conquest is easy, war will erupt when that state turns expansionist and others fail to combine to contain it, as in 1939.

weight, and low cost—ensured that a first-strike capability would be very hard to reach, while a second-strike capability could be sustained at little cost. As a result, the great powers became essentially unconquerable, and even lesser powers could now stand against far stronger enemies. Overall, the nuclear revolution gave defenders an even more lopsided advantage than the combination of machine guns, barbed wire, entrenchments, and railroads that emerged before 1914.

American and Soviet policymakers grasped this cosmic military revolution only slowly, however. At first many feared nuclear weapons would be a boon to aggressors. Even after they lost this fear, they only dimly recognized the vast advantage that nuclear weapons gave defenders, partly because scholars strangely failed to explain it. Thus the nuclear revolution changed realities far more than perceptions. As a result, state behavior changed only slowly, and the two superpowers competed far harder—in both Central Europe and the Third World—than objective conditions warranted. The Cold War was much more peaceful than the preceding forty years, but it could have been still more peaceful had Soviet and U.S. elites understood that their security problems had vastly diminished and were now quite small.

In sum, the events of from 1789 to the 1990s corroborate offense-defense theory predictions—specifically, predictions 1, 2, 4, and 5. These conclusions rest on rather sketchy data—especially regarding predictions 4 and 5—but those data confirm offense-defense theory so clearly that other data would have to be very different to reverse the result.

Periods of war correlate loosely with periods when conquest was easy, and very tightly with periods when conquest appeared easy (for a summary see Table 3). Thus prediction 1 is corroborated.

States that had or perceived greater offensive opportunities and defensive vulnerabilities were Europe's perennial troublemakers, while other states more often accepted the status quo. Prussia-Germany was cursed with the least defensible borders and faced the most offensive temptations. It started the most major wars: those of 1864, 1866, 1870 (sharing responsibility with France), 1914, and 1939. France and Russia, with more defensible borders and fewer temptations, started fewer major wars.[207] Britain and the United States, blessed with even more insulating borders, joined a number of European wars but started none.[208] Spain, Sweden, and Switzerland, also insulated by mountains or oceans from other powers, fought very little. This evidence supports prediction 2.

[207] France can be assigned prime responsibility for 1792 and 1859, and shared responsibility for Crimea and 1870. Russia deserves prime responsibility for the Cold War and shared responsibility for Crimea and the 1904–5 Russo-Japanese War.

[208] Britain does share responsibility for the Crimean War with Russia, France, and Turkey.

Thus the timing of war and the identities of the belligerents fit offense-defense theory's forecasts.

Expansionism was somewhat more prominent during periods of offense dominance (1789–1815, 1859–71, 1930s–45) than at other times, and it was markedly more prominent during periods of perceived offense dominance (1789–1815, 1859–71, 1890–1914, 1930s–45) than at other times. The years 1789–1815 saw a strong surge of French expansionism, nearly matched at the outset by parallel Prussian expansionism. The mid-nineteenth century saw considerable opportunistic expansionism in Prussia and some French expansionism. The years 1890–1914 saw vast expansionist ambitions develop in Wilhelmine Germany and lesser expansionism emerge elsewhere.[209] Large German expansionism then reappeared under the Nazis in the 1930s. During other periods European expansionism was more muted: European powers had smaller active ambitions. This evidence supports prediction 4.

Expansionism was prominent among those states that had or perceived more offensive opportunities and defensive vulnerabilities (especially Prussia-Germany, also revolutionary France), while being more muted among states with secure borders and few offensive opportunities (Britain, the United States, the Scandinavian states, and Spain). This evidence supports prediction 5.

Overall, evidence from this test gives offense-defense theory strong support.

Ancient China

The ancient Chinese multistate system witnessed a long-term shift from defense dominance to offense dominance across the years from 722 to 221 B.C.E.[210] Offense-defense theory predicts that warfare should have increased as this change unfolded (see prediction 1). This forecast is fulfilled: diplomacy grew markedly more savage and international relations grew markedly more violent as the power of the offense increased.

Before roughly 550 B.C.E., the defense held the upper hand among China's many feudal states. Four related changes then strengthened the offense: feudalism declined,[211] mass infantry replaced chariots as the critical military force, conscription was introduced, and armies grew tremendously in size.[212] The two largest Chinese states deployed enormous armies of more

---

[209] See Chapter 7 at notes 28–55.

[210] Concurring is Andreski, *Military Organization and Society*, p. 76.

[211] Noting the decline of feudalism are Griffiths, "Introduction," p. 33; and Li, *Ageless Chinese*, p. 64.

[212] On the growth of armies, the introduction of conscription, and the rise of infantry see Li, *Ageless Chinese*, p. 56; Griffiths, "Introduction," pp. 28, 33; and Wolfram Eberhard, *A History of China* (Berkeley: University of California Press, 1977), p. 49.

Table 4. Testing offense-defense theory: Europe, 1789–1990s; ancient China; the United States, 1789–1990s

Case	Prime predictions:			Explanatory predictions:		
	Prediction 1: is war more common when conquest is easy, or is believed easy?	Prediction 2: do states that have, or think they have, larger offensive opportunities or defensive vulnerabilities initiate and fight more wars than other states?	Prediction 3: do given states initiate and fight more wars in periods when they face, or think they face, larger offensive opportunities or defensive vulnerabilities?	Prediction 4: are intervening phenomena H5A-H5K more abundant when conquest is easy, or is believed to be easy?	Prediction 5: do states that have, or think they have, large offensive opportunities or defensive vulnerabilities more strongly embrace policies that embody phenomenon H5A–H5F, H5H–H5K?	Prediction 6: is there evidence that elites adopted these policies because they thought conquest was easy?
Europe, 1789–1990s	Yes: war is more common when conquest is easy, far more common when conquest is believed easy.	Yes: Europe's less secure and more offensively capable states made more trouble.		Yes: expansionism was more evident in periods of perceived easy conquest.	Yes: expansionism was more evident among states with more offensive opportunities and defensive vulnerabilities.	
Ancient China	Yes: war grew more common as conquest grew easier.					
United States, 1789–1990s		Yes: the U.S. has fought less often than most great powers.	Yes: the U.S. fought less when it felt more secure.		Yes: the U.S. has embraced expansionism, preemptive and preventive war, fait accompli tactics, policies of extreme secrecy, and large military forces less than other great powers.	

NOTE: Cells are blank if evidence to test it was not presented here.

than a million men, and some smaller states had armies numbering in the hundreds of thousands.[213] As armies grew, border forts lost much of their power to stop invaders because invading forces could sweep past after leaving a small force behind to besiege them. Forts also lost stopping power as improved siege engines appeared—battering rams, catapults, and rolling towers—that further eased the conquest of fortified positions.[214] The decline of feudalism eased offensive operations by reducing social stratification, which increased troop loyalty to regimes. This meant armies could conduct long-distance offensive operations without melting away.

The outcomes of battles and wars reveal the shift toward the offense that these changes produced. The number of independent Chinese states declined from two hundred in the eighth century B.C.E. to seven in the late fifth century, to one in the late third century—a clear measure of the growing power of the offense.[215] Before 550 B.C.E. defenders were often victorious. Thus the states of Tsin and Ch'i fought three great battles, in 632, 598, and 567 B.C.E., each won by the defender. Dun J. Li concludes, "If the three battles indicate anything, they meant that neither side was able to challenge successfully the other's leadership in its own sphere of influence."[216] In contrast, the state of Ch'in conquered all of China in a rapid campaign lasting only nine years at the end of the Warring States period (230–221 B.C.E.).[217]

This increase in the power of the offense coincides with a stark deterioration in international relations. During the Spring and Autumn period (722–481 B.C.E.) interstate relations were fairly peaceful and wars were limited by a code of conduct. The code confined warfare to certain seasons of the year and forbade killing wounded enemy troops. It was considered wrong to stoop to deceit, to take unfair advantage of adversaries, to "ambush armies," or to "massacre cities."[218] The subsequent Warring States period (403–221 B.C.E.) was perhaps the bloodiest era in Chinese history. Warfare raged almost constantly,[219] becoming a "fundamental occupation" of states.[220] Restraints on warfare were abandoned. Casualties ran into hundreds of thousands, and prisoners of war were massacred en masse.[221] Diplomatic conduct deteriorated; one historian writes that "diplomacy was based on bribery, fraud, and deceit."[222]

[213] Li, *Ageless Chinese*, p. 56.
[214] Andreski, *Military Organization and Society*, p. 76.
[215] Li, *Ageless Chinese*, pp. 50, 59.
[216] Ibid., p. 52.
[217] Ibid., p. 59.
[218] Griffiths, "Introduction," p. 30.
[219] Ibid., p. 21.
[220] Ibid., p. 24, quoting Shang Yang, prime minister of Ch'in, who conceived war and agriculture to be the two fundamental occupations.
[221] Li, *Ageless Chinese*, pp. 56, 58–59.
[222] Griffiths, "Introduction," p. 24.

In short, the shift toward offense dominance in China during 722–221 B.C.E. correlates tightly with a dramatic breakdown of China's international order.

The United States, 1789–1990s

Since 1815, the United States has been by far the most secure of the world's great powers, blessed with two vast ocean moats, no nearby great powers, and (after 1890) the world's largest economy. In the nineteenth century the United States also had substantial offensive opportunities, embodied in chances for continental and then Pacific expansion against weak defenders. The security endowments of the United States were quite exceptional, however, while its offensive opportunities were more ordinary. Offense-defense theory predicts that such a state will display perhaps average offensive opportunism but markedly less defensive belligerence than other states. Hence it will start and fight fewer wars (see prediction 2).

This forecast fits the pattern of past U.S. foreign policy. The United States has fought other great powers only three times in its two-hundred-year history—in 1812, 1917, and 1941—a low count for a great power.[223] The 1812 war stemmed mainly from U.S. belligerence, but the wars of 1917 and 1941 resulted mainly from others' belligerence. The United States did start some of its lesser wars (1846 and 1898), but it joined other wars more reactively (Korea and Vietnam).

Offense-defense theory also predicts that while the United States will pursue some opportunistic expansionism (intervening phenomenon H5A), it will embrace few policies that embody offense-defense theory's other intervening phenomena (H5B–H5K), since these phenomena are largely responses to insecurity, and the United States was relatively secure (prediction 5). Where the record allows judgments, this forecast is borne out.

Regarding expansionism, the United States has confined itself largely to opportunistic imperialism against frail opponents. Defensive expansionism has been muted, and overall, expansionist ideas have held less sway in the United States than in other powers. The United States has also pursued empire less than other states. The American empire has been limited to a few formal colonies seized from Spain in the 1890s and an informal empire in the Caribbean and Central American areas, with only intermittent control exerted more widely—a zone far smaller than the vast empires of the European powers. The United States has also been slow to resist other great powers' expansion, joining efforts to prevent German hegemony in Europe only late in the game.

The U.S. impulse to engage in preemptive and preventive war has been

[223] Britain, France, Russia, and Prussia-Germany fought other great powers an average of five times over the same two hundred years, by my count. None fought as few as three times.

small. In sharp contrast to Germany and Japan, the United States has launched a stealthy first strike on another major power just once (in 1812) and has jumped through only one window of opportunity (in 1812). Surprise first strikes and window jumping were considered on other occasions (for example, preventive war was discussed during 1949–54 and a surprise attack on Cuba was considered during the Cuban missile crisis), but seldom seriously.

U.S. diplomacy has been strikingly free of fait accompli tactics. U.S. foreign and security policies have generally been less secretive than those of the European continental powers, especially during the late Cold War, when the United States published military data that most powers would highly classify as secrets. The United States arms-raced with the Soviet Union energetically during the Cold War, but earlier maintained very small standing military forces—far smaller than those of other great powers. Overall, intervening phenomena H5B–H5K of offense-defense theory are strikingly absent in the U.S. case.

In sum the United States, though not a shrinking violet, has been less bellicose than the average great power. U.S. conduct contrasts sharply with the far greater imperial aggressions of Athens, Rome, Carthage, Spain, Prussia-Germany, Japan, Russia, and France.

Offense-defense theory further predicts that the level of U.S. bellicosity should vary inversely with shifts in America's sense of security (prediction 3)—as in fact it has.

From 1789 to 1815 the United States saw large foreign threats on its borders. It responded with an active and sometimes bellicose foreign policy that produced the 1812 war with Britain.

From 1815 to 1914 the United States was protected from the threat of a Eurasian continental hegemon by Britain's active continental balancing, and protected from European expansion into the Western hemisphere by the British fleet, which was the de facto enforcer of the Monroe Doctrine. The United States responded by withdrawing from European affairs and maintaining very small standing military forces, although it did pursue continental expansion before 1898 and limited overseas imperial expansion after 1898.

After 1914, Britain was unable to maintain the balance of power in Europe and was unwilling to continue protecting the Western hemisphere from other powers. This deprived the United States of its shield against continental European aggressors. Then followed the great era of U.S. activism—fitful at first (1917–47), then steady and persistent (1947–91). This era ended when the Soviet threat suddenly vanished during 1989–91. After 1991, the United States maintained its security alliances but reduced its troops stationed overseas and sharply reduced its defense effort.

What this evidence indicates

Offense-defense theory passes the tests posed in these three cases. Are these tests positive proof for the theory or mere straws in the wind? The strength of a passed test depends on the uniqueness of the predictions that the test corroborates. The more numerous and plausible the contending explanations for the results we find, the weaker the test.

The three case study tests reported here range from fairly weak to quite strong. They all lack Herculean power, but together they provide strong evidence for offense-defense theory. The test that the case of ancient China offers is a weak one because our knowledge of ancient Chinese society is fairly thin. This leaves us unable to rule out competing explanations for the rise of warfare in China in the Warring States period. The test that the U.S. case offers is somewhat stronger. Plausible alternative explanations can be found for some aspects of this case. For example, some would argue that America's more pacific conduct stems from its democratic character, not from its surfeit of security. Others would contend that the United States has few conflicts of interest with other powers because it shares no borders with them, and it fights fewer wars for this reason. Hence this element of the test posed by the U.S. case is weak. But alternative explanations for the fall, rise, and fall of U.S. global activism over the past two centuries are hard to come up with, leaving offense-defense theory's explanation without strong competitors; so this element of the test posed by the U.S. case has some strength.[224]

The case of Europe since 1789 offers a fairly strong test. There is no obvious competing explanation for the main pattern we observe in the case—greater warfare during 1789–1815, 1856–71, and 1914–45, and greater peace between those periods and after 1945. Offense-defense theory has the field to itself. Competing explanations are offered for specific events within this pattern, but none claims to explain the pattern as a whole. Hence this test seems strong.

How much importance does this evidence assign to offense-defense theory? That is, how potent is offense dominance as a cause of war? In each case, the behavior of states shifted sharply with changes in the actual or perceived offense-defense balance. China saw a dramatic shift toward war as offense grew strong in the Warring States period. U.S. conduct shifted markedly as threats and opportunities came and went. In Europe since 1789, war has been markedly more common when elites believed that the offense

---

[224] Fareed Zakaria offers a competing explanation for the rise of U.S. activism after 1889, ascribing it to the growing strength of the American state. *From Wealth to Power: The Unusual Origins of America's World Role* (Princeton: Princeton University Press, 1998). However, this explanation cannot account for the decline of U.S. activism after 1815 or after 1991, since there was no marked shrinkage of the American state in these periods.

dominated, and states were markedly more belligerent when they perceived large defensive vulnerabilities and offensive opportunities for themselves. This indicates that the offense-defense balance has a large impact on international relations. Offense-defense theory is important as well as valid.

How Much History Can Offense-Defense Theory Explain?

Some valid causes of war have high impact when the cause is present and conditions are right, but these causes and conditions are rare. Such theories explain little history. In contrast, the cause and the conditions required by offense-defense theory are common, and the cases suggest that the theory explains a great deal of war, especially if we expand it to cover the dangers of perceived as well as actual offense dominance. Actual offense dominance has been rather rare—at least in recent times—hence it explains only middling amounts of recent history. But perceived offense dominance is pervasive, and it plays a major role in causing most wars. Knowing exactly which wars still would have erupted in its absence requires a close analysis of each case—impossible here. But the evidence does indicate that it had a vast role, especially in modern times (i.e., since 1789).

This role can be partly measured by asking how much war is driven by the search for security. How common are perceptions of national insecurity? How many wars are justified by claims that this insecurity requires the use of force? If we assume that stated motives express real motives (not always the case but often true), then the incidence of security-driven warfare is a partial measure of offense-defense theory's explanatory power.[225] The more wars that arise from the search for safety, the more wars would be avoided if states were already safe; hence the more wars are explained by their lack of safety; hence the more wars are explained by offense-defense theory.

Security motives for war are in fact ubiquitous. The search for security played a role—sometimes minor, often major—in triggering the vast majority of ancient and modern wars where the motives of the belligerents are known.[226] Often both defenders and aggressors were driven by security concerns; aggressors expanded to gain security, while defenders refused to concede in order to preserve their security.

---

[225] This measure is partial because it captures only the effects of the defensive anxieties that arise when conquest is easy, omitting the effects of the opportunistic aggression that also arise (explanation H5A). To capture these effects we need a second measure, of opportunity-driven wars.

[226] Disagreeing is Zakaria, *From Wealth to Power*, pp. 183, 191, and passim.

Security fears drove both Athens and Sparta in the Peloponnesian War. Thucydides reports that Sparta was driven by fear of Athens' power: "What made war inevitable was the growth of Athenian power and the fear which this caused in Sparta."[227] Athens, in turn, believed that its safety required the ever wider extension of that power. Euphemus explained the Athenians' conduct: "In Hellas we rule in order not to be ruled ... we are forced to intervene in many directions simply because we have to be on our guard in many directions."[228] Athens moved to war in 433 B.C.E. to prevent Corinth from seizing Corcyra's fleet and adding it to the Spartan alliance, since this would challenge the naval supremacy of Athens and thereby threaten its security.[229] Later Alcibiades advised Athenians to attack Sicily by noting the "danger that we ourselves may fall under the power of others unless others are in our power." Hence Athens must "plan new conquests."[230]

Ancient Roman expansion was largely powered by insecurity. I mentioned above R. M. Errington's conclusion that Roman imperialism "aimed to achieve, first and foremost, merely the security of Rome." Another historian notes that Rome's conquest of Italy and the Western Empire was mainly driven by "simple fear, however much that fear may have involved (and, later, been replaced by) a lust for power. Conquest was first the only alternative to being conquered and made subject—by the Etruscans, by the Gauls, by the Samnites."[231]

The Swedes and French joined the Thirty Years' War (1618–48) to limit Hapsburg power before it could dominate the Baltic and Europe. Sweden's King Gustavus Adolphus explained the war to his subjects: "Sweden is in danger from the power of the Hapsburg; that is all, but it is enough ... the danger is great."[232] Later Louis XIV triggered war by seizing buffer room to secure France from invasion, a danger he greatly feared.[233] The coalitions that formed against Louis feared the threat that an uncontained France would pose to their safety.

On their surface the mercantilist wars of the eighteenth century seem to be wars for profit, but beneath they were wars for security. Robert Gilpin writes that the "frequent and seemingly petty commercial wars of the mercantilist era were really conflicts over access to control over the sources of

---

[227] Thucydides, *Peloponnesian War*, p. 49.

[228] Ibid., p. 464.

[229] Donald Kagan, *The Outbreak of the Peloponnesian War* (Ithaca: Cornell University Press, 1969), p. 352.

[230] Thucydides, *Peloponnesian War*, p. 421.

[231] Errington, *Dawn of Empire*, p. 3; John P. V. D. Balsdon, quoted in Klaus Knorr, "Threat Perception," in Klaus Knorr, ed., *Historical Dimensions of National Security Problems* (Lawrence: University Press of Kansas, 1976), pp. 78–119 at 99.

[232] Lynn Montross, *War through the Ages* (New York: Harper, 1944), p. 265. See also Charles Petrie, *Earlier Diplomatic History, 1492–1713* (London: Hollis and Carter, 1949), p. 130; Vagts, *Defense and Diplomacy*, p. 271.

[233] John B. Wolf, *Louis XIV* (New York: Norton, 1968), p. 231; also pp. 189, 214, 403–7, 414.

treasure, markets, and raw materials upon which national security increasingly depended."[234]

The Prussians sought more defensible boundaries in the wars of the 1740s and 1750s. Walter Dorn argues that Prussia's King Frederick believed that "every monarch must seek to expand or perish" and that Frederick launched the Seven Years' War feeling that "he must strike or perish."[235] Security fears also drove Russia to combat Frederick's expansion: Chancellor A. P. Bestuzhev warned the Russian tsar that "the more the power of the King of Prussia grows, the greater the danger for us becomes."[236] Britain and France clashed in 1756 chiefly because each believed that its own security would be threatened if the other gained dominion in North America.[237] Revolutionary France attacked in 1792 partly because it feared attack.[238] Meanwhile the anti-French coalitions of 1792–1815 were largely driven by fear that an unchecked France would threaten their safety.[239]

Competition for security helped kindle all the European wars of the mid-nineteenth century except the war of 1859.[240] Both sides pursued defensive aims in the Crimean War: Russia sought to protect its southern flank, and Britain and France sought to contain the growth of Russian power, which they wrongly thought was already dangerously great.[241] As noted above, Prussia waged the wars of German unification in part to secure its ancient goal of more defensible frontiers, and France accepted Prussia's challenge in 1870 partly from fear of Prussian encirclement.[242]

Both Japan and Russia pursued defensive aims in the Russo-Japanese War of 1904–5. Shumpei Okamoto reports that Japan's leaders chose war "because they regarded Russian activities in Manchuria as a serious threat to

[234] Robert Gilpin, "Economic Interdependence and National Security in Historical Perspective," in Klaus Knorr and Frank N. Trager, eds., *Economic Issues and National Security* (Lawrence: Regents Press of Kansas, 1977), pp. 19–66 at 29.

[235] Walter L. Dorn, *Competition for Empire 1740–1763* (New York: Harper and Brothers, 1940), pp. 300, 316. Likewise arguing that Prussia "had to expand or resign herself to stagnation and perhaps to eventual dismemberment" is M. S. Anderson, *Europe in the Eighteenth Century 1713–1783*, 2d ed. (London: Longmans, 1976), p. 249.

[236] Dennis Showalter, *The Wars of Frederick the Great* (London: Longman, 1996), p. 65.

[237] Smoke, *War*, p. 213.

[238] Blanning, *Origins of the French Revolutionary Wars*, pp. 76, 80–81, 99–101, 111, 123. In 1799 France fought on chiefly for defensive reasons, and Napoleon later claimed defensive motives for his aggressions. See Ross, *European Diplomatic History*, p. 194; and Pieter Geyl, *Napoleon, For and Against* (New Haven: Yale University Press, 1968), p. 252.

[239] See Ross, *European Diplomatic History*, pp. 26–32; Rudé, *Revolutionary Europe*, pp. 202–3; Bruun, *Europe and the French Imperium*, p. 39; also Blanning, *Origins*, pp. 142, 145, 149, 158, 207 (on Britain); 190 (on Russia).

[240] A. J. P. Taylor notes that the war of 1859 was "unique in modern history," being "the only war which did not spring in part from mutual apprehension." *Struggle for Mastery*, pp. 111–12.

[241] On Russia see note 20 above. On Britain and France see Smoke, *War*, p. 155, 162; and Snyder, *Myths of Empire*, p. 172. On post-1815 foreign overestimates of Russian power see also Anderson, *Ascendancy of Europe*, pp. 6–8.

[242] See Smoke, *War*, pp. 115–16.

Korea, and, consequently, to the security of Japan."[243] Ian Nish concludes that the main factors driving both sides to war were "security and fear of armaments policies on the part of the other party."[244]

Austria and Germany sought wider power in 1914 in a search for greater security.[245] The Entente powers resisted because they feared Germany would parlay any gains into further gains and soon become a juggernaut that could overwhelm them. Thus, as E. H. Carr notes, World War I, "in the minds of all the principal combatants, had a defensive or preventive character."[246]

Poland attacked the Soviet Union in 1920 largely to bolster Polish security. As noted earlier, the Polish Supreme Command argued that the "reduction of Russia to her historical frontiers is a condition of [Poland's] existence."[247] The Soviet-Finnish War of 1939–40 stemmed from both sides' security fears. The Finns feared that granting Soviet demands for bases would fatally weaken Finnish defenses,[248] while the Soviets sought these concessions to prevent Germany from using Finland as a springboard to attack the Soviet Union.[249]

Nazi German and Imperial Japanese elites argued for imperial expansion largely on national security grounds. Hitler warned that Germany faced "the greatest danger to the preservation of the German race," a threat that could be removed only by German expansion.[250] Prime Minister Tojo claimed expansion was "a matter of life or death to Japan," and the Japanese navy believed the "very existence" of Japan was at issue.[251]

Beneath the Cold War's ideological justifications lay national security concerns on both sides. As noted above, Soviet expansion was driven in part by the old Russian urge to escape the perils of life on an exposed plain in a

[243] Shumpei Okamoto, *The Japanese Oligarchy and the Russo-Japanese War* (New York: Columbia University Press, 1970), p. 102.

[244] Nish, *Origins of the Russo-Japanese War*, p. 256; see also pp. 2, 11.

[245] See above at notes 22–24, and Chapter 7 at notes 28–43.

[246] Carr, *Twenty Years' Crisis*, p. 112.

[247] Quoted in Wandycz, *Soviet-Polish Relations*, p. 198.

[248] A Finnish newspaper explained that "acceptance of the [Soviet] demands would mean the collapse of the very basis of our independent existence." The *Helsingin Sanomat*, quoted in Max Jakobson, *The Diplomacy of the Winter War* (Cambridge: Harvard University Press, 1961), p. 139; see also p. 133.

[249] Khrushchev, *Khrushchev Remembers* (1970), pp. 151–52; also Jakobson, *Diplomacy of the Winter War*, pp. 8–9.

[250] In November 1937, Colonel Hossbach's paraphrase, in Noakes and Pridham, *Nazism*, 2:681. The anti-Hitler coalition was also driven by national security concerns. See, for example, on the United States, Justus D. Doenecke and John E. Wilz, *From Isolation to War 1931–1941*, 2d ed. (Arlington Heights, Ill.: Harlan Davidson, 1991), p. 98.

[251] Robert J. C. Butow, *Tojo and the Coming of the War* (Stanford: Stanford University Press, 1960), pp. 224, 203; see also 24, 113–14. Their claim was that Japan otherwise might be strangled by enemies who controlled sources of raw materials critical to Japan. Thus, as noted above, Foreign Minister Teijiro Toyoda argued in July 1941 that "our Empire, to save its very life, must take measures to secure the raw materials of the South Seas." Quoted in Yergin, *The Prize*, p. 319.

nasty neighborhood.[252] The United States resisted Soviet expansion largely for national security reasons: U.S. policymakers feared that if the Soviet Union gained hegemony in Eurasia, it would possess a vast industrial base adequate to support a military force that could threaten the United States.[253] These security concerns spawned the Soviet-American military standoff in Central Europe, Soviet military intervention in Afghanistan, U.S. military interventions in Korea and Vietnam, and proxy wars in Nicaragua, Angola, Cambodia, El Salvador, and elsewhere. These interventions in turn aroused others' security concerns: China attacked the U.S. intervention force in Korea because, as General Wu explained, "an aggressor who invades Korea today will certainly invade China tomorrow."[254]

The recurrent Arab-Israeli wars stemmed largely from Israel's security-driven demand for territory and, to a lesser extent, from Arab fears of further Israeli expansion. After 1949 Israel refused to concede any lands seized in the 1948 war partly because it feared that concessions would leave it too weak to defeat a renewed Arab attack.[255] This refusal precluded an early peace. Arab hostility to Israel also had a security component: Nasser explained before the 1956 war: "Fear dominates the area. . . . What do you think I feel when I hear that the Herut Party in Israel wants expansion from the Nile to the Euphrates?"[256]

Many later wars in the Third World also stemmed from competition for security. Iraq unleashed the Iran-Iraq War in 1980 from fear that otherwise Islamic-fundamentalist Iran would subvert and overthrow Iraq's secular Ba'thist regime.[257] Rwanda's Tutsi government warred against Zaire's Mobutu regime in 1996–97 to address the threat of subversion and invasion of Rwanda by Zaire-sponsored Hutus.[258]

In short, perceptions of insecurity are pervasive in international affairs, and the search for security is a pervasive motive for war. Herbert Butterfield notes that this search is "the basic pattern of all narrative of human con-

---

[252] See above at note 31.

[253] Melvyn P. Leffler, "The American Conception of National Security and the Beginnings of the Cold War," *American Historical Review* 89 (April 1984): 346–81 at 356–58, 370, 374, 377; Gaddis, *Strategies of Containment*, pp. 29–30, 57, 201.

[254] Vagts, *Defense and Diplomacy*, p. 350. China's Marshall Peng Dehuai likewise stressed that "if Korea is occupied by the imperialists, the safety of our own country will be directly threatened. To support Korea is also to . . . consolidate our national defense, and to safeguard the industry in the Northeast." Shuguang Zhang and Jian Chen, eds., *Chinese Communist Foreign Policy and the New Cold War in Asia: New Documentary Evidence, 1944–1950* (Chicago: Imprint, 1996), p. 176. See also ibid., pp. 187–88; Jian, *China's Road*, pp. 159, 183–84, 202, 206; Christensen, *Useful Adversaries*, pp. 156–66; and Alan Whiting, *China Crosses the Yalu* (Stanford: Stanford University Press, 1960), pp. 32, 105–6, 127–30, 158–60.

[255] Safran, *Israel*, p. 225.

[256] Donald Neff, *Warriors at Suez* (New York: Simon and Schuster, 1981), p. 82.

[257] Efraim Karsh and Inari Rautsi, *Saddam Hussein: A Political Biography* (New York: Free Press, 1991), pp. 138–39, 145–48.

[258] James C. McKinley, "Rwanda's War Role May Haunt Congolese," *New York Times*, July 12, 1997.

flict." [259] To John Herz it is "the basic cause of . . . 'the urge for power,'" hence of war. [260] If so, offense-defense theory offers a prime answer to the war question, and serves as a master key to the cause of international conflict.

Offense-defense theory explains both specific wars and patterns of warfare in history. I asked above if these patterns conformed to the predictions of offense-defense theory, and found they did. If so, these patterns are also explained by the theory they corroborate. Modern European and ancient Chinese eras of peace and war—the European calms of 1815–53 and 1945–90s, the vast European violence of 1792–1815 and 1914–45, the long Chinese drift from order to chaos across the centuries from the Spring and Autumn period to the Warring States period—can all be explained in large part by offense-defense theory. These shifts had many specific causes, but their roots lay in background conditions that eased or inhibited conquest.

OFFENSE-DEFENSE THEORY IN PERSPECTIVE

Offense-defense theory has the attributes of a good theory. First, it has three elements that give a theory claim to large explanatory power. *Large importance*: Shifts in the perceived offense-defense balance cause large shifts in the incidence of warfare. Shifts in the actual offense-defense balance have less impact because policymakers often misperceive it, but they have a potent effect when policymakers perceive it accurately. *Wide explanatory range*: The theory explains results across many domains of behavior—in military policy, foreign policy, and crisis diplomacy. It governs many phenomena—expansionism, first-move advantage, windows, the use of faits accomplis, secrecy, negotiation failures, crisis management blunders, arms races, tight alliances—that have been seen as important war causes in their own right. Thus offense-defense theory achieves simplicity, binding together a number of war causes into a single rubric. Many causes are reduced to one cause with many effects. [261] *Wide real-world applicability*: Real offense dominance is

[259] Quoted in John H. Herz, *International Politics in the Atomic Age* (New York: Columbia University Press, 1962), p. 234.

[260] Ibid., p. 231. Butterfield and Herz echo Rousseau, who argued that "many wars, even offensive wars, are rather in the nature of unjust precautions for the protection of the assailant's own possessions than a device for seizing those of others." Quoted in Kenneth N. Waltz, *Man, the State, and War* (New York: Columbia University Press, 1959) p. 180.

[261] Offense-defense theory has also been usefully adapted for application beyond the causes of interstate war. For example, it has been used to explain the intensity of war, the causes of ethnic and civil war, the foreign policies of revolutionary states, the size and number of states in the international system, and the alliance behavior of major powers. See Lynn-Jones, "Offense-Defense Theory," pp. 661–62; and Glaser and Kaufmann, "What is the Offense-Defense Balance," pp. 44–45. The theory could also be adapted to explain international economic competition (or cooperation). Thus Jitsuo Tsuchiyama writes of the "prosperity dilemma"—a cousin of the security dilemma in which measures taken by one state to increase its economic well-being decrease another's economic well-being. "The End of the Alliance? Dilemmas in the U.S.-Japan Relations," in Peter Gourevitch, Takashi Inoguchi, and

rare in modern times, but the perception of offense dominance is widespread. Therefore, if perceived offense dominance causes war, it causes lots of war, and offense-defense theory explains a good deal of international history.

Second, offense-defense theory has large prescriptive utility. National foreign and military policy can shape the offense-defense balance, and reasoned argument can correct misperceptions of it. Both the offense-defense balance and perceptions of it are far more manipulable than the polarity of the international system, the strength of international institutions, human nature, or other war causes that have drawn close attention.

Third, offense-defense theory is quite satisfying. In uncovering the roots of its eleven intervening phenomena, offense-defense theory offers a more satisfying—and simpler—explanation than do interpretations pointing directly to these phenomena.

Yet the theory is not fully satisfying. It leaves us wondering why the strength of the offense has so often been exaggerated.

History suggests that offense dominance is dangerous, quite rare, and widely overstated. States are seldom as insecure as they think they are. Moreover, if they are insecure, this insecurity often grows from their own efforts to escape imagined insecurity.

The rarity of real insecurity is suggested by the low death rate of modern great powers. In ancient times great powers disappeared often, but in modern times (since 1789) no great powers have been destroyed, and only twice (France in 1870–71 and in 1940) has any been even temporarily overrun by an unprovoked aggressor.[262] Both times France soon regained its sovereignty through the intervention of outside powers—illustrating the powerful defensive influence of balancing behavior by great powers.

The prevalence of exaggerations of insecurity is revealed by the great wartime endurance of many states that enter wars for security reasons, and by the aftermath of the world's great security wars, which often reveal that the belligerents' security fears were illusory. Athens fought Sparta largely for security reasons, but held out for a full nine years (413–404 B.C.E.) after suffering the crushing loss of its Sicilian expedition—an achievement that shows the falsehood of its original fears. Austria-Hungary held out for a full four years under allied battering during 1914–18, a display of toughness at odds with its own prewar self-image of imminent collapse. With hindsight we can now see that modern Germany would have been secure had it only behaved itself. Wilhelmine Germany was Europe's dominant state, with Eu-

---

Courtney Purrington, eds., *United States-Japan Relations and International Institutions after the Cold War* (La Jolla: Graduate School of International Relations and Pacific Studies, U.C. San Diego, 1995), pp. 3–35 at 5–6, 21–29. (Tsuchiyama wrongly credits me for the prosperity dilemma concept; it was his.)

[262] France helped trigger the 1870 war, hence one could argue that only France in 1940 was overrun by an unprovoked aggressor.

rope's largest and fastest growing economy. It faced no plausible threat to its sovereignty except those that it created by its own belligerence. Later, interwar Germany and Japan could have secured themselves simply by moderating their conduct. This would have assured them of allies, hence of the raw materials supplies they sought to seize by force. America's Cold War interventions in the Third World now seem hypervigilant in the light of its geographic invulnerability, the defensive benefits of the nuclear revolution, and the strength of Third World nationalism, which would have precluded the Soviet Third World imperialism that U.S. interventions sought to prevent. The Soviet struggle to control Eastern Europe and other peripheral areas seems similarly unnecessary for Soviet security.

Paradoxically, a chief source of insecurity in Europe since medieval times has been this false belief that security was scarce. This belief was a self-fulfilling prophecy, fostering bellicose policies that left all states less secure. Modern great powers have been overrun by unprovoked aggressors only twice, but they have been overrun by provoked aggressors six times— usually by aggressors provoked by the victim's fantasy-driven defensive bellicosity. Wilhelmine and Nazi Germany, Imperial Japan, Napoleonic France, and Austria-Hungary were all destroyed by dangers that they created through their efforts to escape from exaggerated or imaginary threats to their safety.[263]

If so, the prime threat to the security of modern great powers is . . . themselves. Their greatest menace lies in their own tendency to exaggerate the dangers they face, and to respond with counterproductive belligerence. The causes of this syndrome pose a large question for students of international relations.

---

[263] Mussolini also provoked his own destruction, but his bellicosity was not security driven.

[7]

Offense-Defense Theory and
the Outbreak of World War I

During the decades before the First World War, a "cult of the offensive" swept through Europe. Belief in the power of the offense increased sharply after 1890 and rose to very high levels as 1914 approached. Militaries glorified the offensive and adopted offensive military doctrines. Civilian elites and publics assumed that the offense had the advantage in warfare and that future wars would be short and decisive. Many foresaw a final winner-take-all struggle for the domination of Europe—a clash that would quickly end in complete victory for the winner and crushing defeat for the loser.

Hence pre-1914 Europe is a good laboratory for testing offense-defense theory. Because belief in the power of the offense was very strong, its effects should be clearly visible. Specifically, the intervening phenomena that offense is alleged to cause should appear in quantity. If these phenomena are observed in their predicted abundance, offense-defense theory is strongly corroborated, because no alternative explanation predicts that such high quantities of these phenomena should appear together anywhere. If they are not observed, offense-defense theory has no excuses: it clearly predicts their appearance in quantity in 1914 Europe, so their failure to appear is powerful evidence against it. Hence the test of 1914 is doubly decisive: passage strongly confirms the theory, failure strongly denies it.

Pre-1914 Europe is also a good test lab because the case is very well documented. Historians have ably recorded the deeds and perceptions of the participants in the 1914 July crisis, compiling an abundant record of the actions, beliefs, and motives of policymakers. Again, this means that the 1914 case offers a strong test of offense-defense theory. We can test predictions of details—for example, about the private speech of government policymakers—that could have no plausible explanation except the operation of offense-defense theory. Passage of these tests strongly supports the theory. Flunked tests also infirm the theory more strongly, because they are harder to explain away as a false negative caused by gaps or flaws in the record.

I argue that evidence from the 1914 case strongly supports offense-defense theory. Nearly all of the theory's testable predictions are confirmed. (For a summary see Table 5.) There is no plausible contending explanation for this general result, hence the theory's success here is strong evidence in its favor. The case studies reported in Chapter 6 offered solid support for offense-defense theory; the 1914 case offers even stronger support.

Study of the 1914 case also indicates that offense-defense theory offers a good explanation for World War I—one far simpler than more popular explanations. (For a summary see Diagram 4.) The cult of the offensive created or magnified many dangers that historians blame for causing the July crisis and making it uncontrollable. It served as a master cause of several of the war's better-known causes.

THE RISE OF THE CULT OF THE OFFENSIVE, 1890–1914

The gulf between the perception and the reality of warfare has never been greater than in Europe during the years before World War I. During the decades after 1850, and especially after 1890, the defense gained a large and growing advantage from five innovations: accurate repeating rifles, the machine gun, barbed wire, elaborate entrenchments, and railroads. In 1914 the power of the defense reached a zenith. In modern times conquest has been harder only deep in the nuclear era (post-1960s).

Yet between 1890 and 1914 Europeans increasingly believed that attackers would hold the advantage on the battlefield and that wars would be short and decisive. They largely overlooked the lessons of the American Civil War, the Russo-Turkish War of 1877–78, the Boer War, and the Russo-Japanese War, which had revealed the power of the new defensive technologies. Instead, Europeans embraced political and military myths that obscured the defender's advantages. This mind-set helped mold the offensive military doctrines that every European power adopted during the period 1892–1913, and primed Europeans to expect a quick, total victory for the stronger side in the next war.[1]

---

[1] As George Quester notes, World War I was "launched on the illusion of offensive advantage." *Offense and Defense in the International System* (New York: Wiley, 1977), p. 11. On the causes of this offensive illusion see Jack Snyder, *Ideology of the Offensive: Military Decision Making and the Disasters of 1914* (Ithaca: Cornell University Press, 1984). On the failure of Europeans to learn defensive lessons from the wars of 1860–1914, see Jay Luvaas, *The Military Legacy of the Civil War: The European Inheritance* (Chicago: University of Chicago Press, 1959); and T. H. E. Travers, "Technology, Tactics and Morale: Jean de Bloch, the Boer War, and British Military Theory, 1900–1914," *Journal of Modern History* 51 (June 1979): 264–86. Also relevant is Bernard Brodie, *Strategy in the Missile Age* (Princeton: Princeton University Press, 1965), pp. 42–52.

In Germany, the military proclaimed the superiority of the offense in strident terms, and infused German society with similar views. General Alfred von Schlieffen, author of the 1914 German war plan, declared that "attack is the best defense."[2] Army propagandist Friedrich von Bernhardi proclaimed that "the offensive mode of action is by far superior to the defensive mode" and that "the superiority of offensive warfare under modern conditions is greater than formerly."[3] The German chief of staff, General Helmut von Moltke, endorsed "the principle that the offensive is the best defense," while General August von Keim, founder of the Army League, argued that "Germany ought to be armed for attack," since "the offensive is the only way of insuring victory."[4] These assumptions guided Germany's Schlieffen plan, which envisaged decisive attacks on Belgium, France, and Russia in quick sequence.

In France, the army became "obsessed with the virtues of the offensive," in the words of B. H. Liddell Hart, an obsession that also spread to French civilians.[5] The French army's 1895 infantry regulations declared that "the passive defense is doomed to certain defeat; it is to be rejected absolutely."[6] Marshall Ferdinand Foch likewise preached that "the offensive form [of war] alone . . . can lead to results, and must therefore always be adopted."[7] Emile Driant, a member of the French chamber of deputies, summarized the common public view: "The first great battle will decide the whole war, and wars will be short. The idea of the offense must penetrate the spirit of our nation."[8]

A related work that explores the sources of offensive and defensive doctrines before World War II is Barry R. Posen, *The Sources of Military Doctrine: France, Britain, and Germany between the World Wars* (Ithaca: Cornell University Press, 1984), pp. 47–51, 67–74, and passim.

[2] Gerhard Ritter, *The Schlieffen Plan: Critique of a Myth*, trans. Andrew and Eva Wilson (1958; reprint, Westport, Conn.: Greenwood, 1979), p. 100.

[3] Friedrich von Bernhardi, *How Germany Makes War* (New York: George H. Doran, 1914), pp. 153, 155.

[4] Imanuel Geiss, ed., *July 1914: The Outbreak of the First World War: Selected Documents* (New York: Norton, 1967), p. 357; Wallace Notestein and Elmer E. Stoll, eds., *Conquest and Kultur: Aims of the Germans in Their Own Words* (Washington: U.S. Government Printing Office, 1917), p. 43. Similar ideas developed in the German navy: see Holger H. Herwig, *Politics of Frustration: The United States in German Naval Planning, 1889–1941* (Boston: Little, Brown, 1976), pp. 42–66.

[5] B. H. Liddell Hart, *Through the Fog of War* (New York: Random House, 1938), p. 57.

[6] Quoted in Luvaas, *Military Legacy*, p. 165.

[7] Quoted in ibid., p. 165. Chief of Staff Joseph Joffre likewise declared that the French Army "no longer knows any other law than the offensive. . . . Any other conception ought to be rejected as contrary to the very nature of war." In 1913, quoted in John Ellis, *The Social History of the Machine Gun* (New York: Pantheon, 1975), pp. 53–54.

[8] In 1912, quoted in John M. Cairns, "International Politics and the Military Mind: The Case of the French Republic, 1911–1914," *Journal of Modern History* 25 (September 1953): 282. In the same spirit the president of the French Republic, Clément Fallières, announced that "the offensive alone is suited to the temperament of French soldiers. . . . We are determined to march straight against the enemy without hesitation." Barbara Tuchman, *The Guns of August* (New York: Dell, 1962), p. 51.

French military doctrine reflected these offensive biases.[9] In Foch's words, the French army adopted "a single formula for success, a single combat doctrine, namely, the decisive power of offensive action undertaken with the resolute determination to march on the enemy, reach and destroy him."[10] Accordingly, France planned an all-out offensive through Lorraine and the Ardennes in the event of war with Germany.

Other European states displayed milder symptoms of the same virus. The British military resolutely rejected defensive strategies, despite grim Boer War experience that showed the power of entrenched defenders against exposed attackers. General R. C. B. Haking argued that the offensive "will win as sure as there is a sun in the heavens," and General W. G. Knox concluded that "the defensive is never an acceptable role to the Briton, and he makes little or no study of it."[11] The Russian minister of war, General V. A. Sukhomlinov, noted that Russia's enemies were directing their armies "towards guaranteeing the possibility of dealing rapid and decisive blows.... We also must follow this example."[12] Russia accordingly adopted an extremely ambitious strategy of attack on both Germany and Austria at the outset of war.[13]

Even in Belgium the offensive found proponents. Under the influence of French ideas, some Belgian officers favored an offensive strategy, evolving the remarkable argument that "to ensure against our being ignored it was essential that we should attack" and declaring that "we must hit them where it hurts."[14]

Illogical or mystical arguments obscured the technical supremacy of the defense, giving the faith in the offense aspects of a cult or a mystique, as Marshall Joffre remarked in his memoirs.[15] For instance, Foch used twisted

[9] On the offensive in French prewar thought see B. H. Liddell Hart, "French Military Ideas before the First World War," in Martin Gilbert, ed., *A Century of Conflict, 1850–1950* (London: Hamilton Hamish, 1966), pp. 135–48.

[10] Richard D. Challener, *The French Theory of the Nation in Arms, 1866–1939* (New York: Columbia University Press, 1955), p. 81. Likewise Joffre later explained that Plan 17, his battle plan for 1914, was less a plan for battle than merely a plan of "concentration." "I adopted no preconceived idea, other than a full determination to take the offensive with all my forces assembled." Theodore Ropp, *War in the Modern World*, rev. ed. (New York: Collier, 1962), p. 229.

[11] In 1914 and 1913, quoted in Travers, "Technology, Tactics, and Morale," p. 275. On British offense-mindedness see also Tim Travers, *The Killing Ground: The British Army, the Western Front and the Emergence of Modern Warfare 1900–1918* (London: Allen & Unwin, 1987), pp. 37–61.

[12] In 1909, quoted in D. C. B. Lieven, *Russia and the Origins of the First World War* (New York: St. Martin's, 1983), p. 113.

[13] Snyder, *Ideology of the Offensive*, pp. 160–62.

[14] Tuchman, *Guns of August*, pp. 127–31. See also Luigi Albertini, *The Origins of the War of 1914*, 3 vols., trans. and ed. Isabella M. Massey (1952–57; reprint, Westport, Conn.: Greenwood, 1980), 3:461.

[15] Joseph Joffre, *Mémoires du Maréchal Joffre* (Paris: Plon, 1932), 33. Joffre speaks of "the cult of the offense" and "a mystique of the offensive of a somewhat irrational kind." Jay Luvaas also quotes a French Captain de Thomasson who, writing in 1920, discussed the "passionate cult of the offensive" that arose before 1914. Luvaas, *Military Legacy*, p. 165.

reasoning to mistakenly argue that the machine gun actually strengthened the offense: "Any improvement of firearms is ultimately bound to add strength to the offensive. . . . Nothing is easier than to give a mathematical demonstration of that truth." Foch explained that if two thousand men attacked one thousand, firing their rifles once a minute, the "balance in favor of the attack" was one thousand bullets per minute. But if both sides could fire ten times per minute, the "balance in favor of the attacker" would increase to ten thousand bullets per minute, giving the attack a larger advantage.[16] He failed to consider that both attacker and defender would have to seek cover against such withering fire, making advance by the attacker impossible. With equally forced logic, Bernhardi wrote that the larger the army, the longer defensive measures would take to execute, owing to "the difficulty of moving masses." Hence the offense would grow stronger as armies grew larger, as they steadily did during 1890–1914.[17] He failed to consider that huge armies could cover an entire frontier, making themselves impossible to outflank, hence impossible to defeat.

British and French officers suggested that higher morale on the attacking side could overcome superior defensive firepower, and that higher morale could be achieved by assuming the role of attacker, since attacking would lift the soldiers' spirits. One French officer contended that "the offensive doubles the energy of the troops" and "concentrates the thoughts of the commander on a single objective,"[18] while British officers declared that "modern [war] conditions have enormously increased the value of moral quality" and that "the moral attributes [are] the primary causes of all great success."[19] In short, mind would prevail over matter; morale would triumph over machine guns.

Some Europeans also discounted the power of political factors that would favor defenders. Many Germans thought that states bandwagoned with other strong, threatening states more often than they balanced against them. Aggressors, they believed, would gather momentum as they gained power because opponents would be cowed into submission and neutrals would rally to the stronger side. Such thinking led German Chancellor Bethmann-Hollweg to hope that "Germany's growing strength . . . might force En-

---

[16] Ropp, *War in the Modern World*, p. 218.

[17] Ibid., p. 203. See also Bernhardi, *How Germany Makes War*, p. 154.

[18] Captain Georges Gilbert, quoted in Snyder, *Ideology of the Offensive*, p. 64.

[19] The *Field Service Regulations* of 1909 and Colonel Kiggell, quoted in Travers, "Technology, Tactics, and Morale," pp. 273, 276–77.

Even when European officers recognized the new tactical power of the defense, they often resisted the conclusion that the defender would also hold the strategic advantage. Thus Bernhardi wrote that while "the defense as a form of fighting is stronger than the attack," it remained true that "in the conduct of war as a whole the offensive mode of action is by far superior to the defensive mode, especially under modern conditions." Bernhardi, *How Germany Makes War*, p. 155. See also Snyder, *Ideology of the Offensive*, pp. 91–92, 138–39; and Travers, "Technology, Tactics, and Morale," passim.

gland to realize that [the balance of power] principle had become untenable and impracticable and to opt for a peaceful settlement with Germany,"[20] and German Foreign Office Secretary of State Gottlieb von Jagow to forecast that Germany's new navy would bring British neutrality in a future European war: "People in England will seriously ask themselves whether it will be . . . without danger to play the role of France's guardian angel against us."[21] German leaders also thought they might frighten Belgium into surrender: during the July crisis, Moltke was "counting on the possibility of being able to come to an understanding [with Belgium] when the Belgian Government realizes the seriousness of the situation."[22] This ill-founded belief in bandwagoning reinforced the general belief that conquest was quite easy.

The belief in easy conquest eventually pervaded public images of international politics and found expression in the widespread application of Darwinist theories to international affairs. In this international social Darwinist image, states competed in a decisive struggle for survival that weeded out weak states and races and ended in the triumph of the strong—an image that assumed that conquest was easy. "In the struggle between nationalities," wrote former German Chancellor Bernard von Bülow, "one nation is the hammer and the other the anvil; one is the victor and the other the vanquished. . . . It is a law of life and development in history that where two national civilisations meet they fight for ascendancy."[23] A writer in the London *Saturday Review* portrayed the Anglo-German competition as "the first great racial struggle of the future: here are two growing nations pressing against each other . . . all over the world. One or the other has to go; one or the other will go."[24] These Darwinist ideas reflected and rested on the implicit assumption that the offense was strong, since "grow or die" dynamics would be impeded in a defense-dominant world where growth could be stopped and death prevented by self-defense.

---

[20] December 2, 1914, quoted in Fritz Fischer, *War of Illusions: German Policies from 1911 to 1914*, trans. Marian Jackson (New York: Norton, 1975), p. 69.

[21] In February 1914, quoted in Geiss, *July 1914*, p. 25. For more examples see Fischer, *War of Illusions*, pp. 133, 227; and Wayne C. Thompson, *In the Eye of the Storm: Kurt Riezler and the Crisis of Modern Germany* (Iowa City: University of Iowa Press, 1980), p. 120.

[22] On August 3, quoted in Bernadotte E. Schmitt, *The Coming of the War: 1914*, 2 vols. (New York: Scribner's, 1930), 2:390n.

[23] Prince Bernhard von Bülow, *Imperial Germany*, trans. Marie A. Lewenz (New York: Dodd, Mead, 1915), p. 291. On international social Darwinism see also H. W. Koch, "Social Darwinism as a Factor in the 'New Imperialism'," in Koch, ed., *The Origins of the First World War* (New York: Macmillan, 1972), pp. 329–54.

[24] Quoted in Joachim Remak, *The Origins of World War I, 1871–1914* (Hinsdale, Illinois: Dryden, 1967), p. 85. Likewise the British Colonial Secretary, Joseph Chamberlain, declared that "the tendency of the time is to throw all power into the hands of the greater empires," while the "minor kingdoms" seemed "destined to fall into a secondary and subordinate place." In 1897, quoted in Fischer, *War of Illusions*, p. 35.

Predictions of Offense-Defense Theory
about Europe, 1890–1914

Europe between 1890 and 1914 is a poor setting for directly testing offense-defense theory's prime hypothesis that offense dominance causes war. The region saw only one major war during this period, providing only one moment of variance that the prime hypothesis makes predictions about. Even if the theory correctly predicts the timing, location, and authorship of that war (as it does),[25] we learn little because many plausible alternative explanations for this single result could be offered. A failed test could likewise be explained away.

Tests of offense-defense theory's explanatory hypotheses are more revealing. In this chapter I test whether offense-dominance causes the theory's intervening phenomena H5A–H5K. (I do not test whether these intervening phenomena cause war because these claims are widely accepted, and some have already been tested.)[26]

Three predictions from offense-defense theory are tested: predictions 4, 5, and 6, listed in Chapter 6. The tests they frame range in strength from weak to strong. Together they pose a very strong test of whether offense-dominance causes intervening phenomena H5A–H5K. If we grant that these phenomena cause war, the whole theory gains credence from passed tests.

Prediction 4 forecasts that intervening phenomena H5A–H5K will be more abundant in periods of large perceived offensive advantage than at other times. Hence it forecasts that phenomena H5A–H5K and their effects should be present in above-normal abundance in 1914 Europe.

Prediction 5 forecasts that states having larger offensive opportunities and defensive vulnerabilities will adopt policies that embody intervening phenomena H5A–H5F and H5H–H5K more often than other states will. Hence these phenomena should be more pronounced in European states that believe they have larger offensive opportunities and defensive vulnerabilities. (Intervening phenomenon H5G, "less negotiation and agreement," is a reaction to other states' reaction to offense dominance; hence it should

---

[25] Belief in the strength of the offense peaked in 1914 in Europe, and Germany had the largest offensive opportunities and defensive vulnerabilities among Europe's powers. Offense-defense theory therefore forecasts that war should erupt in Europe in about 1914, authored largely by Germany.

[26] Claims that expansionism, fierce resistance to expansionism, faits accomplis, failures to reach agreements, and bellicose responses to others' blunders (intervening phenomena H5A, H5B, H5C, H5F, H5G, and H5I) cause war are untested here because they are commonplace. I omit tests of whether first-move advantages and windows of opportunity and vulnerability (intervening phenomena H5D and H5E) cause war because I address this question in Chapters 3 and 4. However, the effects of secrecy and arms races (intervening phenomena H5H and H5J) could use more study. The effect of secrecy on the risk of war has not been examined, and the argument that arms races cause war remains controversial.

be diffused across both vulnerable and invulnerable states and across both offense-capable and offense-incapable states.)

Thus expansionism should be rife in pre-1914 Europe, and should be more pronounced in powers with indefensible borders and vulnerable neighbors (Germany, Austria) and less pronounced in powers with defensible borders and no easy access to others' territory (Britain). Firm resistance to expansion should also be apparent in pre-1914 Europe.

Also, Europe's governments should perceive large first-move advantages and large windows of opportunity and vulnerability. They should adopt fait accompli diplomatic tactics, show reluctance to negotiate, and adopt dark political and military secrecy. The effects of such secrecy (e.g., blunders and miscalculations) should be evident in the diplomacy of the time. Blunders should evoke large and irreversible reactions, and states should arms-race with each other. Governments should adopt policies and hold beliefs that make offense stronger. For example, they might adopt offensive military strategies and offensive alliances, might doubt their opponents' ability to protect one another, and might engage in successful blame-shifting behavior. All these phenomena except reluctance to negotiate should be most pronounced in Germany (and perhaps Austria) and least pronounced in Britain, with intermediate levels in Russia and France.

Prediction 6 forecasts the finding of evidence indicating that elites adopted policies that embodied intervening phenomena H5A–H5J because they believed conquest was easy. Specifically, policymakers should be found arguing that these policies were advisable because conquest was easy.

Thus Europe's elites should recommend expansion for both defensive and opportunistic reasons; they should favor it because national security required it and because it would be easy. They should argue for firm resistance to others' expansion on grounds that unchecked opponents could grow dangerously strong. They should favor preemptive action on grounds that ceding the initiative will leave their country open to conquest. They should favor preventive war on grounds that otherwise their impending decline would threaten national security. They should argue that faits accomplis and dark secrecy are required by imperatives of national security. They should argue against reliance on agreement because others cannot be trusted to keep their word, and because others' secrecy will impede verification of their compliance with agreements. They should argue that national security requires fast and violent reactions to the blunders of others. They should favor military buildups on grounds that national defenses would otherwise be too weak. They should favor policies that make conquest easier on grounds that conquest is already easy. Specifically, they should favor offensive military doctrines and force postures because the offense has the advantage. They should back allies unconditionally because these allies' demise would jeopardize their national safety and because allies having only offensive military options cannot be asked to stand defenseless. They should doubt others' ability to defend third states because these third states could be overrun before they could be defended. And they should argue that the explosive military context of 1914 made blame-shifting possible.

How strong are tests that these predictions set up?

Prediction 4, that intervening phenomena H5A–H5K should be present in above-normal abundance in 1914 Europe, creates a strong test of offense-defense theory. Belief in the power of the offense was far above normal in 1914. Such strong belief should have very visible effects, and such striking effects are not predicted by any competing theory. Hence prediction 4 is both certain and unique, and a test of prediction 4 is doubly decisive: a passed test strongly corroborates offense-defense theory, a flunk strongly disconfirms it.[27]

Prediction 5, that intervening phenomena H5A–H5F and H5H–H5K should be more pronounced among European powers that believe they have larger offensive opportunities and defensive vulnerabilities, creates a weak test. European powers were few in number. Their perceptions of their offensive opportunities and vulnerabilities differed only moderately, hence offense-defense theory predicts only moderate differences in their behavior. Such moderate differences could have many causes other than their differing perceptions of offensive threats and opportunities. Thus this test tells us only a little.

Prediction 6, that policymakers will be recorded endorsing policies that embody the intervening phenomena on grounds that conquest is easy, creates a half-strong test: passage of the test strongly supports the theory, but a flunk only mildly contradicts it. Competing explanations for this testimony seem implausible, so its occurrence is strong corroboration. But leaders seldom record all their reasons for action, hence a failure to find this testimony could arise from gaps in the record. Hence flunked tests supply only weak evidence against the theory, unless we know that our records of elites' thinking and motives are complete.

Since tests of prediction 4 are stronger than tests of predictions 5 and 6, I focus below on reporting data that address prediction 4.

How does offense-defense theory perform? All three predictions are

---

[27] Some would argue that 1914 Europe poses a weak test of offense-defense theory because perceptions of offense-dominance are present in abundance, so their effects are bound to be visible. In this view a stronger test would be found in cases where belief in the offense was weaker. This view misconstrues the attributes of a strong test. Strong tests supply definitive results. A case where belief in the offense is mild supplies a weaker test of offense-defense theory because we have more ways to explain both the passage and the flunking of the test. A flunk could be blamed on our failure to detect the subtle effects of offense-dominance that we should observe in the case. A pass could be blamed on other factors, since many phenomena could be strong enough to cause these small predicted effects. Hence tests in such a setting are more indeterminate and less definitive, i.e., weaker.

broadly confirmed, providing evidence that supports ten of the theory's eleven explanations. Europe in 1914 witnessed widespread expansionism and fierce resistance to expansion. Europe's powers saw very large first-move advantages and windows of opportunity and vulnerability. They resorted to high-risk fait accompli diplomatic tactics, and they enshrouded political and military policies in dark secrecy. They reacted quickly and violently to one another's political missteps. They arms-raced with each other and adopted foreign and defense policies that made conquest easier. These policies and perceptions often were most pronounced in Germany and least pronounced in Britain. Policymakers explained these policies as required by conditions and considerations that had arisen because conquest was easy.

One explanation flunks its tests ("states negotiate less and reach fewer agreements," H5G). The theory can be repaired by striking that explanation.

Offense-defense theory's eleven explanations are considered in turn in the next section. Table 5 summarizes the case results.

EVIDENCE ON OFFENSE-DEFENSE THEORY, 1890–1914

Expansion and resistance (explanations H5A, H5B, and H5C)

In the years before 1914 Germany sought a wide empire, and World War I grew largely from the collision between German expansionism and European resistance to it. This German expansionism bloomed as the cult of the offensive grew in the years after 1890. Bismarck's Germany was sated in the 1880s, and was Europe's peacekeeper. But Kaiser Wilhelm II's Germany adopted large imperial aims and was a major international troublemaker.

Germany framed its imperial aims most clearly in the "September Program," a secret statement of war aims drawn up by Chancellor Bethmann-Hollweg in early September 1914. This program envisioned vast German expansion in Europe and Africa. In Europe, Germany would annex large territories to the east and west, and would create satellite states further afield. France would be permanently crippled and vassalized. All of Luxemburg and parts of France, Belgium, and Poland would be annexed. Russia would be pushed back in the east. Rumania, the Netherlands, a rump Polish state, and the Scandinavian states would become German satellites. Germany would also acquire most of Central Africa, creating a German colonial empire that would extend across the African continent from the Atlantic to the Indian ocean.[28]

The September Program was drawn up after war erupted, but it expressed expansionist ideas that were common currency in Germany before the

---

[28] Fritz Fischer, *Germany's Aims in the First World War* (New York: Norton, 1967), pp. xi, 103–6.

war.[29] Prewar German newsstands and bookstores were filled with expansionist tracts by such authors as Friedrich von Bernhardi, Klaus Wagner, Otto Tannenberg, Daniel Fryman, Ernst Hasse, and K. F. Wolff. The September Program only recycled their ideas.[30]

The logic behind German expansionism rested largely on two widespread beliefs: that German security required a wider empire and that such an empire was attainable, either by coercion or conquest. Thus German expansionism reflected the assumption that conquest would be easy both for Germany and for its enemies.

Prewar statements by German leaders and writers reflected a pervasive fear that Germany was in peril unless it won changes in the status quo. Kaiser Wilhelm declared that "the question for Germany is to be or not to be,"[31] and foresaw a "battle of Germans against the Russo-Gauls for their very existence" that would decide "the existence or non-existence of the Germanic race in Europe."[32] Other Germans warned that "if Germany does not rule the world . . . it will disappear from the map; it is a question of either or" and that "Germany will be a world power or nothing."[33]

Some Germans argued axiomatically that states in Germany's position must grow or die. For example, historian Heinrich von Treitschke forecast that "in the long run the small states of central Europe can not maintain themselves."[34] Some complained more specifically that German borders were constricted and indefensible. One pictured a Germany "badly protected by its unfavorable geographic frontiers"; another complained of German "frontiers which are too long and devoid of natural protection, surrounded and hemmed in by rivals, with a short coastline."[35]

Germans of both views saw a dark future for Germany. Bethmann-

---

[29] Fischer, *Germany's Aims*, pp. 9–11, 28–29, 34–35, 101.

[30] For excerpts from these authors see Notestein and Stoll, *Conquest and Kultur*, pp. 11–12, 19–20, 23, 52–54, 56, 58–59, 72, 81–83, 86–91. On prewar German aims see also Fischer, *War of Illusions*; Imanuel Geiss, *German Foreign Policy 1871–1914* (London: Routledge and Kegan Paul, 1976); Geiss, *July 1914*, pp. 17–53; and Otfried Nippold, *Der Deutsche Chauvinimus* (Berlin: W. Kohlhammer, 1913). A survey of historiographic controversies on the topic is John A. Moses, *The Politics of Illusion: The Fischer Controversy in German Historiography* (London: George Prior, 1975).

[31] In 1912, quoted in Fischer, *War of Illusions*, p. 161.

[32] In 1912, quoted in Thompson, *Eye of the Storm*, p. 42.

[33] Houston Stewart Chamberlain and Ernst Hasse, quoted in Fischer, *War of Illusions*, pp. 30, 36.

[34] In 1897, quoted in Notestein and Stoll, *Conquest and Kultur*, p. 21.

[35] Crown Prince Wilhelm, in 1913, quoted in Fischer, *War of Illusions*, p. 254; and Walter Rathenau, in July 1914, quoted in ibid., p. 450. See also Kurt Riezler, personal secretary to Bethmann-Hollweg and a proponent of German expansion, who saw a Germany "hemmed in by unfavorable frontiers." Quoted in Geiss, *German Foreign Policy*, p. 127. Also General Bernhardi, complaining that "the geographical configuration and position of our country are very unfavorable. Our open eastern frontier offers no opportunity for continued defence," having "no natural obstacle, no strong fortress." Friedrich von Bernhardi, *Germany and the Next War*, trans. Allen H. Powles (1912; New York: Longmans, Green, 1914), p. 151.

Hollweg wondered aloud if there was any purpose in planting new trees at his estate at Hohenfinow, near Berlin, since "in a few years the Russians would be here anyway." [36] A German military officer predicted that "without colonial possessions [Germany] will suffocate in her small territory or else will be crushed by the great world powers." [37]

Germans believed that expansion was feasible—perhaps even easy—as well as necessary. The kaiser told departing troops in early August, "You will be home before the leaves have fallen from the trees," and a German general forecast that the German army would sweep through Europe like a bus full of tourists: "In two weeks we shall defeat France, then we shall turn round, defeat Russia and then we shall march to the Balkans and establish order there." [38] During the July crisis a British observer noted the mood of "supreme confidence" in Berlin military circles, and a German observer reported that the German general staff "looks ahead to war with France with great confidence, expects to defeat France within four weeks." [39] While some German military planners recognized the tactical advantage that defenders would hold on the battlefield, most Germans officers and civilians thought they could win a spectacular, decisive victory if they struck at the right moment.

Bandwagon logic fed German hopes that British opposition to German expansion could be overcome. General Moltke believed that "Britain is peace loving" because in an Anglo-German war "Britain will lose its domination at sea which will pass forever to America"; hence Britain would be intimidated into neutrality. [40]

Victory, moreover, would be decisive and final. For example, Bernhardi proposed that France be "annihilated once and for all as a great power." [41]

Germany's junior partner, Austria-Hungary, also sought wide imperial goals for defensive reasons. Serbia sought Austria's downfall, so Austria had to seek Serbia's downfall. General Franz Conrad, the Austrian chief of staff, later explained that "the Monarchy had been seized by the throat [by Serbia], and had to choose between allowing itself to be strangled, and making a last effort to prevent its destruction." [42] Austria did not seek annexa-

[36] In 1913, quoted in V. R. Berghahn, *Germany and the Approach of War in 1914* (London: Macmillan, 1973), p. 186.

[37] *Nauticus*, in 1900, quoted in ibid., p. 29.

[38] Quoted in Tuchman, *Guns of August*, p. 142; and Von Loebell, quoted in Fisher, *War of Illusions*, p. 543.

[39] The English military attaché in Berlin, quoted in Albertini, *Origins*, 3:171; and Lerchenfeld, the Bavarian ambassador in Berlin, quoted in Fischer, *War of Illusions*, p. 503.

[40] In 1913, quoted in Fischer, *War of Illusions*, p. 227. See also Bernhardi's dismissal of the balance of power in Bernhardi, *Germany and the Next War*, p. 21.

[41] In 1911, quoted in Tuchman, *Guns of August*, p. 26.

[42] Sidney B. Fay, *The Origins of the World War*, 2 vols., 2d ed. rev. (New York: Free Press, 1966), 2:186; see also 1:359.

tions, but it did seek a large reordering of the Balkans. Serbia would be partitioned, with large Serb territories going to Bulgaria, Rumania, Greece, and Albania, and the Serb rump would become an Austrian vassal.[43]

A similar mixture of perceived insecurity and perceived opportunity stiffened others' resistance to Austro-German expansion and fueled a milder expansionism elsewhere in Europe, intensifying the collision between Germany-Austria and their neighbors.

Russia followed a hard-line policy of resistance to Austro-German expansionism that firmed as 1914 approached. After 1908 Russia dropped efforts to co-manage the Balkans through agreements with Austria and instead adopted a policy of building up Balkan resistance to Austrian expansion, a policy embodied in Russian sponsorship of a Serbian-Bulgarian alliance aimed at Austria (and also Turkey) in 1912. This Russian hard-line policy was driven both by the fear that Austrian expansion in the Balkans could threaten Russian security and by the hope that Russia could destroy its Austrian enemy and expand its power if war began under the right conditions. Serge Sazonov, the Russian foreign minister, saw Germany and Austria pursuing a Balkan scheme to "deliver the Slavonic East, bound hand and foot, into the power of Austria-Hungary," followed by the German seizure of Constantinople, which would gravely threaten Russian security by placing all of Southern Russia at the mercy of German power.[44] Eventually a "German Khalifate" would be established, "extending from the banks of the Rhine to the mouth of the Tigris and Euphrates," which would reduce "Russia to a pitiful dependence upon the arbitrary will of the Central Powers."[45]

At the same time, some Russians believed these threats could be addressed by offensive action. Russians considered plans for seizing the Turkish Straits preemptively before Germany could seize them.[46] Russian leaders spoke of the day when "the moment for the downfall of Austria-Hungary arrives" and of the occasion when "the Austro-Hungarian ulcer, which today is not yet so ripe as the Turkish, may be cut up."[47] Russian military officers contended that "the Austrian army represents a serious force. . . . But on the occasion of the first great defeats all of this multi-national and artificially united mass ought to disintegrate."[48]

[43] Ibid., 1:222, 250–51, 544.

[44] Serge Sazonov, *Fateful Years, 1909–1916* (London: Cape, 1928), p. 179. See also Schmitt, *Coming of the War*, 1:87.

[45] Sazonov, *Fateful Years*, pp. 191, 204.

[46] Fay, *Origins*, 1:526, 538, 545.

[47] Izvol'sky, in 1909, quoted in Schmitt, *Coming of the War*, 1:129; and Sazonov, in 1913, quoted in ibid., 1:135.

[48] *Sbornik glavnogo upravleniia general'nogo shtaba*, the secret magazine of the Russian general staff, in 1913, quoted in William C. Fuller, Jr., "The Russian Empire," in Ernest R. May, ed., *Knowing One's Enemies: Intelligence Assessments before the Two World Wars* (Princeton: Princeton University Press, 1986), pp. 98–126 at 113.

Russian leaders encouraged Serbia to prepare a future war of expansion against Austria, to be launched when the time was ripe.[49] Serbia, in its turn, needed little encouragement: it had fond dreams of large expansion at Austria's expense, to include Bosnia, Herzegovina, Croatia, and Slovenia—"the whole Slavic South" in the Serb government's words.[50]

Influenced by a popular nationalist revival, France also adopted a harder line toward Germany after 1911, including strong French backing for Russia's tough Balkan policy.[51] These changes were inspired partly by growing French fear of the German threat after 1911, partly by a related fear that Austrian expansion in the Balkans could shift the European balance of power in favor of the Central Powers and thereby threaten French security, and partly by the belief that a war could create opportunities for French expansion.[52] The stiffer French new attitude on Balkan questions in 1912 was ascribed to the French belief that "a territorial acquisition on the part of Austria would affect the general balance of power in Europe and as a result touch the particular interests of France"—a belief that assumed that the power balance was relatively precarious, which in turn assumed a world of relatively strong offense.[53] At the same time, some Frenchmen looked forward to "a beautiful war which will deliver all the captives of Germanism,"[54] inspired by a faith in the power of the offensive that was typified by the enthusiasm of Joffre's deputy, General de Castelnau: "Give me 700,000 men and I will conquer Europe!"[55] The expansionism expressed in these last two statements was more muted in France than elsewhere on the continent, but was not missing altogether.

Only in Britain—secure with its ocean moats and denied by distance a chance to seize continental empire—was expansionism largely absent. Britain was also the only major power that hesitated to resist German expansion, although in the end it did resist, largely for security reasons.[56]

[49] Fay, *Origins*, 1:383, 399, 543.
[50] Ibid., 1:358, 400, 445–46, 483–86.
[51] L. C. F. Turner, *Origins of the First World War* (London: Edward Arnold, 1970), pp. 33–36; Lieven, *Russia and the Origins of the First World War*, pp. 39–43, 48.
[52] On the growing French fears, see Eugen Weber, *The Nationalist Revival in France, 1905–1914* (Berkeley: University of California Press, 1968), passim; and Snyder, *Ideology of the Offensive*, p. 41.
[53] By the Russian ambassador to Paris, A. P. Izvol'sky, quoted in Schmitt, *Coming of the War*, 1:21.
[54] *La France Militaire*, in 1913, quoted in Weber, *Nationalist Revival*, p. 127.
[55] In 1913, quoted in Turner, *Origins*, p. 53.
[56] During the July crisis, the London *Times* warned that "the ruin of France or the Low Countries would be the prelude to our own," while other British interventionists warned that Antwerp in German hands would be a "pistol pointed at the heart of England" and that the German threat to France and the Low Countries created "a deadly peril for ourselves." The *Times* on August 4, quoted in Geoffrey Marcus, *Before the Lamps Went Out* (Boston: Little, Brown, 1965), p. 305; and the *Pall Mall Gazette* and James Gavin, on July 29 and August 2, quoted in ibid., pp. 243, 268.

Thus the three explanatory predictions of offense-defense theory are fulfilled. Expansionism was rife in Europe before 1914, as was fierce resistance to expansion. Both were largely justified on grounds that conquest was easy—this assumption that made empire building seem feasible and necessary, and made resistance to others' imperialism seem essential. Expansionist ideas flourished most in Germany, a power with insecure borders and wide opportunities to expand.

First-move advantages (explanation H5D)

European policymakers did not explicitly discuss the size of the first-move advantage before 1914. There were no direct debates about how much advantage the side moving first might gain. Three pieces of evidence indicate that governments perceived sizable first-move advantages, however. First, most European leaders thought that a mobilization by either side that was not answered very quickly could affect the outcome of the war. This judgment is reflected in the short time span that officials assumed would constitute a militarily significant delay between mobilization and offsetting counter-mobilization, and in the disastrous effects that they thought would follow if their opponents gained this lead. Second, many officials assumed that significant military preparations could be kept secret for a brief but significant period. Since they also thought that a brief unanswered mobilization could be decisive, they concluded that the side that moved first would have the upper hand. Third, governments carried out some key mobilization measures in secrecy. This suggests that they believed secret measures were feasible and worthwhile.

The perceived significance of short delays

European policymakers widely thought that a mobilization lead of only one to three days would be significant. Austria's General Conrad believed that "every day was of far-reaching importance," since "any delay might leave the [Austrian] forces now assembling in Galicia open to being struck by the full weight of a Russian offensive in the midst of their deployment."[57] In France, Marshall Joffre warned the French cabinet that once German preparations began, "any delay of twenty-four hours in calling up our reservists" would cost France "ten to twelve miles for each day of delay; in other words, the initial abandonment of much of our territory."[58] In Britain, one official believed that France "cannot possibly delay her own mobilization for even the fraction of a day" once Germany began to mobilize.[59]

---

[57] July 29, quoted in Albertini, *Origins*, 2:670.
[58] July 29, from Joseph Joffre, *The Personal Memoirs of Joffre: Field Marshall of the French Army*, 2 vols., trans T. Bentley Mott (New York: Harper, 1932), 1:125.
[59] Eyre Crowe, on July 27, quoted in Geiss, *July 1914*, p. 251.

In Germany, one analyst wrote that "a delay of a single day . . . can scarcely ever be rectified."[60] Likewise Moltke, upon receiving reports of preparations in France and Russia during the July crisis, warned that "the military situation is becoming from day to day more unfavorable for us" and would "lead to fateful consequences for us" if Germany did not respond.[61] On July 30 he encouraged Austria to mobilize, warning that "every hour of delay makes the situation worse, for Russia gains a start."[62] On August 1 the Prussian Ministry of War was reportedly "very indignant over the day lost for the mobilization" by the German failure to mobilize on July 30.[63] The German press drove home the point that if mobilization by the adversary went unanswered even briefly, the result could be fatal. One German newspaper warned that "every delay [in mobilizing] would cost us an endless amount of blood," and moving late "would be disastrous."[64]

Thus time was measured in small units: "three days," "day to day," "a single day," "the fraction of a day," or even "every hour." Moreover, policymakers believed that conceding the initiative to the adversary would bring disaster. The Russian minister of agriculture, Alexander Krivoshein, warned that if Russia delayed its mobilization, "we should be marching toward a certain catastrophe,"[65] and General Janushkevich warned the Russian foreign minister that "we were in danger of losing [the war] before we had time to unsheath our sword" by failing to mobilize promptly against Germany.[66] General Joffre feared that France would find itself "in an irreparable state of inferiority" if it were outstripped by German mobilization.[67] And in Ger-

---

[60] Kraft zu Hohenlohe-Ingelfingen, in 1898, quoted in Ropp, *War in the Modern World*, p. 203.

[61] To Bethmann-Hollweg, on July 29, quoted in Geiss, *July 1914*, p. 284.

[62] Quoted in Schmitt, *Coming of the War*, 2:196.

[63] Ibid., 2:265n.

[64] *Reinisch-Westfälische Zeitung*, on July 31, quoted in Jonathan French Scott, *The Five Weeks*, (New York: John Day, 1927), p. 146.

After the war General von Kluck, who commanded the right wing of the German army in the march on Paris, claimed that if the German army had been mobilized and deployed "three days earlier, a more sweeping victory and decisive result would probably have been gained" against France, and Admiral Tirpitz complained that German diplomats had on July 29 given Britain and Belgium several crucial days warning of the German attack, which "had an extraordinarily unfavorable influence on the whole course of the war." A delay of "only a few days" in the preparation of the British expeditionary force "might have been of the greatest importance to us." Schmitt, *Coming of the War*, 2:148n; Albertini, *Origins*, 3:242n.

A more relaxed opinion was expressed by the Prussian war minister, General Falkenhayn, who seemed to feel that it would be acceptable if German mobilization "follows two or three days later than the Russian and Austrian," since it "will still be completed more quickly than theirs." Schmitt, *Coming of the War*, 2:147. However, he also appeared to express himself in favor of prompt mobilization to forestall or at least keep pace with others at other junctures. See ibid., 1:297; 2:135–36; Albertini, *Origins*, 2:496–97; and Berghahn, *Germany and the Approach of War*, p. 203.

[65] To Sazonov, on July 30, quoted in Geiss, *July 1914*, p. 311.

[66] To Sazonov, on July 30, quoted in Albertini, *Origins*, 2:566.

[67] On August 1, Poincaré reporting Joffre's view, quoted in ibid., 3:100.

many, officials foresaw dire consequences if Germany fell much behind its enemies. Bethmann-Hollweg explained that if German mobilization failed to keep pace with Russian, Germany would suffer large territorial losses: "East Prussia, West Prussia, and perhaps also Posen and Silesia [would be] at the mercy of the Russians." Such inaction would be "a crime against the safety of our fatherland."[68]

Germans also placed a high value on gaining the initiative against Belgium. The Belgian fortresses at Liège controlled a vital railroad junction, and German forces could not seize Liège with its tunnels and bridges intact without gaining surprise. As Moltke wrote before the war, the advance through Belgium "will hardly be possible unless Liège is in our hands . . . the possession of Liège is the *sine qua non* of our advance." But seizing Liège "is only possible if the attack is made at once, before the areas between the forts are fortified," "immediately" after the declaration of war.[69] In short, the entire German war plan hinged on forestalling Belgian preparations to defend Liège.

The belief that secret preparation was feasible

Many officials assumed that military preparations could be concealed for a brief but significant period. Since most officials also believed that a brief unanswered mobilization could be decisive, it followed that the side that mobilized first would have the upper hand.

Russian officials lacked confidence in their own ability to detect German or Austrian mobilization, and their decisions to mobilize were motivated partly by the desire to forestall surprise preparation by their adversaries.[70] Sazonov reportedly requested full mobilization on July 30 partly from fear that otherwise Germany would "gain time to complete her preparations in secret."[71] Sazonov offers confirmation in his memoirs, explaining that he

[68] On August 1, quoted in Schmitt, *Coming of the War*, 2:264n; and in Albertini, *Origins*, 3:167.

[69] Ritter, *Schlieffen Plan*, p. 166. On the Liège attack see also Snyder, *Ideology of the Offensive*, pp. 112, 152–53; Schmitt, *Coming of the War*, 2:149–51; Albertini, *Origins*, 3:459–60; and Chapter 3 above, note 109. Snyder concludes that in fact "had even a few simple, planned demolitions had been carried out [at Liège], they would have devastated German logistics" (p. 112). Accordingly, the sudden seizure of Liège was crucial to the success of the German war plan.

[70] Many observers wrongly suggest that Russia raced to mobilize in 1914 because it mobilized more slowly than Germany. However, mobilizing early could not have helped Russia unless it also mobilized secretly. Otherwise an early move would have simply set off a prompt German counter-mobilization. Moreover, early mobilization could have helped Russia only if it could mobilize secretly, regardless of whether it could mobilize more or less rapidly than its adversaries, because Russia needed every advantage in the coming war and a secret early start provided an advantage. Thus Russia's slow mobilization rate was irrelevant to its haste. Rather, the key to that haste was Russia's belief in its own and its opponents' capacity to mobilize unobserved.

[71] Paléologue's diary, quoted in Albertini, *Origins*, 2:619.

had advised mobilization believing that "the perfection of the German military organization made it possible by means of personal notices to the reservists to accomplish a great part of the work quietly." Germany could then "complete the mobilization in a very short time. This circumstance gave a tremendous advantage to Germany, but we could counteract it to a certain extent by taking measures for our own mobilization in good time."[72]

Similar reasoning contributed to the Russian decision to mobilize against Austria on July 29. Sazonov explains that the mobilization was undertaken in part "so as to avoid the danger of being taken unawares by the Austrian preparations."[73]

Top Russian officials also believed that Russia could itself mobilize secretly, and some historians ascribe the Russian decision to mobilize partly to this erroneous belief. Luigi Albertini writes that Sazonov did not realize that the mobilization order would be posted publicly, and he therefore thought Russia could mobilize without Germany's knowing of it immediately.[74] Albertini reports that the German ambassador caused "real stupefaction" by appearing at the Russian Ministry for Foreign Affairs with a red mobilization poster on the morning of mobilization,[75] and he suggests that the "belief that it was possible to proceed to general mobilization without making it public may well have made Sazonov more inclined to order it."[76]

Like their Russian counterparts, French officials feared that Germany might mobilize in secret, and this fear spurred the French to their own measures. During the July crisis, General Joffre spoke of "the concealments [of mobilization] which are possible in Germany"[77] and referred to "information from excellent sources [that] led us to fear that on the Russian front a sort of secret mobilization was taking place [in Germany]."[78] In his memoirs, Joffre quotes a German military planning document acquired by the French government before the July crisis. The document, which he apparently took to indicate real German capabilities, suggested that Germany could take "quiet measures . . . in preparation for mobilization," including "a discreet assembly of complementary personnel and materiel" that would

---

[72] Sazonov, *Fateful Years*, pp. 202–3. The memorandum of the day of the Russian Foreign Ministry for July 29 records that Russian officials had considered whether Germany seriously sought peace or whether its diplomacy "was only intended to lull us to sleep and so to postpone the Russian mobilization and thus gain time wherein to make corresponding preparations." Quoted in Geiss, *July 1914*, pp. 296–97.

[73] Sazonov, *Fateful Years*, p. 188.

[74] Albertini, *Origins*, 2:624.

[75] Ibid., 2:624, quoting Taube who quoted Nolde.

[76] Ibid., 2:573. Albertini suggests that "Sazonov was such a greenhorn in military matters as to imagine the thing [secret Russian mobilization] could be done, and was only convinced of the contrary when on 31 July he saw the red notices, calling up reservists, posted up in the streets of St. Petersburg." This point "provides the key to many mysteries" (2:584, 624).

[77] On August 1, quoted in Joffre, *Personal Memoirs*, 1:128.

[78] July 29, quoted in ibid., 1:120.

"assure us advantages very difficult for other armies to realize in the same degree."[79] The French ambassador to Berlin, Jules Cambon, also apparently believed that Germany could conduct preliminary mobilization measures in secret, became persuaded during the July crisis that Germany had in fact done this, and so informed Paris: "In view of German habits, [preliminary measures] can be taken without exciting the population or causing indiscretions to be committed."[80]

German leaders apparently did not believe that they or their enemies could mobilize secretly, but they hoped and believed that Germany could surprise the Belgians. German planners referred to the *coup de main* at Liège, and the need for "meticulous preparation and surprise."[81]

Overall, then, Russians feared secret mobilization by Germany or Austria, and hoped Russian mobilization could be secret; French leaders feared secret mobilization by Germany; and German planners saw less possibility for surprise mobilization by either side, but hoped to gain surprise against Liège.[82]

---

[79] Ibid., 1:127.

[80] Cambon dispatch to Paris, July 21, quoted in ibid., 1:119. Joffre records that Cambon's telegram, which mysteriously did not arrive in Paris until July 28, convinced him that "for seven days at least the Germans had been putting into effect the plan devised for periods of political tension and that our normal methods of investigation had not revealed this fact to us. Our adversaries could thus reach a condition of mobilization that was almost complete," reflecting Joffre's assumption that secret German measures were possible. Ibid.

[81] Moltke, quoted in Ritter, *Schlieffen Plan*, p. 166.

[82] During the July crisis adversaries actually detected signs of most major secret mobilization activity within roughly six to eighteen hours, and took responsive decisions within one or two days. Accordingly, the maximum "first mobilization advantage" that a state could gain by forestalling an adversary who otherwise would have begun mobilizing first was roughly two to four days. Orders for Russian preliminary mobilization measures were issued in sequential telegrams transmitted between 4:10 P.M. on July 25 and 3:26 A.M. on July 26; Berlin received its first reports of these measures early on July 26; and at 4:00 P.M. July 27 the German intelligence board concluded that Russian premobilization had in fact begun, for a lag of roughly one and one half to two days between the issuance of orders and their definite detection. Fay, *Origins*, 2:309–15; Ulrich Trumpener, "War Premeditated? German Intelligence Operations in July 1914," *Central European History* 9 (1976): 58–85 at 67–70; Albertini, *Origins*, 2:529. Full Russian mobilization was ordered at 6:00 P.M. on July 30, first rumors reached Berlin very late on July 30, more definite but inconclusive information was received around 7:00 A.M. July 31, reliable confirmation was received at 11:45 A.M., and German preliminary mobilization was ordered at 1:00 P.M., for a lag of roughly twenty hours. Fay, *Origins*, 2:473; Schmitt, *Coming of the War*, 2:211–12, 262–65; Albertini, *Origins*, 3:24–27; Trumpener, "War Premeditated?" pp. 80–83. (However, German mobilization was apparently decided on July 30, before the Russian mobilization order was issued, so the German announcement was less a reaction to news of Russian mobilization than an independent move that Germans might have made in any case. Had the Germans not already been decided on mobilization they might have taken longer to consider their decision, hence reacting in more than twenty hours.) French preliminary measures were begun on July 25, expanded on July 26, further expanded on July 27, and remained substantially undetected on July 28. Secondary sources do not clarify when Germany detected French preliminary measures, but it seems that German discovery lagged roughly two days behind French actions. Schmitt, *Coming of the War*. 2:17–19; Joffre, *Personal Memoirs*, pp. 115–18; Trumpener, "War Premedi-

Secret actions

During the July crisis governments carried out some key military preparations in secrecy. They sometimes informed their opponents before they
moved, but on other occasions they acted secretly. This suggests that they
believed secret measures were feasible and worthwhile and that a desire to
seize the initiative may have influenced their decisions to move. On July 29
German leaders openly warned France of their intention to take preliminary
measures;[83] on July 31 they warned of their ongoing pre-mobilization and
impending mobilization measures;[84] and they openly warned Russia on
July 29 that they would mobilize if Russia conducted a partial mobilization.[85] Russia openly warned Austria on July 27 that it would mobilize if
Austria crossed the Serbian frontier,[86] and then on the twenty-eighth and
twenty-ninth it openly announced to Germany and Austria its partial mobilization of the twenty-ninth.[87] However, Russia, France, and Germany
tried to conceal several major military moves of the crisis: the Russians hid
their preliminary measures of July 25–26 and their general mobilization of
July 30;[88] the French concealed their preliminary mobilization measures of
July 25–29; and the Germans took great care to conceal their planned *coup
de main* against Liège. Thus states sometimes conceded the initiative, but
sought it at key junctures.

In sum, Europe's leaders saw a sizable first-move advantage in 1914. They
thought militarily significant head starts were attainable. This confirms prediction 4 of offense-defense theory. What about predictions 5 and 6? Was belief in a first-move advantage strongest in Germany and weakest in Britain?
Is there evidence that this belief stemmed from Europeans' assumption that
conquest was easy?

As predicted, among European powers Britain was the least jumpy. Per-

---

tated?" pp. 71–73. As for Liège, it was not captured as fast as German planners had hoped,
but it was not yet properly defended when the Germans arrived and was taken in time to allow the advance into France. Germany had scheduled its main armies to start marching
through Belgium on August 15; in fact, the last fort at Liège fell on August 16 and the German march started on August 17, two days late. Tuchman, *Guns of August*, p. 220.

[83] Albertini, *Origins*, 2:491.

[84] Schmitt, *Coming of the War*, 2:267–68.

[85] Ibid., 2:105.

[86] Albertini, *Origins*, 2:529.

[87] Ibid., 2:540, 549, 551; Geiss, *July 1914*, pp. 262, 278, 299.

[88] Albertini, *Origins*, 2:306, 591–92, 620; Geiss, *July 1914*, p. 326. Russian officials did admit
that they had taken some military steps when the Germans asked on July 26, after preliminary mobilization was underway. Sazonov responded that "no mobilization has been ordered but certain military preparations have already been taken to avoid surprises" when
asked by Friedrich Pourtalès, German ambassador to Russia, if Russia had mobilized. Albertini, *Origins*, 2:529. However, Sazonov's response hardly conveys the scope of the Russian
mobilizations then underway, and a blanket denial would have lacked credibility, since the
German military attaché in Russia, Major Eggeling, had already gotten wind of Russian mobilization measures. Thus it seems Sazonov denied as much as he plausibly could.

ceptions of first-move advantage were weaker in Britain than among the continental powers. British officials did not move to seize the initiative or urge allies to do so. Germany, however, was not the most jittery; France and Russia were even more so. German leaders did believe that a successful surprise strike on Liège would provide important rewards. But they were more relaxed about losing the first-mobilization advantage than were Russian and French leaders. Thus prediction 5 fails.

What does this result mean? Perhaps explanation H5D is weak or false. But an explanation consistent with explanation H5D is also plausible. Sentiment for preventive war was widespread in the German military before 1914.[89] Many German officers felt that Germany should start such a war by baiting its opponents into moving first. By putting Russia and France in the wrong, they thought, a baiting strategy would lower the risk of British entry against Germany and bolster German public support for the war effort. If Germans took this approach, they should feed France and Russia false evidence of Germany's ability to mobilize secretly, and they should conceal their confidence in their ability to quickly detect others' mobilizations. This would heighten French and Russian nervousness in crisis, making them easier marks for baiting.

Is this explanation sound? To answer, we need to know why the Russians and French wrongly thought Germany could mobilize "quietly" in July 1914. The historical record is silent on the Russians. We know, however, that Joffre was influenced to this view by a German military planning document acquired by French intelligence. Was this document authentic? Surely not. German planners knew that Germany could not mobilize in secret for any length of time, and a genuine German planning document would never say otherwise. It seems more likely that the Germans planted this document— and perhaps others like it—with the French and the Russians. This would serve German hawks' goals by spurring France and Russia to jump the gun in a crisis. If so, our evidence is consistent with offense-defense theory, if not with its prediction 5. German officers wanted preventive war, in part because they were imbued with the cult of the offensive. Hence they primed France and Russia to act rashly in a crisis by leading them to exaggerate the first-move advantage. If so, the pattern we observe—Germany seeing less first-move advantage than its neighbors—fits with offense-defense theory.

Regarding prediction 6, Europe's leaders said enough to make clear that they perceived a first-move advantage because they assumed conquest was easy. As noted above, they often warned that being late to move could spell their defeat.[90] Such warnings made sense only if enemies could inflict defeat

---

[89] See below at notes 98–105.

[90] See Krivoshein, Janushkevich, Joffre, and Bethmann-Hollweg, quoted above at notes 65–68; also Joffre at note 58.

with the slender resource advantage that a first move would provide—that is, if conquest was easy. Thus these warnings give indirect but clear support to prediction 6.

Windows and preventive war (explanation H5E)

Perceptions of windows and calls for preventive war were rife in 1914 Europe, especially in Germany and Austria. German leaders often warned that German power was in relative decline, and that Germany was doomed unless it took drastic action—such as provoking and winning a great crisis that would shatter the Entente, or directly instigating a "great liquidation," as one general put it.[91] German officials repeatedly warned that Russian military power would expand rapidly between 1914 and 1917 as Russia carried out its 1913–14 Great Program, and that in the long run Russian power would further outstrip German power because Russian resources were greater.[92] In German eyes this threat forced Germany to act. Jagow summarized a view common in Germany just before the July crisis broke: "Russia will be ready to fight in a few years. Then she will crush us by the number of her soldiers; then she will have built her Baltic fleet and her strategic railways. Our group in the meantime will have become steadily weaker. . . . I do not desire a preventive war, but if the conflict should offer itself, we ought not to shirk it."[93] Similarly, shortly before the July crisis, the kaiser reportedly believed that "the big Russian railway constructions were . . . preparations for a great war which could start in 1916," and he wondered "whether it might not be better to attack than to wait."[94] Around the same time, Bethmann-Hollweg declared bleakly that "the future belongs to Russia which grows and grows and becomes an even greater nightmare to us."[95] "After the completion of their strategic railroads in Poland," he warned, "our position [will be] untenable."[96] Wilhelm von Stumm, political

---

[91] Von Plessen, quoted in Isabell V. Hull, *The Entourage of Kaiser Wilhelm II, 1888–1918* (New York: Cambridge University Press, 1982), p. 261. Bethmann-Hollweg summarized German thinking when he suggested on July 8 that the Sarajevo assassination provided an opportunity either for a war that "we have the prospect of winning" or a crisis in which "we still certainly have the prospect of maneuvering the Entente apart." Thompson, *Eye of the Storm*, p. 75.

[92] The Russian program planned a 40 percent increase in the size of the peacetime Russian army and a 29 percent increase in the number of officers over four years. Lieven, *Russia and the Origins of the First World War*, p. 111.

[93] On July 18, quoted in Schmitt, *Coming of the War*, 1:321.

[94] June 21, quoted in Fischer, *War of Illusions*, p. 471, quoting Max Warburg.

[95] On July 7, quoted in ibid., p. 224.

[96] On July 7, quoted in Konrad H. Jarausch, "The Illusion of Limited War: Chancellor Bethmann Hollweg's Calculated Risk, July 1914," *Central European History* 2 (March 1969): 48–76 at 57. On July 20, Bethmann-Hollweg expressed terror at Russia's "growing demands and colossal explosive power. In a few years she would be supreme—and Germany her first lonely victim." Quoted in Richard Ned Lebow, *Between Peace and War: the Nature of International Crisis* (Baltimore: Johns Hopkins University Press, 1981), p. 258n. Friedrich Thimme re-

director of the German Foreign Ministry, likewise explained in early 1915 that Germany had reconciled itself to war in 1914 because "if the war had not come now, we would have had it in two years' time under worse conditions." Had Germany not attacked, "Russia would have attacked us two years later, and then it would have been much better armed. . . . Half of Poland would have been devastated."[97]

Perceptions of windows were especially prevalent among German military officers, leading many to openly call for preventive war during the years before the July crisis. General Moltke declared "I believe a war to be unavoidable, and: the sooner the better" at the infamous "war council" of December 8, 1912.[98] He expressed similar views to his Austrian counterpart, General Conrad, in May 1914: "To wait any longer meant a diminishing of our chances;"[99] and "we [the German army] are ready, the sooner the better for us."[100] During the July crisis Moltke remarked that "we shall never hit it again so well as we do now with France's and Russia's expansion of their armies incomplete," and he urged that "the singularly favorable situation be exploited for military action."[101] After the war, Jagow recalled that Moltke had spelled out his reasoning in a conversation in May 1914: "In two–three years Russia would have completed her armaments. The military superiority of our enemies would then be so great that he did not know how we could overcome them. Today we would still be a match for them. In his opinion there was no alternative to making preventive war in order to defeat the enemy while we still had a chance of victory. The Chief of General Staff therefore proposed that I should conduct a policy with the aim of provoking a war in the near future."[102]

Other officers, sharing Moltke's views, pressed for preventive war because "conditions and prospects would never become better."[103] General Konstantin von Gebsattel recorded the mood of the German leadership on

counted Bethmann-Hollweg's similar explanation after war erupted: "He also admits that our military are quite convinced that they could still be victorious in the war, but that in a few years time, say in 1916 after the completion of Russia's railway network, they could not. This, of course, also affected the way in which the Serbian question was dealt with." Quoted in Volker R. Berghahn and Martin Kitchen, eds., *Germany in the Age of Total War* (Totowa, N.J.: Barnes & Noble, 1981), p. 45. See also Bethmann-Hollweg's 1918 statement, quoted in Chapter 4 at note 23.

[97] John C. G. Röhl, "Germany," in Keith Wilson, ed., *Decisions for War 1914* (New York: St. Martin's, 1995), pp. 27–54 at 33.

[98] Fischer, *War of Illusions*, p. 162.

[99] Berghahn, *Germany and the Approach of War*, p. 171.

[100] Geiss, *German Foreign Policy*, p. 149.

[101] Berghahn, *Germany and the Approach of War*, p. 203.

[102] Quoted in J. C. G. Röhl, ed., *From Bismarck to Hitler: The Problem of Continuity on German History* (London: Longman, 1970), p. 70.

[103] Leuckart's summary of the views of the general staff, quoted in Geiss, *July 1914*, p. 69. For more on advocacy of preventive war by the German army, see Martin Kitchen, *The German Officer Corps, 1890–1914* (Oxford: Clarendon, 1968), pp. 96–114; and Hull, *Entourage*, pp. 236–65.

the eve of the war: "Chances better than in two or three years hence and the General Staff is reported to be confidently awaiting events."[104] The Berlin *Post*, a newspaper that often reflected the views of the general staff, saw a window in early 1914: "At the moment the state of things is favorable for us. France is not yet ready for war. England has internal and colonial difficulties, and Russia recoils from the conflict because she fears revolution at home. Ought we to wait until our adversaries are ready?" It concluded that Germany should "prepare for the inevitable war with energy and foresight" and "begin it under the most favorable conditions."[105]

German leaders also saw a short-term window of opportunity in the political constellation of summer 1914. In German eyes, the assassination of the Austrian Archduke Franz Ferdinand at Sarajevo in June created good conditions for a confrontation. A Balkan flash point ensured that Austria would join Germany against Russia and France (as Austria might not if war broke out over a colonial conflict or a dispute in Western Europe), and the assassination gave the Central Powers a plausible excuse for war, which raised hopes that Britain might remain neutral. On July 8 Bethmann-Hollweg reportedly remarked that "if war comes from the east so that we have to fight for Austria-Hungary and not Austria-Hungary for us, we have a chance of winning."[106] Likewise, the German ambassador to Rome reportedly believed on July 27 that "the present moment is extraordinarily favorable to Germany."[107]

Austrian leaders had similar visions of gaping windows. Like their German counterparts, many Austrian officials feared that the relative strength of the Central Powers was declining, and in Sarajevo they saw a fleeting opportunity to halt this decline by force. The Austrian war minister, General Alexander Krobatin, argued early in July 1914 that "it would be better to go to war immediately, rather than at some later period, because the balance of power must in the course of time change to our disadvantage."[108] The Austrian foreign minister, Count Berchtold, favored action because "our situation must become more precarious as time goes on," warning that unless

---

[104] On August 2, quoted in Fischer, *War of Illusions*, p. 403.

[105] On February 24, 1914, in Schmitt, *Coming of the War*, 1:100n; and Fischer, *War of Illusions*, pp. 371–72.

[106] Jarausch, "Illusion of Limited War," p. 58. Earlier, Bülow had explained why the Agadir crisis was an unsuitable occasion for war in similar terms: "In 1911 the situation was much worse. The complication would have begun with Britain; France would have remained passive, it would have forced us to attack and then there would have been no *casus foederis* for Austria ... whereas Russia was obliged to join in." In 1912, quoted in Fischer, *War of Illusions*, p. 85.

[107] Schmitt, *Coming of the War*, 2:66n. The German ambassador to London even warned the British Prime Minister that "there was some feeling in Germany ... that trouble was bound to come and therefore it would be better not to restrain Austria and let trouble come now, rather than later." Ibid., 1:324, quoting Lichnowsky, on July 6.

[108] On July 7, quoted in Geiss, *July 1914*, p. 84.

Austria destroyed the Serbian army in 1914 it would face "another attack [by] Serbia in much more unfavorable conditions" in two or three years.[109] The Austrian Foreign Ministry reportedly believed that "if Russia would not permit the localization of the conflict with Serbia, the present moment was more favorable for a reckoning than a later one would be."[110] Conrad lobbied relentlessly for war on preventive grounds before 1914, warning in 1912 that Austrian survival required the "overthrow of Serbia by war" and that if Austria "does not settle this life-or-death question now, it will be forced to solve it within a short time and under much more unfavorable circumstances."[111] The Austrian ambassador to Italy thought an Austro-Serbian war would be "a piece of real good fortune," since "for the Triple Alliance the present moment is more favorable than another later."[112]

Visions of windows shaped Germany's Schlieffen plan. Two windows of opportunity, one for the French and one for the Germans, persuaded German war planners to include the plan's ambitious western attack on Belgium and France. First, they foresaw that a German-Russian war, by tying down German troops in Poland, would create a ripe opportunity for France to recover the territories it lost in 1870–71.[113] Hence Germany might as well launch a forestalling attack on France if a Russo-German war loomed. Second, German planners knew that German armies could mobilize faster than the combined Entente armies, hence the ratio of forces would most favor Germany just after it finished mobilizing. Germany would therefore do best to force an early decision. This required that Germany assume the offensive, since otherwise its enemies would not offer battle until they mobilized. As one observer explained, Germany "has the speed and Russia has the numbers, and the safety of the German Empire forbade that Germany should allow Russia time to bring up masses of troops from all parts of her wide dominions."[114] France was the logical target of this offensive because French forces were in closer reach of Germany, hence Germany could inflict more damage on them than on the Russians before the window closed.

[109] On July 7, quoted in ibid., p. 81; and on July 31, quoted in Schmitt, *Coming of the War*, 2:218.

[110] Ibid., 1:372, quoting Baron von Tucher on July 18.

[111] Alfred Vagts, *Defense and Diplomacy: The Soldier and the Conduct of Foreign Relations* (New York: Kings Crown, 1956), p. 303. The *Militärische Rundschau*, an Austrian newspaper, likewise argued that "since we shall have to accept the contest some day, let us provoke it at once." On July 15, 1914, quoted in Schmitt, *Coming of the War*, 1:367. For more on preventive war and the Austrian army see Gerhard Ritter, *The Sword and the Scepter: The Problem of Militarism in Germany*, 4 vols., trans. Heinz Norden (Coral Gables, Fla.: University of Miami Press, 1969–73), 2:227–39.

[112] Count Merey, on July 29, quoted in Albertini, *Origins*, 2:383.

[113] General Bernhardi, among others, warned of "the standing danger that France will attack us on a favorable occasion, as soon as we find ourselves involved in complications elsewhere." Quoted in *Germany's War Mania* (London: A. W. Shaw, 1914), p. 161. See also Bethmann-Hollweg, quoted in Schmitt, *Coming of the War*, 2:269.

[114] Goschen, in Schmitt, *Coming of the War*, 2:321.

Finally, France (like Germany) also saw a political window of opportunity in the July crisis.[115] France feared a one-on-one war against Germany with Russia on the sidelines. Hence like Germany it preferred a war that emerged from a Balkan crisis, since this would guarantee Russian involvement. The French therefore took a Clint Eastwood "go ahead make my day" attitude in the July crisis. They did nothing to provoke the crisis, but nothing to ease it.

In sum, European policymakers saw windows everywhere in 1914, confirming prediction 4. What about predictions 5 and 6?

Perceptions of windows were most conspicuous in Germany and were weakest in Britain, as prediction 5 forecast. Germans of all stations and persuasions saw large windows for Germany, and many advised preventive war, as noted above. By contrast, in Britain there was little expressed fear of relative decline and no serious talk of preventive war, even though Britain was in fact suffering a long-term relative decline in economic and military strength against Germany.

European leaders did not explain in detail why they saw large windows, but they said enough to make clear that their logic rested on the belief that conquest was easy. As noted above, they often warned that unshut windows could spell their doom,[116] a warning that made sense only if enemies could inflict doom with a slender resource advantage—in other words, if conquest was easy. These warnings give indirect but clear support to prediction 6.

Brinkmanship and faits accomplis (explanation H5F)

Two faits accomplis by the Central Powers shaped the 1914 July crisis: the Austrian ultimatum to Serbia on July 23 and the Austrian declaration of war on Serbia on July 28. The Central Powers planned to follow these with a third fait accompli: quickly smashing Serbia on the battlefield before the Entente could intervene. These plans and actions reflected the German strategy for the crisis: "fait accompli and then friendly towards the Entente, the shock can be endured," as Kurt Riezler, Bethmann-Hollweg's top aide, summarized on July 8. One German diplomat explained that Austria declared war on Serbia "in order to forestall any attempt at mediation" by the Entente; another noted that the rapid occupation of Serbia was intended to "confront the world with a 'fait accompli.'"[117]

The Entente powers reacted quickly and fiercely to the Austro-German

---

[115] Obviously either France or Germany was wrong, since the crisis could not have favored both sides.

[116] See Jagow, Bethmann-Hollweg, and Moltke, quoted above at notes 93, 95, 96, 102.

[117] Riezler quoted in Moses, *Politics of Illusion*, p. 39; Tschirschky quoted in Schmitt, *Coming of the War*, 2:5; Jagow quoted in Albertini, *Origins*, 2:344; see also 2:453–60. For more on faits accomplis in pre-1914 German thought see Moses, *Politics of Illusion*, pp. 31–32, 35–39.

faits accomplis. Russian leaders agreed to fateful military steps, including the launching of preliminary military mobilization on July 24–25, when they first learned of the Austrian ultimatum to Serbia. France also quickly ordered preliminary military mobilization measures (on July 25). Russia answered the July 28 Austrian declaration of war on Serbia by promptly ordering mobilization against Austria. Entente troops moved almost as soon as Austro-German faits accomplis became known.

Thus 1914 saw broad resort to faits accomplis by the Central Powers and a violent reaction by others, as prediction 4 forecast. What about predictions 5 and 6? Was fait accompli thinking most prevalent in Germany? Is there evidence that policymakers resorted to faits accomplis, or reacted strongly to faits accomplis, because they thought conquest was easy?

Germany was the main instigator of Austro-German faits accomplis of 1914. It also was the clear locus of fait accompli ideas. Kurt Riezler even wrote a book that extolled what he called the diplomacy of "overbluffing"— of faits accomplis—as a means of peaceful German expansion.[118] Such ideas were scarce elsewhere in Europe, and no other power rested important policies on them.

Bethmann-Hollweg and Riezler favored faits accomplis as a risky but effective expedient to redress the grave dangers they thought Germany faced. Bethmann-Hollweg was awed by Russian military strength and often expressed acute fears of Russian invasion. Shortly before the war he voiced terror at Russia's "growing demands and colossal explosive power. In a few years she would be supreme—and Germany her first lonely victim."[119] Such a menacing threat justified perilous countermeasures: he later explained his resort to faits accomplis by noting that Germany's precarious security had "forced us to adopt a policy of utmost risk."[120]

French and Russian policymakers explained that national insecurity compelled a firm reaction to Austro-German faits accomplis. Russians feared that their security would be directly threatened if Austria crushed Serbia. Serbia added important power to their alliance, they argued, and Serbia's demise would trigger a domino effect that would run through the Balkans to Russia. After Serbia fell, Bulgaria would follow. Germany would then be on the Black Sea, able to project power directly into southern Russia. In Sazonov's words, this would be "the death-warrant of Russia."[121]

French elites voiced similar views. During the July crisis, one French ob-

---

[118] On Riezler's thought see Thompson, *Eye of the Storm*; and Moses, *Politics of Illusion*, pp. 27–44. On overbluffing see ibid., pp. 31, 35–39.

[119] On July 20, 1914, quoted in Lebow, *Between Peace and War*, p. 258n. Riezler likewise believed that Germany must grow or die, writing during the war that "we will in the long run be crushed between the great world empires . . . Russia and England" unless Germany gained a wider sphere of influence in Europe. Thompson, *Eye of the Storm*, p. 107.

[120] Jarausch, "Illusion of Limited War," p. 48.

[121] Sazonov, *Fateful Years*, p. 179. See also Chapter 6 at notes 54–56.

server warned that Serbia's demise would directly threaten French security: "To do away with Serbia means to double the strength which Austria can send against Russia: to double Austro-Hungarian resistance to the Russian Army means to enable Germany to send some more army corps against France. For every Serbian soldier killed by a bullet on the Morava one more Prussian soldier can be sent to the Moselle. . . . It is for us to grasp this truth and draw the consequences from it before disaster overtakes Serbia."[122]

Thus predictions 5 and 6 also fit the available evidence. Germany was the chief practitioner of fait accompli diplomacy, which it adopted because German leaders thought they faced grave security threats. French and Russian leaders reacted fiercely because they feared their national survival would otherwise be threatened.

States negotiate less and reach fewer agreements (explanation H5G)

Offense-defense theory predicts that agreements should often be broken, seldom trusted, and hard to reach during the run-up to 1914.[123] These predictions fail, leaving explanation H5G as the one explanation of offense-defense theory that flunks the test of 1914. There is no clear basis for saying that diplomacy deteriorated as the cult intensified after 1890, or that agreements were few circa 1914. Active international deal making continued up to 1914, embodied in the Anglo-German détente of 1912–14 and the peaceful partition of Africa, completed at Agadir in 1911.

We do see signs of mistrust and expectations of broken deals. States feared that others would attack when it suited them ("then she will crush us by the number of her soldiers")[124] and accused others of perfidy—for example, "perfidious Albion." In the July crisis, leaders widely assumed that others might strike by surprise. Thus the kaiser reached a hasty and wrong conclusion, stemming from his misreading of a telegram, that the tsar had betrayed him by mobilizing early in the crisis.[125] In short, we see a suspicious mind-set, which should impede negotiation. And, of course, the conflicts of the July crisis were not resolved by diplomacy.

Nevertheless, the predicted decline in the quantity of successful diplomacy, and in the general climate of diplomacy, do not appear in the diplomatic record of 1890–1914. This casts a shadow on explanation H5G. Either

[122] J. Herbette, July 29, in Albertini, *Origins*, 2:596.

[123] These expectations are inferred from offense-defense theory prediction 4. Prediction 6, that policymakers should blame their reluctance to negotiate on factors stemming from the cult of the offensive, is moot if there is no reluctance to negotiate. Prediction 5, that the phenomenon should be concentrated in states with large offensive opportunities and defensive vulnerabilities, does not apply to explanation H5G, as noted above.

[124] Jagow, referring to Russia, on July 18, quoted in Schmitt, *Coming of the War*, 1:321.

[125] For the Czar's telegram see Geiss, *July 1914*, p. 291. For the kaiser's reaction see ibid., pp. 294–95.

it requires conditions that were missing in the 1914 case, or it fails and should be struck from offense-defense theory.

Military and political secrecy and their effects—first-move advantages, false optimism, and blunders (explanation H5H)

Before 1914 all the European powers enshrouded their military and political policies in a secrecy so tight that top civilians were often unaware of the basic shape and nature of military plans. This secrecy, in turn, raised a host of secondary dangers.

In Wilhelmine Germany, secrecy was so tight that Chancellor Bethmann-Hollweg, Secretary of State Jagow, Admiral Tirpitz, and probably even the kaiser were unaware that the Schlieffen plan required an immediate attack on Belgium once German mobilization began.[126] Bethmann-Hollweg heard of the Belgian surprise attack plan only on July 31, 1914, after the start of Russian mobilization had made German mobilization (with its built-in Belgian attack) inevitable.[127]

As a result, top Germans failed to grasp the immense dangers of their strategy of fait accompli against Serbia and the Entente. If that strategy triggered mobilizations by any other power, war would explode immediately; there would be no weeks of bargaining during which Germany might peacefully wrest spoils from the Entente, or back off if they stood firm. There is no record of the crisis scenario that Bethmann-Hollweg and Riezler expected, but it seems likely that they blithely assumed they would have some days or weeks to negotiate after the Austrian ultimatum to Serbia and, perhaps, to organize a retreat if the Entente stood firm. We can only imagine their horror when, too late, they learned the truth. Their blunder stemmed from keeping Germany's military plans secret from Germany's own top leadership.[128]

German secrecy also fostered key blunders by other European powers.

---

[126] See Chapter 3, note 111.

[127] L. C. F. Turner, "The Significance of the Schlieffen Plan," in Paul M. Kennedy, ed., *The War Plans of the Great Powers, 1880–1914* (London: George Allen & Unwin, 1979), pp. 199–221 at 213.

[128] The political secrecy entailed in Germany's fait accompli strategy also left other powers unable to warn Germany that they would oppose the German-Austrian smashing of Serbia. This lack of warning fostered false German hopes that others would stand by without fighting, or might even side with Germany in event of war. Many German leaders falsely thought Russia would accept Austrian vassalization of Serbia without fighting. Albertini, *Origins*, 2:158–61, 301–2; Schmitt, *Coming of the War*, 1:317–20. Albertini writes that Germany "took the plunge reckoning on the acquiescence of all three *Entente* Powers and at the worst on the neutrality of England. An extraordinary illusion! . . . The World War sprang from this miscalculation" by Germany. Albertini, *Origins*, 2:161. Germany also badly misread political sentiment elsewhere in Europe, hoping that Italy, Sweden, Rumania, and even Japan would fight with the Central Powers, and that Belgium would stand aside. See ibid., 2:334, 514, 520, 673, 678; 3:233, 469–70; Geiss, *July 1914*, pp. 226, 255, 302, 350–53; Schmitt, *Coming of the War*,

Britain committed two. First, because British leaders were unaware that German mobilization meant war, they were unaware that peace required restraining Russia from mobilizing as well as attacking. As a result, the British took a relaxed view of Russian mobilization during the July crisis, while frittering away their energies on schemes to preserve peace that assumed that war could be averted even after the mobilizations began.[129] This British ignorance reflected German failure to explain clearly to the Entente that mobilization did indeed mean war—German leaders had many chances during the July crisis to make this plain but did not do so.[130] We can only guess why Germany was silent, but a desire to avoid throwing a spotlight on the Liège operation—itself a key reason why mobilization meant war— probably played a part. This desire lead German soldiers to conceal the plan from German civilians, which meant concealing the political consequences of the plan from the rest of Europe.[131] Thus German military secrecy obscured the mechanism that would unleash the war, leaving British leaders not knowing what they had to do to preserve peace.

Second, German secrecy led Britain to fail to clearly warn Germany that Britain would fight if Germany attacked westward. Britain did not clearly threaten intervention until after the crisis was out of control. The Germans apparently were misled by this. Jagow declared on July 26 that "we are sure of England's neutrality," while during the war the kaiser wailed, "If only someone had told me beforehand that England would take up arms against us!"[132] Britain failed to warn because British leaders were unaware of the

---

1:72–74, 322; 2:52–55, 149, 390n; Lebow, *Between Peace and War*, pp. 129–32. Also relevant is Albertini, *Origins*, 2:308–9, 480, 541.

[129] Albertini, *Origins*, 2:330–36, 393, 540; Geiss, *July 1914*, pp. 198, 212–13, 250–51; Schmitt, *Coming of the War*, 2:41n. In his memoirs, Grey later explained that "I did most honestly feel that neither Russian nor French mobilization was an unreasonable or unnecessary precaution. . . . How could any one urge on Russia or France that the precaution of mobilization was unreasonable? . . . I believed the French and Russian mobilizations to be preparation, but not war." Quoted in ibid. Albertini concludes that Grey "never made any attempt to prevent the various mobilizations, in fact regarded them as inevitable." Albertini, *Origins*, 2:393.

[130] See Albertini, *Origins*, 2:479–81; 3:41–43, 56, 60–65. Albertini writes that European leaders "had no knowledge of what mobilization actually was . . . what consequences it brought with it, to what risks it exposed the peace of Europe. They looked on it as a measure costly, it is true, but to which recourse might be had without necessarily implying that war would follow." This reflected German policy: Bethmann-Hollweg's ultimatum to Russia "entirely omitted to explain that for Germany to mobilize meant to begin war," and Sazonov gathered "the distinct impression that German mobilization was not equivalent to war" from his exchanges with German officials. Ibid., 2:479; 3:41, 43.

[131] Kautsky and Albertini suggest that the German deception was intended to lull the Russians into military inaction, but it seems more likely that they sought to lull the Belgians into nonprotection of Liège. Ibid., 3:43.

[132] Ibid., 2:429; Tuchman, *Guns of August*, p. 143. See also Albertini, *Origins*, 2:514–27, 643–50; Jarausch, "Illusion of Limited War"; Lebow, *Between Peace and War*, pp. 129–32; and Levy, "Preferences, Constraints, and Choices," pp. 163–70. Marc Trachtenberg has argued that Germany was not confident of British nonintervention; see Marc Trachtenberg, *History and Strategy* (Princeton: Princeton University Press, 1991), pp. 85–86. I am more persuaded

nature of the German policy until very late. This left them little time to choose and explain their response. Lulled by the Austro-German fait accompli strategy, they were unaware until July 23 that a crisis was upon them. On July 6, more than a week after the Sarajevo assassination, Arthur Nicolson, undersecretary of the British foreign office, cheerfully declared that "we have no very urgent and pressing question to preoccupy us in the rest of Europe."[133] British leaders also were apparently unaware that a continental war would begin with a complete German conquest of Belgium, thanks to the dark secrecy surrounding the Liège operation. During the July crisis, Lloyd George falsely hoped that the Germans would cross only the southern tip of Belgium: "It is only a little bit, and the Germans will pay for any damage they do."[134] The British decision to enter would have been clearer to the British, hence to the Germans, had the German operation been known in advance.

German secrecy also fostered two key Russian errors. First, because the Liège attack was secret, Russian leaders began preliminary mobilization on July 25—a step that set the stage for later mobilizations—without realizing that for Germany "mobilization meant war."[135] Second, Russia exaggerated

---

by Levy's argument that German leaders were fairly confident (though not completely confident).

[133] Schmitt, *Coming of the War*, 1:417–18; see also 1:392.

[134] Quoted in Lord Beaverbrook, *Politicians and the War 1914–1916* (1928; London: Archon Books, 1968), p. 23. In 1911 General Henry Wilson, British director of military operations, predicted that Germany would not attack Belgium in event of a Franco-German war; such an attack would be "much too dangerous." Ernest R. May, "Cabinet, Tsar, Kaiser: Three Approaches to Assessment," in May, *Knowing One's Enemies*, pp. 11–36 at 13. The French general staff expected only a modest German flanking assault through Belgium, confined to the area below the Meuse river. Paul M. Kennedy, "Great Britain before 1914," in May, *Knowing One's Enemies*, pp. 172–204 at 189; also Snyder, *Ideology of the Offensive*, pp. 44, 86, 99.

[135] Albertini, *Origins*, 2:308–9, 479–81, 515, 541, 551, 558, 574, 579–81; 3:36, 41–43, 56, 58, 60–65, 105; on the ignorance of high Russian military officers see Schmitt, *Coming of the War*, 2:207. It also seems likely that this Russian illusion persisted into the crisis and influenced Russia toward full mobilization on July 30. On July 26, after Russian preliminary mobilization was underway, the German ambassador to Russia, Friedrich von Pourtalès, warned Sazonov in general terms that mobilization meant war for Germany. Pourtalès recorded later that Sazonov asked him: "'Surely mobilization is not equivalent to war with you, either, is it?' I replied 'Perhaps not in theory. But . . . once the button is pressed and the machinery of mobilization set in motion, there is no stopping it.'" Albertini, *Origins*, 2:481. Bethmann-Hollweg also warned the Russians on July 29 that continuation of Russian preliminary mobilization "would compel us to mobilize and then a European war could scarcely be prevented." Ibid., 3:43; and for other oblique warnings see ibid., 2:549, 3:64. And on July 29 Sazonov spoke in a manner suggesting that this warning had sunk in, explaining that "in Russia, *unlike western European states*, mobilization is far from being the same as war." Ibid., p. 549, emphasis added. Sazonov's reference to Western European states must refer to Germany. Later on July 29 and again on July 31, however, Sazonov still seemed unclear on the matter. Most striking, Sazonov endorsed full mobilization to the Czar on the twenty-ninth with claims that mobilization was not tantamount to war. Ibid., 2:558. He returns to the question of whether mobilization means war on July 31, again asking the Germans if they could mobilize without war—which suggests he was still unconvinced. Ibid., 3:62, 64–65. It may be that by July 29–31 Sazonov realized that mobilization meant war, and he deliberately

the extent of German mobilization measures during the crisis, a miscalculation that helped spur Russia's fateful July 30 mobilization. German secrecy left Russia guessing at the scope of German actions, and Russia guessed on the high side—an error that hastened the rush to war.[136]

The other European powers also closed most military and political matters in dark secrecy.[137] In Britain, Foreign Secretary Edward Grey was even unaware that the British and French military staffs were developing plans for wartime Franco-British military cooperation during 1906–11.[138] In Austria the army chief of staff and his senior military officers shared only fragments of information with civilians.[139] In Russia, the military also withheld crucial data from civilians;[140] as one historian notes, this fostered "mutual incomprehension between statesmen and soldiers."[141] As a result, on July 24–25 Russian civilians began moving toward a partial south-only mobilization against Austria, unaware that this would cripple a later Russian general mobilization and hence was infeasible—Russia had to mobilize fully or not at all.[142] Thus the Russians began the slide toward mobilization unaware that the endpoint they envisioned—a Russian face-off with Austria that left Germany unthreatened—was technically impossible, and instead they would soon face an all-or-nothing mobilization choice.

In sum, dark secrecy in military and diplomatic affairs was the norm in Europe before 1914, and it had a host of dangerous effects. This confirms prediction 4.

Our data are too thin to support judgments on predictions 5 and 6. Was

---

misled the Czar because he (Sazonov) by then favored war. If so, the story still reveals that the argument that mobilization did not mean war could still be seriously made and could affect vital policy decisions (if the Czar was swayed by it—we cannot know if he was) on July 30.

Moreover, it remains possible that Sazonov never fully grasped that mobilization inexorably meant war. All German warnings were somewhat indefinite (for example, "scarcely be prevented" instead of "not be prevented" and "perhaps not in theory, but . . ." instead of "yes"); and the reason why mobilization meant immediate war—the Liège-attack mechanism that connected mobilization and war—was never explained, leaving room for misunderstanding.

Oppositely arguing that European leaders took the key decisions of the crisis knowing that mobilization meant war is Trachtenberg, *History and Strategy*, pp. 73–74, 76–80.

[136] Albertini, *Origins*, 2:566–67, 576; Schmitt, *Coming of the War*, 2:225, 237–38.

[137] Sidney Fay generalizes that the plans of Europe's militaries were held in "absolute secrecy. Not only were they unknown to Parliament and the public; they were often not even known to the Minister of Foreign Affairs, or at least their details and significance were not grasped by him." Fay, *Origins*, 1:41.

[138] Ibid., 1:41.

[139] Samuel R. Williamson, Jr., *Austria-Hungary and the Origins of the First World War* (New York: St. Martin's, 1991), pp. 102–3. Williamson notes that "Conrad seldom had to explain his analysis or submit to a counter-factual set of arguments. He had the intelligence; he drafted the war plans; he made the mistakes." Ibid., p. 103.

[140] Fuller, "Russian Empire," p. 190. This secrecy left the Ministry of Foreign Affairs "ignorant of the real state of the army."

[141] Lieven, *Russia and the Origins of the First World War*, pp. 152–53.

[142] Albertini, *Origins*, 2:292–94.

secrecy tightest in Germany, loosest in Britain? Why did Europe's leaders impose it? The historical record is too sketchy to let us make reliable cross-national comparisons. One gets the impression that secrecy was tighter in Germany than Britain, but this is a guess, inferred from the wider public discussion of military affairs in Britain. And Europe's elites left the reasons for this secrecy unexplained.

Blunders have larger and less reversible consequences (explanation H5I)

Europe's governments reacted fast and hard to each others' blunders during the 1914 July crisis, quickly making these blunders irreversible and propelling the crisis into war. In Chapter 6, I noted Russia's quick military response to Austria's ultimatum to Serbia and Germany's quick military response to Russia's military move.[143] These rapid reactions left Germany and Russia little time to retrace their steps and left Britain little chance to reverse its disastrous decision not to restrain Russia from mobilizing. This chain reaction corroborates prediction 4, which forecasts fast and violent reactions to other states' errors in 1914 Europe.

Prediction 5 forecasts that powers that thought they faced above-average offensive opportunities and defensive vulnerabilities should react more forcefully to others' blunders in 1914. This prediction fails. Germany saw more offensive opportunities and defensive vulnerabilities in 1914, but Russia and France were more jumpy. But this pattern could be explained in a way consistent with offense-defense theory, if French and Russian perceptions of a first-move advantage were planted by German officers who sought a war begun by France or Russia, as I speculated above. If so, French and Russian jumpiness was sown by Germany. Events are then consistent with offense-defense theory, if not with prediction 5. Germany's insecurity led it to foster anxiety in France and Germany in order to get them to begin a preventive war that Germany desired.

Prediction 6, that policymakers should explain their rapid and violent reactions as required by offense-dominant conditions, cannot be tested because policymakers did not record their reasons for these decisions in any detail.

Arms racing (explanation H5J)

The years before 1914 saw a burst of naval arms racing between Britain and Germany (1898–1912) and a ground arms race between Germany and the Franco-Russian alliance (1912–14).[144] Contemporary Europeans widely

---

[143] See Chapter 6 at notes 99–103.

[144] On the ground arms race see David G. Herrmann, *The Arming of Europe and the Making of the First World War* (Princeton: Princeton University Press, 1996), pp. 173–237; for data on

felt they were witnessing an intense arms race, and historians have characterized the 1898–1914 era as one marked by arms racing. The percentage of the national population in military service was higher in every European power in 1914 than in 1890.[145] These facts corroborate offense-defense theory prediction 4, which forecast above-average arms racing in 1914.

Military spending as a share of GNP, however, was lower in 1914 than during the European arms race in the late 1930s or the Soviet-American Cold War arms race.[146] Hence the intensity of the arms race of 1914 depends on the baseline used for comparison. The 1914 race was intense compared to late-nineteenth-century arms competition, but tame compared to the 1930s or 1950s.

How to interpret this pattern? The increase in the percentage of national income spent on armaments after 1918 probably reflects the growing power of modern states to extract resources from society. If so, it seems plausible that military spending in 1914 might have reached later levels had nations in 1914 possessed the extractive capacities of later powers. Hence it seems fair to discount straight comparisons to later decades as a measure of arms racing in 1914 and conclude that 1914 did see above-average arms competition, as prediction 4 forecast.

The most secure European powers spent the least on defense in 1914, but the least secure did not spend the most. Of the six major powers, the most secure powers, Britain and Italy, spent the smallest share of their national income on the military. However, Russia and France devoted a greater share of national income to the military than did Germany, and Russia also spent more than Austria. Overall we see a faint correspondence between insecurity and arms racing, as prediction 5 forecast. The test is passed, but just barely.

---

army personnel and expenditures see pp. 234, 237. For data on military and naval personnel and on warship tonnages during 1880–1914 see Paul Kennedy, *The Rise and Fall of the Great Powers: Economic Change and Military Conflict from 1500 to 2000* (New York: Random House, 1987), p. 203. Hermann's figures shows a spurt of continental ground arms racing from 1912 to 1914. Kennedy's figures shows a spurt of Anglo-German naval racing after 1900 (compare tables 17 and 20, which show British and German warship tonnage growing markedly faster than national industrial potential during 1900–13). Another estimate of army and navy spending is A. J. P. Taylor, *Struggle for Mastery in Europe, 1848–1918* (New York: Oxford University Press, 1954), p. xxvii–xxviii.

[145] From 1890 to 1914 the percentage of national population in military service rose from 1.02 to 1.33 percent in Germany; from 1.42 to 2.29 percent in France; from .58 to .77 percent in Russia; from 1.12 to 1.17 percent in Britain; from .81 to .85 percent in Austria-Hungary; and from .95 to .98 percent in Italy. Calculated from Kennedy, *Rise and Fall*, pp. 199, 203. My percentages for 1914 divide military personnel figures for 1914 by population figures for 1913.

[146] A. J. P. Taylor reports the percent of national income devoted to armaments by the major powers in 1914 as follows: Russia, 6.3 percent; Austria-Hungary, 6.2 percent; France 4.8 percent; Germany 4.6 percent; Italy 3.5 percent; Britain 3.4 percent. *Struggle for Mastery,* p. xxix. In contrast, Paul Kennedy reports the percent of national income devoted to armaments in 1937 as follows: Japan, 28.2 percent; the Soviet Union, 26.4 percent; Germany, 23.5 percent; Italy, 14.5 percent; France, 9.1 percent; and Britain, 5.7 percent. Kennedy, *Rise and Fall*, p. 332.

In accord with prediction 6, European leaders explained that their arms racing was required to address threats to national survival. Bethmann-Hollweg justified the German military buildup on security grounds, proclaiming that "for Germany, in the heart of Europe, with open boundaries on all sides, a strong army is the most secure guarantee of peace." The German kaiser likewise wrote that Germany needed "more ships and soldiers . . . because our existence is at stake."[147]

In sum, arms racing was probably above average in 1914. Leaders explained this arms racing as a response to security threats that were magnified in their minds by their perceptions of offense dominance. Military spending by the powers correlates with their offensive opportunities and vulnerabilities, but only very loosely. Thus two predictions of offense-defense theory have modest support, and one barely passes.

Conquest grows easier (explanation H5K)

As belief in the power of the offensive spread before 1914, four related phenomena appeared that made conquest easier, or appear to be easier. The European powers adopted increasingly offensive military doctrines and force postures; Europe's alliances drifted from defensive to defensive-and-offensive; Germany's respect for Britain's capacity to intervene against a continental aggressor declined; and Germans hoped and planned to shift blame for a future war onto others.

Military posture and doctrine (explanation H5K1)

The military doctrines and force postures of Europe's major powers grew increasingly offensive during the decades before 1914, and reached an offensive extreme during 1913–14. In 1879–90 Germany had embraced Moltke the Elder's plan for a defensive stand in the west and a limited offensive in the east in event of war with Russia and France.[148] This plan was then replaced by Schlieffen's far more grandiose plan for two decisive offensives, first to the west and then to the east, developed during and after Schlieffen's tenure as chief of staff of the German army (1891–1905).[149] In 1913, Germany's commitment to the offensive reached a new extreme. Until 1913 the army annually updated an alternative plan for an Elder Moltke–style initial

---

[147] Both in 1912, quoted in Konrad Jarausch, *The Enigmatic Chancellor: Bethmann Hollweg and the Hubris of Imperial Germany* (New Haven: Yale University Press, 1973), p. 95; and Fischer, *War of Illusions*, p. 165.

[148] Snyder, *Ideology of the Offensive*, pp. 130–32; Ritter, *Schlieffen Plan*, pp. 17–21.

[149] On the Schlieffen plan see Snyder, *Ideology of the Offensive*, pp. 132–56; Ritter, *Schlieffen Plan*.

concentration in the east (which presumed defense in the west). Thereafter it updated only Schlieffen's scheme for sequential west-then-east attacks.[150]

Russia's 1875 and 1880 plans for a future war against Germany and Austria were more defensive than offensive: they charted early defensive operations followed later by a counteroffensive.[151] Russian doctrine then grew more offensive during 1880–1905. The Russian plan of 1900–1902 outlined an offensive in the first month of a war.[152] Russian planners returned to a more defensive approach after Russia's defeat in the 1904–5 Russo-Japanese War, and they adhered to a defensive doctrine until 1912. Then, during 1912–14, they embraced the highly offensive Plan 20—the plan with which they went to war.[153] It posited an ambitious three-pronged offensive against Germany and Austria-Hungary.

French doctrine was largely defensive before 1884, became more offensive beginning in 1887, and achieved an offensive extreme with Plan 17, which was adopted in 1913.[154] It posited an all-out offensive against Germany's stout defenses in Lorraine and the Ardennes, conducted under the guiding principle that "whatever the circumstances, it is the . . . intention to advance with all forces to the attack."[155]

Defensive vs. defensive-and-offensive alliances (explanation H5K2)

The alliances of 1914 began as defensive agreements, but evolved over time into more offensive partnerships. By 1914 the Austro-German alliance and the Franco-Russian-British Triple Entente were de facto offensive alliances, and they operated as offensive alliances in the July crisis. Germany backed Austria unconditionally—indeed, pushed Austria forward—largely because German leaders believed that German security required Austria's survival, and that Austria's survival was threatened by Serb subversion. Russia likewise backed Serbia unconditionally, and Britain and

---

[150] Fischer, *War of Illusions*, p. 173. The Schlieffen plan's finishing touch—the fateful Liège attack that melded mobilization and war—was also adopted at this time (specifically, and appropriately given its flaws, on April 1, 1913). Ritter, *Sword and the Scepter*, 2:266.

[151] Lieven, *Russia and the Origins of the First World War*, p. 101.

[152] Ibid.

[153] On the evolution of Russian doctrine see Snyder, *Ideology of the Offensive*, pp. 157–98. Plan 19 Revised was technically still in effect in August 1914, but the Russian concentrations reflected its successor, Plan 20. Ibid., p. 183.

[154] Jay Luvaas, "European Military Thought and Doctrine, 1870–1914," in Michael Howard, *The Theory and Practice of War* (Bloomington: Indiana University Press, 1965), pp. 69–94 at 80–81; Gerd Krumeich, *Armaments and Politics in France on the Eve of the First World War: The Introduction of Three-Year Conscription 1913–1914*, trans. Stephen Conn (Leamington Spa, England: Berg, 1984), p. 119. On French doctrine see also Snyder, *Ideology of the Offensive*, pp. 41–106; and Samuel R. Williamson, Jr., *The Politics of Grand Strategy: Britain and France Prepare for War, 1904–1914* (Cambridge: Harvard University Press, 1969), pp. 115–30, 205–26.

[155] Foch, quoted in Luvaas, "European Military Thought," p. 81. Austrian doctrine also was highly offensive in 1914, charting sequential offensives against Serbia and Russia. Norman Stone, "Austria-Hungary," in May, *Knowing One's Enemies*, pp. 37–61 at 38.

France backed Russia unconditionally.[156] As a result, Europe's most bellicose states could drag the rest into their local disputes, creating a general war.

The Austro-German alliance was offensive simply because its members had compatible aggressive aims. The Entente was offensive because security interdependence among its members was high and because its most excitable member, Russia, had no defensive military options.

Britain and France feared they might fracture the Entente if they pressed Russia too hard for restraint, so they tempered their demands to preserve the alliance. Raymond Poincaré, the president of France, wrote later that France had been forced to reconcile its efforts to restrain Russia with the need to preserve the Franco-Russian alliance, "the break up of which would leave us in isolation at the mercy of our rivals."[157] Likewise, Winston Churchill recalled that "the one thing [the Entente states] would not do was repudiate each other. To do this might avert the war for the time being. It would leave each of them to face the next crisis alone. They did not dare to separate."[158] These fears were probably overdrawn, since Russia needed Britain and France as much as Britain and France needed Russia, but they affected French and British behavior.[159] Such fears in turn reflected the assumption in France and Britain that the security of the Entente members was closely interdependent.

Britain and France also were hamstrung by the offensive nature of Russian military doctrine, which left them unable to demand that Russia confine itself to defensive preparations. The British ambassador to St. Petersburg warned that Britain faced a painful decision, to "choose between giving Russia our active support or renouncing her friendship."[160] Had Russia confined itself to preparing defensively, it would have sacrificed its Balkan interests by leaving Austria free to attack Serbia, which it would have been very reluctant to do. However, the British government was probably willing to sacrifice Russia's Balkan interests to preserve peace;[161] what it could not do was to frame a request to Russia that would achieve this, because there

---

[156] As Albertini summarized, if Sazonov "committed a terrible mistake in resorting to mobilization before diplomacy had irreparably failed to compose the [Austro-Serbian] dispute, no influence was exercised by France or England . . . to hold him back from the fatal step he was about to take. Paléologue urged him to be unyielding, Grey thought it natural . . . that Russia should mobilize against Austria." Albertini, *Origins*, 2:540.

[157] Ibid., 2:605.

[158] Winston Churchill, *The Unknown War* (New York: Scribner's, 1931), p. 103.

[159] Grey later wrote that he had feared that a German diplomatic triumph "would smash the Entente, and if it did not break the Franco-Russian alliance, would leave it without spirit, a spineless and helpless thing." Likewise, during July 1914 Harold Nicolson wrote: "Our attitude during the crisis will be regarded by Russia as a test and we must be careful not to alienate her." Schmitt, *Coming of the War*, 2:38, 258.

[160] Buchanan, in Fay, *Origins*, 2:379.

[161] See Geiss, *July 1914*, p. 176; Albertini, *Origins*, 2:295.

was no obvious class of defensive activity that it could demand. Edward Grey, the British foreign secretary, wrote later: "I felt impatient at the suggestion that it was for me to influence or restrain Russia. I could do nothing but express pious hopes in general terms to Sazonov. If I were to address a direct request to him that Russia should not mobilize, I knew his reply: Germany was much more ready for war than Russia; it was a tremendous risk for Russia to delay her mobilization."[162] This statement reveals a losing struggle to cope with the absence of defensive options. Russia was threatened, and it must mobilize. How could Britain object?

German contempt for British capacity to defend France (explanation H5K3)

Wilhelmine German military planners thought the Germany army could overrun France before Britain could move large forces to its defense. Hence they discounted the British backlash that their invasion of Belgium and France would provoke. Schlieffen declared that if the British army landed, it would be "securely billeted" at Antwerp or "arrested" by the German armies,[163] while Moltke said he hoped that it would land so that the German army "could take care of it."[164] German leaders also hoped that German power would cow Britain into neutrality or that Britain would hesitate before entering the war and then quit in discouragement once the French were beaten. Schlieffen expected that "if the battle [in France] goes in favor of the Germans, the English are likely to abandon their enterprise as hopeless." This hope led the Germans to further discount the risk of British opposition.[165]

Such thinking was a marked change from that of Bismarck's era (1862–90), when German leaders feared British strength and made no move on the continent before ensuring that Britain would not oppose it with force.

Blame shifting (explanation H5K4)

Many Germans who favored war also thought Germany had to avoid blame for its outbreak, to preserve British neutrality and German public support for the war. Moreover, they seemed confident that Germany could shift blame for the war onto its opponents. Moltke counseled war but noted that "the attack must be started by the Slavs," seemingly confident that this could be arranged.[166] Bethmann-Hollweg decreed that "we must give the

[162] Ibid., 2:518.

[163] Ritter, *Schlieffen Plan*, pp. 71, 161–62; Geiss, *German Foreign Policy*, p. 101. But see also Moltke quoted in Turner, *Origins*, p. 64.

[164] Ritter, *Sword and Scepter*, 2:157.

[165] Ritter, *Schlieffen Plan*, p. 163. See also Bethmann-Hollweg, quoted in Fischer, *War of Illusions*, pp. 169, 186–87.

[166] In 1913, in Albertini, *Origins*, 2:486.

impression of being forced into war" if war broke out, and declared it "imperative" that responsibility for the war "should in all circumstances fall on Russia."[167] Admiral von Müller summarized German policy during the July crisis as being to "keep quiet, letting Russia put itself in the wrong, but then not shying away from war."[168] "It is very important that we should appear to have been provoked" in a war arising from the Balkans, wrote Jagow, for "then—but probably only then—Britain can remain neutral."[169] And as the war erupted, von Müller wrote, "The mood is brilliant. The government has succeeded very well in making us appear as the attacked."[170]

These and other statements reveal a German confidence that German responsibility for the war could be concealed. This confidence was well placed. World War I was, in a sense, the international "crime of the century"; Germany sparked a world war but escaped blame for decades. Germany's wartime and postwar innocence campaign enjoyed huge success.[171] During the war the German public accepted official claims of German innocence, Russian aggression, and British encirclement. After the war the myth of German innocence flourished in Germany and spread to Britain and the United States, where it fostered an isolationism that left Hitler uncontained and helped cause World War II. The success of this innocence campaign reflected the impact of the cult of the offensive. The war developed from an explosive chemistry of provocation and response—a chemistry made explosive by the cult of the offensive—that could easily be misconstrued by a willful propagandist or a gullible historian. To the untrained eye, defenders seemed like aggressors because all defended quickly and aggressively.

[167] On July 27, 1914, in Fischer, *War of Illusions*, pp. 486–87.

[168] On July 27, in J. C. G. Röhl, "Admiral von Muller and the Approach of War, 1911–1914," *Historical Journal* 12, no. 4 (1969): 669. In the same spirit, Bernhardi (who hoped for Russian rather than British neutrality) wrote before the war that the task of German diplomacy was to spur a French attack. He continued: "We must not hope to bring about this attack by waiting passively. Neither France nor Russia nor England need to attack in order to further their interests. . . . [Rather] we must initiate an active policy which, without attacking France, will so prejudice her interests or those of England that both these States would feel themselves compelled to attack us. Opportunities for such procedures are offered both in Africa and in Europe." Bernhardi, *Germany and the Next War*, p. 280.

[169] In 1913, in Fischer, *War of Illusions*, p. 212.

[170] Röhl, "Admiral von Müller," p. 670.

[171] On this innocence campaign, see Holger H. Herwig, "Clio Deceived: Patriotic Self-Censorship in Germany After the Great War," *International Security* 12 (Fall 1987): 5–44; and Imanuel Geiss, "The Outbreak of the First World War and German War Aims," in Walter Laqueur and George L. Mosse, eds., *1914: The Coming of the First World War* (New York: Harper & Row, 1966), pp. 71–78.

In sum, in the years before 1914 Europe's leaders adopted policies and beliefs that made conquest easier, or made it seem easier. This supports prediction 4.

What about predictions 5 and 6? Was commitment to an offensive military posture and doctrine more pronounced in Germany than elsewhere? Did elites testify that they embraced offense-easing policies and beliefs because they believed conquest was easy?

Commitment to offensive military postures and doctrines reached a fairly uniform extreme across the European continent by 1914. No power could possibly have had a more offensive doctrine than Germany's 1914 Schlieffen plan, but France, Russia, and Austria all matched German enthusiasm for offense. Russian and French offensive enthusiasm did temporally lag behind German enthusiasm, however. Russian doctrine went through a defensive phase from 1905 to 1912, and France did not reach the offensive extreme of Plan 17 until 1913. As late as 1910, Russia had a very defensive war plan and France a relatively defensive one.[172] If, therefore, we consider the entire latter part of the era of the cult of the offensive (1900–14), offensive war planning does seem somewhat more pronounced in Germany, an observation that mildly supports prediction 5.

Elites justified the adoption of offensive military doctrines and postures on grounds that the offense was strong.[173] Leaders who gave allies unconditional backing claimed they were compelled to do so by their inability to demand that allies with no defensive military options conduct themselves defensively,[174] and by the threat to national security that would arise if they left their allies in the lurch.[175] Germans who dismissed British capacity to defend France argued that Germany could overrun France before large British forces could cross the channel,[176] and that Britain might be cowed into inaction.[177] Thus three elements of prediction 6 are supported.

The reasons why Germans believed they could shift blame to their enemies and why they succeeded in doing so are more obscure. German leaders did not record why they thought blame shifting would succeed, and those who were gulled never explained why they were fooled. So this forecast of prediction 6 is untested.

[172] Snyder, *Ideology of the Offensive*, p. 10.
[173] See, for example, the statements by August Keim and the French army's 1895 infantry regulations, quoted above at notes 4 and 6.
[174] For example Grey, quoted above at note 173.
[175] See, for example, Poincaré and Churchill, quoted above at notes 157 and 158.
[176] Schlieffen's plan assumed victory over France in a month or less. Snyder, *Ideology of the Offensive*, p. 109.
[177] For example, Schlieffen, quoted above at note 165.

OFFENSE-DEFENSE THEORY AND THE TEST OF 1914

The 1914 case supplies strong support for offense-defense theory. It allows a test of twenty-seven predictions from offense-defense theory (see Table 5).[178] The phenomena that these twenty-seven predictions forecast—above-average levels of expansionism, fierce resistance to expansionism, first-move advantages, windows of opportunity and vulnerability, fait accompli diplomatic tactics, secrecy, rapid and violent responses to others' blunders, arms racing, policies and beliefs that make conquest seem or become easier (here embodied specifically in offensive military doctrines and alliances, German dismissal of British power, and German confidence in its ability to shift blame for war to others), a focus of these phenomena in Germany, and arguments by elites that policies embodying these phenomena were expedient because conquest was easy—constitute a disparate and fairly uncommon group whose simultaneous appearance in 1914 Europe is not forecast by any competing explanation. Most of these predictions (twenty-four of the twenty-seven) are fulfilled (see Table 5). Two of the three unfulfilled predictions (explanation H5D, prediction 5; explanation H5I, prediction 5) may be non-predictions: offense-defense theory may not really make the falsified forecast. The other is hard to explain away (explanation H5G, "less negotiation and agreement," prediction 4), but it casts doubt on only one strand of offense-defense theory. We can repair the theory by removing that strand.

The strongest pieces of evidences are the observations that corroborate prediction 4, forecasting an abundance of intervening phenomena H5A–H5K in 1914. The presence of these phenomena together in such profusion in Europe in 1914 is a striking oddity that has no plausible explanation aside from the action of offense-defense theory. Their appearance is powerful evidence for the theory.

Where does this leave offense-defense theory? Clear passage of a strong test gives a theory strong support. The 1890–1914 case poses a number of tests. Some are weak but some are strong, and together they pose a very strong test. Offense-defense theory clearly passes. Its predictions are quite congruent with the observed realities of 1914, and the three instances where its predictions fail inflict no fatal wounds on the theory. Ergo, offense-defense theory has a strong claim to credence. We have a verdict: war is markedly more likely when conquest is easy, or is believed easy.[179] This

---

[178] I am counting as "tested" all predictions other than those labeled "Don't know" and "Doesn't apply."

[179] Some argue that no single case study can tell us much. However, a single case that tests unique and certain predictions can be very decisive. I suggest two examples from hard

Table 5. Testing offense-defense theory: World War I

Predicted Phenomenon	Prediction 4: Was the intervening phenomenon present in above-average amounts in Europe in 1914?	Prediction 5: If the intervening phenomenon is a national attribute, was it more prominent in states with large offensive opportunities and defensive vulnerabilities (e.g., Germany) and less prominent elsewhere (e.g., Britain)?	Prediction 6: Did elites claim that policies that embodied the intervening phenomenon were required or invited by offense dominance, or by its effects?
Expansionism, and firm resistance to expansionism (H5A–H5C)	Yes: expansionism was abundant in 1914 Europe; resistance to it was fierce.	Yes (for expansion; firm resistance to expansion was diffused everywhere).	Yes: expansionists evoked need for secure borders as a key argument for their program; proponents of fierce resistance to expansion also made security arguments.
Perceived first-move advantages (H5D)	Yes: 1914 was a rare case of preemptive war.	No, but . . . the theory may predict the pattern we see.	Yes: elites thought first-movers would make big gains.
Perceived windows (H5E)	Yes: elites saw many windows, and struck for preventive reasons.	Yes: Germans saw large windows for Germany, Britons did not see windows for Britain.	Yes: elites foresaw decisive wins for window-jumpers.
Fait accompli diplomacy (H5F)	Yes: 1914 saw major use of faits accomplis.	Yes: Germany and Austria authored the faits accomplis of 1914.	Yes: security fears drove the German-Austrian faits accomplis and strong Franco-Russian reactions to them.
Less negotiation and agreement (H5G)	No.	Doesn't apply.	Doesn't apply.
Dark military & political secrecy (H5H)	Yes: Europe's powers hid policy in dark secrecy.	Don't know (thin data).	Don't know (thin data).
Blunders have larger & less reversible effects (H5I)	Yes: the July crisis saw fast, strong reactions to blunders.	No, but . . . the theory may predict the pattern we see.	Don't know (thin data).

Table 5. (continued)

Predicted Phenomenon	Prediction 4: Was the intervening phenomenon present in above-average amounts in Europe in 1914?	Prediction 5: If the intervening phenomenon is a national attribute, was it more prominent in states with large offensive opportunities and defensive vulnerabilities (e.g., Germany) and less prominent elsewhere (e.g., Britain)?	Prediction 6: Did elites claim that policies that embodied the intervening phenomenon were required or invited by offense dominance, or by its effects?
Arms racing (H5J)	Tentative yes—depends on how arms racing is measured.	Yes—barely.	Yes: buildup advocates used national security arguments.
Offensive force postures and doctrines (H5K1)	Yes: European doctrines were offensive.	Tentative yes.	Yes: offense proponents argued that offense was strong.
Offensive alliances (H5K2)	Yes: European alliances were offensive.	Doesn't apply.	Yes: leaders backed allies unconditionally for security reasons.
German dismissal of British capacity to defend France (H5K3)	Yes: Germany dismissed British capacity to help France in 1914.	Doesn't apply.	Yes: Germans expected victory over France before Britain could intervene.
Confidence in blame shifting (H5K4)	Yes: Germans thought they could shift blame.	Doesn't apply.	Don't know (thin data).

claim is further strengthened by the theory's passage of the three tests reported in Chapter 6.

Do these tests close the case on offense-defense theory, or is there more to know? They show beyond much question that the theory is valid and important. But a glance at other cases shows that offensive capabilities and beliefs do not always raise the risk of war. In the late 1930s, Soviet, French, and British belief in the power of the *defense* contributed to the outbreak of World War II. In the early 1950s, an offensive U.S. military buildup probably

science in Van Evera, *Guide to Methods for Students of Political Science* (Ithaca: Cornell University Press, 1997), pp. 66–67.

caused a Soviet political stand-down. Clearly, the dangers of offense dominance have important bounding and limiting conditions, missing in these
cases. These conditions need specification and testing. (I offer my guesses
on what these conditions are in Chapter 6.)

EXPLAINING WORLD WAR I

Offense-defense theory passes the test of World War I. It also offers a
simple and satisfying explanation for the war.

Older explanations for World War I hold that a number of disparate dangers appeared together in Europe in 1914 by tragic coincidence, bringing
about the war. Historians dispute which dangers mattered most. Fischer
school adherents point to Austro-German expansionism, German hunger
for preventive war, and reckless Austro-German fait accompli tactics. Their
opponents emphasize Russia's precipitous mobilizations, which pushed the
July crisis over the brink. Others point to the "tight" nature of Europe's alliance systems (which spread a local Balkan war to the rest of Europe), to the
naval and land arms races, to the inflexibility and multifront nature of German and Russian war plans, to the imperative that "mobilization meant
war" for Germany, to British failure to take early steps to deter Germany and
restrain Russia, and to Russian or Austrian blundering in the July crisis. But
most agree that several causes mattered, and none explain why they appeared together in 1914.

Offense-defense theory suggests that all these causes stemmed from a
common source, the prevalent belief that conquest was easy. German expansion stemmed from German security fears and from German faith in the
feasibility of quick victory in a war of conquest. Insecurity also fueled Austrian expansionism and inspired sharp Franco-Russian resistance to Austro-
German expansionism. German desire for preventive war stemmed from
German fears that a small relative decline would open Germany up to conquest from without. Austro-German fait accompli tactics reflected their
leaders' gloomy belief that their states had to grow or die, hence that large
risks had to be run to win wider spheres of influence. Russia's quick mobilizations reflected Russian belief that a small material advantage could be
parlayed into decisive victory and that a preemptive mobilization would realize it.

The tightness of the Triple Entente and the Russo-Serbian alliance
stemmed, first, from British, French, and Russian fears that the loss of a
single ally could spell their own demise and, second, from the offensive
shape of Russian war plans, which precluded British demands that Russia
confine itself to defensive military preparations in July 1914. Russian and
German war plans required early offensives in all directions because the

Diagram 4. Complex and simple explanations for World War I

"That which is simple is also good"—Moltke the Elder

Complexity: A traditional explanation for the origins of the First World War

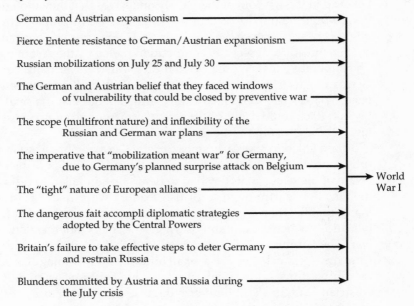

German and Austrian expansionism

Fierce Entente resistance to German/Austrian expansionism

Russian mobilizations on July 25 and July 30

The German and Austrian belief that they faced windows
of vulnerability that could be closed by preventive war

The scope (multifront nature) and inflexibility of the
Russian and German war plans

The imperative that "mobilization meant war" for Germany,
due to Germany's planned surprise attack on Belgium

The "tight" nature of European alliances

The dangerous fait accompli diplomatic strategies
adopted by the Central Powers

Britain's failure to take effective steps to deter Germany
and restrain Russia

Blunders committed by Austria and Russia during
the July crisis

→ World
War I

Simplicity: The "cult of the offensive" explanation for the origins of the First World War

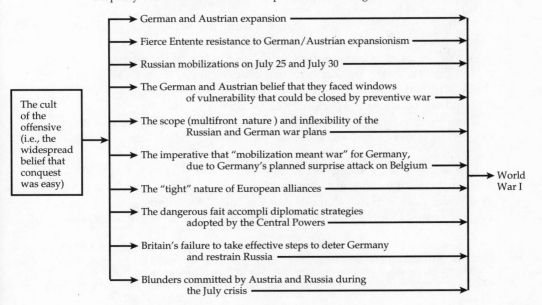

The cult
of the
offensive
(i.e., the
widespread
belief that
conquest
was easy)

German and Austrian expansion

Fierce Entente resistance to German/Austrian expansionism

Russian mobilizations on July 25 and July 30

The German and Austrian belief that they faced windows
of vulnerability that could be closed by preventive war

The scope (multifront nature) and inflexibility of the
Russian and German war plans

The imperative that "mobilization meant war" for Germany,
due to Germany's planned surprise attack on Belgium

The "tight" nature of European alliances

The dangerous fait accompli diplomatic strategies
adopted by the Central Powers

Britain's failure to take effective steps to deter Germany
and restrain Russia

Blunders committed by Austria and Russia during
the July crisis

→ World
War I

Russian and German militaries believed that the only successful strategy was to launch early offensives against every actual and potential enemy: otherwise opponents would strike at an opportune moment and bring them ruin. These plans were inflexible because European militaries so strongly believed in the wisdom of these early offensives that they thought other options would be unwise to choose, hence unwise to prepare since civilians might unwisely choose them in a crisis. The European arms races of 1898–1914 stemmed from security competition fueled by the cult of the offensive. The imperative that "mobilization meant war" for Germany stemmed from Germany's decision to launch a surprise attack on Belgium even as it mobilized. This decision stemmed from German belief that the small gains won by this attack could decide the war for Germany, and German ruin could follow if these gains were foregone.

Britain failed to take early steps to deter Germany because Germany carefully concealed its planned attack on Belgium, which left British leaders unaware of the deeds that they had to deter. Britain failed to restrain Russian mobilization partly because British leaders were unaware that, for Germany, mobilization meant war; hence they were unaware that Russian mobilization, which would surely trigger German mobilization, also meant war. The German secrecy that produced these British blunders stemmed from the German belief that a small information advantage could mean victory in wartime, and a small disadvantage could bring ruin. Russian and Austrian leaders also blundered because they lived in a world of dark, security-driven secrecy and had to act quickly in a fast-exploding crisis; others then reacted with security-driven haste and violence, leaving Russia and Austria unable to recover their errors.

All these causes of trouble stemmed from the widespread belief that conquest was easy. All would have abated or disappeared had the actual power of the defense been recognized. Thus the cult of the offensive was a master cause of many mechanisms that brought about the war. Without it, the Austro-Serbian conflict of 1914 would have been a minor and soon forgotten disturbance on the periphery of European politics.

If so, we can simplify the traditional rococo tale of First World War's origins. Its many causes are subsumed in a simple rubric, summarized in Diagram 4.

This, at any rate, is the argument. Is it valid? This chapter is formatted to test a theory, not to explain a case, but I have argued elsewhere (largely on evidence reported in this chapter) that the cult of the offensive was an important cause of World War I.[180] If that argument is accepted, then offense-

---

[180] Stephen Van Evera, "The Cult of the Offensive and the Origins of the First World War," *International Security* 9 (Summer 1984): 58–107.

Contrary views, doubting the role of the cult of the offensive in causing the war, are Trachtenberg, *History and Strategy*, pp. 64–95; Patrick Glynn, *Closing Pandora's Box: Arms Races,*

defense theory offers an elegant explanation for 1914. It cannot explain every factor at work in 1914. Other important war causes likely include: the rabid nationalist mythmaking that infected European societies after 1870; the bizarre false optimism with which all belligerents entered the war, which cannot be fully explained by concealments stemming from the cult of the offensive; the strange general belief that war was a positive and healthy activity; Kaiser Wilhelm II's marked personality disorders; and "social imperial" motives that led politically frail regimes—above all the German regime—to seek to strengthen themselves by pursuing foreign conflicts that would solidify their popularity. But offense-defense theory does offer an explanation for many factors that historians agree were central to the outbreak of the war.

Arms Control, and the History of the Cold War (New York: HarperCollins, 1992), pp. 1–44; David Kaiser, "Deterrence or National Interest? Reflections on the Origins of Wars," *Orbis* 30 (Spring 1986): 5–12; and David M. Keithly, "War Planning and the Outbreak of War in 1914," *Armed Forces and Society* 12 (Summer 1986): 553–79. A more mildly skeptical view is Scott D. Sagan, "1914 Revisited: Allies, Offense, and Instability," *International Security* 11 (Fall 1986): 151–76.

[8]

The Nuclear Revolution
and the Causes of War

What are the effects of the nuclear revolution? Has it made the world more or less violent? Is there a safer alternative to the current nuclear order? These are the questions this chapter addresses.

Scholars have disagreed on these issues since the nuclear revolution began. Most have viewed nuclear weapons as a curse and a danger. In the early atomic era many believed that nuclear weapons would multiply the violence of the next war without making it less likely. In 1944 a U.S. government panel viewed the impending nuclear age with foreboding: "The whole history of mankind teaches . . . that accumulated weapons of destruction 'go off' sooner or later, even if this means a senseless mutual destruction."[1] In 1946 Lewis Mumford echoed the opinion of many in warning that the nuclear revolution "will lead eventually to the destruction of mankind."[2]

Others warned that nuclear weapons were instruments of surprise attack and aggression that made war more likely as well as more destructive. In 1945 Robert Oppenheimer saw atomic weapons as means "of aggression, or surprise, and of terror."[3] NSC-68, a key U.S. strategy document of 1950, states that atomic weapons put "a premium on surprise attack" and "a premium on piecemeal aggression."[4] In 1954 Stanislav Andreski likewise ad-

[1] The Jeffries Committee of the Manhattan Project, quoted in Lawrence Freedman, *The Evolution of Nuclear Strategy* (New York: St. Martin's, 1981), p. 41. William Borden likewise warned that "an armed peace cannot persist indefinitely . . . in time an attack on the United States will surely come." In 1946, quoted in Gregg Herkin, *Counsels of War* (New York: Knopf, 1985), p. 12.

[2] Lewis Mumford, "Gentlemen: You Are Mad!" in Milton L. Racove, ed., *Arms and Foreign Policy in the Nuclear Age* (New York: Oxford University Press, 1972), pp. 391–94 at 391.

[3] Freedman, *Evolution of Nuclear Strategy*, p. 65.

[4] Thomas H. Etzold and John Lewis Gaddis, *Containment: Documents on American Policy and Strategy, 1945–1950* (New York: Columbia University Press, 1978), p. 414.

vised that nuclear weapons "made the military conquest of the world quite feasible."[5] Others warned that the nuclear revolution required prudent political leaders and could not tolerate the recklessness or lunacy that some leaders displayed.[6]

These fears led many to call for nuclear disarmament or for world government.[7] Some endorsed other alternatives, including defenses to protect populations from nuclear attack, and unilateral U.S. nuclear superiority—a solution that would let the United States escape the nuclear terror but enlarge it for others.

A few observers argued that the nuclear revolution promotes peace. Some noted the governmental caution that nuclear weapons create; others believed they bolster peace in other ways. Bernard Brodie argued in 1946 that nuclear weapons were "a powerful inhibitor to aggression," hence an asset to peace.[8] Jacob Viner declared that "the atomic bomb is a war deterrent, a peace-making force."[9] Alex Roland found nuclear weapons "an instrument of war so terrible that other means [must] be found to settle political conflicts."[10] Kenneth Waltz called them "a great force for peace."[11]

[5] Stanislav Andreski, *Military Organization and Society*, 2d ed. (Berkeley: University of California Press, 1971), p. 78. In 1985, Fred Iklé argued more specifically that the nuclear stalemate favored Soviet aggression: "the 'balance of terror' cannot favor the defense of a democratic alliance. Sooner or later, it will favor those most at ease with, those most experienced in, the systematic use of terror." Quoted in McGeorge Bundy, *Danger and Survival: Choices about the Bomb in the First Fifty Years* (New York: Random House, 1988), p. 576. Also skeptical that nuclear weapons bolster peace is Robert Gilpin, *War and Change in World Politics* (London: Cambridge University Press, 1981), pp. 216–18.

[6] Fred Iklé, in 1973, summarized in Freedman, *Evolution of Nuclear Strategy*, pp. 349–50; also Freeman Dyson, *Weapons and Hope* (New York: Harper & Row, 1984), p. 246.

[7] Calls for nuclear disarmament include Jonathan Schell, *The Abolition* (New York: Knopf, 1984); Jonathan Schell, *The Gift of Time: The Case for Abolishing Nuclear Weapons Now* (New York: Holt, 1998); and Barry M. Blechman and Cathleen S. Fisher, "Phase Out the Bomb," *Foreign Policy*, no. 97 (Winter 1994–95): 79–95. An assessment is Joseph Rotblat, Jack Steinberger, and Bhalchandra Udgaonkar, eds., *A Nuclear-Weapon-Free World: Desirable? Feasible?* (Boulder: Westview, 1993).

[8] Herkin, *Counsels*, p. 9.

[9] In 1945, quoted in Fred Kaplan, *Wizards of Armageddon* (New York: Simon and Schuster, 1983), p. 27.

[10] Alex Roland, "Keep the Bomb," *Technology Review*, August/September 1995, pp. 67–69 at 68.

[11] Kenneth N. Waltz, "The Origins of War in Neorealist Theory," in Robert I. Rotberg and Theodore K. Rabb, eds., *The Origins and Prevention of Major Wars* (New York: Cambridge University Press, 1989), pp. 39–52 at 48. Other studies on the consequences of the nuclear revolution include William Liscum Borden, *There Will Be No Time* (New York: Macmillan, 1946); Bernard Brodie et. al., *The Absolute Weapon* (New York: Harcourt, Brace, 1946); Shai Feldman, *Israeli Nuclear Deterrence* (New York: Columbia University Press, 1982); Charles L. Glaser, *Analyzing Strategic Nuclear Policy* (Princeton: Princeton University Press, 1990); Robert Jervis, *The Meaning of the Nuclear Revolution: Statecraft and the Prospect of Armageddon* (Ithaca: Cornell University Press, 1989); Michael Mandelbaum, "International Stability and Nuclear Order: The First Nuclear Order: The First Nuclear Regime," in David C. Gompert et al., *Nuclear Weapons and World Politics* (New York: McGraw-Hill, 1977), pp. 15–80; Michael Mandelbaum, *The Nuclear Revolution* (New York: Cambridge University Press, 1981); Kenneth N. Waltz, *The*

This chapter applies theories of military power and war to these questions. I assess the dangers of six alternate worlds: the past pre-nuclear world, the present nuclear world, and four possible future worlds. These worlds are:

- PAST (Pre-Atomic State). This is the world before 1945. Nuclear technology is absent and unknown.
- MAD (Mutual Assured Destruction).[12] The leading powers have secure nuclear deterrents that could annihilate an attacker's society even after suffering an all-out surprise attack. MAD has governed the world since the 1950s or 1960s.
- MARNE (Mankind Absolutely Rejects Nuclear Explosives). All powers have dismantled their nuclear capabilities. Nuclear technology is absent but known.
- BAD (Both Are Defended).[13] States maintain nuclear forces but also have defenses that could protect their populations from nuclear attack. Hence no major power could promptly inflict large damage on another society.
- WORSE (Winning Only Requires Striking Early). States maintain nuclear forces, but these forces are vulnerable to surprise attack. As a result the first side to attack can gain victory.
- USA (Unilateral Superiority—American). The United States has the world's only secure deterrent: it can annihilate an attacker's society after absorbing its all-out first strike, but others cannot do likewise to the United States. In an enhanced variant, the United States also has defenses that can prevent damage to U.S. society if others launch a first strike against U.S. cities.

I argue that the effects of MAD depend on the kind of states that comprise it. A MAD world of deterrable states—that is, states that are sensitive to costs, clearly perceive other states' interests and intentions, and value conquests less than others value their independence—is profoundly peaceful. In such a world MAD erases major causes of past war. States fight far less than in the pre-nuclear era.

But a MAD world of states that are nondeterrable—that is, in some combination are insensitive to costs, misperceive other states' motives and intentions, and highly value new conquests—is very dangerous. Such states are unresponsive to threats of punishment because they do not feel the pain

---

Spread of Nuclear Weapons: More May Be Better, Adelphi Paper no. 171 (London: International Institute for Strategic Studies, 1981); Kenneth N. Waltz, "Nuclear Myths and Political Realities," *American Political Science Review* 84 (September 1990): 731–45.

[12] Donald Brennan's term. Bundy, *Danger and Survival,* p. 552.

[13] Robert Art's term. Art, "The Role of Military Power in International Relations," in B. Thomas Trout and James E. Harf, eds.,*National Security Affairs: Theoretical Perspectives and Contemporary Issues* (New Brunswick, N.J.: Transaction, 1982), p. 23.

of punishment, or they are willing to take great pain to gain their goals, or they fail to see the punishment coming. Hence they are hard to deter. When such nondeterrable states appear, the pacifying effects of MAD disappear and large new dangers arise, making a MAD world more violent than PAST.

MAD also grows dangerous if nuclear actors can use nuclear weapons and escape punishment. This occurs if states can use nuclear weapons anonymously, or if terrorists with no identifiable state sponsorship acquire nuclear weapons, leaving no clear target for retaliation. Both risks might increase with wide nuclear proliferation.[14]

Despite these downside risks, we must learn to live in a MAD world, because all escapes from it are both infeasible and undesirable. Escapes are infeasible because technology strongly favors MAD. All non-MAD world military orders are very hard to achieve, and would soon degrade back to MAD if they were ever gained. Efforts to escape MAD will be swamped by powerful technical forces running the other way. Escapes are undesirable because they would raise large risks of war. All alternate military orders are more dangerous than MAD.

Thus the effects of the nuclear revolution depend in part on whether governments accept and adapt to the MAD world that it creates, or try to build another. Nuclear technology will probably preserve MAD even if governments try to escape it, but any exit they do find will lead to disaster.

An imagined exit from MAD would be even more dangerous than an actual exit. An imagined exit would unite MAD's unlimited capacity to destroy with the motives to destroy that appear in alternate worlds (MARNE, BAD, WORSE, and USA)—a worst-case combination.

In sum, a MAD world of deterrable states is far safer than a PAST world; MAD inhabited by nondeterrable rogue states or anonymous nuclear users may be more dangerous than PAST; MAD departed is very dangerous; and MAD misconstrued as MAD departed is the worst world of all.

MAD AMONG DETERRABLE STATES

Many observers note that MAD raises the cost of war, making governments more careful to avoid war.[15] If this were MAD's only effect, there would be little net gain for peace. Wars would take roughly the same number of lives in a smaller number of more violent conflicts.

---

[14] The proliferation of other technologies of mass destruction (for example, biological and chemical killing agents) pose parallel dangers.

[15] See, for example, John Lewis Gaddis, "The Long Peace: Elements of Stability in the Postwar International System," *International Security* 10 (Spring 1986): 99–142 at 120–23; and Roland, "Keep the Bomb."

But MAD also has other pacifying effects. Most important, under most conditions it erases the five causes of war outlined in Chapters 2–6.

False optimism

The use of nuclear weapons under MAD has very certain results. This certainty lowers false optimism about relative capabilities. States cannot mistake what their military forces can and cannot do. They can annihilate the other's society and cannot protect their own society from annihilation. These facts are hard to misconstrue.

Before MAD, wars were decided by a complex collision of military forces. Outcomes were hard to predict. Under MAD, nuclear forces collide with cities. Anyone can predict the outcome without thinking long.

As Thomas Schelling notes, conflicts in MAD are settled less by tests of force than by tests of nerve. "Issues are decided not by who can bring the most force to bear . . . but by who is eventually willing to bring more force to bear."[16] Miscalculations of the balance of assets matter less because the balance of assets matters less.

In short, MAD clears the "fog of war" by removing the relevance of the clash of military machines. The calculus of relative capabilities drops from the calculus of war. Leaders can still miscalculate relative will, but relative capacity cannot be misconstrued. Room to miscalculate remains, but there is less room overall.

First-move advantage

Under MAD, first-move advantages largely vanish. Even large shifts in relative force levels have little effect on relative power; hence even a first strike that shifts relative force levels has little effect on the balance of power; hence it provides little or no reward.

Once the opponent's major cities are targeted by secure nuclear forces, more forces are a useless excess. A first strike that changes the ratio of this excess has little meaning. States cannot destroy each other more than once; an attack that confers or removes the ability to destroy for a second or third time has no utility.[17]

Also, the surprise that a first move requires is harder to gain in a MAD world. As I observe below, MAD bolsters the defense. Secrecy is looser in a defense-dominant world, hence surprise is more difficult.

---

[16] Thomas C. Schelling, *Arms and Influence* (New Haven: Yale University Press, 1966), p. 94.

[17] Nikita Khrushchev explained his indifference to superior U.S. nuclear force levels: "We're satisfied to be able to wipe out the United States the first time around. Once is quite enough. What good does it do to annihilate a country two times over?" Nikita Khrushchev, *Khrushchev Remembers*, trans. and ed. Strobe Talbott (Boston: Little, Brown, 1970), p. 517.

Windows of opportunity and vulnerability

Under MAD, windows largely disappear. Again, the reason is that even large shifts in relative force levels have little effect on relative power. A declining nuclear power can view its descent with calm, knowing that its relative power will be unaffected as long as it retains a secure deterrent. Hence its decline poses no threat that needs forestalling. Preventive war makes no sense because there is no future danger to prevent. The future looks like the present: force ratios may change but decliners know they will remain sovereign and secure.

Moreover, states can build their way out of trouble far more easily than they can fight their way out. A secure nuclear deterrent is much easier to build than to threaten. Hence states that face future threats to their nuclear deterrent can address these threats better by building up their forces than by using force. Preventive war loses its logic partly because shutting windows by military buildup is far more effective.

Cumulative resources

Under MAD the cumulativity of material resources is sharply reduced, because less can be done with the forces that could be distilled from these resources. More forces are a useless excess if states can already destroy each other; thus, the resources that could provide these forces are also useless excess. Their gain or loss has little effect on a state's ability to gain or defend other assets.

Buffer room and military bases are noncumulative under MAD for a second reason: nuclear weapons can easily be hurled across great distances.[18] This makes geographic assets less significant. Wide buffer room cannot impede nuclear delivery, and the possession of distant bases does little to make it easier.

Hence it makes less sense to fight to control or destroy bases, territory, or military or economic resources under MAD. States can worry less about places endowed with these resources since their gain or loss has less effect on the balance of power.

Capabilities are absolute under MAD, so disputes are decided more by the balance of resolve. Hence national welfare depends more directly on others' estimates of one's national resolve and, therefore, on the credibility of threats that express this resolve. Hence credibility becomes more cumulative under MAD than under pre-nuclear conditions.

As noted in Chapter 5, however, most evidence suggests that states gain

---

[18] Noting the devaluation of strategic depth under MAD is Klaus Knorr, *On the Uses of Military Power in the Nuclear Age* (Princeton: Princeton University Press, 1966), pp. 86–87.

little credibility by using force.[19] Credibility is a cumulative resource, but one that does not accrue to the warlike. Hence the greater cumulativity of threat credibility under MAD should create little temptation to war, as long as policymakers understand this reality.

Offense dominance

Most important, MAD gives defenders a large advantage over aggressors.[20] As noted above, capabilities are absolute under MAD, so disputes are decided by the balance of resolve. Defenders are big winners under these rules. They value their freedom more than aggressors value conquest, so they are willing to run greater risks and pay a higher price to prevail. Hence they can dominate the contest of pain-taking that MAD creates. Knowing this, aggressors back down first.[21]

Hence conquest among great powers is almost impossible in a MAD world. Even powers with far superior assets cannot use this advantage to subjugate other powers, as long as the others maintain secure deterrents.

States also can better defend third parties against aggressors under MAD. If they have superior resolve they can force the aggressor to back down by facing it with a losing contest in pain-taking, much as they would in a one-on-one confrontation. They can also deploy "tripwire" forces to threatened third parties in order to catalyze war between themselves and an invader, as the United States deployed troops to Germany as a tripwire during the Cold War. This device can extend states' nuclear protection over threatened allies even when their resolve is no greater than the aggressor's.

The intensity of war under MAD

Some argue that MAD brings no net gain for peace because war in MAD is more destructive, so that total casualties will remain high although wars are fewer. Is this so?

The answer depends on our theories of warfare intensity. In one view the

---

[19] See Chapter 5, note 27.

[20] Developing this argument is Jervis, *Meaning of the Nuclear Revolution*, pp. 4–5, 19–21, 29–35.

[21] Egyptian President Anwar Sadat explained that Egypt could not destroy Israel because "we know the Jews will go to the very end to preserve this state of theirs. . . . Even if we were to put them in a position where we could wipe them off the map, we know what would happen. They would not go down without trying to wipe us out with them." In 1974, quoted in Thomas Kiernan, *The Arabs* (Boston: Little, Brown, 1975), p. 276. Nikita Khrushchev likewise noted that neither side would concede defeat "before resorting to the use of all weapons, even the most devastating ones" in a Soviet-American war. "The trouble is, the losing side will always use nuclear weapons in the last resort to avoid defeat. . . . If a man thinks he's going to die he'll take any steps." In 1961 and 1964, quoted in Thomas W. Wolfe, *Soviet Power and Europe, 1945–1970* (Baltimore: Johns Hopkins University Press, 1970), p. 145.

intensity of war depends on the destructive power of the belligerents' forces: "In wartime, states destroy what they can. Destructive forces make for destructive wars." A second view holds that warfare intensity depends on the belligerents' ability to avoid unwanted harm to civilians; hence it depends on whether their weapons are discriminate: "In wartime, states destroy what they cannot avoid destroying. Indiscriminate forces make for destructive wars." Both views suggest that MAD will magnify warfare by putting weapons of vast and indiscriminate power in the hands of belligerents.

But a third view argues that the intensity of warfare depends on the size of the stakes at issue: "In wartime, states make large violence when large interests are at issue. Big stakes make for big wars." In this view MAD dampens warfare by making belligerents more secure from conquest, which removes national sovereignty from the stakes when states fight. A fourth view holds that the intensity of warfare depends on the ability of each belligerent to punish the other for escalating: "In wartime, states destroy in inverse proportion to the punishment they will receive in return. Mutual deterrence makes for small wars." In this view MAD limits warfare by letting belligerents compel each other to show restraint.

Thus the assumption that MAD expands the violence of warfare is too facile. Plausible arguments can be made both ways, and it seems possible that wars will be less violent, as well as fewer, under MAD.

Overall, then, MAD among deterrable states is far more peaceful than PAST. I argue in Chapters 2–6 that false optimism, first-move advantage, windows of opportunity and vulnerability, high cumulativity in resources, and especially offense dominance are potent causes of war. MAD largely removes these problems, and in so doing it prevents the wars they cause. It cannot prevent false perceptions of the last four of these problems (first-move advantage, windows, resource capability, and offense dominance). Such misperceptions cause even more war than the problems themselves, because they are more common. Nevertheless, by removing the problems themselves MAD does prevent a good deal of war.

MAD among Nondeterrable States; MAD among Many States

MAD strengthens peace only under certain conditions. States must be deterrable; that is, they must adapt their conduct to avoid the punishment that others could impose. Specifically, states must be sensitive to costs, must perceive the world well enough to know when others plan to impose costs, and must value conquests less than others value their independence. This describes most states, so MAD is pacifying under most conditions.

But if these conditions are missing, MAD's prime pacifying effect— bolstering the defense—largely disappears. If aggressor states are not cost

[247]

sensitive—that is, if their governments do not value their citizens' lives and property—MAD gives defenders little advantage because their threats to punish aggressors cause little fear. If aggressor states badly misperceive others, they may be undeterred by defenders' threats because they mistake them for bluffs or fail to hear them. If states value conquest very highly—that is, if they are willing to pay as much to conquer neighbors as their neighbors will pay to stay free—defenders no longer have superior resolve. Aggressors can match defenders in a contest of pain, hence they face each other on more equal terms.

MAD's other pacifying effects also diminish. False optimism becomes more possible if states are not cost sensitive. Because the balance of will no longer decides everything, the balance of capabilities starts to matter again. Hence misreadings of the balance of capabilities also start to matter again. For the same reason, first-move advantages and windows reappear if states are not cost sensitive: the balance of will no longer decides everything, so the material advantages that might be gained by moving first or moving early begin to matter once again. And material resources become more cumulative because, once the balance of will no longer decides everything, these resources again have significance.

Moreover, new dangers arise as MAD's pacifying effects disappear. These dangers stem from the possibility of wanton violence by nondeterrable rogue states and from fears of such violence among normal states. Nondeterrable states are more dangerous to others under MAD than PAST. Under PAST such states had to conquer before they could destroy. Under MAD they can destroy even those they can not conquer. All states lie at the mercy of their violent impulses, even those with secure nuclear deterrents and strong conventional defenses. War could erupt either from violence by these nondeterrable states or from forceful moves by normal states to forestall their violence. As a result, a MAD world of nondeterrable states is more violent than a PAST world of such states. Nondeterrable states have a greater capacity for violence in such a world; this gives other states more reason to use violence in self-defense.[22]

Could nondeterrable nuclear states appear? The danger seems remote but

---

[22] These dangers point to a cause of war not framed in Chapters 2–6—what might be called the danger of destruction-dominance. If states can easily destroy each other's societies, war becomes likely if states also feel that they cannot rely on deterrence to stay others from destructive acts. They will then feel compelled to erase others' destructive power, despite the great cost this could involve, because the alternative could be worse. Specifically, they might deploy forces that neuter others' deterrents—a choice that could drive others to extreme steps to preserve or regain their deterrents, thereby risking war—or they might opt directly for war. This danger arises under two conditions: the destruction of opposing societies is easy, while their defense from destruction is difficult; and states are largely nondeterrable. The problem could also be called the "survival dilemma": a situation where measures taken to ensure one's physical survival threaten others' survival and sovereignty.

possible. Governments insensitive to their nation's suffering have not been unknown. Joseph Stalin and Pol Pot horribly punished their own societies. Others' threats to punish these societies would have struck them as a quaint redundancy unless their own power or lives were also threatened. Hitler had contempt for the German people, cared little about the suffering his wars inflicted on them, and had little regard for his own life; this made him hard to deter.[23] Extreme delusions have shaped policy in many states. Wilhelmine Germany, Nazi Germany, imperial Japan, and Saddam Hussein's Iraq are fine examples of how modern states can badly misperceive the realities they face. Whether any state has valued conquest more than its victims valued freedom is more doubtful, but Hitler's Germany, with its rabidly expansionist leadership, came close.

On the other hand, no major power has shown significant signs of being nondeterrable since World War II. This danger is not at the world's doorstep.

Thus the effects of MAD depend on the nature of the states that comprise it. They may also depend on the number of nuclear actors. A world of many nuclear powers raises the possibility that a state hiding in the nuclear crowd could use nuclear weapons anonymously. Weapons also could leak to nonstate actors that are less deterrable because they have no fixed homeland or population that could be held hostage for their good behavior. A MAD world of many nuclear powers could be violent if these problems arose.

The second danger seems larger than the first. Anonymous use by states will remain difficult in a world of many nuclear powers. Only states with powerful motives would run the risk that such use would involve; but such highly motivated states are easy to spot, so they have limited ability to act anonymously.[24] Use by nonstate actors is more worrisome. Such use might be deterred by holding states strictly accountable for violence emanating from their territory, as Israel has often done with its neighbors. This policy works only with strong states, however; it breaks down with the world's weak and failing states, whose control of their territories is tenuous. Terrorists hiding in these states could be hard to deter.

In summary, MAD is what we make of it. It will punish a world where states suffer large misperceptions or communicate poorly. It will punish a world of regimes led by elites indifferent to the suffering of their people, or fanatically dedicated to expansion. It will punish a world that allows the spread of the capacity to use nuclear weapons anonymously. But if these dangers are avoided, MAD liberates the world from some potent causes of war. It makes conquest nearly impossible, erases first-strike advantages

[23] On Hitler's hostility toward Germans see Sebastian Haffner, *The Meaning of Hitler*, trans. Ewald Osers (Cambridge: Harvard University Press, 1979), pp. 120, 149–65. On his suicidal streak see ibid., pp. 4, 20–21.

[24] Moreover, possible motives for anonymous use are obscure. Coercion is the most likely purpose of nuclear use, but anonymous use achieves no coercion.

and windows, precludes false optimism, and eases competition for power-generating resources. With these dangers at bay, the risk of war is sharply reduced.

ALTERNATIVES TO MAD: MARNE, BAD, WORSE, AND USA

MAD is hardly perfect. It becomes a nightmare if nondeterrable nuclear actors appear. However, all alternative worlds are worse. Even if nuclear disarmament could be achieved, PAST would not be restored because nuclear knowledge cannot be erased. Instead, nuclear disarmament would create a MARNE world of disarmed states with nuclear knowledge. Such a world would be far more dangerous than PAST or MAD. Other nuclear worlds would also raise large risks of war.

Because technology strongly favors MAD, any exit from it is very unlikely. A secure nuclear deterrent is easy to build and hard to threaten, so any great power can impose MAD by its unilateral choice to build a deterrent. Hence MAD is bound to last for a very very long time. But if an exit were somehow possible, it would spell disaster. All alternatives are far more dangerous than today's MAD world.

MARNE

Under MARNE, nuclear forces are abolished but nuclear knowledge is not. This nuclear knowledge makes any MARNE world very frail. Even small crises will spur states to try to break out of MARNE by building a nuclear capability, for both opportunistic and defensive reasons. Better endowed states will be tempted to try a breakout by hopes of gaining unilateral nuclear superiority. All states will be driven to try a breakout by hopes of stealing a march on their opponent, and by the fear that otherwise their opponent will steal a march on them. These temptations will be strong because the stakes are high: the loser of a breakout race will be at the winner's mercy. Moving quickly can mean the difference between supremacy and subjugation.

Thus an early race back to nuclear capabilities is likely if MARNE is ever achieved. This race, in turn, will raise large dangers of preventive war.[25] Any state that gains a fleeting lead will be tempted to strike to consolidate its advantage, if only to avert the risk of later losing the race or of suffering preventive attack when the lead briefly swings to the other side.

These dangers could be averted only by a collective security system whose

---

[25] Noting these dangers is Schelling, *Arms and Influence*, pp. 249–50; also Herman Kahn, *On Thermonuclear War*, 2d ed. (New York: Free Press, 1969), p. 230.

members agreed to disarm any state trying a nuclear breakout, combined with a verification regime that created full military transparency, letting all states see each other's nuclear efforts almost in real time. A collective security system would face breakout states with arrest by a stronger coalition. Full transparency would remove hopes of stealing a march on others and fears that others are stealing a march. However, collective security has never worked, and governments have never been willing to accept the intrusive verification measures that full transparency would require. Hence states in MARNE will always hope they can win a breakout race, and they will always fear that if they don't do it now, another will do it later. Hence they will always be nervously watching for the right moment to move, and will be quick to seize it.

For these reasons, MARNE would be far more prone to war than MAD or PAST.[26]

BAD, WORSE, and USA

Many believe that BAD—a world of population defenses—offers an escape from the terrors of the nuclear age. Like MARNE, however, BAD would be immensely dangerous. Population defenses are far harder to maintain than to defeat.[27] Hence if BAD is ever achieved, it will not last long. One side will soon crack the other's defenses, whether by deploying new arms or by breaking the other's defense in battle. At that point BAD (both are defended) will degrade into OID (one is defended). In this new order, one side gains dominance and the other suffers decisive defeat. The defenseless state will stand at the other's mercy, forced to submit or be destroyed.

Thus BAD, despite its defensive look, is an offense-dominant world. The lives of states in BAD will be brutal and short. They will conquer and be conquered at a fast pace. Hence BAD has the many dangerous attributes of an offense-dominant world. States in BAD will be tempted by the possibility of conquering others and frightened by the specter of being conquered. Hence they will compete fiercely for advantage—pursuing wide expansion, fiercely resisting others' expansion, striking first or early to gain even small material rewards, adopting fait accompli diplomatic tactics, enclosing their

---

[26] Another discussion of the risks of MARNE is Glaser, *Analyzing Strategic Nuclear Policy*, pp. 166–203.

[27] The cost-exchange ratio between antimissile defenses and offsetting responses was estimated at 5:1 during the U.S. debate over population defenses in the mid-1960s. In other words, a dollar invested in defenses could be neutralized by 20 cents invested in offensive countermeasures. In the 1980s this ratio was conservatively estimated at 3:1. James R. Schlesinger, "Rhetoric and Realities in the Star Wars Debate," *International Security* 10 (Summer 1985): 3–12 at 7–8. Schlesinger argues that "the ratio is still strongly weighed against defense and will remain so" (p. 8).

On BAD's lack of robustness see also Glaser, *Analyzing Strategic Nuclear Policy*, pp. 119–24.

policies and forces in dark secrecy, and pouring great effort into offensive military buildups. Governments will spend their days considering how and when BAD will degenerate, and they will hatch violent schemes to ensure that they are the ones that can still defend after it does. They will live in fear of surprise attacks and will plan ways to forestall them with their own. Peace will be rare and brief. This is the violent world that population defenses, seemingly so benign, will create.

WORSE has no proponents. Everyone understands that it would raise the widely recognized dangers of first-move advantage. Less recognized is that BAD and WORSE are often one and the same. The coming of BAD will often bring WORSE as well. The secrecy that BAD fosters eases surprise attack. And, as just noted, the competitive nature of BAD puts a premium on any material gains that can be gained by striking first. Hence first-move advantages are likely to appear in BAD. If these first-move advantages are sizable, a WORSE world emerges. With it come the great dangers that arrive with large first-move advantages. Hence the shortcomings of WORSE should also be assigned to BAD.

USA has many fans in the United States but, like BAD, it raises more risks than it dampens. USA leaves other states insecure. Insecure states are risk takers. They resort to dangerous tactics to escape their vulnerability, such as the Soviet Union's secret missile deployment to Cuba in 1962. They may resort to force, if by using force they can restore their nuclear deterrent. This is the flaw with USA. It presses others to the wall, spurring them to lash out even if they must fight at a marked disadvantage.[28]

USA is therefore both dangerous and frail. States will struggle hard to escape it. This struggle could hold the seeds of war. If war is avoided, states are bound to struggle out at some point, erasing USA and restoring MAD. Thus an effort to reach USA offers short-term risks without promising any ultimate change in the world military order.

Imagined exits to MARNE, BAD, and WORSE would be even worse than the real thing. False belief that MAD had been escaped would leave states with the unlimited capacity to destroy that comes with MAD and the motives to destroy that arise in non-MAD worlds. War would then be both cataclysmic and hard to avoid. Thus peace requires that MAD persist and be understood to persist. Its reality must be recognized.

Past observers have sometimes lost their grip on this reality. In 1979 General Daniel Graham, former director of the U.S. Defense Intelligence Agency, wrote that "nuclear war cannot destroy the world, but may conquer it less damaged than Europe and Japan were damaged by World War II"—this at a time when both the Soviet Union and the United States could annihilate

---

[28] On the provocative effects of USA see Glaser, *Analyzing Strategic Nuclear Policy*, pp. 158–61.

the other's society several times over even after absorbing an all-out attack.[29] Thomas K. Jones, a deputy undersecretary of defense in the Reagan Administration, opined in 1981 that "if there are enough shovels to go around, everybody's going to make it" through a general thermonuclear war by using simple do-it-yourself civil defense measures, and that the United States could fully recover from such a war with the Soviet Union in two to four years.[30] Two leading American strategists published an article in 1980 that claimed in its title that "victory is possible" in nuclear war, and in its text that nuclear war "can be won or lost," a claim at odds with MAD's realities.[31] Soviet military officers also insisted repeatedly that nuclear war could somehow be won. One wrote in 1972 that the nuclear revolution creates "extensive new opportunities for waging actual offensive operations."[32] Other Soviet officers claimed that mass nuclear missile strikes "can determine the victory of one side and the defeat of the other at the very beginning of the war."[33] Still others noted the "profound error and harm in the disorienting claims of bourgeois ideologues that there will be no victor in a thermonuclear world war." Rather, in the next war "the peoples of the world will put an end to imperialism."[34] Such doubts about MAD's reality would risk war if they came to govern the policies of great powers.

THE JANUS-FACED REVOLUTION

Like the god Janus, the nuclear revolution has two faces, one benign and one malign. It has a benign face if states are deterrable and punishable, and if states recognize and accept the MAD order that it creates. It has a malign face if states are hard to deter or punish, or if states somehow escape— or believe they have escaped—from MAD. Thus the effects of the nuclear

[29] Daniel O. Graham, *Shall America Be Defended: Salt II and Beyond* (New Rochelle, N.Y.: Arlington House, 1979), p. 108.

[30] Robert Scheer with Narda Zacchino and Constance Matthiessen, *With Enough Shovels: Reagan, Bush, and Nuclear War* (New York: Random House, 1982), pp. 18, 23, 25. Louis Giuffrida, head of the Federal Emergency Management Agency in the Reagan Administration, similarly argued that nuclear war "would be a terrible mess, but it wouldn't be unmanageable." Ibid, p. 1.

[31] Colin S. Gray and Keith Payne, "Victory is Possible," *Foreign Policy*, no. 39 (Summer 1980): 14–27 at 14.

[32] Marshall of Armored Troops P. A. Ropmistrov, quoted in William R. Van Cleave, "Soviet Doctrine and Strategy: A Developing American View," in Lawrence L. Whetten, ed. *The Future of Soviet Military Power* (New York: Crane, Russak, 1976), pp. 41–71 at 60.

[33] Colonel B. Byely et. al, *Marxism Leninism on War and Army* (Moscow: Progress, 1972), p. 217.

[34] N. B. Karabanov and V. F. Khalipov, "The Modern Era and Problems of War and Peace," in Major-General A. S. Milovidov and Colonel V. G. Kozlov, eds., *The Philosophical Heritage of V. I. Lenin and Problems of Contemporary War*, trans. U.S. Air Force (1972; Washington, D.C.: U.S. Government Printing Office, 1974), pp. 7–22 at 17.

revolution are indeterminate. They hinge on the perceptions and policies of governments.

In future centuries, the year 1945 will be marked as the greatest watershed in international history, the year that international relations were forever changed. But how will it be marked—as a dawn of a peaceful age or the beginning of a catastrophe? The answer lies with nuclear societies themselves. They will decide if the nuclear revolution is a curse or a blessing.

[9]

Conclusion

This book advances four main arguments. First, states' perceptions of the structure of international power strongly affect the risk of war. States fight when they think they will prevail, when they think the advantage will lie with the side moving first, when they believe their relative power is in decline, when they assume that resource cumulativity is high, and, most important, when they believe that conquest is easy. Together these perceptions explain a great deal of modern war. In their total absence, war rarely occurs.

Second, the actual structure of international power also affects the risk of war, but it matters less because states often misperceive it and because they react only to what they perceive.

Third, the structure of power has been quite benign in modern times. First-move advantages have been small, the relative strength of great powers has rarely fluctuated sharply, resource cumulativity has been low, and conquest has been very difficult. These dangers were small in the decades before 1945, and shrank further with the nuclear revolution. In the MAD world that nuclear weapons create they nearly vanish.

Fourth, modern states have recurrently believed that the structure of power was malignant. Often they wrongly judged that the side moving first would gain a large advantage, that they faced large windows of opportunity or vulnerability, that resource cumulativity was high, and that conquest would be easy for themselves or for their opponents. A great deal of modern war has flowed from these fallacies. Many modern wars have been wars of illusions, waged by states drawn to war by misperceptions of international power realities.

These arguments support two conclusions about the much debated and much maligned Realist paradigm.

First, Realists are right to make strong claims for the virtues of their paradigm. If, as I argue, the theories explored here are strong, their luster also reflects on the parent paradigm—Realism—they represent. The common dismissal of Realism as a barren paradigm with few explanations and fewer prescriptions is wrong. Realism offers strong explanations for war and feasible solutions to war.

Second, Realists have misdirected their attention toward Realism's weaker theories of war, and away from its stronger theories. Their favorite theories have focused on the effects of the gross structure of power—that is, the distribution of aggregate capabilities. Thus Realists have dwelled at length on the impact of the bipolar or multipolar structure of international power, and on the equal or unequal distribution of power among states. However, the fine-grained structure of power—including the size of first-move advantages and windows, the degree of resource cumulativity, and the ease of conquest—has far more effect on the risk of war. Realism becomes far stronger when it includes these fine-grained structures and perceptions of them. Yet most Realists have strangely failed even to claim these ideas for their paradigm.

Thus this book supports Realists' claims to the power of their paradigm, but suggests that Realists have focused on its weak ideas while neglecting the strong.

What causes misperceptions of the structure of power? Why is it often believed more malignant than in fact it is? Four explanations will be explored in another book.

One explanation holds that war-causing national misperceptions flourish when professional militaries dominate national ideas about international and security affairs. It rejects the common view that militaries live by war, hence prefer war to peace, and hence cause war. Rather, militaries cause war as an unintended side effect of their efforts to protect their organizational welfare. Their welfare is best secured when civilian society believes a range of war-causing ideas: that conquest is easy, that windows of vulnerability are large and common, that empires are valuable, that other states are hostile, that threatening diplomatic tactics will produce better results than accommodation, that war is cheap or even beneficial. These ideas emphasize the necessity and rewards of possessing or using force, and the importance of the military to the nation. As such they help militaries protect their institutional size, wealth, and autonomy. Accordingly, militaries often purvey these ideas to the wider society, and if the military dominates national perceptions, the ideas may take hold.

Such military dominion of national perceptions has been rare in history, but disastrous when it occurred. Prime examples include Wilhelmine Germany and Imperial Japan. Lesser examples include Austria-Hungary, Russia, France, Serbia, and Turkey before World War I, and Hungary before World War II. There are many wars that this problem cannot explain, but it does cover some major calamities: World War I and the Pacific theater of World War II.

A second explanation holds that states tend to infuse themselves with chauvinist myths about their own and others' conduct and character. These myths fall into three types: self-glorifying, self-whitewashing, and other-maligning. All three are purveyed largely through national educational systems. Elites purvey them for reasons both legitimate and dubious: to persuade people to sacrifice for the common good and to bolster public support for elites.

If believed, these myths fuel spirals of international conflict. Myth-ridden states underestimate their own role in provoking others' hostility; hence they find others' answering hostility unreasonable and overreact to it, provoking still more hostility. Chauvinist myths also foster false optimism. Myth-ridden states over-glorify their past national achievements and leaders ("we are a great people who did great things"); this feeds their arrogance about their prospects in future wars. They also exaggerate the legitimacy of their own claims; hence they underestimate the resolve of opponents and exaggerate their own international support. As a result, they exaggerate their adversaries' willingness to concede to threats or violence, and they overestimate the willingness of third states to back their cause. This leaves them unduly hopeful on the likely results of using force.

A third explanation holds that states often fail to evaluate key policy ideas; this allows misperceptions to pass unexamined. As Aaron Wildavsky suggests, large bureaucracies are inept at evaluating their own ideas and performance because the bureaucracy attacks its evaluative subunits.[1] Whole states suffer the same syndrome. Governmental and nongovernmental evaluative institutions, including academe and the press, often fail to evaluate national policies and perceptions from fear of retribution by interests harmed by evaluation. Speaking truth to power is seldom rewarded and widely penalized, hence important truths are often unspoken. This syndrome lets national misperceptions develop and persist unchallenged.

A fourth explanation suggests that states tend to leave their national strategies undefined because well-defined strategies provide a clear target for outside evaluation, which governments seek to evade. But without clear strategy, official thinking deteriorates. Unframed, official ideas cannot be audited and so cannot be cured of error. Vagueness in strategy also leaves states less able to divine one another's interests and intentions, raising the

---

[1] Aaron Wildavsky, "The Self-Evaluating Organization," *Public Administration Review* 32 (September/October 1972): 509–20.

risk of inadvertent collisions between states that are blind to the other's concerns. Lastly, vagueness in strategy raises the relative importance of credibility: inarticulate states fall back on demonstrating credibility as a way to convince others that they mean business. Wars for the preservation of reputation ensue.

Appendix: Hypotheses on Power and the Causes of War

H1.   War is more likely when states fall prey to false optimism about its outcome.

H2.   War is more likely when the advantage lies with the first side to mobilize or attack.

    H2A.   A first-move advantage improves an attacker's prospects for victory, since the attacker claims the first move and enjoys the benefits that come with it. This causes war by tempting states to play the attacker.

    H2B.   A first-move advantage raises the military cost of letting an opponent move first. It also raises the odds that the opponent will move first unless forestalled by preemptive action, since the opponent also is tempted to jump the gun by the first-move advantage. Hence restraint in a crisis is more dangerous, and preemptive mobilization or attack is more expedient.

    H2C.   A first-move advantage leads states to conceal their grievances, military capabilities, military plans, and political strategies from opponents. States conceal their grievances because honesty could trigger an opponent's preemptive attack. States conceal their military capabilities and their political and military plans to avoid rousing opponents to take countermeasures that negate their ability to strike a telling first blow. These concealments cause war by impeding diplomacy, by raising the risk of military missteps in crisis, by leading opponents into military overconfidence, and by preventing others from correcting conflict-producing national misconceptions.

    H2D.   A first-move advantage confronts states with a deadline: they must make decisions and complete diplomacy before the other preempts. Haste hampers diplomacy and magnifies the risk of war-causing errors.

H2E. A first-strike advantage invites states to adopt offensive force postures. It also makes them slower to mobilize for self-defense in a crisis, from fear of triggering preemption by the other side. Hence conquest is easier, raising the risks outlined under H5.

H3. War is more likely when the relative power of states fluctuates sharply—that is, when windows of opportunity and vulnerability are large.

H3A. Impending power shifts tempt declining states to launch an early war before the power shift is complete, to avoid having to fight a war later under worse conditions or to avoid being compelled later to bargain from weakness.

H3B. Impending power shifts lead declining states to risk war more willingly. They regard even unwanted wars as less calamitous because their coming decline makes standing pat look relatively worse. As a result they adopt more high-risk policies.

H3C. Impending power shifts reduce the credibility of the offers of rising states and the threats of declining states. As a result, states are less able to resolve disputes peacefully. Even states that could agree on substance may fight because the other's compliance with the agreement is less certain, hence an agreement is less valuable, hence a forceful solution is relatively more attractive.

H3D. Impending power shifts raise the risk of war. In so doing they magnify the risk posed by war causes that are catalyzed by expectations of war—including first-move advantages and power shifts.

H3E. Rising states conceal their grievances against others from fear of triggering preventive attack. This causes war by impeding diplomacy and deterrence. Conflicts are not resolved because they are not acknowledged. If the rising state intends aggression after its rise, its lulled targets may form a defending coalition too late to deter it. If its grievances rest on misperceptions, these cannot be addressed because they are not acknowledged.

H3F. Like first-move advantages, impending power shifts force states to hurry diplomacy or to end it before it bears fruit. Declining states rush to secure agreement before their bargaining power vanishes, or to use force while they can still win on the battlefield. This hasty action raises the risk that workable diplomatic solutions will be overlooked, that deterrence will be attempted too late, and that dangerous misperceptions will shape decisions because they escape scrutiny.

H3G. Even power shifts that pass without war leave danger in their wake. The powers and privileges of states are now in disequilibrium, and the process of restoring equilibrium may trigger war. Risen states demand new privileges to match their new power, but declined states cannot concede without inviting blackmail from others. As a net result, risen states demand their "place in the sun" but declined states often refuse to yield it. This causes collisions between risen and fallen.

H4. War is more likely when resources are cumulative; that is, when the control of resources enables a state to protect or acquire other resources.

H5. War is more likely when conquest is easy.

    H5A. When conquest is hard, states are dissuaded from expansion by the fear that it will prove costly or unattainable. When conquest is easy, expansion is more alluring: it costs less to attempt and succeeds more often. Thus even aggressive states are deterred from attacking if the defense is strong, and even temperate powers are tempted to attack if the offense is strong.

    H5B. When conquest is hard, states are blessed with secure borders; hence they are less expansionist and more willing to accept the status quo. They have less need for more territory because their current territory is already defensible. They are less anxious to cut neighbors down to size because even strong neighbors cannot conquer them. They have less urge to intervene in other states' internal affairs because hostile governments can do them less harm. Conversely, when conquest is easy, states are more expansionist because their present borders are less defensible. They seek wider territories to gain resources that would bolster their defenses. They find strong neighbors more frightening; hence they are quicker to use force to destroy their neighbors' power. They worry more when hostile regimes arise nearby because such neighbors are harder to defend against; hence they are quicker to intervene in neighbors' domestic politics. These motives drive states to become aggressors and foreign intervenors.

    H5C. When conquest is easy, states resist others' expansion more fiercely. Adversaries can parlay smaller gains into larger conquests, hence stronger steps to prevent gains by others are more expedient. This attitude makes disputes more intractable.

    H5D. When conquest is easy, the benefits of mobilizing or striking first are greater. Hence offense dominance raises all the risks that arise when it pays to move first (see H2).

    H5E. When conquest is easy, shifts in the relative power of states are more pronounced, and declining states are more tempted to respond to their decline with force. Hence offense dominance raises all the risks that impending power shifts generate (see H3).

    H5F. When conquest is easy, states adopt more dangerous diplomatic tactics—specifically, fait accompli tactics—and these tactics are more likely to cause war.

[261]

H5G. When conquest is easy, states have less faith in agreements because others break them more often; states bargain harder and concede more grudgingly, causing more political deadlocks; compliance with agreements is harder to verify; and states insist on better verification and compliance. As a result, states negotiate less often and settle fewer disputes; hence more issues remain unsettled and misperceptions survive that dialogue might dispel.

H5H. When conquest is easy, governments cloak their foreign and defense policies in greater secrecy. An information advantage confers more rewards, and a disadvantage raises more dangers: lost secrets could risk a state's existence. Hence states compete for information advantage by concealing their foreign policy strategies and their military plans and forces. Such secrecy raises the risk of wars of false optimism, inadvertent war, and other dangers.

H5I. When conquest is easy, political and military blunders have larger and less reversible effects. States see larger threats in others' moves, and so respond faster with more violent moves of their own. Hence errors are often irreversible, and they trigger war more quickly.

H5J. When conquest is easy, arms racing is more intense. Arms racing in turn raises other dangers: windows of opportunity and vulnerability, false optimism, and militarism. Thus offense dominance is a remote cause of the dangers that arms racing produces.

H5K. Offense dominance and defense dominance are self-reinforcing. This gives offense dominance a self-sustaining character that makes an offense-dominant world hard to escape. States cannot leave without swimming against a strong current.

Index

CORNELL STUDIES IN SECURITY AFFAIRS

edited by Robert J. Art, Robert Jervis,
and Stephen M. Walt